D1797237

The Monetary System

For other titles in the Wiley Finance series
please see www.wiley.com/finance

The Monetary System

Analysis and New Approaches to Regulation

JEAN-FRANÇOIS SERVAL AND
JEAN-PASCAL TRANIÉ

WILEY

Library of Congress Cataloging-in-Publication Data
Serval, Jean-François
  The monetary system : analysis and new approaches to regulation /
  Jean-François Serval and Jean-Pascal Tranié.
      pages cm. — (The Wiley finance series)
  Includes bibliographical references and index.
  ISBN 978-1-118-86792-1 (hardback)
  1. Money. 2. Finance. 3. Financial institutions. 4. Monetary policy.
  I. Tranié, Jean-Pascal   II. Title.
  HG221.S4857 2014
  339.5′3–dc23   2014022364

A catalogue record for this book is available from the British Library.

ISBN 978-1-118-86792-1 (hardback)   ISBN 978-1-118-86785-3 (ebk)
ISBN 978-1-118-86791-4 (ebk)   ISBN 978-1-118-86780-8 (ebk)

Cover design: Wiley
Cover Image: ©iStock/TheRugPile (top); ©iStock/andrearoad (bottom)

Set in 10/12pt Times LT Std by Aptara, Inc., New Delhi, India
Printed in Great Britain by TJ International Ltd, Padstow, Cornwall, UK

Table of Contents

List of Figures

List of Tables

Acknowledgements

We must first pay tribute to our ancestors – the ones who invented money. We don't know who they were, but they left us with a way to organize society. We especially have to revere those of German origin who, in horrible circumstances, invented relativity and linked sociology and money: Von Mises, Hayek and their successors Allais and Mundell, to name just a few. Without them – without the appropriate basis – this work would not exist.

Also, of course, our families have to be thanked. They fiercely and fully supported us when we were reading, thinking and writing, despite perhaps being a little neglected.

Many of our friends helped us by reading, unaided, numerous drafts which were difficult to understand. We mention Gilles Godefroy, who believed that a book on this subject was possible and useful and brought us through the advanced mathematics; George Ugeux, who is our reference in terms of ethics and market functioning but also did us the favour of reading and commenting on some of our drafts; Antoine Treuille, who has been patient in reading and commenting on our papers since we started this work in 2010; René Pierre Azria, the banker and great philanthropist; Donald Lamson, the law specialist in sovereign debts and US monetary regulation; Antoine Maffei, expert in international regulatory matters; Patrice Durand, who is knowledgeable about so many aspects of the entrepreneurial economy and now exposed to the security issues of modern means of payments. They are all great specialists in their field. Without their support and comments, this book would not exist. This year, Robert Mundheim was honored by the American Lawyer as a "Lifetime Achiever" which is one of the most recognized distinctions that a US lawyer can get. Robert Mundheim has served in senior positions at the US Treasury and the Securities and Exchange Commission. He has wide experience in the academic world and in corporate and private practice. We had many discussions, particularly at early morning breakfast meetings in NYC. I am grateful for his sharing, his expertise and his values which help make this book what it is. We are also grateful to President Jacques de Larosière who agreed to read our global document and being the President of the high committee on regulation he inspired the general design of the European Union Financial Surveillance framework. He is the one in the world who had been exposed at IMF level to all possible situations and negotiations after having witnessed as Head of a Central Bank all post war monetary cycles. Off course his sharp comments have been priceless to us.

Special thanks are due to Patrick Barth, the respected New York lawyer and Raphaël Douady, the great mathematician and the head of the Paris 1 Panthéon-Sorbonne Labex research center on financial regulation who contributed to the modelling and also gave us some insights about risk modelling and appraisal. Thomas Serval helped us with aspects of the new Internet age. Without them we would not have reached our goals. Long discussions were necessary.

We should not forget those who reviewed our use of the English language – Roger Hanwehr, Nancy Marchand and Elanor Clarke. We are also indebted to our publisher at John Wiley & Sons Ltd., his team and independent professionals for supporting this work.

To all we are deeply indebted. They brought this work into existence.

Foreword and Introduction

One evening in June 2008 served as the pivotal backdrop for a critical meeting between this work's authors, Jean-Pascal Tranié and Jean-François Serval. Wrapped in thought, and sitting in the kitchen of Jean-Pascal's Bourville–Normandie country manor, the authors pondered an uncertain economic future – one that could profoundly impact their lives and the financial future of their respective families. At the centre of their dilemma was the question of how to balance actions based on short-term decision horizons against the uncertainty of impending long-term change in the economic environment. Clearly, this was a central theme in deciding how the head of a family should plan, work out his strategic position and then act to preserve his family's best financial interests. The same might be expected of a corporate CFO/CEO, financial industry professional, government treasury or central banking official, or any other leader engaged in an analytical, strategic planning, risk mitigation or fiscal decision-making position.

In the course of their discussion, Jean-François and Jean-Pascal concluded that the prevailing make-up of the existing financial world would likely undergo an enduring multi-stage transformation in the months and years to come. Accordingly, the authors felt that it was essential for them to understand and characterize the key distinguishing factors which would help shape a future global financial environment. The authors also recognized the collective value of their shared, as well as divergent, personal and professional lives. Linked by a common financial industry pedigree, Jean-Pascal Tranié and Jean-François Serval were financial professionals endowed with a western perspective – nevertheless, both authors keenly appreciated that a newly emerging financial world would look very different from the traditional environment that they had become accustomed to. Jean-Pascal's long experience in Asia, coupled with the value of his partner's broad North American background, would be decisive in helping them circumnavigate beyond a strictly European view of the questions at hand, and in considering both the Asian and emergent economic points of view.

Simply due to the scope of the proposed project, it was concluded that the best approach would be to write a book on the subject. This undertaking would require them to understand intimately how the world's financial system had arrived at its current fragile impasse – and how adjustments to future trends within a transforming economic environment might be anticipated, for instance based on a comprehensive and cogent forward-looking analysis. Moreover, since Jean-Pascal (a former civil servant and now private equity investor) and Jean-François (an expert in public accounting) both valued the importance of serving the public interest, the publication of a book was equally well suited in this regard. The authors agreed that such a work needed to address a number of major questions: what logical underpinning of democratic society had facilitated a transition to the economic realities of June 2008, what were the major drivers that characterized the current economic impasse and how could one forecast future trends? Moreover, given a sense of the potential directions in which the global economic society was headed for, what could be done to "fix" the present economic system?

The seminal idea for pursuing this set of questions originated in the authors' previous book, entitled *The Virtual Money We Live With*. The conclusion originally reached by the authors was that the monetary system created at Bretton Woods in July 1944 had become obsolete, and needed to be revisited and broadly reformed. A central impetus for global monetary and fiscal structural reform was the fact that the level of worldwide private and sovereign debt had reached a staggering level. In the authors' opinion, this in turn necessitated a radical restructuring of endpoint monetary exchange, at the outset centring on the recognition that creditors would ultimately not be repaid. A defining prerequisite for hitting a global "economic reset button" was to organize the best approach for exiting from this historic monetary failure in an orderly manner – a process that needed to be sufficiently equitable so as to prove sustainable, without triggering social revolution on a global scale.

To arrive at a single-step, precedent-setting conclusion seemed too simplified, particularly in the context of the authors' committed belief in democracy, rooted in the heritage and proud traditions of the French Revolution and rule of law in the modern French State – where liberty begins at the point where restrictions on others' liberty ends.

Arising from their respect for the legal framework governing the financial systems of modern nation-states, and sharing similar concepts to those espoused by great economic minds of the US and Austrian schools of economics, the authors recognized that they needed to understand not only the causes of the current crisis but also the millennial evolution of monetary systems from pre-antiquity to the 1944 Bretton Woods Treaty – a foundation on which a post-war monetary and financial order would enjoy a lifetime of many decades. The authors were also interested in the events that led to the financial and monetary collapse of Germany from 1919 to 1925, subsequently hurling Central Europe into the crisis of 1929 and the Second World War. These events profoundly shaped the philosophy and economic thinking of leaders born in the late 19th and early 20th century, individuals of historical standing who would later organize and implement the post-1944 Bretton Woods monetary regime.

As a follow-up from their previous published work, the authors additionally realized that they needed to consider a worldwide global market structure, which more recently began to replace the strict confines of the original Bretton Woods system. Globalization is a key differentiating factor that sets our world apart from that of the early and mid-20th century and in recognition of this fact, the authors specifically adapted their analysis, conclusions and projected models for reforming the monetary system.

If – with a dose of vanity – the authors could affirm a personal belief in their conclusions, then it also follows that despite their extensive best efforts to achieve clarity and broad understanding among all readers, the previous work on "virtual money" could not be mastered fully by a lay reader. Admittedly, to do so would demand all readers to draw on a similar background rooted in the operational aspects of a specialized economic and financial culture, not to mention personal or professional exposure to the dynamics of financial and monetary markets. As such, this precedent work may have missed its mark in galvanizing grass-roots support for the acceptance of broadly based reforms designed for the western financial world, as well as for Asia – where financial markets emulate and accept the validity of western financial systems, without fully merging into them.

As a result, the authors decided that a different and more comprehensive approach to what money was and how it operates nowadays should now be accessible to a broad cross-section of society, and not only to members of the financial industry, leading economists and political leaders. In preparing such new work in the form of this book, the authors have attempted to eliminate any focus on technical regulation and abstract concepts, and in their place adopt methods for a transparent explanation of existing concepts of financial organization – particularly in a manner that would be easy to understand for a large public constituency impacted by changes in the world economic system, and eventually by the consequences of its wide ranging reform.

In addition, the authors felt that the objectives underlying a new book reflected not only a duty to the democratic tradition, but also an integral prerequisite for winning and maintaining the vital public support required to implement economic reforms – the impact of which would be felt most by our children's generation, who are intended as the beneficiaries of reform. Ideally, effective reforms would result in a world endowed with durable economic improvement and transnational political stability. In the authors' view, a globally reformed environment would reflect a fiscally improved world with reduced aggravation, rather than a continuing state of crisis and collective social pain likely to ensure a lack of hope, alongside certain political risk.

In essence, we had to discover what money really was, and then form a supportable basis for defining today's monetary system and its flows, in order to have it understood from all points of view. In doing so, we need to understand and communicate how money is used and what it means collectively for society, as well as for individual citizens who generally embrace an ancient social contract that accepts money as a method for fulfilling price obligations. Such a definition would need to be intellectually accessible to the public and lay the groundwork for an essential conceptual breakthrough required to generate the acceptance of impending economic reform which, regardless, will ultimately emerge as compulsory. In considering the exorbitant privilege that governments exercise to issue the form of wealth we know as money, and how income and wealth are appraised or coveted through its use, the authors review a range of concepts and definitions in their ultimate quest to find a common basis for best describing the role of money in our troubled economic system.

As much as all concerned may dream of a perfect world lacking misery (where the impact of money would be solely to generate prosperity rather than provide a cause for disorder and inequity), money remains a quantitative instrument. As such, an enduring and stable monetary system must inspire the trust of rank-and-file citizens, including a broadly accepted system for associated metrics and regulations governing the use of money and the preservation of the social contract that legitimizes money as tender. To be effective and to form the basis for an ongoing fiscal consensus between the citizenry, regulatory agencies and banks, as well as governments worldwide (who are tasked with ensuring that a global monetary system functions and provides long-term stability), money must meet the highest standards as the ultimate social contract of our time. Let's start with how our discoveries have been organized to build up the basis of this book.

In Chapters 1 and 2 we cover the history of money from antiquity to modern times, and why it is necessary to have it available. We also try to show the link between the expansion of money's qualities and the scope of its use, which has come with huge progress in exchanges and general prosperity. However, in doing so we discover the accompanying change in nature of what money is and what are still its key attributes, comparable through the support of universal measurement sampling means with, in later times, a nominal value on the support. We explain the link between the rise and fall of civilizations and money: a reserve allowing the financing of education, philosophers and statesmen.

In Chapter 3 we look at the reasons why precious metals became the staple for money – due to their universal acceptance as a means of payment, because of their unique stable chemical formulae which allow a sampling capacity when associated with a specific weight and therefore a guarantee of acceptance by a wide number of participants in the exchanges. We find out why sampling and acceptability, combined with stability, are conditions for the definition of money and for economic growth as a result of specialization in production and scale economies. This specialization, based on the comparative advantages and scale economies that economists and policy makers have discovered and favoured, is the cause of this extraordinary growth that humanity has achieved. Like many other authors, we lead the reader to rediscover that the "Pax Romana" – the first example of economic integration and prosperity over not a continent but, at that time, the known world; the Mediterranean – was accompanied by monetary unification as a parallel development. We also explain why precious metals are still in existence as reserves but no longer fit the needs of a modern economy. The shortage explains the emergence of script money, with the need to fill the timing gaps of wider geographic exchanges from antiquity to modern times. Transportation of goods over long distances required time and pre-financing. Chapter 3 also describes what needs money has fulfilled – such as payment, measurement and reserve – and how it has expanded into new territories, with new monetary instruments complying with the definition of being accepted by a sufficient number of participants in the exchanges to satisfy a payment. This is how the reader is led to a definition of money that includes, potentially, any receivable that can be exchanged – new aggregates covering every receivable or debt showing on a balance sheet "M5" and for the total of the balance sheets "M6". To operate these exchanges, and to replace gold's virtue of being a fixed sampling instrument with fixed chemical formula associated with weight to a physical reality as a unification factor – but no longer practical, and limited in its flexibility – our central thesis is that a new universal language (accounting) for participants to agree upon when exchanging is now the mechanism. The monetary units and numbers to be used for a contract are linked. By human construction they are universal, but the numbers used to operate accounting are transcendental, out of reach for humans in the same way that gold's chemical formula is independent of human beings. This is their second key discovery. However, users of exchanges, ordinary people as well as finance professionals, are becoming confused about what is conventional, what is value and what are numbers.

Von Mises, the great Austrian economist of the early 20th century, had already told us that a repeated statement irrelevant of its original veracity may become an everlasting truth as it is no more than a statement and obsolete. Chapter 4, on accounting language and its main general principles, is necessary for us to ground this discovery about the use of numbers as a replacement for precious metals, and to show the various errors of the type that Von Mises talked about. Financials are taken as realities; they are not. Aggregates are held as realities; they are not. The numbers used are like a precious metal chemical formula. Only transactions with a number attached to them, and taken one by one, are realities. The link between numbers and other non-universal realities like time and values creates uncertainties for market participants, as well as nominal values on bills and coinage and any other monetary instrument. Being linguistic by essence, accounting is of limited nature. The question that has to be asked when using numbers as an operational tool and applying them to formulae to deliver an image of financial operations and situations is: how do we analyse the reality underlying the image separately from the latter? At the same time, this chapter – with a reminder of the double-entry system of posting – will explain the reasons for contagion when a party to a transaction fails, and again show that images can become realities, especially on a legal grounding of insolvency. It will remind the reader that to any debt corresponds a receivable, and that the language to record the transactions on the balances has not only been unified to enable governments to collect taxes and survey them, for individual profits and enterprises, but also made compulsory with the aim that markets (owing to such unification) are more efficient and bring better competition. In summary, we have established that in a matter of decades since World War II, coinage has been replaced by financial instruments that are contracts and coins struck by accounting standards.

Helped by the digital revolution, accounting standards have merged with money both as an accepted measurement language, like gold was, and also as a language describing the transmission and availability of money. It changes the world when economic agents have to communicate to exchange, and to define the way they meet or receive what they expect from a transaction. Therefore, with a unified monetary language, productivity is enhanced by wider competition. If anyone sees the same image of a product and service and the corresponding prices, as well as the financial situation of a company or government, efficiency is improved. We are reminded of the concepts, rules and problems, as well as the fact that this immense breakthrough of financial information is also the root of contagion. Contagion goes through this direct interconnection, but also through price variations that will trigger imbalances in balance sheets' equity. The firewall[1] of ignorance about corporations' financial situations has disappeared. Rules have to be sensible for spectators and users, otherwise they don't fulfil their information objective and precious metal, which is no longer usable, has to be replaced by other bases and mechanisms to operate as switches. The amounts of debt and assets have to be related to the revenues and profits shown in financial statements.

This quick reminder moves us on to Chapter 5, which is aimed at explaining how the need for monetary regulation to satisfy the request for stability and coherent monetary zones was brought into the current monetary organization – which was drawn up after the war but is no longer appropriate – with aggregates based on banking credit distribution and its classical multiplier to cope with the new challenge. Even with the current reforms, the surveillance system is still based on outdated aggregates which themselves started from attempts to keep the banking sector a monopoly, to distribute loans and see society trying to define a regulatory scope. This approach does not correspond to the modern world of exchanges and disintermediation that we wanted to free the barriers to exchanges. The system is not only leaking due to the refinancing being operated through banks by non-bank financial entities outside the scope of surveillance, but also companies can now operate directly between themselves as well as individuals can. The revolution in payments, electronic devices and telecommunication hubs will accelerate the phenomenon. We explain shadow banking, and why the notion itself is insufficient.

Chapter 6 details how, in the new environment, new aggregates would better follow on exchange and money velocity, and what new definitions will bring in terms of containing risks, improving security and, as a result, improving the economy. By providing the economy with good money, governments are letting producers enlarge their territories and take more development risks. Our thesis, as already developed in our previous book, is that in the deregulated context of modern economies with their financing mostly made on debt and equity financial markets, the old aggregates will no longer be able to give proper warnings to governments to act in due time. Lobbies do what they are designed for and act separately to promote their members' business, irrelevant of monetary interconnections. We explain that

---

[1] See Glossary for definition.

any receivable which is now convertible or exchangeable is potentially a monetary instrument if accepted by a sufficient number of actors. We consequently explain how we see today's money – the new aggregate M5 resulting not only from central banks' and regulated financial institutions' balance sheets, but from any balance sheet. It covers not only potentially all instruments, meaning any receivable, but also any actor of a balance sheet as counterpart. The money concept of M5 is being extended to allow a follow-up of transformation (between instruments) and velocity of flows which will determine the volume of money needed for exchanges. It is distinguished from shadow banking in the sense that shadow banking surveillance is an attempt to apprehend what has flown away from the banks and is now with the retirements systems, hedge funds and money market funds, while all the data exists to get a global picture. The world has changed, with no territorial or jurisdictional borders that governments have agreed to suppress over the years (they fight against trade barriers and currency exchange freedom with no intervention from monetary authorities) to achieve a wider world competitive marketplace. Monetary surveillance can only be renovated to encompass the entire space of monetary exchanges and all operating actors. We do not divide the monetary space between banks and other registered financial institutions, but between all financial entities combined with other non-specifically financial entities issuing financial statements and the public (households). In doing so, we resolve the issue of the scope of regulation and surveillance that encompasses all the first categories. Of course, especially due to major changes in economic equilibrium between nations since the war, and to the economic and demographic growth in general, the Bretton Woods monetary system has been dismantled. The 2007–2008 financial crisis, which needed government intervention to avoid collapse, has trigged new international forums such as the G20 and new laws which create new patterns of regulation and international cooperation.

In Chapter 7 we describe where we stand in respect of the fluidity of money inside zones as well as the interconnections between zones; what is aimed at and what is missing. We uncover the problem already taken care of by Robert Mundell of optimum monetary zones – an issue that creates a dispute between the objectives of gain from larger-scale and resulting efficiency savings, and better serving citizens placed in totally different social patterns and production capabilities depending on where they are located.

In Chapter 8, in light of this analysis, we reconsider what needs "extended money" should comply with in terms of trustworthiness and stability to guarantee the flow of exchanges and the functioning of the financial markets as they now exist. After having resolved the key issue of what conceptually designed modern money is, we address the matter of its contractual nature and why it does not oppose regulation, laws and where the resulting new seignorage stands. We also address the topic that claimable money, by being better able to flow through, can also accumulate wrongly – due to the behaviour of financial agents – in non-productive safe assets instead of feeding the economy. This is what we address as the money trap; the fact that after being issued and before the end of its term, if any, money can only be deposited somewhere, creating excesses within some instruments and shortages elsewhere. Interest rates can be linked not to risk taking as in classical approaches, but rather to risk avoidance. This trap – finding its roots in the general accounting standard of double entry, combined with the *de facto* monopoly of financial institutions to open payment accounts – is the new basis for seignorage that is now shared with governments; the one that has allowed the extraordinary salaries some bankers receive. Commissions or margins on passing flows can logically explain these bonuses. Once explained, we see the way that the power over money issuance functions today can be handled. We propose mathematical research and a mathematical formula to comprehend today's monetary system, which is described as a hot air balloon transporting passengers with leaks in the envelope and a furnace to balance the hot air leaks that are accumulations.

Chapter 9, after exposing the effect of electronic markets on exchanges from both operational and structural points of view, raises the question of the resulting lack of individual accountability. It also raises the topic of deciding how to determine the most efficient money endowment for each agent. This analysis supports our thesis of a need in the new environment for surveillance that only extended money can provide, combined with better principles to let it flow freely. This allows us to come back again to the difference between numbers, conventions and values – prices becoming the first variable with the other factors being contained or tangible. The new transparency brought about by electronic markets and clearings is not only a complication but also an opportunity, as it provides a possible view on transactions and uncleared amounts. Mathematicians may operate with tools that have been developed for physics, with the notions of time and speed that accountants are not able to comprehend. The static formulae and slice-by-slice observation can no longer apply to determine a rating or valuation risk without misleading the public about what can be done to have it properly informed. New topics are appearing that were previously hidden, such as money being guaranteed by general principles and becoming more transparent as to the observation of its flows. The described monetary world being global, it is no surprise that price fluctuations (which are different from values if the latter have any meaning besides being exchange ratios), becoming visible instrument by instrument and market by market, create a systemic risk through the mere accessibility of their image and obvious gigantic size. This exists out of necessity, but the increased visibility adds to the speed of irrational movements. This is the matter dealt with when raising the topics issuing from the new, targeted set-up with centralized counterparties (CCPs) for credit default swaps. This topic regards how central banks can operate their stabilization duty under the Democratic control of parliaments and install the necessary market breakers, as well as who should do this. Five years after the crisis, these topics are still on the tables of policy makers on both sides of the Atlantic and are of great concern for all citizens.

At the end of our journey we propose an entire upheaval of the current approach to money. Any economic transaction potentially triggers money issuance or use. Today's money is no more than a piece of equity or a receivable with an exchange right attached to satisfy a commitment but no more claimable at a Central Bank. Nominal values, conventional exchange ratios, prices and values are different dimensions than the monetary unit standard and its physical or digital support. Because of the general individual identification of all participants in monetary exchanges throughout the Western world, observation of flows that old aggregate did not permit is now possible. The resulting granular data, modern mathematics and sociology can be used to diagnose some of the causes of the current crisis and suggest some possible ways to fix them.

Ultimately a new surveillance system with condition to stability open the possibility, with new knowledge to cure discovered anomalies in flows and values, is not alone in wanting to avoid a collapse of the current monetary set-up without the development of strategies to deal with them. We believe that both the implementation of such a surveillance system and the new lights it will bring will show the need for a general reform.

CHAPTER 1

From Antiquity to Modern Times; Monetary Development Over 5000 Years. What History Explains and Comparison within New Contexts

"We are used to setting a company either for our entire assets or for a specified business purpose: such as the buying and selling of slaves. There was a dispute over whether a company could be set in order to have one of the participants granted a bigger part of the profit and less of the losses; Quintus Mucius considered this to be against the mere nature of a partnership while Servius Sulpicius, whose decision prevailed, considered that a partnership could be set in order to have one of the partners not participate in the losses while sharing in the profits subject to the fact that his personal contribution was precious enough to make such provision equitable"[1]

— Gaïus, *Institutes*, III, pp. 148–154

THE ORIGIN OF MONEY; FROM ANTIQUITY TO MODERN TIMES

Money is a central component of civilization's evolution from subsistence and barter economies into finance and trade societies. The initial step in economic development usually involves the bartered exchange of goods and then physical-value equivalents, in a manner that validates simultaneous transactions between two or more parties. Heralding further transition into a financial economy, the potential issuance of currency-based tender subsequently enables legal contractual consideration and a range of transactions via a monetary standard that favourably supports economic development and labour specialization.

---

[1] This refers to the first century BC (author's own translation).

A Metallic System Allowing Intrinsic Measurement Stamping: Ingots to Coinage

Consistent with prevailing knowledge, it is generally accepted that money appeared in Mesopotamia concurrent with the emergence of an alphabet and a written system of Cuneiform language, around 2900 BC.[2] Excavations have uncovered numerous terracotta tablets stamped with cuneiform signs, and detailing inventories, entries and exits of valuables.[3] Examples of valuation in metal weight appear much later, around the time of the "Hammurabi Code", or 1650 BC. Within the "Hammurabi Code" itself there are several references to the prices of goods and services.[4]

Through archaeologically recovered remains of palaces and both inscribed stones and Cuneiform terracotta tablets, a detailed description of organized Sumerian society and ruling structures has been compiled by experts. This includes the characterization of a general system of laws required for qualifying and distinguishing monetary tender from other value standards such as goods.

Precious metals such as gold and silver (or their electrolytic mix) were recognizable by anyone, regardless of language or regional culture. The rapidly appearing utilization of weight standards for value measurements provided a form of monetary unification that facilitated trans-Mediterranean trade, as well as trade between "capital kingdom" cities and states such as Egypt throughout the greater Middle East, prior to the introduction of coinage and before the Hellenistic period (8th to 2nd century BC). Further west, from Mesopotamia towards the Mediterranean, it is believed that the Greek Attic *Talent* of around 26 kg in metal ingots was one of the usual units of trade between palaces, temples and then cities.[5] It was the equivalent of modern central bank money; only usable to clear what would be today's international trade but not money that a citizen could carry to satisfy their day-to-day needs and pay for them. It was probably not the first monetary unit to be used. Without coinage artefacts dating back to the period of the Hammurabi Code, one does not know exactly when and where coinage appeared first.[6] Nevertheless, it is hard to understand how monetary references such as prices could have existed without a tangible supporting means of payment, which a coinage system would

---

[2] Kremer, S.N., *History begins at Sumer*; Bottero, J., *Mesopotamus, Writing, Reasoning and the Gods*; Roux, G., *Ancient Iraq*. See References.

[3] Such tablets can be seen at the Metropolitan Museum of New York.

[4] Numerous copies of the Hammurabi Code exist and can be seen in Western museums such as Le Louvre in Paris. Without certitude about date, the Talmud (Exodus XXX 11–15) was written much later in time, in the 1st century AD at a time when the Mediterranean civilization became Roman after being under Greek domination. The Talmud refers back to Abraham concerning several money prices. The census was based on one-and-a-half shekel coinage per adult male of 20 and over. Abraham is deemed to have lived in a similar period to the Hammurabi's time, that is the 17th century before Christ.

[5] The Athenian currencies can be described as the "mina" equivalent to 434 grams, they were 60 mina for a Drachma. The "obole" was 1/6th of a Drachma or 72 grams. The mina itself was supposed to refer to the weight of water required to fill an amphora, but amphoras were different depending on the city. An Attic Talent could pay a month's wages of a trireme crew of 20 men. Hellenistic mercenaries were commonly paid one Drachma per day of military service. The Athenian Drachma was recognizable; struck with the owl of goodness, the olive branch and the crescent moon. It is the one we refer to here.

[6] An article on the website of a coin broker (*your online guide to coin trading*) dates a coin found in Ephesus (Coast of Asia Minor, today's Turkey) back to 2700 BC but the attached image, said to be of a starter struck with a lion on one face visible at the British Museum in London (Department of Money and Medals), is similar in shape and appearance to one we refer to here dating from the 6th century BC (see footnote 8). However the Hammurabi Code, dating back to 1650 BC, already set prices for goods and services or sanctions.

provide when paper did not exist. We can already note the distinction between the means of payment though, the coin or metal ingot, and the accounting records found on terracotta tablets.

Claimed by Herodotus[7] to have been introduced later (after the Hammurabi Code) as an invention of the Lydians established alongside the Pactole River (in today's Turkey), coinage was subsequently struck to be used as monetary tender. The oldest existing examples of such coins from the ancient Greeks date back to between the 8th and 9th centuries BC.[8] Controversy over the chronological appearance of coinage guarantees and units did not abate until the 19th century. Sovereign guarantees attached to coinage and units became historical with the Athenian civilization[9] of the 5th century and much later, under the Roman Empire, as we will see later. Historical analysis of the interaction between political power and currency then reveals deepening thought on the historical evolution of a role for monetary currency in society.

Grounding the Guarantees of Stamping: From an All-Metallic System to Paper Bills

The split between the management of sovereign assets versus those belonging to the people, and the complexity of currency flows in the Roman Empire, are topics that have inspired many authors since the 18th century.[10] After the disappearance of collectivist economies where property belongs to no one, including the sovereign (for example, ancient Egypt),[11] this topic became important to the understanding of the guarantees and trust that an issuer of coinage or scriptural money may grant, or merely inspire. Analytical emphasis is frequently centred on the sovereign power to strike coinage (money species) versus the state allowing or disallowing a sovereign to issue money notes and bills-of-credit. The power to print notes with bargaining power (commercial notes and then note bills) gives those deemed to be in possession of coinage or paper counter value the capability to exchange goods in a manner that others would lack. The debate about whether the issuance of money should be a privilege of the sovereign, of the people collectively or be left to private initiative will go on subject to the limitation of the single or small number of stamping recognitions over a territory that efficient trade requires. We will see later that measurement stamping and its guarantee require authority. Specific topics include where such authority may derive from, and through which mechanisms.

---

[7] Herodotus (423–348 BC), *Histoire*, I, p. 94, Les Belles Lettres, Paris, 1970: "to our knowledge the Lydians were the first to mint and use gold and silver coinage".

[8] A "creseïde" Lydian coin is to be found in the collections of the Monnaie de Paris, the Central Minting Institution of France. It dates back to the 5th century BC (ref. Catalogue of Monetary Treasuries Exhibition, Sept–Nov 1996, p. 12). The attribution to the Lydian King and the naming of the coin is based on the struck image of a lion on a tiny ingot. Herodotus also gives two anecdotes making the link with the lion: first, as a common symbol of royal power in the Middle East where Crassus gives a lion to Delphi (Hdt. I 50); second, the carrying of a lion around the city of Sardis to protect it from its enemies (Hdt. I 84). Other numismatists think that coinage started during the same period as the first Achemidides (6th century BC), from what is today Iran, Iraq and the Black Sea, but also conquered Egypt and Libya.

[9] Rostovtzeff, M.I., *The Social and Economic History of the Hellenistic World*. See References.

[10] Locke, G., *Montesquieu*. See References.

[11] The Battle of Actium in 31 BC, when the Romans defeated the Egyptian fleet gathered by Mark Antony, put an end to Egyptian independence and brought to a close the Hellenistic period of Alexander the Great's successors around the Eastern part of the Mediterranean, including Asia Minor down to Mesopotamia.

Fluctuations in financial power characterize the core of market economies – in particular from the time of the 15th-century Lombardy traders to the 19th-century English Industrial Society, where the Bank of England's power to print bills dates back to a charter instituted in 1694. (26 years before, the Swedish Risken Ständers, acting as a central bank, was accorded the same privilege as successor to a failed private bank whose privilege had already been granted in 1656.) The French Banque Royale, chartered in 1718 and having the monopoly to issue bank notes with the guarantee of the King, was the first to operate as a modern bank and to be used by a government to finance a war and reimburse budget deficit with paper. It also allowed a reduction in public debt. It dragged a large public of 2 million citizens out of public debt and brought forward the concept that gold should be put aside. People were forbidden to hold gold. It also facilitated the development of colonial trade companies, such as one for Louisiana, one for India and one for China. France's yearly external trade with its colonies was multiplied threefold by volume (number of boats sent) after 1719 due to the capacity to finance its cargo. The bank failed because of an uncontrolled speculation on its shares and bonds; the first example of the possible disconnection between price determination processes for financial instruments, Banque Royale shares and realities. Even more interesting was its organized liquidation, with over 2,000,000 creditors, 251,000 depositors, holding up to 100 gold Louis, will be reimbursed totally while larger depositors, 100,000 with over 2,000 gold Louis would not, and 185 speculators would be sanctioned with penalties amounting to 137 million Louis. The resolution process for Cyprus's 2013 process on a much smaller scale was not much different. Nothing is new in the world but France, like the USA later, was very much against pure paper money for 200 years, and both returned to gold worship.

Of course, Europe was only following a process already known in the east as a promise to pay the bearer. They were made on leather and appeared in 118 BC during the Han Dynasty. In fact, public literature says that even prior to China's 7th-century Tang dynasty, paper bills guaranteed by the state were being issued. As claimable instruments, these issued bills were differentiated from instruments issued between private individuals as promissory notes, and utilized to clear a trade. In these evolving systems of currency-based economic societies, democracy or liberty was defined as the power of the individual to act without coercion, thus linking economic commerce with the freedom to trade – and limited only by the capability of traders to come into possession of valuable coinage, goods, notes or their equivalents.

In many settings, the scarcity of metal – and consequently of metal coinage – was the reason for the emergence of paper bills (Massachusetts Bay Colony, 1690),[12] as had occurred at earlier points in history. By serving to eliminate the transport of heavy currency metals and decreasing the motivation for theft thereof, the utilization of paper bills appeared to favour long-distance trade as did loan contracts in ancient times.[13] Compared with metal coinage,

---

[12] For their local needs, the colonies issued 20 shilling bills in 1690 and a six shilling and eight pence bill on February 4, 1736. It was stated at the time: "The bill of six shilling and eight pence due by the province of the Massachusetts Bay in New England to the possessor thereof shall be in value equal to one ounce of a coin's silver troy weight of sterling; alloy gold coin at the rate of four pounds eighteen shillings per ounce, and shall be accordingly accepted by the treasurer or receiver subordinate to him on all payments." The colony's treasury defaulted, and the resulting "sour-grapes" souvenir of defaulted Massachusetts Bay Colony bills explains why the wording of the subsequent US Constitution referred only to metal coinage.

[13] Venture loans for sea transportation. Charles-Picard, G. and Rougé, J., *Texts and documents relating to economic and social life in the Roman Empire 31* BC–AD *223*, p. 167 (Vienna papyrus no. 19972). See References.

paper bills lacked intrinsic value as goods; the holder had to be recognized by the receiver, and the use of recognition codes facilitated the use of carriers unknown to the receiver.

Viewed as a whole, bills or credit issued by sovereign authorities and/or chartered banks (the system that prevailed in the USA until 1913) in essence constituted a loan to the beneficiary of the bills. The growth in use of paper bills paved the way for the birth of a fractional reserve banking system. A fractional reserve did not require the issuer to meet an eventuality where all bearers and depositors could simultaneously demand execution of all guarantees, in total, at the same point in time. However, the reserve issuer could be liable for reimbursement of a large fraction of the deposits on hand.

Regulations were required to maintain some discipline, but extenuating circumstances, such as extraordinary government expenses or wars, led to relaxation of the rules and issuance of credits where an inherent complicity between governments, central banks and chartered banks (with authorization to issue paper bills) inevitably developed. Such collusion could predispose to instability.

THE RISE AND FALL OF CIVILIZATIONS

Civilizations are characterized by their populations' acceptance of common values; overall cultural ones such as language and religion. They also correspond to a political and military common space. However, they don't always have all of these attributes. An organization's exchanges and what it shares with the public characterize best what a civilization is, and through economic exchanges will tend to use common price sampling mechanisms such as that brought about by a generally accepted monetary unit over a territory. Money will ever more cause an extension of such civilizations outside their own territory as a result of superiority in trade. Civilization, currency and political unification are parallel phenomena, if not closely interlinked. On the contrary, financial difficulties of the head of state, whatever they are caused by, may lead to monetary decline and the extinction of a civilization by reducing exchanges between the populations from which it is composed, or the centralized power to regulate wealth and taxes.

What differentiated successful public issuance of paper money from instances that failed was the quality of the issuer or authority that represented the mandate to levy taxes, and the potential capability to redeem the issued bills with levied taxes. The value of bills to be issued was pegged in relation to the magnitude of expected tax levies. The link between what characterizes a civilization and the capability to gather forces, including a military to defend its future, does not have to be demonstrated here. The forces are, out of necessity, economic ones as those in military service are retrieved from production, and money and taxes are the tools for the consequent required transfers.

Already, in ancient times, many authors denounced the pattern of an exploding distribution of credits followed by impaired liquidity, which frequently presaged a major crisis. Greek philosopher, trader and statesman Solon,[14] deemed to be the father of Athenian "democracy", issued laws cancelling the debts of peasants unable to repay and therefore at that time

---

[14] Solon (640–558 BC). Moses, F., *La servitude pour dettes: Revue technique de droit Français et Etranger Série 4*, XLIII, pp. 159–184, 1965. Aristotle, *Athenian Politician*. He also reformed the measurement units AR (Athe 10.1–2) and the calendar (Plut Solon XXXV).

condemned to slavery. Again, referring back to Greek antiquity when philosophical ideas traced their ancestry to Sumerian times, and when 4th century BC trans-Mediterranean trading flourished, Rostovtzeff writes: "Systematization and regulation of commerce widely benefited from the development of banks which professionalized. Banks were practicing on a regular basis monetary transactions that included a wide variety of credits."[15] Yet, why did an ensuing economic crisis fall over Greece – was it primarily due to the nation's political evolution?

Rostovtzeff's comments sum up the essential societal value and perception of what money represented during the pinnacle of ancient Greek civilization, starting in the 5th century BC – namely, a monetarily unified economic exchange system based on both coinage and standardized "letters-of-credit", which recognized the metrics of time and transactional duration. This system thereby facilitated the requirements of advanced monetary commerce, specifically in allowing for the clearance of an exchange transaction during the period beginning with a decision to ship the merchandise, to the end point where the merchandise was delivered to and accepted at the buyer's end of the transaction pipeline. Implementation of this type of system represented major progress in economic society, considering the risk and time involved in having ships transiting the Mediterranean Sea, and in continuing maritime commerce even during periods when sea travel was precluded every winter due to inclement weather.

The historical interaction between the rise and fall of civilizations, regional and distant trading patterns, the emergence of philosophical ideas, the political evolution of democracy and tyranny, as well as the emergence of increasingly complex means of economic exchange represents a continuum in the human experience. The exchange of goods (as well as intangible assets such as ideas) by electronic means of transport, namely the Internet, remains to be completely standardized in the monetary context. Ultimately, these patterns bear continuing relevance to the concept of prosperity, described by Adam Smith[16] as arising by consequence of improved efficiency and the advantages of competitive processes.

With globalization, goods not readily available in one region may be located elsewhere in an instant and transacted by means of the Internet, solely due to the options provided by the existence of monetary currency and advanced technology. There are, however, innumerable detractors of the monetary system of commerce, who since the dawn of "money" disdain its perverse impact on society – a point of view that can be extended to suggest that money is to blame for underlying causes leading to the decline of civilization, solely based on adversely interpreted issues involving systems of monetary commerce.

The Greek economic crisis of antiquity described by Rostovtzeff demonstrates parallels with our contemporary financial crisis. The Greek model was a unified political assembly of independent cities with common cultural elements assembled around the leadership of Athens or Sparta. Greek civilization was extending its economic and cultural influence across the entire littoral regions of the Middle East,[17] including areas under the political domination of the Persians – the naval Salamine Battle in 480 BC, won by the assembled Greek cities, marked the peak period of its civilization but also the start of its decline. The Parthenon monument in Athens, ordered by Pericles as a development, is proof of the degree of sophistication reached by the ancient Greeks with their mathematical expertise used to determine how to calculate optic effects of dimensions in order to correct them for the eyes of citizens passing

---

[15] Rostovtzeff, M.I., *The Social and Economic History of the Hellenistic World.* See References.

[16] Smith, A., *The Wealth of Nations.* See References.

[17] Today's Turkey.

by this sacred area. Many dedications record in stone the cost in Drachma of the huge constructions launched in this period, but sometimes interrupted by wars requiring other priorities. Democracy has also left behind proof, in the form of stone slot machines to count votes, to demonstrate the link between state resources (treasuries) and their allocation.[18]

A major factor in the rise of regional Athenian influence may be attributed to the Athenian currency, the Drachma. We note that Athenian prosperity allowed the Greek government of that time to indemnify citizens who participated in public charges, making possible the recruitment of competent citizens irrespective of their class.[19] In the same way, the Greeks had the monetary resources to be educated and to become scientists, philosophers and teachers (usually all at the same time). Eventually, however, the Drachma's value declined, triggered by the combined effects of ancient Greece's growing debt, a loss of competitiveness in its economic structure and output, and an associated decline in Athens' military superiority.[20] The inherent domination of Greek culture in the Mediterranean and Middle Eastern regions then began to wane, as its commercial/monetary strength and competitiveness weakened – in part as a consequence of and due to the costs of multiple foreign wars against the Medes and Phoenicians, as well as domestic exhaustion from internal strife involving civil wars between Greek cities and social revolutions. The Peloponnesian wars started the decline that ended the brilliant 5th century BC.[21]

In contrast to the ancient Greek model, the patterns of Roman military and political expansion that took hold after their destruction of Phoenician Carthage[22] in 146 BC resulted in social and economic structures that would prove more resilient in terms of handling monetary crises. The natural geographical space extended by the Pax Romana[23] facilitated the Roman power structure annexing large, economically exploitable territories – which in turn allowed for the development of highly diversified and robust monetary and economic exchange systems. This pattern of acquisitions led to gains in productivity through specialization of populations and economies of scale, and included benefits derived from North African and Egyptian imports and Sicilian corn, to mention only a few examples. A quasi-globalized international economic system triggered cyclical enhancement of prosperity, and repeatedly countered or delayed the impact of other factors that could have prematurely weakened the Roman Republic and its successor, Imperial Hegemony. In contrast, the Imperial Hegemony and resulting deeper economic integration of its territorial components made each of its centres, such as Rome, dependent on imports of food and luxury goods triggering monetary needs, especially when importing from Asia and delivering gold to do so.[24]

---

[18] Visit the new Athens' Archaeological Museum.

[19] Kagan, D., *Pericles: The Birth of Democracy*, p. 184; Theucydides, *History of the Peloponnesian War*, pp. 2, 37. See References.

[20] After the Romans took control of Greece with Octavian, who became Emperor Augustus after he took power in AD 31 with the Actium naval victory. The Greek civilization and culture survived, but in AD 267 the Roman Empire was no longer able to protect Athens. The city was destroyed by a German invading tribe – the Urules.

[21] Described by Theucydides. See References.

[22] In today's Tunisia.

[23] 799 years after the mythological birth date of Rome in AD 49, Emperor Claude decided to have Thracian – at the current border of modern Turkey, Greece and Bulgaria – conquered. The Mediterranean Sea, a lake, was then dominated entirely by Rome for two centuries.

[24] Temin, P., *The Roman Market Economy*. See References. Temin shows the degree of interdependency of the Roman economy with a unified flour market favoured by the "Pax Romana".

The concept of territorial space acquisition as a driver for monetary unification originated with the Sumerians and Athenians, and would develop further as a major underpinning for both Carthage and Rome – both in terms of their sovereignty and in enhancing efficiency for trade and wealth accumulation. However, in terms of historical analysis, it is essential to distinguish between political and monetary unification. For instance, in a more recent setting, this issue arose within the Eurozone of the European Union – where the "Fathers of Europe"[25] originally decided to reverse the previous political pattern of nations and law, and thereafter decided that economic integration was a prerequisite for the ultimately intended trans-European political integration, which should eventually follow as a preventative institutional state structure designed to avoid future armed conflict. The Fathers were taught by the never-ending European wars that followed the final collapse, in AD 476, of the Western Roman Empire.

We believe that the economic and monetary crisis of our time spreading over non-politically unified territories is more similar to the Greek crisis of antiquity than to models of cyclical Roman economic instability. After all, the extension of commerce in the manner known during ancient Greece was not primarily defined by political borders, as economic structures in the Roman Imperial state hierarchy were. The issue of an inherent gap between sovereignty and political/economic and cultural realities represents a primary challenge impeding financial regulation in today's politically heterogeneous world order. A curious anecdote may underscore this contention. The unification of Italy, before it was split between the Greeks and Phoenicians under rule of the Roman Republic in 211 BC, led to the murder by a legionary of the most extraordinary inventor, Archimedes.[26] The successive Roman Imperial era never demonstrated the creativity and intellectual/scientific renaissance that had characterized the decentralized environment of competing cities in ancient Greece and indeed, much later in Western Europe, the so-called "Renaissance".

However, it became imperative for the sophisticated and "westernized" exchange system of the Roman Empire to require that coinage be struck again, as it was under the Greek era, not by cities but on a global territorial basis where it should be accepted. In the 1st century AD, Emperor Augustus (63 BC–AD 14) unified the coinage system across the Empire to allow both an easier long distance trade and a State (Empire) global budget. At the end of the 3rd century AD, Emperor Aurelian (AD 214–275), trying to restore the breaking imperial system which was plagued for a century by continuous political unrest, usurpers and invasions, triggering military costs and reduced tax collection, as well as fake struck coinage, pioneered a new metallic but fiat[27] currency (money) that would more or less survive until the successive Eastern Roman Empire (Byzantium). He would mint a new currency – showing for some coinage a "XXIKA" mark for a metallic formula – which acted as a kind of implicit guarantee

---

[25] Jean Monet, Konrad Adenauer, Robert Schumann, Paul Henry Spaak, Count Carlo Sforza, Joseph Bech and others, because of the painful scars of World War II, decided to start the rebuilding of Europe with a progressive process of economic integration (CECA Treaty of April 18, 1957 between Belgium, France, Germany, Luxemburg, the Netherlands and Italy; Rome Treaties of March 25, 1957 establishing the European Community with a single market and the Euratom). Later, statesmen like Altiero Spinelli proposed the first Constitution.

[26] Archimedes (287–212 BC) was an inventor in all fields, and was also a gifted military architect and engineer. He was the architect who conceived the fortress of Syracuse, built to protect the city against Phoenician assaults.

[27] Fiat money is a currency with an exchange value higher than its corresponding content of metallic weight at price. Aurelian also imposed fixed prices on basic goods.

of content that would distinguish it from previous fake or poor-quality struck coinage.[28] In turn, this would constitute another advance in "money", until the Renaissance and subsequent emergence of the next form of "money" – paper bills.

WHAT CAN WE LEARN FROM ANCIENT AND MORE MODERN HISTORY?

History reveals how certain monetary mechanisms were introduced to satisfy specific transactional needs in society, and how the resultant impact of monetary development triggered economic growth. Such mechanisms include: (1) a unified and universally recognized monetary instrument that is a weight measurement of a transaction-specific precious metal that is, by itself, a factor of economic unification, as indeed paper currency became; (2) a potential shortage of metal as a driver for the development of bills-of-credit; (3) the ability to repeatedly address necessary timing issues for transactional exchanges via such bills-of-credit (requirements that passive metal coinage could not satisfy); as well as (4) the authorities' right to set money-standard measurement metrics and to guarantee them. Subsequently, throughout history, monetary jurisdictions accepted the inevitable deviances that resulted from the introduction of fiat money – an evolutionary economic process that descends from the emerging privilege of seignorage.[29] The latter development presents an inherent paradox that has been highlighted by the economist Robert Mundell (see Chapter 7: The Growing Issues of the Size of the Monetary Zones – Research for Optimum) – the practical infeasibility of simultaneously satisfying all functional requirements that money should be expected to provide in a complex society administered using purely monetary systems based solely on fiat "monies".

Overall, we see in ancient history that money already allowed education and public service. Advanced civilizations existed alongside money. The ancient Greek democracy, a social contract, came with monetary strength and declined when the monetary system weakened.

Even a cursory review of ancient history (as shown in Figure 1.1) reveals how excessive acceptance of overvalued struck monetary coinage can destroy domestic industries and favour imports (a major issue for the upper-crust lifestyle of many Roman citizens, whose consumer demands drove the substantial import of luxury goods from eastern territories and later from Byzantium – following oriental division of the Empire). Other negative factors impacting economic stability included the tendency for those centres of government that enjoyed a strong political and military position to issue too large a quantity and value of "money", especially that which was seignorage-derived.[30] The 1492 discovery that led to colonization of the Americas, and the resulting access to large South American gold reserves, demonstrates how economic destruction can be triggered by uncontrolled access to resources considered as representing the equivalent of wealth. Although understood only as the cause of major inflation at the time, this and related phenomena throughout history exemplify the ultimate examples of monetary disorder.[31]

---

[28] Summary of Eliot, S., *Catalogue des monnaies de l'Empire Romain*, pp. 39–49. See Selection of Articles.

[29] Fiat money derives its value from government regulation.

[30] Derived from the sovereignty privilege to issue and impose coinage.

[31] Jean Bodin (1529–1596), French jurisconsult and economist, declared "there is no other wealth than man". See References.

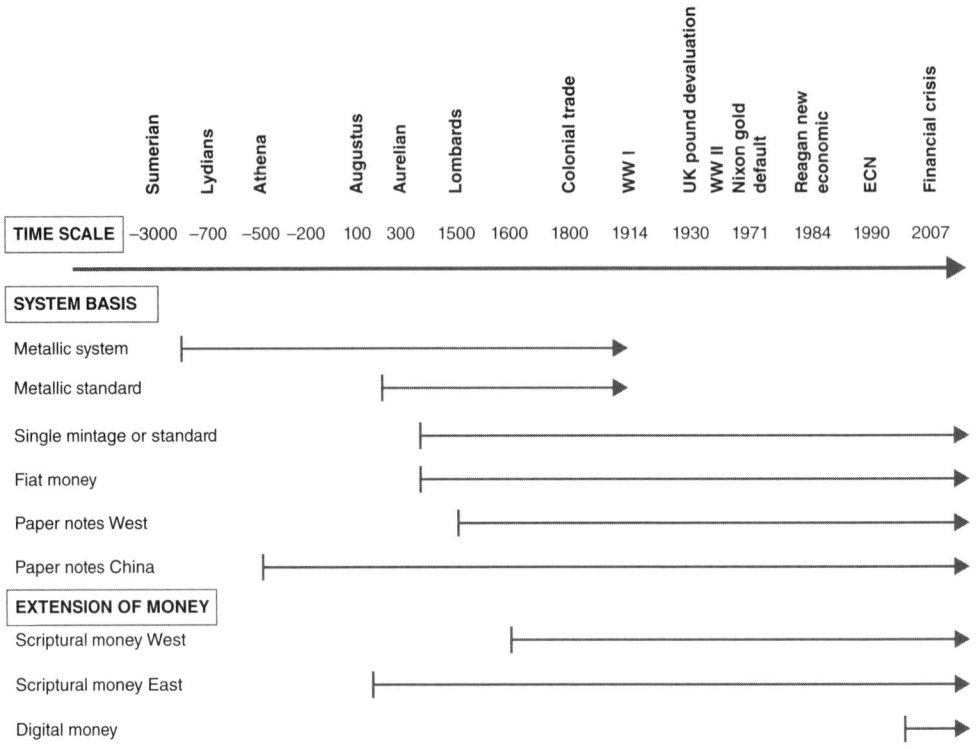

ECN: Electronic Communication Network – the original term for electronic marketplaces was created in the 1990s, linking market participants without using any intermediary. As a result of their competitive development, brokers' fees went down. Non-regulated, they mixed the transaction and clearing functions. Since then, they have agreed to be separately regulated for each function. A repository for electronic marketplaces was created during the 1990s.

FIGURE 1.1   Historical chart (author's view)

Through the evolution of "money", it was possible via revolution or social unrest for the rich to be defeated by the poor. With a shortage of agricultural goods to feed populations, and of tangible goods to bring comfort, we can explain – from Solon to Marx – how, because money was looked at to advise or promote reforms for the happiness of the population, the existence of a sovereign was necessary. History provides many examples where different forms of "money" and various monetary policies characterized different societies. It also explains that fully linking currency with a universal and fixed physical reference will not allow for the necessary flexibility of monetary systems in terms of providing the quantity, price adjustments to values and ultimately the fixing of targets to rotation needs. In our contemporary crisis, liberated from the metal link, a different paradox has emerged. The overvaluation of western non-manufacturing "service industry" wage structures pegged against the undervaluation of manufactured goods shipped by emerging economies presents monetary imbalance. In such an environment, the consumers of our time can be defeated by both the suppliers of goods and a mismatch of tangibles versus intangibles (services) that are arbitrarily and differentially valued after the sociological realities of a special continuous online digital relationship between the service provider and its receiver, which is different from that between vendors and users of tangible goods. A range of monetary instruments and related fiscal policies has been developed by central governments of larger monetary zones, as well as national budgets to keep up consumption and the resulting exchanges to satisfy their citizens. There are no clues and no scientific papers drawing up a general framework of what is to be expected from such long-term policies. The expectations are to be considered as part of the sociological issue of who wishes to be part of a society and who is not; a base for further conflicts not only inside a defined national society, but also between zones of economic influence. This is the target of the present book, which aims to bring the reader through these topics.

We also see, with the Banque Royale failure, a new mechanism at the time that allowed disconnection between the price-setting mechanisms of goods and services and financial instruments, with the need for understanding and regulation to set reconciliation.

Modern 21st-century "money" is clearly different from its predecessors in the ancient world. Following the Second World War (WWII), financial democracy and its attendant creativity led to broadened transactional exchange capabilities worldwide. As a lesson from history, the Fathers of the European Union understood that exchanges should be the basis for economic development and a guarantee of peace, at least within a geographic zone. Their successors also considered that a monetary union was the corollary to a trade union. They were helped in achieving such a goal by all the changes in the intrinsic nature of money. Monetary instruments have come a long way from the simple definition of deriving monetary value from any metal weight measurement or its scripted equivalent – that is, monetary elements that are merely designed for the clearance of an exchange transaction. It can be seen that today's "money" has been extended not only in a technical context (e.g., supporting hypothetical value on the Internet) but also from the standpoint of legal definitions governing non-physical electronic payment transactions that are no longer limited to cash equivalents and that are not necessarily executed with a cheque, "money bill" or wire transfer, but rather via any number of alternative exchange formats.

QUESTIONS AND ANSWERS

From antiquity to modern times: monetary development over 6000 years. What history explains and comparison with new contexts

When did money appear?
  Probably at the same time as writing; 2900 BC.

What was money originally made from?
  Metal; some civilizations used other goods they had available, like shells, but these were limited.

What did metal allow?
  Weight as a measurement and stamping as a reference to it; also, it was easy to carry.

What was the evolution?
  From metallic money to derived paper bills.

Since when do we have proof of money existing?
  In the Hammurabi Code of 1650 BC and other slightly more ancient literature we have references to monetary measurement of prices.

How and since when have we had proof of coinage?
   Since the 8th/9th centuries with Asia Minor coins.

Why did paper bills appear?
   A shortage of metal, they are easier to transport and adapted to long distances, for long-duration lending and better safety against theft because of a possible holder's check on identity.

What are the other advantages?
   Paper bills can be coupled with infinite contractual conditions and attached to a purpose to be achieved, such as the transport of goods.

Is there a link between civilization and money?
   Yes. A civilization gathers humans together as a single society with a culture. The gathering is linked to the exchange and accumulation of wealth and means, including military, to defend them. To conduct its exchanges, a society needs monies that each participant will recognize.

What is the first example of a chartered bank?
   The Bank of England in 1694.

What is the first example of a modern central bank, and why?
   The French Banque Royale. It disconnected paper bills from guaranteeing reserves, allowing financing of both government and trade.

Why did it fail?
   Speculation on its equity and lack of trust in the royal guarantee for depositors in the absence of metallic reserves.

Is there something to learn from history?
   Yes, the irresistible evolution towards less and less tangible money and the above link between civilization and money. Further, a need for regulation to replace the constraint of metallic-based money and to survey its use by market participants when not for exchanges.

CHAPTER 2

Modern Times – Liberation and Growth of the Money Supply. The Facts Presented in Monetary Units and Resulting Regulatory Needs

"As soon as Blaise Pascal[1] has convinced scientists about air pressure, it will be easy to deduct that the Archimedes push will also operate on any corpse put in gas and especially into air. The theory will then be ready for hot air balloons to fly into the sky."

— **Gilles Godefroy**[2]

From a monetary point of view, modern times start with the fall of the Berlin Wall, which can be seen symbolically as the final end of WWII or of the so-called "Cold War". Since military budgets shrank for a while both in the western world and Russia, finance became the core topic of policy makers. If we had to be historians and explain in two sentences what happened, we would say that this starting period was a period of continuous war effort dedicated to scientific development primarily for weapons, with few human resources to use. It was also characterized by the dogmatic fight between the communist centralized economic model on the one side and the free-market economic model on the other. It has to be noted that in the common continuous war effort both were engaged in they started out with similar resources, both human and tangible, also dedicated to economic development. What brutally changed the pattern was, with the fall of the Berlin Wall, the liberation of a huge number of disciplined human resources for whom safety and comfort were a real achievement. Overall, better communication after the war let the citizens of both economic models compare their situation. The very different outcome over the transitional period between 1945 and the 1970s,

---

[1] 17th-century French philosopher and scientist.

[2] Godefroy, G., *Mathematics. Directions for use*, p. 70. See References.

with a continuous flow of human resources from the east towards the west, along with the overwhelming superiority of US monetary resources after WWII, were components in the liberation of money and basically explain the evolution of monetary regulation. The opening to a market economy of the entire Eastern Europe as well as China and their Dominion previously operating on a barter system changed the necessary volume of monetary instruments in the context of a fast-growing population.

Some significant population data (just estimates, besides the USA and EU)

Greek Empire (5th century BC)	3.5–15 million
Medic Empire (5th century BC)	50 million
Roman Empire at peak (2nd century AD)	100 million
China (18th century)	100–200 million
China 2013	1360 million
France (18th century)	24 million
France 2013	65.7 million
UK (18th century)	6 million
UK 2012	63.7 million
USA 2013	316 million
EU (28 countries currently)	510 million
India 2013	1224 million
World	7111 million

Note: The figures for ancient times are estimates from various specialized sources. Indian, US, EU and German figures for the 18th century do not represent the same geographic sovereignty and so are not given because they are not sensible of comparison. For the same reason, Greek and Medic figures are provided (Greece and Iran in modern times).

MONETARY EVOLUTION BACKED BY ECONOMIC GROWTH

Since the end of WWII, global wealth and the liquidity of the world's financial exchanges have grown at an extraordinary pace. The money required to handle the corresponding increases in industrial output, service sector productivity, expanded financial exchange activity and the concurrent need to post this wealth into corporate financial statements all depends on the capability to enhance both the nominal value and availability of the world's monetary pool.

This, in turn, raises the inevitable challenge of how best to fulfil the requirements in question. The answer is to simultaneously increase the monetary volume while concurrently reducing the requested need for money – in part by accelerating financial transactions and expanding their volume (the latter in large part by augmenting monetary velocity and improving flow efficiency inside the system). Thus, fluidity and volume are key targets, provided that their accurate measurement can be determined and the required processes to attain these objectives effectively developed.

DEVELOPMENT OF A GLOBAL FINANCIAL MARKET ECONOMY

The contemporary financial exchange-based market economy that we live with is enduring a growth crisis. Relevant data are necessary to understand the scope and dimensions of historical and recent developments.

Between 1970 and 2011, the gross domestic product (GDP) of the USA increased 15-fold, that of France 21-fold and the estimated Chinese GDP grew by a multiple of 51.[3] With almost 1.4 billion inhabitants, China reached only half of the actual US with 9.2 billion versus 16.8 billion for US with 310 million inhabitants (IMF data). However, in terms of dollar valuation, the achievement is far greater when characterized by bargaining power parity. In fact, following only a few years of exponential growth, China has become the world's second-largest economy (see Figure 2.1).

This pattern of accelerating GDP growth is a recent phenomenon. Historians usually consider that the standard of living on the globe remained unchanged from antiquity up until the 18th century. Furthermore, and until the 1970s, this phenomenon was mostly limited to western economies – aside from isolated and uncommon exceptions, such as Japan.

A historically derived economic analysis will point to various determining factors that favour the growth of predominantly market-driven economies, including: economic freedom, free enterprise, freedom for the exchange of ideas and commercial goods, as well as the right of individuals to travel freely. Over time, the liberalist model of a market economy has repeatedly overwhelmed authoritative political regimes incapable of integrating market

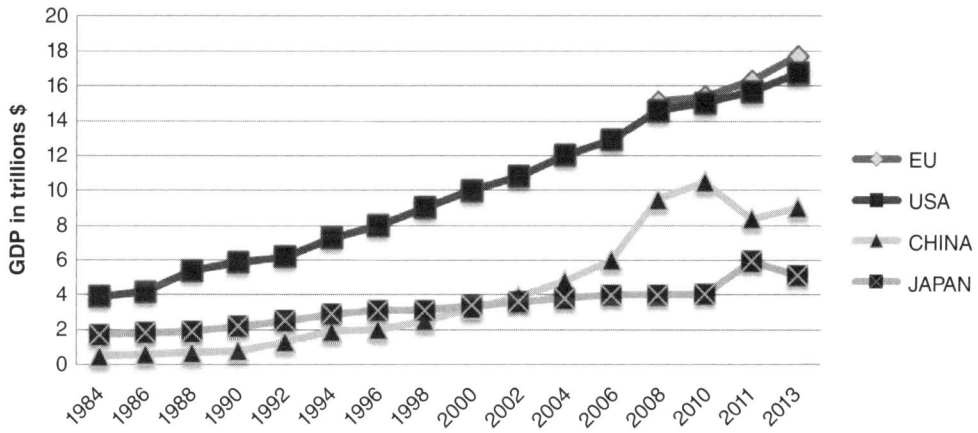

Total world GDP at current prices in 2013 is $74.71 trillion.
The EU, because of its geographic extension over the years, has not been considered pro-forma for the period.
Besides China at 8% forecast growth, this figure only gives trends.
Various sources: CIA world facts, OECD, World Bank, etc.

FIGURE 2.1   Face value of GDP in trillion dollars (after adjustment for buying power)
Source: Authors' creation.

---

[3] Source: Data.worldbank.org.

forces. When a people sharing the same culture and common roots have been separated into two adjacent nation-state entities, one with a centralized economy and the other with a market economy – as occurred with Germany and Korea – the state with the market economy has experienced stronger and more rapid sustained growth.

The growth in GDP parallels the evolution of other parameters: growth in household wealth, development of international trade and interaction between markets, as well as commercial monetization of economies.

The growth in household wealth is particularly evident in western countries with so-called developed economies. For instance, according to the INSEE,[4] wealth in France for a household represented 8 years of net available income in 2012 compared with only 4.4 years during the period 1978–1997. Unprecedented growth is also a recent phenomenon in the great emerging countries, including India and China. The urban Chinese middle class (income over RMB 25,000 ($5400)) represents 19% of the urban population compared with less than 1% five years earlier, with a growth rate of 25 million inhabitants per year. In India, the middle class (annual income of $4500) was on the order of 50 million in 2007; the McKinsey Global Institute estimates that it will grow to 580 million by 2025. In most countries, household assets are growing faster than GDP, and thus represent most of the observed increase in progressive enrichment.

In France,[5] the number of households retaining a stock portfolio increased from 1 million in 1978 to 12 million in 2007. For many developed, western economies this rise in financial wealth relates to the transition from a growth-based economic model to an economic model where an aging population expects additional income from capital accumulation that this segment of the population does not generate, develop or otherwise contribute to on an active wealth generation basis. In most developed countries, this trend has triggered a reorientation of savings asset deployment towards "ostensibly safe" financial instruments, thereby disregarding more risk-prone industrial investments.[6]

This pattern corresponds to a different allocation for GDP within such nations, leading to more emphasis on monetary transfers and to a larger role for currency-based assets. For instance, additional growth in savings led banks widely to increase their lending activities – supported by new high-yield financial products, including "sub-primes", which were originally claimed to be risk-free instruments. The proportion of worldwide financial assets compared with GDP reached a peak in 2007, with over $300 trillion compared with a world GDP of over $57 trillion.[7]

With regard to the global capitalization of market-listed companies, the ranking of banks has grown substantially and the weight of the financial sector now carries an ever-growing position in the composition of western GDP. Unlike the manufacturing sector, the market share for the service sector has experienced robust growth and, until 2000, the fractional GDP contribution from financial assets alone continued to increase – such growth has been fed by the development of financial transactions between residents of developed western economies.[8]

---

[4] French Governmental Statistical Office. See Glossary.

[5] Updated figures for France as well as comparable figures for the USA have not been found. Pension plans (401(k)s and others) only exist in the USA.

[6] Filippi, C.-H., *L'argent sans maître*. See References.

[7] McKinsey Global Institute (MGI) report of March 2013 on "Financial Globalization: Retreat or Reset".

[8] Bulletin de la Banque de France no. 175, 1st trim. 2009.

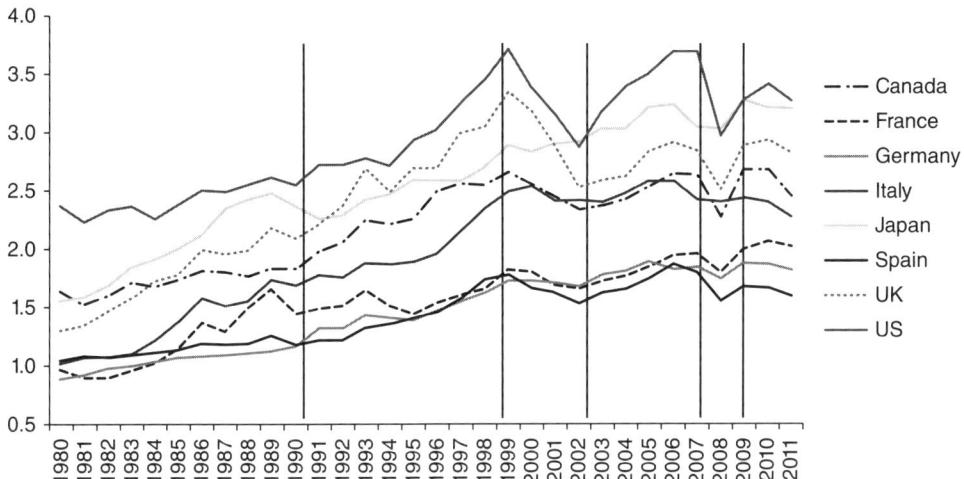

FIGURE 2.2 International comparison of the evolution of household wealth
Source: OECD. *18-Dec-2012 – COM/STD/DAF (2012)8*

Beginning in the 1980s, the growing interaction between an increasing number of national economies contributed to this dynamic of world economic growth, as did the emergence of new players with now predominating influence, the penultimate example being China.

Regarding the US the financial crisis of 2007, an April 2013 release from the Federal Bank of St. Louis[9] shows that 115 million households in the USA have not fully recovered in terms of net value, and we can see that real estate is their main asset while the partial recovery of 91% (with growth in number of households the figure is reduced to 81%) of 2007 values for the middle classes is due to an increase in share values. International comparisons are to be taken cautiously because they depend on asset classes, governmental interest, quantitative monetary policies and social set-ups, all of these being subject to further analysis about the "value" effect but certainly impacting consumption and savings (see Figure 2.2).

The growth of international trade is also noteworthy, as it not only reflects the development of globally interconnected market economies but also the interdependence of currency zones and both domestic and transnational enterprises operating within these zones. As shown in Table 2.1, the transactional volume of financial market exchanges has increased 14-fold since 1950.

This table evidences the fantastic growth of exports and exchanges that has outpaced overall growth in GDP during the historical period since WWII. It also reflects the globalization of the economy and the progressive internationalization of enterprises,[10] as many corporations have expanded to a transnational presence or in terms of their market position. The data also highlights changes in the relative strengths of regional economic systems, reflecting the emergence of Asia

---

[9] Emmons, W.R. and Noeth, B.J., Issue 4-2013, Short essays related to research on understanding and strengthening of the balance sheet of Americans households.

[10] The WTO 2009 report also contains developments on the transformation of international trade because of the rise in integrated groups that would partially explain the more than proportional to GDP growth of exchanges for the period 1948–2009.

TABLE 2.1   Export of merchandise (billion dollars and percentages)

	1948	1953	1963	1973	1983	1993	2003	2012
	Value							
World	59	84	157	579	1838	3677	7380	17,930
	Share							
World	100.0	100.0	100.0	100.0	100.0	100.0	100.0	100.0
North America	**28.1**	**24.8**	**19.9**	**17.3**	**16.8**	**18.0**	**15.8**	**13.2**
United States	21.7	18.8	14.9	12.3	11.2	12.6	9.8	8.6
Canada	5.5	5.2	4.3	4.6	4.2	3.9	3.7	2.5
Mexico	0.9	0.7	0.6	0.4	1.4	1.4	2.2	2.1
South and Central								
America	**11.3**	**9.7**	**6.4**	**4.3**	**4.4**	**3.0**	**3.0**	**4.2**
Brazil	2.0	1.8	0.9	1.1	1.2	1.0	1.0	1.4
Argentina	2.8	1.3	0.9	0.6	0.4	0.4	0.4	0.5
Europe	**35.1**	**39.4**	**47.8**	**50.9**	**43.5**	**45.3**	**45.9**	**35.6**
Germany[a]	1.4	5.3	9.3	11.7	9.2	10.3	10.2	7.8
France	3.4	4.8	5.2	6.3	5.2	6.0	5.3	3.2
Italy	1.8	1.8	3.2	3.8	4.0	4.6	4.1	2.8
United Kingdom	11.3	9.0	7.8	5.1	5.0	4.9	4.1	2.6
Commonwealth of								
Independent States								
(CIS)[b]	–	–	–	–	–	**1.5**	**2.6**	**4.5**
Africa	**7.3**	**6.5**	**5.7**	**4.8**	**4.5**	**2.5**	**2.4**	**3.5**
South Africa[c]	2.0	1.6	1.5	1.0	1.0	0.7	0.5	0.5
Middle East	**2.0**	**2.7**	**3.2**	**4.1**	**6.8**	**3.5**	**4.1**	**7.5**
Asia	**14.0**	**13.4**	**12.5**	**14.9**	**19.1**	**26.1**	**26.1**	**31.5**
China	0.9	1.2	1.3	1.0	1.2	2.5	5.9	11.4
Japan	0.4	1.5	3.5	6.4	8.0	9.9	6.4	4.5
India	2.2	1.3	1.0	0.5	0.5	0.6	0.8	1.6
Australia and								
New Zealand	3.7	3.2	2.4	2.1	1.4	1.4	1.2	1.6
Six East Asian Traders	3.4	3.0	2.5	3.6	5.8	9.7	9.6	9.7
Memorandum item:								
EU[d]	–	–	24.5	37.0	31.3	37.4	42.3	32.4
USSR (former)	2.2	3.5	4.6	3.7	5.0	–	–	–
GATT/WTO members[e]	63.4	69.6	75.0	84.1	78.4	89.3	94.3	96.6

[a] Figures refer to the Federal Republic of Germany from 1948 to 1983.
[b] Figures are significantly affected by including the mutual trade flows of the Baltic States and the CIS between 1993 and 2003.
[c] Beginning with 1998, figures refer to South Africa only and no longer to the Southern African Customs Union.
[d] Figures refer to the EEC(6) in 1963, EC(9) in 1973, EC(10) in 1983, EU(12) in 1993, EU(25) in 2003 and EU(27) in 2012.
[e] Membership as of the year stated.
Note: Between 1973 and 1983 and between 1993 and 2003 export shares were influenced significantly by oil price developments.
Source: WTO international trade statistics 2013 (http://www.wto.org).

and the rapid decline of the USA. The relatively stable initial ranking for Europe is multifactorial, that is the initial success of post-WWII recovery serves to statistically obscure the impact of subsequent intense exchanges within a single, unified EU market leading up to 2010. Since 2011, interstate commerce within the EU has been neutralized, reducing the uptrend rate but still showing European resilience within its world trade market share. In contrast to its continuation within the ALENA inter-trade, which was not neutralized, the reduction of the US share in the world exchange in favour of Asia is obvious. As noted by Pascal Lamy, former General Manager of the WTO, these statistical trends still fail to reflect the worldwide expansion of several major companies[11] as monetary measurements that impart substantial economic weight.

Within the USA, household wealth and its components can easily be appraised (see Table 2.2). In 2007, 93.3% of families held at least one type of financial asset – 52.6% having retirement accounts and 17.9% holding equity stocks. Households in possession of benefit accounts realized returns of only 37.9% in 1992. The growth in retirement accounts reflects the aging population and the changes in both distribution and utilization of wealth. During the same period, growth in private holdings of stock increased by only 1.0%. Even more demonstrative is the growth of (nominal) wealth, evolution assets and liability allocation. Although total wealth increased 57-fold between 1952 and 2010, not surprisingly a significant fraction of this growth is concentrated within pension plan reserves that represent 27.3% of overall wealth (a 39.5-fold increase). As for home mortgage liabilities, these increased 173-fold during the same 58-year period. If we compare financial assets between 1952 and 2012, from 830 million they reached 47,739 billion (a multiplication factor of 57).

TABLE 2.2 Wealth of households and non-profits in the USA

	1952	%	1972	1992	2010	%
Total financial assets	830	100	3,220	16,906	47,639	100
Deposits (including money market)	143	17.2	766	3,281	7,931	16.6
Credit market instruments	105	12.7	255	1,886	4,355	9.1
Corporate equities	151	18.2	921	3,094	8,514	17.9
Pension fund reserves	33	0.4	349	4,139	13,025	27.3
Equity in non-corporate business	322	38.8	783	2,899	6,251	13.1
Total liabilities	98	11.8	583	4,122	13,918	29.2[a]
Credit market instruments	94	11.3	555	3,970	13,357	28[b]
Home mortgage	58	7	343	2,840	10,070	21.1[c]

[a] Bureau of Census gives 23.5%.
[b] Bureau of Census gives 22.6%.
[c] Bureau of Census gives 15.5%.
Source: Table 1169 US Census Bureau extract.

---

[11] On June 6, 2011, Pascal Lamy, General Manager for the WTC at that time, declared: "Trade expressed in value-added is a better (than gross amounts) measurement of world trade. By focusing on gross value of exports and imports, traditional trade statistics give us a distorted picture of trade imbalance between countries. The picture would be different if we took into account, how much value added is embedded in these flows." Since 2013, the WTO gives some insights on value added per country allocation carried with trade exchanges in its report.

CITIZENS EMERGING IN THE PROCESS OF FINANCIALIZATION

Employment in the financial services sector has expanded tremendously throughout western countries, without even considering its specific concentration of staffing in financial centres such as New York, Frankfurt, Paris and Luxembourg. Expressed as a percentage of total employment we have the following figures:

	1970	1993	2007
USA	4.1	5.0 [5.7[a]]	
Germany	2.9	3.6	3.9
France	2.5	3.2	4.7
Luxembourg	4.3	10.0	28.3

[a] 2012 Bureau of Labor.
Source: Edey, M.L. and Hviding, K., OCDE/6D(95) Economics Department Working Paper no. 154, Economic Studies no. 25, "An assessment of financial reforms in OCDE countries", Paris, 1995.

Ultimately, some research centres have developed, based on BIS statistics, a concept to measure the use of money in economies. It includes, as we will see later, all financial instruments, equity, bonds, bank claims, secured and unsecured lending. This is the **financial depth**, defined as the ratio between GDP and the financial wealth made up of the financial instruments for each country, and globally for developed and emerging countries. Not surprisingly, it confirms the link between GDP growth and financial depth. Quickly growing since WWII until the 2007 crisis, it has since been rather stable at 325%.

In reviewing this period of economic history, we note not only the growth in wealth and the progressive major allocation of such wealth into financial instruments – such as pension plan systems and direct debt instruments – but also a dual debt structure that accompanies this trend. Today's pension plan reserves are adapting to longer life spans and retirement period expectancies that did not exist 60 years ago. Given the reality that money plays a key intermediate role as regards asset transfers (even beyond the role that debt exerts on inter-generational inheritance), monetary structure is undergoing substantial change as the split between active and non-active citizens continues to widen.

The Realities

Citizens in contemporary society are confronted with the impact of financialization through available sources of information and educational options, increasingly scarce job availability, as well as various options for management of personal financial assets. Nevertheless, financial activities and key aspects of decision making are highly concentrated within regional financial centres, whereas the impact on citizens is universal. Limited curricula relevant to these issues have been developed in both MBA and engineering degree programmes, including specialized courses in finance, financial instruments and mathematics, as well as accounting/auditing – where students cannot escape discovering the major changes involving the role of enterprises and the evolution in the general principles of accounting.

It is a fundamental and inescapable reality that – beyond the traditional and functional bookkeeping requirements that already rule the foundations of a now global system of commerce – the financial services sector constitutes an ever-growing stakeholder in the world economy.

The long-term statistics show a strong growth of financial sector employment in the entire western world until the 2007 crisis, with a concentration in certain cities. Statistics since the crisis are rare, but just looking at Western Europe we see a great resistance to contraction. Nevertheless, regarding this resistance one should be cautious about the statistics as the banking sector was, and still is, subsidized by low interest rates.

What one has to consider is the financial sector consolidation following the 2008 crisis, with the demise of some major corporate financial actors: Lehman Brothers by failure; Merrill Lynch, JP Morgan and Bear Stearns through buyouts. The resulting consolidation of power continues to generate a major threat to the economy in terms of continuing systemic risk and diminished fair competition. A citizen may rely on too limited a number of financial institutions for daily transactions. Moreover, recent events confirmed that many instruments and transactions (as well as financial industry players) were insufficiently regulated and not protected from bankruptcy. As seen from a geographical point of view, the growth of the financial sector is primarily limited to selected countries and economic zones: China, the UK, the USA and Europe, and some centres that have been termed "cores" by Fernand Braudel[12] and Jacques Attali[13] : New York, London, Dubai, Shanghai, Paris and Frankfurt.

The share of financial sector activities as regards employment is also very significant in major capital cities. With 310,000 salaried employees in the financial sector for 2012, the Ile de France region concentrated 41% of employment in this sector, compared with 665,700 positions in London and 737,500 in New York.[14] Furthermore, these figures do not include indirect sector activity, such as audit, legal and related supporting services – telecommunications, real estate, hospitality services, etc.

What is even more striking is that the share of financial intermediation in the global economy has not decreased significantly with the crisis. Without the US statistics, which are not available to us as we write, we can look at the UK and the Eurozone (18) countries taken as a whole. The rate remains at around 3% even if we see a stress on the UK that does not reflect the pressure on the City.

	1999	2010
Total employment (000):		
UK	29,340	31,213
Eurozone	134,269	146,273
Financial intermediaries (000):		
UK	1,130	1,118
Eurozone	4,041	4,245

Source: OCDE.

[12] F. Braudel: "Splendor, wealth and happiness convene together in the core of the world economy, in its heart. It is there that the sun of history is shining and that it has the brightest colors, where prices are the highest, salaries the best, the bank, the royal merchandises, the profitable industries, the capitalist farmers: there that are located the starting and arrival spots of lengthy traffics, the flux of precious metals, of hard currencies and credit bills. All an advanced economic modernity is located there: the traveler seeing Venice in the 15th century or Amsterdam in the 17th, or London in the 17th, or New York today will notice that." Extract from La Dynamique du Capitalisme, 1976 Conference. Editions Flammarion, collection "champs", 1988. (This footnote is author's own translation.)

[13] Jacques Attali, former president of BERD and author of *Une Brève Histoire du Temps*, Fayard, 2006.

[14] Statistics provided by Europlace, London City and Department of Labor. New York statistics include banking and insurance as well as pension sectors. In New York, financial employment represents, in 2012, 8.3% of total employment.

The consequences of ongoing financialization continue to raise concerns, as we see no real decrease in employment figures since the 2007 crisis. Over the past 10 years, the weighting of financial products has continued on an exponential upslope, alongside the evolution of financial techniques, technology and engineering of new instruments. A prime example of this may be found in the opinion of leading experts,[15] some of whom now consider the total value of "futures and derivative instruments" on world markets to equate to $600 trillion (with 10% for SDR only), thus representing a concerning 15-fold excess leverage against world GDP.

The impact of these and other complex phenomena has accelerated with the development of new and sophisticated information management and delivery systems, software and Internet interfaces. Although the resulting effect has been concentrated in some regional financial sector "cores", the resulting daily end-user implementation of financial service innovation (for instance through credit card payment transactions) has worldwide import. Accordingly, such trends beg consideration of two basic questions: is the financialization of our economy a positive development, and does it provide effective services to all citizens or is it just focused on benefit to a "happy few"?

Lord Adair Turner, one-time Chair of the UK Financial Services Authority (FSA) (its new denomination being the Financial Conduct Authority (FCA)), raised the real question that considers not the need for financial services or their legitimacy but rather the concerning uncertainties raised by "hypertrophy" of the financial sector: "Have all trading activities an economic justification or do they carry a withholding on the real economy?"[16]

Causes Underlying Emerging Macroeconomic Realities

Despite the foregoing realities that are not entirely positive, there remain underlying needs for the financialization that we have witnessed. Throughout both the western world and China, populations in many countries are confronting low birth rates which – alongside the changing demographics of aging – increasingly mandate that societies accrue the necessary financial resources to provide for adequate retirement benefits and stable systems of benefit dispensation. Since the required reserves that need to be "shown on the books" in fact constitute constituency beneficiary rights, such reserves need to be protected by regulations and professionals tasked with guaranteeing regulatory compliance. Further complicating shifts in demographics are the continuing rise in healthcare costs, and the accompanying expectation of populations that financial coverage will be maintained in proportion to changing healthcare cost structures.

The protection and administration of retirement and healthcare benefits are both challenges that involve GDP redistribution – a process that can be operated only via organized and regulated institutional systems. Such social institutional systems are of extreme importance to national GDPs and include the expectation of a temporal dimension in terms of timely monetary reserve availability to meet the requirements for redistribution of accrued amounts. These accruals are, in turn, based on a capitalization system that needs to receive recurring investment, which in turn depends on eloquent management and posting capability.

---

[15] Christophe Donay, research specialist, Landsbanki Kepler, September 2008, slate.fr, December 2009; figure quoted again by the ISDA General Manager Conrad Voldstad during a conference in New York on September 16, 2010.

[16] *Les Echos*, December 2, 2009.

The requirements for managing such society-wide benefit infrastructures imply corresponding future growth of applicable financial industry subsectors.

Resulting Needs for Standardization, Regulation and Supervision

As observed specifically through statistics on financial vehicles and instruments, these extraordinary patterns of growth in financial depth required the development of business and government infrastructures that were designed to ensure citizens were not only guaranteed their rights to participate in the benefits of such growth, but would also receive their due share.

Struck coinage and stamped bank bills have, over the years, lost their meaning in terms of guaranteeing the instrument of debt repayment. They are now of limited use. Sampling what is exchanged is now necessary to be able to articulate a price, and to do sampling financials are needed.

The government, if able to regulate, cannot sample all transactions and financial statements. An actor independent from the parties is required – the Certified Public Accountants (CPAs). This rationale provided the basis for legal innovation dating back to the 1929 economic crisis (1934 securities laws establishing the US Securities and Exchange Commission (SEC)). More recently, and in the wake of the Enron and Worldcom scandals, contemporary legislation (Sarbanes–Oxley 2001) imposed compliance with new external standardized audit standards that replaced the accounting profession's existing internal quality control methods. So as to address the weakness of previous securities laws that regulated publicly listed companies and the accountability of their financial executives, newer legislation strengthened sanction regimes as well. The most recent 2008 economic crisis resulted in the Dodd–Frank legislation passed by US Congress, which is still in the process of being implemented – with the objective of reorganizing the US financial system and improving financial consumer protection. During the same period of time (2008–2009), the EU began to introduce a global system of regulation which was nevertheless handicapped by the absence of coordination rules and provisions of executive power sharing between member states.[17]

Besides the issue of financial regulation per se, such regimes have been intended to ensure that accounting data disclosed in financial statements accurately reflect: comparable corporate performance statistics, "best practices", corporate resource allocation serving primarily the interests of investors, and a verifiable basis on which public trust in financial market exchanges may be preserved. Although publicly chartered (i.e., government) independent auditors were placed in charge within the US system, the regulatory auditing process has remained largely in private hands. Thus, in the Anglo-Saxon world, the accounting/auditing profession (charged with warranting the integrity of financial auditing information and practices) remained mostly self-regulated until Sarbanes–Oxley created the PCAOB. The converse is true in continental Europe, where the accounting/auditing profession has been legally regulated since WWII.

As a consequence of the growth in world trade, corporate internationalization and the globalization of financial markets, today's accounting profession has become an international oligopoly. Power and influence is consolidated in an unprecedented group of four major firms delivering opinions on the financials underlying 95% of the securities issued by publicly listed western companies. With increasing concerns raised by the US government and the European

---

[17] This handicap was later corrected with the European Stability Mechanism (ESM), the tax package and the Banking Union, which gave coordination power to the European Central Bank.

Commission, the globalized accounting/auditing industry wields self-generated accounting and auditing methodology that claims both independence and integrity – and that is now globally accepted as the prevailing system of extra-governmental corporate accounting and auditing standards.

This excessive consolidation of the global financial audit system is centred on the largest accounting firms, known as "The Big Four" (Price Waterhouse Coopers, KPMG, Ernst & Young and Deloitte), organizations which each command a staff of between 135,000 and 165,000[18] mid- and senior-level professionals. Although it has not been blamed for financial crises as such, this concentration of power has been implicated in terms of the absence of early warnings of corporate or economic crisis, and potentially in terms of impending publicly listed institutional collapse – for instance, in cases where clear opinions were issued only weeks in advance.

This was a primary argument that led the European Commission to propose reform. Since "The Big Four" presently control compliance with standards set by professional bodies (the International Accounting Standards Board (IASB) and the Financial Accounting Standards Board (FASB)) said to be "independent", but to whose function the four leading firms contribute, this has raised concerns. Such concerns include the question of governance for these bodies, issues relating to the handling of and follow-up on financial information, as well as the question of how to ensure the necessary degree of independence for external audits that are appointed and paid for by the audited entity. Additional issues raised have involved the question of potentially insufficient competition within "The Big Four" oligopoly, a state of affairs that would reduce both quality and innovation – particularly in the light of technological advances, which have significantly changed those information technologies and infrastructures that provide the data to be audited.

On October 13, 2010, the European Commission issued a green paper on these topics, subsequently transitioned into a white paper (submitted for active parliamentary consideration). After a lengthy consultation process, this new regulation approved by the trilogue on December 17, 2013 was concluded mid 2014 in the form of a Directive and Regulation[19] by the beginning of 2014.[20] It is aimed at reinforcing auditors' independence by forbidding them to practice anything other than audits (excluding any other kind of consulting work such as tax and legal or organizational) and reinforcing independence by obliging companies to change audit firm at least every 10 years, or 24 years in the case of a joint audit. The details of enforcement of the rotation of auditors is still being discussed.

Following the fall of the Berlin Wall in 1989 and the subsequent epoch of financialization, it is evident that world governments have been progressively overwhelmed by the rapid spread of globalizing market economies. Prior to the fall of the Russian communist empire, centralized economies somehow provided a balancing counterweight to free market economies. Late players in this process of free market evolution endeavoured to harness the inevitable growth differential, and never gave up on a comeback. This race notwithstanding, progressive deregulation originally intended to attract capital was heavily promoted, despite insufficiencies in

---

[18] Source: OXERA Report 2004, European Commission on the audit market concentration.

[19] A Directive in the EU is only applicable when transposed into the national legislation of member countries. A Regulation is immediately applicable throughout the EU. The new Directive will be enforceable on January 1, 2016.

[20] EU, Brussels, October 2011, White Paper final – Audit policy: lessons from the crisis. Directive 2014/56/European Union, regulation 537/2014 both published in OJ L 158 on May 27, 2014.

analytical statistical systems, over-consolidation of supervisory structures, and governance rules that were no longer appropriate and required revision.

Seen as the period that blunted the risk of war, the 1989 collapse of the Berlin Wall in fact liberated world finance without checks and balances of power. In a setting of insufficient competition (in part resulting from a concentration of players as well as inadequate laws and governance), key constituencies as well as their auditors failed to demonstrate the ability to generate advance warnings about inherent risks. Such pitfalls were illuminated by data that revealed unbridled economic growth and monetary expansion, and that suggested an eventual predisposition to collapse – thus underscoring the need for advance consideration of effective preventative measures.

QUESTIONS AND ANSWERS

The liberation and growth of money supply. Economics is represented in monetary units and resulting regulation needs

Modern times

When did modern times start in terms of money?
In the 1970s and 1980s, which is called the transitional period, with the disappearance of the link with gold and the fall of the Berlin Wall. Money became almost book money with digital support.

What backed the evolution of money?
The growth of both population and wealth backed a need for more money to flow and allow exchanges.

What other phenomena occurred?
Globalization and a development of exchanges as a parallel extension of the role of finance in society have to be noted, as does the emergence of new kinds of money with new guarantee attributes based on legal set-ups – that is, securitization.

How is employment in the financial sector important?
As a percentage of total global employment, with growth of population increase in employment, it remains marginal (with the exception of capital cities such as Luxembourg, London, New York, Hong Kong and Paris). The opposite is true in some core cities, such as those noted above, where with concentration and consolidation the financial employment sector is of paramount importance.

What is the result of monetary growth in terms of requirements?
There is a need for more standardization and regulation to provide better transparency for the public regarding the instruments and assurances about the guarantees derived from book balances. There is also a need for an independent third party to assess and guarantee data and financial statements. Quality of standards, professionalism of auditors and independence are all at stake.

CHAPTER 3

Past and 21st-Century Money Analysis

"Monetary calculation as a method of thinking."
"Monetary calculation is the guiding star of action under the social system of division of labour."

— L. Von Mises

DEFINING "TODAY'S MONEY"

Beginning with the classical concept of money and its use, one may witness the brutal historical transformation of monetary coinage into its contemporary form – that of purely *conceptual money* that lacks any constraints previously imposed by a gold-backed monetary standard. The scope of *today's money* has been extended to include financial instruments that are complementary to banknotes and that may be warranted either by tangible assets, government agencies or systemic financial institutions – the latter ultimately also backed up by the guarantees of governments and taxpayers.

Based entirely on a free market economy devoid of any banking monopoly, and not strictly imposed by law as merely coinage or bills, today's new concept of money is highly dependent on external drivers such as free trade and telecommunications. Impacted by new market regulations and the effect of digitalized market exchanges, contemporary actors in the monetary system cannot escape the question of whether even tacit acceptance of today's "new money" constitutes a social contract – where the ever-changing definition of money reflects its increasingly diverse functionality.

MONEY DEFINED BY ITS FUNCTIONALITY

Following an ancient Aristotelian[1] analysis, money fulfils three economic functions: (1) a price measurement standard that allows the price of goods to be fixed; (2) an exchange and

---

[1] Greek philosopher, born in 384 BC and died in 322 BC. See References.

trading instrument that provides a stable means of payment; and (3) a reserve depository of defined valuation that supports a given level of bargaining power.[2]

In comparison with pre-monetary barter economies, which required complex analytical methods (thereby impeding the development of monetary exchange-based transactional systems), the use of money provides a simple and measurable first-tier pricing standard for comparing different goods. The second function, namely for money to serve as a means of payment, requires some qualitative attributes to ensure its fluid use: broad *acceptance* of what mandates the "desirable" choice of precious metals, *durability* (non-oxidation of gold), a *user-friendly weight/volume* limitation and the *divisibility* of monetary currency. Ultimately, its third attributed economic function presupposes that money received in exchange for the sale of goods can be held as a value reserve over time, with a low risk of loss.

Money allows for the measurement of most economic activities; similar to the arithmetic summation of tangible or intangible transactions – however, in today's environment, monetary metrics themselves can no longer effectively reflect growing transactional complexity in the absence of reliance on transparent financial reporting and accounting. Inarguably, the nature of simple, real-time transactions between only two parties (for instance, cash payment against remittance of a product) has changed appreciably in our contemporary era. Just as bills of payment first appeared in 14th-century Europe (thereby replacing the use of metal coinage with script-based transactions), cheque payment methodology is rapidly being supplanted by today's electronic payment modalities, at the same time as traditional clearing procedures on bankers' books are being replaced by specialized commodities, financial instruments, industrial goods or services, or general clearing platforms that balance debits and credits between registered parties, without requirements for any physical transfer of currency.

Reflecting such an evolution of economic exchange methods, the role of money is expanding beyond a mere script-based means of payment, which corresponds linearly to account postings. Rather, a central question today is where the limits on potential uses of money may be found. For example, a recent issue of contention involved the mandate – if any – for central banks to regulate Internet customer software interfaces (originally developed from platforms supporting various airlines' frequent flyer mileage programmes) that exchanged miles as currency-convertible denominations on "peer-to-peer" sites, which in turn are capable of indefinitely archiving electronic-value equivalents – in the absence of any legally validating statute of limitations. Is the self-regulation of such platforms a sufficient guarantee and competition between currency qualities a possible answer to the need for safety of the actors?

To better understand the issues raised by the complexity of today's transactional exchanges and associated reporting via accounting standards, it is illuminating to examine the core elements comprising most monetary transactions as Aristotle defined them, namely: (1) the reproducible setting of a fixed or variable price; (2) a means of payment accompanying a transactional exchange between parties; and (3) a value repository. At the outset of any such analysis, it is essential to understand that as monetary-driven transactions are posted on accounting ledgers, the relationship between these three functional roles for monetary instruments can be distorted or unfavourably altered as a result of how financial accounting statements are interpreted. Increasingly – and particularly in terms of transmitting information about monetary instruments – the required trust in analysis is no longer driven by the quality

---

[2] Economists sometimes add a fourth economic function to define money as a "means of enrichment" derived from interest earned on a given amount of money invested.

and fixed valuation of metal coinage, but rather by the accounting interpretations that are imposed externally on the monetary transaction environment.

The First Function: Price Setting – Money as a Measurement Standard-Based Source of Information

The price is the result of a transaction by which two or more participants agree to pay for the transfer of property of an asset or a service delivery. It has to be expressed by a number of units that are monetary units. The price, as a result, is temporally and numerically unique for all participants in the transfer. As such, it differs from value, which could be different for each of the participants in the transaction. It is because of this major conceptual difference between price and value that transactions happen. However, from the unity of the price resulting from a meeting of wills between participants, it results that money is required to be used as a sampling instrument so that they can refer to the same counterpart for commitment and acceptance. Acceptance grounds the basis for any money instrument's existence. It has to be expressed – either in a contract or not – driving a need for stamping a number on the instrument itself. This stamping, combined with the offer or agreed-upon price, is the instrument's information. We will note that in its information or referential role, money does not need to exist physically or contractually. It will only necessarily appear when a transaction is concluded (for instance, the asking price for an asset such as a real-estate property is neither a price nor a value – it is information). Nevertheless, the information provided by a publicized price or tentative transactional price may have different interpretations depending on the instrument which is then used to clear the transaction.

The transactional price, that is to say the expressed par value, is the first exchange factor between two parties. In simpler terms, this concept is analogous to equating a fixed price with a universal exchange ratio; that is, a given weight in metal represented by a specific numerical notation, as imprinted on the surface of a coin or banknote. Money standards developed during antiquity – Sumerian (27th century BC) and Greek (7th century BC) first,[3] and then Roman coinage,[4] which we already talked about in Chapter 1, did not bear a face value (Drachma, Denarius, Aureus, Sesterce, etc.).

However, their weight-equivalent metal content imparted these currencies with an implicit payment value. Examples of weight-equivalent precious metals include coinage standards of that time consisting of precious metals: gold, silver and electrolytic forms (for instance, a naturally occurring alluvial mixture of gold and silver said to be found alongside the Patroclus River, near Sardis). Notwithstanding the absence of any struck number on their surface, coins could still be counted. With weight being a universal physical measurement standard, and with differences in size recognizable by the diameter and thickness of struck coinage, complex and sizable transactions were possible. Moreover, the utilization of a defined metal weight standard constituted an innovation that provided a semblance of monetary unification,

---

[3] Herodotus: *History*, "To our knowledge, the Lydians were the first to stamp gold and silver, and to then use gold and silver coinage…" The Bible also refers to land transactions and a census conducted by Abraham in "shekels". If Abraham is dated back to the 16th century BC, there is nevertheless an absence of proof as to this date – as opposed to ancient Greece, we thus have no tangible proof about coinage in this primeval instance. Furthermore, the Hammurabi Code refers to money as "giving prices to things and services". See Bottero (1995).

[4] Pliny the elder, "King Servius is the first to have stamped bronze".

in that exchange transactions across vast geographical regions, and between distant or remote territories, were readily facilitated.

Other unifying factors included organized reconnaissance for suitable precious metal deposits and sources, required for mass striking of coinage. The Divine[5] Emperor Augustus (63 BC–AD 14, according to the Julian calendar) as already noted in Chapter 2, instituted monetary unification of coinage rights over the entire Roman Empire that he had conquered. This imperial expanse comprised all of the Mediterranean coasts, and the entire Roman Imperial state with its advanced administrative set-up. Unofficially emulating procedures already in existence with the Greek Drachma, various types of Roman struck coinage were differentiated and valuated as visibly distinct measurement instruments – that is, not recognized solely by the weight of metal they contained. With this advance in monetary coinage, the concept of a legal tender device (meaning that creditors were obliged to accept the coinage by law) was born.[6] Fiat money was subsequently introduced in parallel with this cycle of monetary innovation.

For almost a century the Roman Empire stood prosperous on the consistency and weight standards of precious metal coinage. A century of disorders followed and the Emperor Aurelian (AD 270–275) decided to issue the first Roman "guaranteed" coinage,[7] which introduced the stamping of weight and consistency on the surface of the coin itself. Although basic metal coinage would remain the general monetary standard over centuries to come, the appearance of a stamped figure as an exchange value disconnected from variations in precious metal valuation, which presaged the eventual emergence of other monetary formats, first appeared in 7th-century China, along with the emergence of fiduciary money in the west. Derived from the Latin term *fides* or "trust", fiduciary money relies fundamentally on the public's trust in the issuer – for instance, the example of a guarantee of face value, as shown on a 100 Indian Rupees bill: "I promise to pay the bearer the sum of one hundred Rupees", and bearing the facsimile signature of the Governor of the Indian Central Bank, though few people would be able to verify the validity of the counterparty.

Nevertheless, convertible or claimable money became the reference for good script money, and eventually emerged as the principal gold reserve-based currency paradigm that western countries such as the UK, France, Germany and the USA utilized, until the advent of the First World War (WWI). In other words, the fact that the money was redeemable via a government bank issuer known to have sufficient gold reserves constituted an otherwise reliable guarantee.

Maintenance of sufficient gold reserves became an essential element for sustaining reliable currency/gold conversion ratios, but 20th-century history would reveal that major economic and political crises could overcome monetary systems designed to maintain the

---

[5] The "divine" qualification is only used to raise dispute from the reader, and to underline that he did not consider himself divine. His contemporaries granted him such a qualification after his death. In many respects, such as that of economic monetary regulation, his achievements were extraordinary considering the size of the Empire he helped grow, the period and available tools. He was a great ruler, handling matters as they were for the benefit of the Empire's citizens and the Empire as a whole.

[6] During the Peloponnesian war (777 BC), the Greek Drachma representing 4.5 grams of silver was imposed on Delos league members as legal tender. A subdivision of the Drachma, 1/6th of it, was the "obole", which became a word meaning a very small gift in French.

[7] As a matter of fact, the nature of this guarantee did change with the disappearance of the gold exchange standard, which occurred during the 1980s for most currencies.

stability of currency valuation and convertibility against a gold standard. An interesting example can be found in the case of the *franc Germinal*; France's imperial currency that was created on April 4, 1804 under Napoleon I, and that followed on the heels of unrealized financial reform attempted by his predecessor Louis XVI of France and his Finance Minister, Charles Alexandre de Callone.

Napoleon's franc Germinal had a fixed conversion ratio of 322.56 milligrams of 90% pure gold per franc, and the ratio remained unchanged for more than a century, outlasting the abdication of Napoleon I, Napoleon III's military defeat against Prussia at Sedan,[8] and forward in history until the point where France was drawn into WWI. More than just representing a national currency, the franc Germinal became the basis for a major international monetary agreement. Known as the Union Latine, this first inter-European monetary union was established in 1865 under Napoleon III. The Union Latine linked France, Belgium, Switzerland (later Greece) and ultimately 32 countries (other than Germany and the UK) through a bimetallic (gold, silver) metal coinage system throughout which coinage was redeemable at face value in any member country. The bimetallic system was based on the Napoleonic Germinal franc (GF), with an equivalency of one gold unit to 15.5 silver units.

At the inception of this monetary union, the bimetallic design included rights for currency holders to exchange gold coins for silver coins (and vice versa) at a central bank. Inevitably, variable shortages of available coinage supplies emerged, specifically as a consequence of metal price fluctuations driven by speculation – a trend that magnified any existing variations in supply-chain availability of both coins and precious metal supplies. Ultimately, silver had to be abandoned as a monetary metal standard, thereby underscoring the need for a unique unified measurement standard.

During the post-WWI period – under the leadership of the then French Prime Minister Raymond Poincaré, and following a devaluation that reduced the franc's value to 0.0655 grams of gold – the French government attempted a return to a stable gold exchange standard. However, given the rapid impact of the 1929 US financial crisis on Europe, the UK was obliged in 1931 to undertake a harsh devaluation of the pound sterling. This in turn impacted on the competitiveness of the French economy, triggering a large decline in France's share of worldwide exports following strong growth after its Poincaré devaluation and return to the traditional gold standard. It ultimately led to the 1936 election of the left-wing *Front Populaire* (along with the institution of two weeks' paid leave for all French working citizens). A subsequent October 1936 currency devaluation brought the venerable French franc to a value of between 43 and 49 milligrams of gold from its 1914 original germinal value of 322 milligram. In 1925 Churchill, as Chancellor of the Exchequer, after a long dispute between its advisors and contrary to Keynes' opinion, re-established the link between the British pound and gold, driving high unemployment and difficulties in Britain.

Financially speaking, though a return to the old parity would not have been possible, a return to a pre-WWI gold backing would have been, had the defeated country (Germany) paid war reparations, as had been the rule in Europe for thousands of years. However, the defeat conditions in the period between WWI and WWII were different from before. France had borrowed debt capital from the USA and the UK, so as to finance its military role in WWI – a devastating conflict for France that destroyed infrastructure throughout the north and east of the country, including its most industrialized regions. Despite a clear intent to pay down its national debt to

---

[8] In 1870.

the USA, and backed by the expectation of receiving war reparations from Germany, France met resistance from the USA against attempts to conditionally monetize transatlantic remuneration to the USA by using post-war restoration proceeds due from Germany. After reimbursing the USA in full, France would ultimately be short-changed, as Germany would pay out only 9.5 billion gold Marks of the 68 billion Marks in fixed damages that had been mandated by a 1931 US-driven settlement. The issue in contention was not of parity, but rather that the debt was linked to the most recent prevailing value of gold, and could no longer be repayable at the gold value that was in force during the immediate post-war period.

Nevertheless, one has to remember that symbols are important to the public, and thus to politicians as well.[9] A simple approach can be made today by comparing where gold was accumulated the most – in the USA – then after 1925 in France, or where in counterpart it was missing; in the UK and ruined Germany with political disorders. Also, the financial history of great economies would demonstrate the impossibility of the gold model standard and why the crisis came from the USA and not from Germany. In Germany Hjalmar Schacht, the Minister of Finance, had re-established the currency situation of the country using the hyperinflation caused by the distrust in the Reich Mark to buy it back with a new invented currency – the Renten Mark – which was created in November 1925 with no real guarantee other than a theoretical promise that it was grounded on farm land and industry.

By the end of 1925, Schacht had stopped the hyperinflation and was able to start borrowing again, especially from the US banks. In the meantime, as a process that we will experience again, excess money was retreating from safe assets to others such as gold or shares in the USA, while US industry was discovering cars and refrigerators and experiencing scale economies more than other countries. Gold was frozen by central banks, with the USA not to use it, and borrowing was being made available through excess money already floating around in nominal amounts over the debt created by the war, which had been wiped off by inflation. For the first time, the conditions for a money retrenchment were created. This happened on the Black Thursday of October 1929. The assets in exchange price value would not meet the nominal value of the loans distributed through the economy. Due amounts were in nominal value, counterparts at price amounts. Value and prices were concepts that most refused to consider as different because of this original, still prevailing, mental reference to a metallic system.

We can observe this prevailing mainstream idea when analysing the attempts that were made to form regulated monetary systems for pricing during the inter-war period. The May 1922 Genoa Agreements instituted an intermediate system intended to replace the prevailing standard of universal convertibility. The new system established a short-lived "gold exchange standard" between central banks, pegged against the US dollar and the British pound sterling. Given prevailing pre-WWII world trade markets characterized by competitive currency devaluations, the financial environment was no longer compatible with a long-lasting fixed link between currencies and the gold standard. However, keeping the reference to a past period where the west dominated the world economically, no attention was given by political leaders to the new context of the worldwide exchange economy. Strongly impacted by the 1929

---

[9] In 1958, as part of a "balanced budget recovery plan" designed by Armand and Rueff and under the tutorship of French General de Gaulle (who strongly favoured the link to a gold standard), the franc's nominal value was divided by a hundred (e.g., 100 old francs were required to be exchanged for 1 new franc). New 5 franc coins made of silver were a return to the traditional coinage that France had known for more than a century. Not in silver, the 1 franc coin was also a replica of the old 1 franc coin that France had known. 15 years later, the US mint would start removing its silver dollar coins.

world economic crisis, however, this putative gold exchange standard was abandoned prior to WWII. Naturally, this occurred for a number of reasons, which included: (1) inflationary pressures driven by pre-WWII trade barriers and (2) economic adjustments in response to insufficient offers of reparation, as well as (3) economic drivers necessitated by mobilization efforts required to repair the destruction of war.

Though direct financing of the economy did not yet exist, nevertheless no macro-economic statistics were available in countries where a sufficiently stable currency existed to measure the money which is genuinely in circulation, through lending. It was only when a crisis had already broken out that those western countries tried to implement systems – some because of crises like in the USA, others because they were preparing a war effort.

Again, the topic changed. The forgotten topic of pricing was no longer important in a war economy where loans and taxes had to balance expenses and barter came back into use between nations, especially communist ones.

With the adoption of the Bretton Woods Agreements in July 1944, a robust universal system of free monetary exchange and semi-fixed currency trading rates between nations was reintroduced. The long-established convertibility between the dollar and the pound qualified these as internationally recognized reserve currencies, while gold was re-legitimized as an international reserve reference designed to provide stability, back up the dollar and maintain its value. However, the Bretton Woods Agreements made a semi-final change in concept; if gold were not available against outstanding money in other central banks, the pricing function of the central bank had disappeared. The stored gold was only a reserve, and the system a commitment to currency exchange stability action. When we see that the FED maintained the price of gold unchanged for a decade, it does not mean that prices were stable. After the Korean war broke out, inflation rose. Gold was neutralized by the mere fact that it could not be used to neutralize excess money.

In its practical implementation, the Bretton Woods regime only survived a finite number of decades. Because of the accumulated deficit on its balance of payments, on August 15, 1971 the USA gave up on the dollar's gold convertibility – primarily because existing gold reserves were no longer sufficient to universally back up the dollar. To date, precious metals are no longer a universal standard, and most world currencies derive their source of valuation from margins on immediate exchanges and from the pegged value of loans, currency market trading instruments and credit spreads. In fact, the contemporary face-equivalent monetary note value for most transnational bulk currency loans is based either on the available GDP for the nation in question, or on the capacity of the "currency note-issuing" government to balance its budget. The latter fiscal watershed for balancing debt versus revenues reflects three essential elements: the ability to levy taxes on all elements of national production, the potential to employ political or military leverage to impose the terms of monetary exchange, and the capability of monetary or treasury bond reserve credit holders to obtain credits in exchange.

Moving away from the fixed Bretton Woods currency system after 27 years was a daunting task, and in December 1971 the "Smithsonian Agreement"[10] introduced a transactional role for free-floating currency markets – alongside introducing an increase in the allowable currency fluctuation rates from 1% to 4.5%. Concurrently, in April 1972, the common market – then West Germany, France, Italy, the Netherlands, Luxembourg and Belgium – established the European Joint Float. Under that protocol, individual member countries could allow their currency to fluctuate within a 2.5% band, and collectively (known as "the tunnel") within a 4.5% band against the US dollar.

---

[10] From the name of the Smithsonian Institute in Washington where it was signed.

In January 1976, the "Jamaica Agreements" officially ended the multi-decade Bretton Woods regime of fixed exchange rates and replaced it with a formally recognized floating-rate exchange system. Technically in force up to the present day, the components of the Jamaica Agreement were these: floating rates were legitimized and signatory states could enter the foreign exchange market to even out "unwarranted" speculative fluctuations; gold was abandoned as a reserve asset; the IMF returned gold assets to member nations at current market prices (diverting the resultant trading proceeds into a support fund aimed at helping poorer nations); and IMF quotas paid by member states to the IMF were increased to $41 billion, a value that has since increased to $180 billion. Most notably, it was now an accepted fact that money functioning as a metric standard was based on member state self-evaluation.

The Jamaica Agreements may have resolved the arithmetic of measurement standards, but not the trust in those measurements and in the unit denomination values of individually fluctuating currencies. In fact, from December 1976 onwards, currency metrics could be based only on relative parities between units (more or less pitting the dollar against other currencies). The Jamaican regime relied on the fact that currencies were legal tenders that obliged holders to use such currency units alongside both legal and de facto banking monopolies for the purpose of receiving deposits, including record-keeping and payment service management. As such, the "legal tender concept" that obliges a creditor to accept a monetary unit as payment for a transactional obligation was now solely grounded on the credibility of the monetary note issuer, rather than on the absolute or even inherent right to convert that note into a corresponding weight of a precious metal standard that no longer existed.

The Jamaica Agreements consequently and logically converted the previous metrics-based approach into a voting system of member states. In order to change currency parities and flotation bands, an 85% quorum of membership votes was required, including a "declaration of intention" about what additional factors should determine parities between currencies.

A contemporary example that supports the importance of credibility assigned to the issuer of a currency may be found in 2012 the recent Greek sovereign debt instrument crisis. During this phase, the state issuer's credibility has been challenged, based on the debatable quality of statistical data on the Greek budget. Although potentially an extreme example, the Greek sovereign crisis underscores the importance of trust factors.

In practical terms, there are two basic trust factors: (1) the capacity to levy taxes to an extent proportional to the sovereign debt that has been issued and (2) trust in, or doubt about, the fair representation of the financial situation as reflected in the statistics provided by the state issuer (including trust in data elements provided with the help of bankers).[11]

When considering the foregoing, an immediate follow-on question might be this: are there additional aspects of misrepresentation relating to other countries that the primary overwhelming focus on the modern Greek fiscal crisis will, in fact, obscure, especially when examined by professional observers based in nations that have a secure tax system?

Two issues relate to the topic – the capacity to levy taxes and the capacity to collect them. The USA, before an agreement was made by Congress, was confronted with the first one while Greece had been experiencing both.

Decades before our current 21st-century issues came to the forefront of economic debate, a visionary economist, Friedrich A. Hayek (1899–1992), understood the importance of

---

[11] Goldman Sachs was held responsible for helping the Greek government hide some of its debt through financial instruments.

financial statements arising as the result of price measurement. He wrote: "uncertainty in valuation results from the liability in the variation of the value of money itself. Of this the merchant, the accountant, and the commercial court are alike unsuspicious. They hold money to be a measure of price and value, and they reckon as freely in monetary units as in units of length, area and weight."

The implication is that the prevailing trust in the expression – *money par value* – has been overvalued. Again Hayek writes: "If old truths are to retain their hold on men's minds, they must be restated in the language and concepts of successive generations. What at one time are their more effective expressions gradually become so worn with use, that they cease to carry a definitive meaning. The underlying ideas may be as valid as ever, but the words (even when they refer to problems that are still with us) no longer convey the same convictions; the arguments do not move in a context familiar to us, and they rarely give us direct answers to the questions we are asking."[12]

The question of "par value money" as a measurement standard has also changed consistently with the way modern trade is operated – namely utilizing very few physical transactions compared with the vast number of purely financial and electronic transactions receiving the same contractual support. When markets are efficient, the matter of money as an intermediate valuation tool has lost some, if not all, of its paramount importance. The concept of monetarily defined price is no longer pricing at market support levels, but at times has emerged as a mere figure quoted from a transactional or brokerage insurance premium for hedging activities.

Today's money has changed in terms of how it is used consistently. Money is now: (1) *dynamic* (e.g., flow overrides stock value, thus determining the rising importance of transactional speed); (2) *dematerialized* (virtual transactions); and (3) *conventional* (i.e., grounded in accounting ledgers and standards). Providing a revised modern basis for currency durability, trust and credibility can no longer be based on gold. In today's monetary environment, precious metals only represent mere tangible goods that are unfit to be a standard for an essentially non-tangible economic system – one lacking any limits on the type, frequency and number of transactions (especially digital) that a plethora of economic and commercial actors can generate. However, given that transactions must be posted and amounts added or subtracted accounted for, more than ever today's money retains its numbering measurement function.

Accordingly, a prerequisite of the contemporary transactional environment is awareness of which individuals and entities (including institutional mechanisms) will guarantee the measurement function required of contemporary money. In past eras, officers of the King (or Queen) inspected markets to control and ensure that merchants were not embezzling data on precious metal weights, etc. In contrast, our present environment requires that trust in the monetary system is maintained in the context of appropriate regulatory regimes (commercial law for exchanges, clearing rules between nations, etc.) – regimes which help maintain stable valuation for money. Notwithstanding, in a broader context money remains a mere financial instrument, since other conflicts impacting trust can emerge in terms of the extent to which the currency issuer is able to confirm national economic health and sound budget policy that supports the tender value of a nation's currency.

---

[12] F.A. Hayek (1899–1992). *The Constitution of Liberty*, introduction.

The Second Function: A Payment and Trading Instrument[13]

Being denominated in increments, money can be used transparently to clear a transaction. The applicable transactional spectrum may range from an exchange against tangible goods (food, appliances, etc.) or intangible services (e.g., downloading music from the Internet), to a simple reciprocal monetary contract (lending, deposit, etc.). Liberated from the burden of physical metal currencies or direct links to a precious metal standard, today's money transfers (payments, deposits or withdrawals) can be made by straightforward posting on physical or electronic ledgers. These postings are equivalent to closed transactions contingent on time-specific proof of the debtor's acceptance and the bookkeeper's (bank or payment service provider's) confirmation as to a repository of and command over money or lending capability.[14]

Considering the small and still diminishing volume of remaining coinage and bills, modern money is mostly scriptural in nature (see Chapter 5). New attributes and risks are emerging alongside the non-material or intangible consistency of contemporary money. In the electronic age, money can circulate and be exchanged at the speed of light, without limitation on transactional speed – especially compared with any other means of payment. The proof of such circulation rests on electronic means and auditing follow-up. The process can be prone to forgery in a manner analogous to the risk of absence of material proof – or its verification – that democratic laws require in order to convict the dishonest. In other words, a forged paper does not necessarily designate the counterfactors specific to a transaction, but nevertheless constitutes proof in and of itself.

Given that monetary transactions require recorded evidence (physical or electronic) as proof, this fact raises new issues in the contemporary monetary environment; for instance, the need for adaptive posting methodology on regulated books (in the face of a virtual lack of any limitations on transactional speed), as well as attendant issues that relate to balancing and clearing functions, and categorization and choice of ledgers that should be utilized for recording and tracking activities – which in themselves are in a nearly constant state of evolutionary flux. A few examples may be noted: what if all transactions were to be kept open indefinitely without balancing and clearing? The resulting record-keeping function would rapidly become untenable, particularly in terms of summating transactional flow. Moreover, questions of how and when transactions should be cleared, and what constitutes a clearing function, all become critical issues in the auditing world that tracks the exchange of modern monetary bills and instruments. In addition, there are legal issues regarding competent jurisdictions and geographical territories, notions of which are increasingly impaired in the electronic age.

The Third Function: A Reserve

When issued, money may exist by itself without any use for immediate transaction. It is a storage hall for value. By virtue of their underlying guarantee, different types of monetary instruments (as well as mainstream forms of fiduciary money notes) all constitute a *value-equivalent*

---

[13] We use the words "payment" and "trading" combined for simplicity to focus later on the fact that exchanges may be paid in the sense of being cleared with any kind of exchangeable financial instrument and not only with bank bills.

[14] This is the purpose of the European directive for a Single Euro Payment Area (SEPA), EU no. 2007/64, creating an automated European system of payments and regulation EU no. 260/2012 – issued as of March 2012 – for the purpose of setting technical constraints on wires and transfers.

reserve for their holders. Viewed as a whole, scripted money can accumulate on accounting ledgers without limits imposed by regulatory regimes (e.g., prudential ratios), or management constraints imposed by entities that handle the flow of trade balances or that accept deposits (not necessarily only banks or savings institutions). When the balance of cash or other liquid assets referable to one specific source of ownership exceeds the levels of capital required to clear expenses or guarantee operations, then the concept of a monetary "reserve" invariably enters into play. Of course, it remains axiomatic that each individual account holder or enterprise may be characterized by differences in the volume of disbursements and collections.

Accordingly, the appropriate determination of what fraction of a balance corresponds to a reasonable reserve volume will differ between diverse business sectors and individual account holders. The variable concept of how to define appropriate reserve levels is important simply in the context of the overall impact that countless such determinations have on monetary capital flow through the economy, particularly when considering the measurement function of money.

Throughout the applicable technical literature, this is described as the determination of the "needed endowment".[15] The question raised at that stage is about reserves and savings in the Keynes formulae, and what share of available money is going to be limited in availability, and to what extent. We are talking about households' free money compared with committed money, and we can immediately say that there is no set material border between the two categories, not even talking about individual liberty and different psychological profiles. Many authors have discussed extensively how to operate the Keynesian functions individually and combined, and how they will interact with prices, changing therefore the borders between reserves and total money issuance.

LINKS BETWEEN MONETARY FUNCTIONS

Although links between the three described functions (measurement standards, payment instruments and reserve function) are obvious, both the nature and flexibility of their interactions – particularly in terms of the trust issue – are subject to substantive variability. Unlike some contemporary economists, Von Mises, Hayek and Keynes understood[16] that assigning a par value to a monetary species is an enabling valuation facility subject to market-driven variation, but not an absolute physical measurement. In an October 2011 public speech,[17] European Internal Market Commissioner Michel Barnier reminded us that the convenience of ignoring this reality is one underlying cause of failure for auditors of financial records.

A classic example of this phenomenon can be encountered upon the convergence of business records as a consequence of a legal merger, where two participating legal entities

---

[15] Aubin, J.-P., *How Much Money Endowment is Needed?*; Aubin, J.-P., *et al.*, *Applied Functional Analysis. Economic Theory & Philosophy*. See References.

[16] F. Hayek, writing in *The Constitution of Liberty*. At the head of his chapter "The Monetary Framework", Hayek quoted the work of Keynes (*The Economic Consequences of the Peace*, 1919, pp. 220–221): "there is no subtler, no surer means of overturning the existing basis of society than to debauch the currency. The process engages all the hidden forces of economic law on the side of destruction, and does it in a manner which not one man in a million is able to diagnose."

[17] FEE Brussels.

remit all of their issued shares as proceeds in exchange for a single new set of shares. Another variant is a single entity absorbing a second corporate entity and issuing new equity shares to the absorbed entity's existing shareholders against the net equity brought into the transaction. The disclosed price for the transaction bears little effect on nominal remuneration and is, in essence, irrelevant – being intended merely to satisfy bookkeeping and taxation purposes. Only the securities exchange ratio is of importance to the stock holders of both entities – in other words, whatever transactional price may have been set, the key issue is the specific number of new shares that stockholders will receive in exchange for their original shares (i.e., preservation of an acceptable percentage of equity ownership is of primary transactional importance to the investor).

When the Roman Emperor Aurelian had metal coins stamped, or more recently in the 20th century when F.A. Hayek, the prominent economist and advisor to the Austrian government from 1926–1929, recommended that a different quantity of coinage be issued than the government had intended, it was necessary to disconnect the value of coinage from price structures.

These examples underscore the realization that money has no greater intrinsic role than as a contractual instrument aimed at effecting payments (i.e., the discharge of an obligation). One may also recall that the first bills-of-credit issued in North America (Massachusetts Bay Colony, 1690) had a limited time of validity, ensuring that this type of currency could not be used to form or hold a long-term value-equivalent reserve. We focus on this issue because the ongoing evolution of money towards an immaterial instrument adds greater importance to our remarks, for instance when considering the potential destabilizing role and impact of flash trading or black pool market exchanges.

THE INTRINSIC DEFINITION OF MONEY

Money is not only functional, for being so it needs to be able to provide the user with a fixed sampling unit (see the Glossary), which allows the value measurement and price setting of any good or service and comparison from that perspective. Of course, for exchanges to operate successfully, this unit must be a number combined with a fixed reference. Precious metals were the most commonly used references. The point is made here – as further on, during later developments – that gold disappeared as such, or at least became much disputed. We need to explore in detail what is needed to replace it, or what has already stealthily replaced it.

A Trifunctional Monetary Support System

Gold as a Universal Standard – Evolving from an Intrinsic Value Basis for Metal Coinage into a Reference, and Beyond into a Reserve

At this point in our discussion, we can hardly avoid the question of why gold – at times disparagingly labelled a "Barbarian relic" – always returns to human consciousness when any monetary purpose with broad implications is considered. There is a mystic quality imparted to gold, one that cannot be simply disregarded when several billion earthly inhabitants use gold as jewellery, or in exemplifying individual and collective dreams of beauty, wealth and social status. Moreover, gold is deemed valuable under conditions of conflict, when it is still universally accepted as having an exchange value; this is easily understood for many parts of the world that are exposed to social and political unrest, where local tenders are of doubtful use to holders who are potentially exposed to the threat of displacement.

Sharing a common view with Charles de Gaulle, Rep. Ron Paul[18, 19] and Edwin Vieira Jr.,[20] many politicians and economists have acknowledged the virtues of gold; a durable and electrochemically neutral metal not in the sole possession of any source. Recently discovered Byzantine coins have been found to be in splendid shiny condition. In comparison, had they been buried only a century ago, paper dollar bills issued by the US FED would have decomposed well before our time. Yet, the historical and enduring trust placed in a precious metal whose prime use is in jewellery consistently drives savings, induces confidence and hoarding and, not infrequently, fuels destructive speculation. In fact – where diversion and hoarding of metal coinage for profit resulted in a metals market price for coinage that was higher than its face value – speculative destabilization has triggered restrictions on the mining and minting of precious metals at different historical moments.

In our time, the link between money and gold (only available in limited quantities,[21] while fiat money is not) either rests on direct convertibility via the currency issuer (the so-called but presently inactive universal gold standard) or on a counterpart system between central banks (the gold exchange standard). Without returning to a *precious metal weight/purity*-defined currency model (X ounces of gold = $Y \times 1$ monetary unit – as with the Germinal franc),[22] as utilized by the monetary agreement known as the Paris Convention of 1865 (Union Latine)[23] – for instance, were gold retained by any nation's central bank, say to make payment on a transnational deficit on the balance of payments between two nations – it is fairly unlikely that any voluntary transfer and delivery of precious metal to a counterparty central bank would actually transpire.

This was the essential rationale that US President Nixon's Administration was obliged to adopt, in order to justify its historical mid-1971 disconnection of the US dollar from its previous link to the gold standard. Since that moment, gold has become a mere reserve of value for central banks, as it is for individuals. The resulting magnitude of this residual global gold reserve appears insignificant, specifically in comparison with the size of the presently circulating worldwide scripted money supply.

---

[18] Monetary history from antiquity to the Middle Ages, and beyond into the 19th century, was characterized by the problem of how best to compare the respective values of precious metals (silver and gold). A further consideration was the minting cost of small bronze coinage that was produced at a lower price than the value of the metal it contained, but that (due to its low value) did not need to be saved as a reserve or withdrawn from circulation for speculative purposes.

[19] Ron Paul, Member of the US House of Representatives. Author of *The End of Fed*, Grand Central Publishing, 1989.

[20] *Piece of Eight. The monetary power and disabilities of the US constitution*, revised edition, 2002.

[21] Projections claim that an estimated 140,000 tons of gold have been extracted since the beginning of human history, 120,000 of these still being in existence. Currently, in rough figures, 1/3 of the available planetary gold is used for jewellery, 1/3 is acquired by banks or for savings reserves, and the balance of gold has been acquired by central banks – despite an official decision in force since 1971 for central banks to sell their reserves of gold as these are no longer intended to back up the value of world monetary supplies. From 1959 until today, between 2000 and 2500 metric tons (MT) of gold have been produced every year, with the USA contributing 230 MT/yr to that figure. At $1800 an ounce (0.031104 metric grams), the present levels of gold production would represent a value of $1.5tn a year, to be compared with a US monetary base of $2tn, a Eurozone base of 1.2tn euros, and a world GDP of $57tn.

[22] 0.32256 grams of gold for 1 franc. See "The First Function: Price Setting" earlier in this chapter.

[23] That will set the exchange rate with gold for 100 francs (called the gold franc) at 3.25 grams with grade 900.

The real reason for gold is the reserve functional role of money. As such, gold is durable. Gold is both a physical unit (its weight as coinage) and inviolable as a support (the metal). These imperative qualities of reserve money will still be required over time, whatever the chosen unit and its support. Only the means to reach them may change with technical and sociological progress.

There are two key aspects pertaining to the role of gold as a monetary instrument. The first aspect is that gold disappears (speculative profit-driven diversion/hoarding) when not available in sufficient quantities to satisfy the ongoing needs for either coinage (ancient history)[24] or a given volume of issued script money (including treasury bonds or claimable public debts), as experienced in modern times. Moreover, history has shown that paper currency-to-metal convertibility is negatively impacted when precious metal demand is not satisfied – the most recent example being the August 1971 disconnection of the US dollar from the gold reserve standard.

As we have already noted, the trust factor surrounding the stability of fiduciary and script money implicates the need for a credible guarantee. As such, even if disputable gold were to be accepted in exchange for monetary tender, the trust requirement would, by necessity, impose a stable ratio of exchange between the weight of precious metal that was set to define units of value, and then the expressed value itself. If such conditions were not to be satisfied, then only metal transfers using weight-based guarantees could be retrieved. Of course, disconnection of monetary systems from the gold standard does not imply that gold has disappeared from the monetary economy; it has not. It simply denotes that gold stocks are now held by central banks and other interests, and not surprisingly that the value of gold has risen for the reasons discussed, as well as a number of unrelated macroeconomic factors.

The second aspect of interest relates to gold's measurement function. The existence of a measurement standard used to clear foreign exchange balances is a need that only money itself can satisfy. Such balances are, by definition, a reserve for any and all entities that at the outset (prior to transactions) have no determined counterparty. In general, such holders of "balances due" request validation via a reserve value measurement standard, a number of defined units. Other ways to avoid detaining balances that cannot be cleared or can only be cleared with instruments that cannot be used because of their lack of standard value, economic agents will stop exchanging with all consequences.

Since Bretton Woods, there have been discussions on what should constitute an appropriate monetary reference basis. If gold no longer satisfies a range of requirements in this regard (in the preceding discussion we already mentioned the issue of limited availability of precious metals under a range of potential circumstances), it stands to reason that consensus is lacking as regards acceptable new measurement and reference tools for defining and standardizing monetary systems – aside from propositions and rejections made at Bretton Woods, which involved a basket of choices in raw and natural materials.[25]

In the absence of a broad consensus in the post-Bretton Woods era, central banks still retained their gold stockpiles as a reserve, equivalent in value to a large fraction of their monetary note assets:[26] 65% for the USA, 80% on average for Germany, France and Italy,

---

[24] Ancient coinage more frequently consisted of silver than gold, even if both metals were available. Reasons included a more readily available supply of silver, or the need to avoid intentional or speculative diversion by individuals when the value ratio changed in favour of gold.

[25] "Bancor", proposed by K.M. Keynes. See Glossary.

[26] IMF publishes the tonnage of gold held by central banks. As of June 13, 2014 data published on website at "about international", the EU Eurozone stands first at 346,50 Million troy ounces and the US at 261,5 Million troy ounces.

2% for China[27] and 18.7% for the UK (which did not comply with this general under-standing). This situation began to evolve further with Eurozone financial consolidation prac-tices that provided for maintaining currency reserves. In regard to China, despite the Yuan's non-convertibility there is an observable trend in that direction, for instance with the issuing of Yuan-traded bonds by the Chinese central bank – whose current policy is to diversify and grow gold reserves by purchasing all Chinese gold production at around 400 MT per year.[28]

In addition to the key aspects of supply/demand and measurement function that character-ize the role of gold as a monetary instrument, precious metals have an additional virtue. Given their fluctuating availability in different quantities, precious metals can be used in a variety of ways, have different users and can be substituted for one another during shortages. This trend has characterized the history of gold and silver over millennia. Historical experience illu-minates the need for segregated currencies that can be circulated concurrently, depending on exchange pricing and on the accumulation potential of the economic agent. These patterns of variability have related to numeration tooling and have led to the formation of different classes of coinage, for instance the Aureus and Sesterce used in Roman times.

Table 3.1 shows the price of gold in troy ounces [oz.] (one troy ounce = 31.1034768 grams) at year-end, from 1921 until 1965. As may be seen for the 50-year period beginning after WWI and extending well past the Korean war, the price of gold nearly doubled, from $20 to $37.44 per troy ounce.

TABLE 3.1   Gold prices in US$ per troy ounce 1921–2013

GRAB			
	Table of historical price		
Gold spot $/oz. price			
Period:	**December 1921–December 2013**		
Currency:	**US$**		
DATE	**PRICE**	**DATE**	**PRICE**
Dec-13	1207.00	Dec-70	37.44
Dec-11	1563.70	Dec-65	35.12
Dec-05	517.00	Dec-60	35.27
Dec-00	272.25	Dec-55	35.03
Dec-95	387.10	Dec-50	34.72
Dec-90	382.80	Dec-45	34.71
Dec-85	326.80	Dec-40	33.85
Dec-80	589.75	Dec-35	34.84
Dec-75	140.25	Dec-30	20.65
Dec-71	43.48	Dec-25	20.64
		Dec-21	20.58

1931 was the year for devaluations (major currencies against gold) and 1971 was the year of dollar disconnection.

---

[27] China may be buying gold directly from Chinese mines; most of their production is estimated at 900 tons a year, therefore this figure may be totally understated.

[28] The latest report of Thomson Reuters GFMS (Gold Field Mineral Services), dated January 16, 2013, indicates net buying by central banks of 536 tons (equivalent to 18.7% of mining production). Gold is defined there as a safe asset alternative to sovereign debt.

The End of Gold

As already discussed, the 1976 Jamaica Agreements mandated de facto separation of the gold standard and reserve backing from the world central bank monetary system. As shown in Table 3.1, as the world banks attempted to terminate interbank and exchange gold sales – despite market resistance to the Jamaica injunction – the price of gold experienced a 30-fold rise in the 35-year period between 1975 and 2013 (i.e., from $140 to around $1250 per troy ounce).

Benefits Arising from the End of the Gold Standard

As had been recommended by Belgian/US economist Robert Triffin,[29] the release of precious metal links with limited availability allowed for the formidable development of script money. However, this new direction in monetary policy required an improvement in diagnostic oversight as to the economic health of currency-issuing nations – particularly since their national debt structures were no longer limited by the gold reserves of their respective central banks.[30] On the contrary, a pure monetary supply (decoupled from gold and thus less dependent on constraints imposed by national debt) could now be more easily adjusted in volume, for instance to meet the needs of public exchange markets while adapting to external economic dynamics and growth.

The nature of money had changed. Now defined in currency-denominated units monitored by accounting standards, the concept of debt and both the rules and process set up to monitor financial data had assumed a new level of importance, as predicted some decades earlier by Hjalmar H. Schacht,[31] architect of the German economic recovery following that nation's historic post-WWI monetary collapse. Moreover, with post-"gold era" bargaining power increasingly leveraged through assets and liabilities (as posted in detailed financial statements – including those of governments), these are now linked to levels of liquidity and solvency, reflecting the depth of financial markets and other factors such as transparency with regard to tainted information on the quality of counterparty-dependent instruments. One example of the latter may be found in the August 2008 suspension for a few weeks by BNP (Banque Nationale de Paris-Paribas) of reimbursements on treasury-backed market and ABS

---

[29] Born in Belgium, Robert Triffin (1911–1993) was a Yale University professor and economic advisor to President Kennedy. Triffin explained the paradox of a reserve currency – due to its dual role both as a standard and as trading money – such that the maintenance of its quality valuation required limitations placed on gold's availability. This constraint in turn was in direct opposition to the need to maintain a needed supply of gold flowing into central bank reserves, so as to back up economic growth and the expanding monetary base. This opposing duality in the monetary reserve-linked role of gold is referred to as "the Triffin paradox".

[30] *Currency Wars: The making of the next global crisis* by James Rickards gives, on p. 243, the implied price of gold needed to cover US M1 at a 40% rate. This price as of 2011 M1 level would be $2590, and $12,347 for M2. Combining the USA and China, the required value would have been $6993 for M1 and $44,552 for M2.

[31] Hjamar Horace Greely Schacht (1877–1970), President of the Reichsbank from 1924–1939. Despite his release from all public assignments in 1939 (and with the exception of the BIS seat that he retained during the war) he was tried at the Nuremberg War Crimes Tribunal, but was not sentenced.

money market mutual funds.[32] For several weeks, BNP honestly declined to pay out on the hosted instruments, as they had lost their market liquidity, with the consequence of losing total price value on many of the instruments.

HOW TO GROUND TRUST IN MONEY: AUDITED FINANCIAL STATEMENTS FOR GOVERNMENT AND CENTRAL BANKS

Aware of their growing dependency on "non-gold-backed" currency trust issues, most governments proceeded to set up financial statements, the conceptual design of which today closely parallels that of financial statement methodology and structures used in the private sector. Naturally, central banks had already long followed this practice, since their institutional origin had been privately set up and subsequently chartered by governments to issue bills-of-credit or coinage. In the modern era, however, with the complete disappearance of privately issued money – and as the sole issuers of national currencies – governments needed to gain the confidence of markets and thus regularly submitted their yearly financials to accredited independent external audits (in the same manner as any market-listed company is required to do, i.e. when accepting (borrowing) capital from public market-based investors).[33]

SEIGNORAGE AND THE PRIVILEGE OF ISSUING AND STAMPING[34] MONEY

Traditional Seignorage in General

The right to coin money and stamp it, as seen in ancient times, belongs today to the state. It is usually included in their Constitution. To give two examples, let's quote those of the USA and UK. For the USA, Section 8 of the Constitution provides for the power in paragraph 5: "To coin money, regulate the value thereof, and of foreign coins and fix the standards of weight and measures." In the UK, the 1706 Treaty of the Union, which merged the Kingdom of Scotland and of Great Britain in article 16, paragraph 5 unified money. With additional legal texts, such as the US legal tender act of 1862, the issuance of paper money was authorized but had actually already happened much before or at the same time as the coinage privilege. The

---

[32] Not able to ascertain the value of its own vehicles, BNP decided to suspend reimbursement of its shares for a few days.

[33] Following a protracted period of high public deficits, and as a result of reforms aimed at instituting a balanced budget, Canada became the first western country whose books were subjected to a clear opinion from auditors. While serving as Canada's Finance Minster from 1993–2002, Paul Martin (b. 1938) led the revolutionary effort to successfully implement a progression of balanced budgets. Despite this milestone, the IMF criticized Canada for not aggressively employing new types of financial instruments, a fact that would eventually prove advantageous. Benefiting from a very high concentration of fiscal resources, a relative paucity of "toxic paper" and strict prudential ratios, Canadian banks were effectively immunized from many of the effects that their US counterparts encountered during the 2007–2008 financial crisis. Unlike the USA, where GDP fell to 3.4%, Canada's robust economy did not require monetary injection in the face of a solid 8.5% GDP. See also Edey, M.L. and Hviding, K., OCDE/6D(95) Economics Department Working Paper no. 154, Economic Studies no. 25, "An assessment of financial reforms in OCDE countries", Paris, 1995.

[34] See the Glossary for stamping being distinguished from sampling.

constitutionality of money issuance combined with the right to levy taxes brought something new and necessary – generality and the legal tender concept. Governmental money has to be accepted by citizens and legal tender may be used to pay taxes. Between citizens, the nation's currency (from the word "curraunt" – circulating) cannot be refused as a medium of exchange. A nation's currency becomes a medium for its holder to satisfy an obligation for a value struck on a coin or stamped on a paper bill. The right for the sovereign to play on values is derived from this set-up, and is a very controversial topic of monetary policy that grounded, after financial failures, the stream of ideas pleading for a return to the gold standard.

With the absence of gold as a monetary reference and given an internationally adopted philosophy that opposes intervention on currency exchange markets, the monetary privilege of seignorage has all but disappeared – notwithstanding its ancient roots. Traditional seignorage persists in a tiny niche area, where it is invoked by former minting administrations for the sale of collection coinage to the public (essentially pocket money without monetary effect). Historically, however, any effective impact of seignorage had already dissipated when Germany and France went to war, and when the gold reference was abandoned. In prior centuries, however, seignorage provided a useful tool for governments, due to the difference between the intrinsic metal value of the struck coins and their face value – the resulting margin allowed for generation of a profit that could be used to finance government operations. This historical anachronism constitutes one reason why, in the wake of the French Revolution, Jefferson and other like-minded statesmen opposed to autocracy were equally ill-inclined to embrace the concept of a seignorage-mandated central bank that could yield institutional power outside the purview and even support of an elected Congress.

The Modern Seignorage Privilege

There are two privileges to be distinguished, the first being a *monetary issuance privilege* or the authority to issue paper bills or script money, and the second being a *stamping privilege* to designate a "par value" stamp or figure as an indication of value for a given denomination of money.

The Issuance Privilege

One justification originally supporting the argument for a gold standard was the link benefit of committing governments and their central banks to a limit on the accumulation of metal reserve equivalent to the level of national wealth. Even without a gold standard, chartered banks (at least in the USA) were limited in equating their fair reserves to the level of so-called "good deposits". When combined with a gold standard, that concept was acceptable, if not favourable.

However, when the rules changed to "our institution will only buy your commercial bank papers and treasury bonds", by artificially impacting values, interest rates and liquidity volumes this approach could be interpreted as equivalent to embezzlement. It served to obscure the multiplier effect of credit and, with direct and indirect tax exemptions, impacted treasury bond values. These exemptions comprise the government bonds and debt issuances withholding tax exemption, municipal bonds not taxed at the local level, and/or special vehicles (insurance companies, pension plans, etc.) enjoying a range of tax benefits. All these instruments could have "obscured" taxation benefits inside their currency zone of origin, or taxation advantages outside the respective primary currency zones – with such zones being designated as reserve territories by corresponding central banks.

In view of the above and depending on how it was practiced, the pure monetary issuance privilege may thus be termed as "exorbitant", for instance when a currency was to be accepted on a larger scale than defined by its own territory or regional monetary zone. In this context, the IMF website even refers to the classic comments of the then French Minister of Finance, Valéry Giscard d'Estaing, when talking about the US dollar. The IMF uses elements of his classic quote in referring to the special case of the US dollar as: "the existence of a greater macroeconomic space accorded to a country, issuing a major reserve currency by virtue of the greater liquidity of its market, the ability to borrow in its own currency abroad at lower cost, and the seignorage earned from issuing an internationally used currency (distinct from, but associated with, its role as a reserve asset)."[35]

The issuance privilege is a trust requirement to adjust the quantity of available instruments to current needs, and therefore guarantee the stamping value we talk about. As we will see later, the pricing mechanism of monetary instruments is not linked to real transactions and therefore no longer naturally limited as it was with, for instance, the gold standard. Therefore, a trustworthy third party and a stable mechanism are necessary to determine the quantity of money that should be available. This concept by itself supports the existence of compensation for intermediation, the seignorage. One will see that the question is whom and how. An issuer who declares that they will limit the quantity of instruments if credible will gain trust in the same way as any rare object has value. Should seignorage be a monopoly or not? That is the question.

The Stamping Privilege[36]

Granting a constitutional right to set the value of a national currency denomination is equivalent to granting the right to use an imprinted measurement tool designed to support monetary exchange mechanisms. In many settings, the precise definition of this right is widely open to debate.[37] In the USA, such a right should be interpreted in the historical context of coinage, and the failure of the original continental bonds (issued during the War of Independence). In this narrow case, the stamping privilege was initially intended to guarantee the face value and exchange value of the US dollar against a range of foreign coinage then in use in the post-revolutionary United States.

Before constituencies enable democratic governments to exercise such a right, there is an implicit (but practically unrecognized) duty to consider whether a government will behave as any responsible private entity would to limit indebtedness. Hence, an unlimited monetary stamping privilege has generally not been considered historically (and if it were, it would have been condemned). One example supporting this position can be found in the discourse between the ailing pre-revolutionary French monarchy and both Thomas Jefferson and Benjamin Franklin – all parties that were intimately familiar with the financial reform projects of the then French Finance Minister de Calonne. These reforms were rejected by the "Etats Généraux", so called by Louis XVI, but after subsequent monetary failure the second

---

[35] See the IMF website at imsrefor.org/about/glossary – Reforming the International Monetary System, Commonly used terms and concepts.

[36] See the Glossary entry for stamping.

[37] Article One, section 8 of the 1788 Constitution states: "The congress shall have power (…) to borrow money on the credit of the United States (to coin money, regulate the value thereof, and of foreign coin, and fix the Standard of Weights and Measures…"

generational iteration of financial reform was ultimately adopted by the new French Republic in 1791 (see our previous discussion on the evolution of the Germinal franc). Of course, such historical examples are of interest only to the extent that the respective economic, fiscal and political environments are reproducible.

From a cursory 5000-year review of economic historical precedent, however, no single relevant example that illuminates this issue equivalently may be reproduced in our time. As the underlying privilege of monetary stamping survives and prevails in our time, it continues to be legitimized by a combination of societal trust and free market forces. Thus, one must accept its existence, albeit pondering the best methods for reigning in a privilege of otherwise immense state power.

It is generally agreed that governments have a public service duty to keep their constituencies prosperous but also to collect tax levies, as the very governments tasked with maintaining economic prosperity need to be kept in fiscally sound status – not prone to economic collapse or sovereign default. In other words, the consequence of fiscal state failure rapidly impacts the public, which is dependent on state-issued currency. This is of considerable importance when considering self-destructive societal processes. When the "Schumpeter creative destruction"[38] effect is applied to entire economic systems and societies, the impact is not self-limiting as it might be for an individual company entering bankruptcy. Even recently, however, the financial world has witnessed the global impact that the collapse of bulge bracket banks or transnational insurance conglomerates can generate. Nevertheless, the consequences of a self-destructive societal economic collapse generally have even more deleterious outcomes, frequently ending in external military conflict and civil warfare.

The preceding theory points out the fact that both monetary measurement standards and multilateral surveillance of money stamping and issuance are necessary in tandem – and are preferable, if not superior, to a gold standard function that is required to combine all these aspects in one level of functionality. Any present or future international monetary agreement or regime thus needs to address the methodology to be adopted for measuring and defining the unit of currency. This includes the conditions for warranting the measurement unit as well as the conditions for insuring public trust and sustainability of the currency system – in the public interest of conditionally securing the best optional position for a society to maintain prosperity. To further expand on this issue, one needs to consider the new global monetary environment that contemporary society is confronting today.

Nevertheless, even if backed up by metal reserves, there is confusion in the minds of many between the "value", stamping[39] and nominal face value of a struck or printed money instrument. The confusion is linked to the guarantees given to a bank bill or coinage (often in the hands of the public) and the trust given to figures due to the respect in which the government may be held. Even if not formally, the government is often deemed to be, in the public's mind, the warrantor. We will review later (in Chapter 8) the topic of warrantees and warrantors, which will create distinctions between several kinds of money. At most, when backed, it is a metal weight equivalent. When not backed, as has been the rule since 1971, it is a derivative of a transferability commitment from the central bank that gives "legal tender" to what is called money. Stamping is now a mere numbering system to help measurement by comparison

---

[38] Schumpeter, J., *Capitalism, Socialism and Democracy*. See References.

[39] The word "stamping" is used as an action to give a figure to a measurement in reference to an independent unit system. The nominal value does refer to a figure referring to a monetary unit.

with totally transferable instruments, and is to be distinguished from "value", which results from an exchange ratio.

Legal Tender and Seignorage

Legal tender just means that a government will agree to deliver its currency against other instruments, and that a legal tender instrument has to be accepted by any existing counter-parties within a defined territory. However, since gold is no longer a monetary basis, it is not really a more claimable instrument when issued by a government central bank than when issued by any private issuer. As commented long ago by Von Mises, some repeated sayings may be held as becoming the truth, when they are not.[40] A bank statement representing a deposit or a bank bill, which are both denominated instruments, has long been considered to have a fixed value, while conceptually it does not. Somehow, the essence of seignorage has changed as at the same time the monopoly to trade "money" has been scattered between new players and is no longer the sovereign's privilege. However, at the same time, through regulation tax policies and other strategies, governments may change the value of the instruments they have issued. They may tax or exempt an instrument, they may raise or reduce the values of an instrument which has already been stamped through interest rate strategies at the central bank, and they may reduce the exchangeability of instruments by creating regulated vehicles that they will be driven into, such as pension plans or insurance policies.

We note that the concept of legal tender is weakened or reduced by the broadening nature of what money is. No longer redeemable, what is M1 money or central bank money is now only an exchangeable instrument with limits set by laws, regulation and practice, which has modified the potentiality of seignorage. Exchangeability is the synonym for competing monetary instruments. The seignorage right to stamping relies mainly on sovereignty and the related monopoly of issuing money. What it will rely on in the future is at stake[41] if money becomes mainly immaterial, not redeemable and digital. We have doubts about the understanding by central banks that even the most recent regulations do not address the topic, and are outdated for reaching the goals to be assigned to an efficient currency instrument.[42]

EVOLUTION OF MONEY INTO A SEGREGATED INTERMEDIATION TOOL WITH IMPRECISE FRONTIERS

Linguistic Definition of the Word "Money"

If we consult the *Oxford Dictionary*, money is defined as "a current medium of exchange in the form of coins and banknotes; coins and banknotes collectively". As today's guardians of this dogma (recognized as being foreclosed since the 1971 demise of the Bretton Woods

---

[40] Human action.

[41] European Directive 2007/64 CE of December 13, 2012 DSP for instance defines electronic money to be accepted.

[42] Banque de France, Focus no. 10, "Dangers relating to the development of virtual moneys; an example, the Bitcoin", December 5, 2013.

monetary regime), both the IMF and the central banks define liquidity in a restricted context. However, included in the word "legal" is the inherent liberty for individuals and enterprises to engage in trade. A more restrictive definition of the legal aspects pertaining to money is provided by the French *Larousse* dictionary.[43] This source refers to the "currency exchange rate of a note" – which in turn is contingent on the currency denomination having received a specific stamp from the central bank guaranteeing a monetary note's reimbursement value (either in metal or in exchange to a specific quantitative level of release from debt).

These two "at variance" definitions of money reflect a philosophical divergence with regard to two issues: (1) the trend that a central bank or equivalent authority needs to define money tends to hide the last 20 years of innovation and (2) an evolving reality that governments or their central banks are – in the public mind – no longer able to guarantee convincingly the potential conversion of the money supply into an acceptable counter form or other asset value derived from the sale of assets or tax levies that would be recognized by creditors. In other words, what is at question here is the reliability of a sovereign privilege that, in essence, cannot (over a predictable period of time) support the reimbursement of government debts or guarantee equivalent convertibility of an issued monetary supply to potential subscribers.

In raising this issue, one may return to Chapter 2 and reconsult Table 2.2, which reflects the relationship between merchandise exports versus US household and non-profit wealth. These parameters are reflective of systems involving exchange volumes without imposed constraints with regard to the speed, frequency or total number of applicable transactions per unit time or per market size. This limits any understanding of how such transactions are compensated for either in cash-value or in non-cash-value equivalents, thus necessitating revision of the existing limits that govern an increasingly outmoded definition of money.

MONEY TODAY

A wider approach to defining today's money needs to consider practically all categories of receivables and debts, as well as any asset or liability that reflects an economic system based on multivariate interaction between enterprises, entrepreneurs and money – all linked to a common exchange contract and the inherent concept of potential exchange value. It is necessary to remind ourselves that money is merely a back-up to "real-world economic dynamics" that undergo evolutionary adaptation. As Braudel has written: "money is a very old invention, if I consider by that any means that accelerate exchanges and with exchanges, not society. One could say that money issued by cities had created modernity. At best, statistics about economy are just a flow analysis of national income but not of the volume extent. But this volume has to be analysed."[44]

In considering the rapidly transforming exchange mechanisms underlying the extraordinary developments of an early 20th-century world economy rattled by change, it was logical that money would emerge as a prime supporting factor underlying such evolution, and reflecting mutations in the ongoing process – especially when considering money's function as an intermediate for most transactional exchanges.

---

[43] French equivalent to the *Oxford Dictionary* or US *Harraps*.

[44] Braudel, F., *La Dynamique du Capitalisme*, ch. 2, p. 120.

As an anti-analogical aside, one may consider the case of 1789 France, where metal coinage represented 96% of the money supply, as opposed to less than 1% 200 years later. Script money was, in fact, absent at the eve of the Revolution. In 1989 it represented 84% of monetary supply, the balance (16%) being fiduciary money. This development of script money into the predominant form of currency – which developed to its present level in modern times – may be considered a historically remarkable world phenomenon.

It would be absurd to believe that this mutational trend is limited only to consideration of script money issued by banks. Rather, with the development and spread of the global digital economy (coupled with the imagination, innovation and economic requirements of the global financial sector), entirely new genres and forms of contract relating to money have emerged. Provided that frontiers, which once helped define classical money, can be repositioned, such new forms of financial quasi-monetary compacts can be qualified as liquid assets, albeit with inherent transitional challenges involved.

Perhaps not surprisingly, some writers like Ron Paul[45] (Member of the US House of Representatives and well known for his presidential debate positions on the role of money and current financial reforms) join F.A. Hayek[46] and go to the extreme in recommending the abandonment of legal money issued by central banks. In Congressman Paul's view, legal money represents only a tiny fraction of all types of circulating monetary species or equivalents, such as bartered goods, securities, derivatives, bonds, credit or debit notes, bearer bonds, natural resources and commodities, etc. Although accurate with regard to the disproportion of currency to other forms of money, extrapolating a subsequent conclusion that the FED concedes a loss of control over the monetary supply and comes to an end is a highly controversial position. In the eyes of most experts, these are non-mainstream positions – particularly when viewed in the context of today's world economic structures. Clearly, though, governance issues at central banks cannot be reformed internally or warranted effectively to the citizenry by existing means of guidance and control. The essential issue is how to manage and proctor an international reform process – on a basis that is acceptable to the widest constituency possible. Such a globally scalable monetary institutional reform effort would require a body of mandated but independent political power, a body that would convene and establish new reform principles, structures and operational mechanisms – including recommendations on their implementation, necessary accountability and a determination as to which governing bodies would provide the oversight needed.

The topic of granting an authority the right to stamp, or of defining the stamping measurement unit, is key and whoever is chosen is requisite for exchanges based on a single language in that respect. One has to remember that the end of the chartered bank system's ability to issue money with the creation of the FED in 1913 was caused by having different values for the dollar depending on the bank which issued it, which was a deterrent to exchanges. The need for a monetary instrument to exchange and a guarantee of scale do not impose a central bank, though. What imposes centralized regulation of scale is the need for its guarantee, and further the need for stability during the time of the production phases of any service or product. Money as a toll for exchanging easily can only exist if it covers a sufficient number of market participants over a sufficient economic space. Having different values and volatility would jeopardize the target of level plain markets. Money has to be secured and stable, the resulting price of exchanged goods and services are the adjusting factors.

---

[45] Paul, R. *End the FED*. See References.

[46] Hayek, F. *Prices and Production* (1931); *The Road to Serfdom* (1944). See References.

THE DEMISE OF TRADITIONAL CONCEPTUAL APPROACHES

Focusing solely on the opinions of classical economic theorists, one may overlook alternative viewpoints such as those of Malthus, which may be of passing interest but no longer bear immediate relevance to the current global economic environment – where a cogent analytical approach requires consideration of a range of societal factors, such as "asset preservation" (including savings), trends and investment factors. Once again fashionable in our time, Keynesian thinking (so attractive to the monetarists and physiocrats of the past) nevertheless has limits, and requires reformulation to maintain relevance vis-à-vis rapid changes in our global financial system. When participating in the Bretton Woods Conference Keynes was, after all, a civil servant beholden to the British Crown, and thus promoted a composite currency then known as the "Bancor". A central underlying motivation for this was his intent to maintain a significant global presence for the UK pound sterling that commanded monetary dominance over an immense colonial Empire and Commonwealth, while nevertheless exhibiting stress in the face of an impending exit from an immense war effort.

However, the emerging supremacy of the US dollar dominated thinking in the 1944 environment – one that projected a vast financial challenge in terms of impending European reconstruction. It is not surprising in hindsight, then, that an inevitable outcome of Bretton Woods was the rejection of a pound sterling-centric Keynesian world. In the interim decades, however, the negative reciprocity and lack of vigilance that accompanied the dollar's global reign (not to mention the deviant use of such monetary supremacy) paradoxically facilitated the gradual weakening of US economic predominance alongside the rise of Asia. Although implausible at the time, a "Bancor"-type currency system might one day re-emerge as a consideration in a globalized, multi-polar financial environment of the future.

Considering the evolution of political thought in 1944, one limitation in proposing alternative options to a dollar-dominated system was the reality that a post-war monetary system organized solely around central banks was no longer a practical consideration after 1929. The fact that a future globalized supply-side monetary pool would consist only partially of a monetary compartment destined purely for exchange functions was originally noted even by Braudel, an intellectually sharp academic known for his politically neutral positions. Drawing an analogy to Lavoisier's earlier genius in changing the mainstream view of molecular chemistry, the 20th-century anti-Keynesian neutralist view of economic systems also sought to escape the confines of an inexistent narrow, linearly bordered space, much like Lavoisier had done for the field of 18th-century chemistry.[47]

Today's financial environment operates within new legal, accounting and financial territories set by innovative as well as short-sighted human forces alike. Yesterday's formulae are no longer adaptable for the purposes of efficiently organizing management of the contemporary

---

[47] Wrongly summarized in the saying: "Nothing is created, nothing disappears, it only changes." Thomas Jefferson, Benjamin Franklin, Irénée Dupont de Nemours and Lavoisier knew each other. Benjamin Franklin's mission in France was to obtain financing from the French Court for the US War of Independence, but also to buy saltpeter for the purpose of manufacturing gunpowder. This explains the subsequent monopoly granted to Dupont de Nemours to manufacture gunpowder. In addition, Lavoisier and Franklin were close friends.

1. What is an exchange & the money issuance process

An exchange:- of an asset or service against another asset or service = BARTER
- an asset or service against a book balance or a cradit note

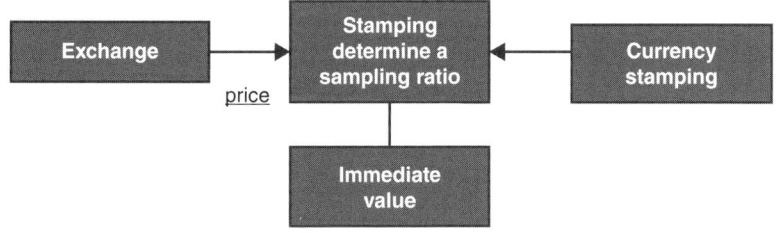

Production of financial
instruments as money

2. The production scheme

| Exchange | → | Stamping determine a sampling ratio | ← | Currency stamping |

price

Immediate value

3. Consequences

- Value is not stamping
- Value is instantaneous
- Value is volatile over time
- Stamping concept is attached to repayable or transferable money
- Value is not price
- Price is determined by sampling
- Sampling is not stamping

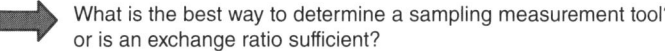

What is the best way to determine a sampling measurement tool?
or is an exchange ratio sufficient?

FIGURE 3.1   Currency and stamping value: today's money issuance

world economy. Many experts would argue that a global economic environment with flexible limits is likely more favourable to democracy and economic development in our time than it was in the immediate post-war era – when the operational aspects of national economies were focused on a wartime footing and emerging Cold War military challenges. However, historical experience also teaches us that going beyond "flexible approaches" to an unbridled "laissez-faire environment", as Quesnay advocated,[48] would likely prove an unworkable basis for harmonious economic growth in democratic societies. Rather, through an entirely revamped system of modernized money and exchanges (Figure 3.1), the implementation of a new and balanced economic set-up deserves consideration – an approach suggested by Braudel in proposing the re-examination of current statistical approaches.[49]

One may also note again that both monetary velocity and related concepts such as the multiplier fail to cover the entire operational scope of exchanges, and as a result tend to gloss over interconnected effects on sampling that are associated with a range of related mass

---

[48] François Quesnay (1694–1774), French Physiocratic School.

[49] See the Conclusion to this book: namely, how – in a conference at Johns Hopkins University – Braudel incites researchers to begin statistical research anew, so as to best characterize economic phenomena that more effectively reflect a global financial environment.

accumulation effects – hence, such approaches also present drawbacks. Across the board, then, the "lenses of observation and scrutiny" applied to ongoing changes in the post-war economic system have been richly opaque, and characterized by unclearly formulated concepts.[50]

THE OPERATIONAL SCOPE OF MONEY AND ITS USE

Following the demise of the gold-to-currency reserve link, our common understanding of money and its role in world society was irreversibly altered. Ronald Reagan's 1984 election to the US Presidency ushered in the belief system of the Chicago school of economic thinking, which promoted the thesis that financial resources would be more efficiently used by entrepreneurs rather than by the government.[51] Even with the Cold War still in progress, colonial conflicts were largely resolved, along with a reduction in colonial territories open for non-remunerated resource exploitation. Economic stimuli for the US economy were now generated through massive research and development of new defence technologies, rather than primarily by means of forward deployment of military forces. Arising from these new economic points of view, a US-instigated pattern of tax reductions was emulated by most western nations (see Table 3.2).

(a) In 1944, following the Great Depression and to contribute to the war effort, the top brackets of US income tax reached a 94% rate and stabilized around 90% till the end of the Kennedy era.
(b) The US rate for individuals at 45% is without state tax. State tax can vary, but a standard 10% can be added for comparison when the taxpayer is a resident of a major industrial state.
(c) The French marginal rate for individuals was reduced to 40% in 2010 and raised again in 2013 to 45%, to which 15.5% must be added as social contributions on passive income for 2013, part of which was deductible. The cumulated taxation with an existing wealth

TABLE 3.2   Marginal individual income tax rates evolution

	USA		France		China		Germany	
	Corporation	Individual	Corporation	Individual	Corporation	Individual	Corporation	Individual
1960	47%	90%	50%	60%	NA	NA	15/51%	53%
2007	39%	35%	33.33%	50%	25%	45%	29.80%	45%
2013	39%	45%	33.30%	45%	25%	45%	29.80%	45%

Source: Finance laws.

---

[50] Scientific papers on both sides of the Atlantic seem to view market statistics as the major determinant for "rules of observation". This viewpoint reflects the belief that the historical origin of such statistics imparts truth. In doing so, and in building mathematical models on such a basis, the implementation of such positions aggravates the potential dysfunction of markets involved in trading financial instruments. Worse yet, superimposed human input and gregarious, contagious general speculative behaviour may uncover both truths, as well as contribute to catastrophic economic outcomes.

[51] See the Foreword to this book for mention of the relationship between finance law and economic recovery.

tax on non professional or art assets was capped at 50% from 2008 to 2010. The new French Presidency in 2012 raised the capping to 75% maximum tax rate on income over 1 million euros (1.3 million dollars at 2013's exchange rate with the euro) yearly taxable income, but the Constitutional Court censured that proposal and set a referential maximum bracket limit of 66% over which tax would be considered confiscatory.

(d) 2007 shows a turn in fiscal policies since, on both sides of the Atlantic with the exception of the UK, finance laws tend to increase marginal rates for individuals by reducing special exemptions, capping limits and raising rates. Basic general rates go up to 45% and long-term or ordinary capital gains as passive income niche safe heavens are reduced (USA) or mostly cancelled (France).

(e) 2013 sees a further upturn on individual taxation.

In distinct variance to the pattern of tax reductions between 1985 and 2004, since the 2007–2008 economic crisis, marginal tax rates for individuals have demonstrated a rising trend (for both general income and capital gains tax rates), especially for the period 2012–2013 when considering the need for balancing budgets to reduce the growth of governmental debt levels. Concurrently, the continuing impact of deregulation and resulting global competition has restrained price increases and inflation on industrial products, or led to deflation where possible, so as to balance price increases in some necessary and limited-availability natural raw materials. Contrary to this global deflationary environment, rare fixed assets like well-located real estate have been hit by the excess of liquidity and the refinancing system extension with uninterrupted price increases.

In the post-2009 environment, private and corporate sources of capital are accessible on an increasing scale with a trend towards corporate balance sheets that reflects factual refinancing proceeds and accumulating deficits, but to some extent the deployment of scripted money is hemmed in by regulation. Money has changed in nature – every conceivable model of financial engineering or instrument appears to generate today's "new money", and both banks and markets continue to embrace a brave new world that appears to thrive on an ever-expanding global currency, which continues to evolve in a historically unprecedented direction.

Meanwhile, professional actors in the banking playing field seek to: (1) increase personal compensation by inducing monetary velocity through accelerated transactional rotation of money and (2) reduce institutional risk by shunting that risk externally through third-party financing arrangements, which use protective formulae and legally safe packaging. Income generated by commissions and transaction margins – rather than by sound economic expansion – has become the basis of the banking sector's primary growth. It is interesting to examine the diverse tools that have been used by the financial sector to maintain profitability.

THE EXTENSION OF MONEY WITH DISINTERMEDIATION

Direct Financing and Hedging of Risk

Since the Reagan era of the 1980s, under the influence of Milton Friedman and other economists from Chicago, deregulation coming from an over-regulation due to past wars being necessary became the motto, if not the Holy Grail. The refinancing of economies was no longer limited to bank financing, as we have already seen when describing financial depth (Chapter 2). Securitization granting equivalent guarantees to paper holders was the main engine, and the deficits of both trade and budget the fuel for it. Financial instruments, including mortgage-backed securities becoming monetary instruments, were moving faster and outside the boundaries of the banking system.

REPLACEMENT OF BANK LOAN FINANCING BY SECURITIZATION AND THE IMPACT OF PRO-CYCLICAL EFFECTS[52]

The Origin of Securitization

A primary reason for debt securitization was to allow banks not to carry the risk of loans they produced or were rewarded for. This objective was enabled by ongoing evolution in economic conditions. These included deficit spending by governments or industry, and the matured savings (albeit dwindling) resources of an aging population. Thus, a new form of monetary sourcing and leverage was available on financial markets. This in turn opened the window for widespread sales of new financial instruments, both from within originating monetary jurisdictions and in a cross-border international context. Moreover, as the administration of loans is not specifically a banking activity and can be subcontracted to specialists, effective externalization of associated expenditures and financial risks served to reduce banking overheads. Ultimately, this overall strategy of debt securitization was intended to reduce banks' balance sheet liabilities, and as a consequence enhance return on equity for banks.

Over the past 35 years, financial engineering options have also increased in sophistication, and the impact of their implementation has fundamentally changed the financial structure of the economy. Concurrently, the traditional oligopolistic sources of commercial bank financing have progressively been supplanted by the role of markets and securitized debt instruments. In the USA, the most active players on these secondary markets have been financial institutions with total assets that exceeded those of traditional commercial banks, particularly as of 2007 Q3.[53] One example of such secondary market instruments are mortgage-backed securities, which have enjoyed a historically disastrous upsurge, due in part to the massive pre-crisis expansion of the housing sector – a key contributor to the domestic US economy. This occurred in parallel with another trend, namely the progressive transference of US manufacturing capability to foreign nations that offered low-cost offshore production environments.

This dynamic provided players in the securitization sector with a false sense of abundant and rapidly accessible liquidity. However, economic history showed that such hubristic liquidity presaged a coming crisis, one which was heralded most recently by a massive rise in household debt coupled to mortgage-backed securities, a wave that by mid-2001 had already reached a domestic value of $11 trillion for the US housing sector.

Alongside these real-estate-sector securitization options and trends, the facile financing of heavy infrastructure and transportation capabilities (rail or sea, and aircraft) was also facilitated in the context of reducing the required scope of government participation. Such financing was enabled through the sale of receivables, the management of which could also be subcontracted. The role of bank financing was increased by the sale of loan portfolios, and by

---

[52] See further, note 88 in D'Austra and Schlessinger (1993) regarding securitization alongside a parallel banking system, as well as our previous book.

[53] $17.6tn for market institutions (including $4tn for ABS issuers) and $12.6tn for banking institutions. *Source:* US Federal Reserve.

the release of corresponding hedging equity that was available for new credits (under Cooke and Basel ratios). By capping the ratio between loan commitments and available core equity, Basel II regulations actually favour the securitization process.

This process is not a very recent phenomenon – that is, many years of growth in the US home construction sector (that contributed to the set-up of the 2008 crisis) had long been "pushed" by government-chartered agencies set up for the purpose of warranting fiscally compromised loans, and then allowing their direct or secondarily securitized sales on organized financial markets – or by artificially clearing such loans from the ledger sheets of commercial banks that were previously saddled with such failing loans.

We note that this evolution of factors accelerated the disintermediation of lending activities, which were subsequently reduced to redistribution activity, and thus escaped from the need for refinancing internal to a given commercial banking institution. In turn, this pattern influenced direct central bank interventions, for instance in response to negative assessments on the capabilities of various commercial banks to self-finance their internal loan portfolios. Not surprisingly, under such conditions "interest spreads"[54] have emerged as a determinant factor. If spreads are high and allow coverage of the default rates, this induces banks to lend. Conversely, if spreads narrow and become too low, banks abstain from accumulating additional lending risk.

As we know, the above description is problematic. During the starting phases of the 2007–2008 crisis, the liquidity erosion within the financial markets would not have been readily perceived, particularly if observers' viewpoints were limited to the classical analysis of cash money and bank credits to the economy. In other words, not all the intermediary financial institutional parties (including commercial banks, whose public customer deposits do not cover the entire scope of operational refinancing capital requirements) inevitably engage in large-scale borrowing on the financial markets. However, unlike the precarious position of pure brokerage houses, whose operating reserve liquidity rapidly eroded during the crisis period, diversified "multi-activity" banks cross-retained liquidity resources to allow for continued operational stability. That is, multifunctional mega-banks with sizable commercial operations or mainstream commercial banks exert a so-called protective "bumper role" – as the sheer size of their balance sheet can cover the marginal effects of defaults, at least in those instances where banks do not surrender to the market sirens of unrestrained proprietary capital trading or whose organizational structure is heavily skewed away from maintaining a sizable commercial banking operation.

The pro-cyclical effect of market refinancing and interbank deposits (REPO)[55] reveals a major reason for the brutal credit crunch and resulting novel aspects of the 2008 crisis. As suggested by knowledge gained during that crisis, future doubts about overall macroeconomic accounting-level reconciliation between "values of debts" in the banking system (including sovereign debts and the projected global capacity of economies to eventually reimburse those debts) are unlikely to be ameliorated by mere application of "stress-testing" parameters. In other words, new and potentially misleading accounting standards may not provide more than

---

[54] Difference between interest rates for borrowing money versus the lending rate applied to borrowers.

[55] Contractual sale and repurchase agreement by which two parties agree to the sale by one of them of a proportion of securities (that will be used as collateral for the other buyer against a loan of lower value), with both parties agreeing to subsequently reverse the transaction by a repurchase transaction at some later date.

a distorted picture of individual or grouped banking status, since the economic link between such financial institutions (including their fiscal vulnerabilities) has assumed a historically new pattern of interdependence – one that remains largely undefined with no accepted, crisis-tested or proven formula for its global analysis. Moreover, "stress test"-defined and capital requirements-driven accounting standards have, to date, not adequately considered accounting-induced microeconomic "book effects" which can result from the impact of how securitization trends are analysed or inadequately considered.

Thus, the potential for banks to experience instability as a consequence of pro-cyclical market behaviour will not be reduced by links to such accounting standards – at least not in the absence of wide-reaching intrinsic reform. Without such far-reaching fundamental reform, central banks would have to provide substitute liquidity in future crisis settings where a focal lack of liquidity could emerge in the financial sector, and for which a replacement monetary supply would not exist outside the central banks themselves. This potential scenario remains a major challenge for today's central banks.

With securitization's global role extending far beyond the intent of any original design, a financial Excalibur emerged – a double-edged sword with the potential to drive future transactional flow in the face of an uncertain and potentially deleterious outcome. A suitable analogy might be a football championship with sizable quantities of pre-reserved tickets, subject to potential cancellation on the basis of non-predictable inclement weather. Such financial uncertainty for both organizers and ticket holders would, in turn, be compounded through insurance premium liabilities for the organizers and inflated ticket costs for football fans.

It may be said that securitization has been a victim of its own success. Through the securities sorting phenomenon, stakeholders were separated from immediate fiscal impact and remained largely concerned only with the financial health of underlying primary warrants and their owners. Little concern was directed towards the impact on the larger population of retail-level public market investors – in essence, the citizens who were potentially most vulnerable to variances in the financial health of underlying warrantees.

In a real sense, securitization allows for de facto transformation of a "receivables portfolio" into a new secondary (derivative) financial instrument, which becomes independently tradable on public markets. Prior to the 2007–2008 crisis, this had been allowed to occur even if primary "receivables" warrants underlying the new financial instruments were of uncertain long-term stability. In this manner, an entire market sector (in this case real estate and the credit industry) could be exposed to non-sector-applicable market-driven variations in value, without links to the overall economic situation or that of the impacted sector (e.g., real estate and credits).

The challenge of maintaining balance in this macabre new financial reality involved offsetting the greed of the financial world against the weakness of prevailing accounting standards.

The Securitization Concept and Its Implementation

The design of a securitization derives from the archaic idea that any receivable may be sold, and combines this precept with the concept of "fair value" – for example, since the sale of a receivable can (legally speaking) be performed only at a fair value-based equitable price.

To perform the sale of a portfolio containing many receivables, one has to determine individual and composite pricing. One also needs to carefully design the legal mechanisms by which sales of the receivable, and recovery of both interest flux and reimbursement flow, will benefit the buyer. In other words, the securitization process converts a receivable into a "warranted right" to regularly receive (usually as a lump sum) remuneration, in the form of interest and future financial revenue flows. Depending on the degree of certainty as regards the debtor's capability to insure the instrument over time (and the strength of the warrantees and their sale in case of default), the projected flow of remuneration can be quantitatively projected.

The use of trusts and similar legal bodies located in "ad hoc" favourable legal and tax jurisdictions also serves to enhance legal protection for the warranted beneficiaries of the securitized instruments. When utilizing such legal options, the critical objective is to minimize or eliminate the tax-withholding liabilities that could reduce buyer yield or incur sell-side expenses (the latter model exempting situations where sellers are government entities). It may also reduce the risk of claims resulting from the financed investments (vessels for instance).

The determination of the securitized portfolio's value requires knowledge of the average statistical risk for default, the underlying value of the warrant and its execution costs. Prior consideration is also accorded to the probability of anticipated changes in reimbursement levels by debtors, and/or of the eventuality that an adverse interest spread emerges during the life of the security – that is, interest rates decline in comparison with those at the start of the securitization and valuation process.

This overall securitization process is then rendered feasible and practical by bundling a sufficient number of individual, securitized receivables warrants that share a common or homogenous legal design. From observations based on previous default patterns, it is possible to extrapolate future event probabilities. Upon quantification, this risk appraisal forms the basis for implementing forward-hedging strategies – for instance in the form of corresponding front deposits or by purchasing premiums from an independent insurer.

Via such a securitization process, an industrial company or financial institution can sell its receivables to a third party at a set price with immediate payment. One example of this is the use of a unit investment trust. Operating through a suitable securitization specialist, the receivables warrants can be placed into a dedicated trust, the unit shares of which are tradable. This trust is comprised of warranted shares and risk shares which are synergistically grouped within the trust, for the purpose of establishing a reserve capable of absorbing potential defaults, covering anticipated reimbursements – and to a defined extent offering protection for both categories of shares. The eventual seller of the receivables is therefore discharged of the collection burden delegated to specialists. These securitization set-ups then generate commissions, fees and margins – whose extent and significance is linked to the underlying risks and the complexity of the design.

The existing market for secured receivables is mostly related to home financing (mortgage-backed securities), but also exists in the field of consumer lending and leveraged assets (ABS) – for instance, enabling the producers of such loans to immediately cash out receivables. The various processes for receivables selling have contributed to the functional repertoire of financial institutions and industrial corporations alike, thereby ensuring faster and at times safer monetary flow for the economy. Securitization is merely one of these processes, and each nation has its own unique origination mechanism (for instance not only in the home building sector, but also in the heavy equipment and transportation sectors).

Securitization has also been used to access tax havens. For instance, given the financial surplus of the 1980s, Japan and other countries instituted legal mechanisms (set by laws and tax treaties) for avoiding tax withholding and double taxation on returns from shares and bonds – for instance, those which involve the flow of money emanating from countries not linked by tax treaties. The use of trusts and similar legal bodies located in "ad hoc" nations also serves to enhance legal protection for the warranted beneficiaries of the securitized instruments. When utilizing such legal options, the critical objective is to minimize or eliminate the tax-withholding liabilities that could reduce buyer yield or incur sell-side expenses (the latter model exempting situations where sellers are government entities).

Securitization Financing via Trust-Derived "Shadow Capital" Originating from Retirement Accounts, Direct Savings and Trade Deficits

A US importer receives a product from Asia. They credit their export vendor's account for a set amount, for instance $100, posted at the vendor's central bank. In the case of international trade transactions, all dollar transactions are centralized for the US FED via a US clearing central bank – in the EU, an analogous system involves the ECB, which centralizes all transactions in euros.

On the US-side of the transaction accounting system, a debt against the Asian system does not appear on the books. As a consequence, the $100 receivable can then circulate freely. Depending on applicable regulations, this amount could remain under the exporter's control, except for the obligation to sell the foreign currency equivalent in that exporter's possession to the applicable central bank. By virtue of that obligation, the $100 is held and processed through the exporter's commercial bank.

In cases when the importer has an account outside the jurisdiction where the importer is domiciled – for instance in Dubai, London or Hong Kong – the entitled bank will be able to operate this "non-resident account" and apply the deposited $100 as if it were fundable. This sum can then be exchanged between non-residents of the USA or sold against other currency. Nothing happens at the US national account level, as the balance there remains unchanged. As a single example that has broader implications, the use and destination of the $100 in funds can follow a number of pathways, exemplifying the movement of trade capital across the globe:

- Either such trade capital can be invested in US financials or debt instruments bought on US markets, and then rerouted through the banking system assigned to the benefit of the US FED.
- Or, trade capital can be used for tangible investments in US companies, in which case the $100 also returns to the USA.
- Or, the $100 is used for an import transaction from the USA.
- Or, such capital is used for tangible investments of purchases abroad, in which case the $100 in this example is lost to the US system and trade balance.

Through this and similar processes, the accumulated US deficit has fed the capacity for banks to levy the financing needed to operate major export transactions denominated in US$, but originating from non-US monetary zones. In doing so, banks rely on refinancing mechanisms beyond their control, and thus on the good will of outside sources willing to loan them capital. The latter sources of offshore capital are then in a position to appraise the good quality of the assets they hold in the role of a counterparty, but as a general policy will maintain a generous "security" margin in their favour. In case of a microeconomic drop in value for a given economic subsector, the commercial banking and reserve will be compromised, and central banks will have to come to the rescue with equivalent amounts to replace the liquidity that has evaporated.

The saying that "bad money drives out good"[56] is applicable to this example, since the availability of currency will induce traders to invest and will also motivate the primary government or central bank issuer to release additional monetary reserves to compensate for the rising trade deficit. In a free currency exchange system, our hypothetical $100 is fairly volatile, since its fate will depend either on the choices and priorities of the central bank to which it has been sold or assigned, or on the owner of a non-US-resident bank account where these funds have been deposited – that is, a financial counterparty who can freely use those funds, including withdrawing them from circulation or deployed investment in the USA.

The transitional fate of the $100 will additionally depend on the interest rates prevalent for the dollar market at that time, and on the decisions of other central banks that are impacting international currency markets and relevant interest spreads. In particular, the Chinese central bank retains an inventory of $3 trillion, which only represents funds that are specifically deposited in the Chinese banking system, by virtue of China's degree of exposure to the accumulated US trade and budgetary deficit.

Because of free trade and the market-driven circulation of such accumulated transnational capital balances, knowledge about likely monetary retention or recirculation patterns generates purely hypothetical projections. The impact of globalization trends and banking secrecy ensures that the ultimate detainee of the liquid financial power of these dollars remains mostly anonymous, the counterpart of the deposits with the central banks being shielded by these or by bank secrecy when the currency market has no constraints.

GUARANTEES ON RECEIVABLES: A SECURITIZATION MULTIPLIER

Warrantee mechanisms structurally enhance the value of both primary and secondary financial instruments, primarily by reducing carried risk and by enhancing liquidity. Both third-party guarantees and second-level warrants (FED, governments, civil agency, CDS, etc.) have fundamental advantages over asset backing – particularly in allowing for final severance between seller and buyer. This functional property alone renders such types of secured instruments extremely liquid, as if they were legal money tender – that is, analogous to any currency benefiting from government or central bank warrants (applicable to other governments or market-based parties). For instance, securitized instruments may be utilized directly as primary warrants, by virtue of their investor subscription. As a result, refinancing may predispose a range of parties – not necessarily banks – to partial or total reimbursement liabilities, in the event that the estimated face value of the warrant declines.

Given the above, it should be noted that securitized warrants originally arose from the process of debt production, a process that may be viewed as virtuous because its underlying intent is to finance or capitalize investments for the purpose of creating wealth. Case in point: because of the very low household savings rate in the USA, the US government set up warranted security agencies or granted similar status for mortgage-backed securities (Fanny Mae

---

[56] Termed the "Gresham law" after Sir Thomas Gresham – an agent of Queen Elizabeth I of England – who explained in a report the use of the English bad shilling, which had a 40% reduced weight in silver, over the good shilling which would be saved by its holder and therefore disappear. The concept was used by the English economist Henry Dunning Macleod.

and Freddie Mac[57]), allowing for maintenance of lower rates to borrowers whose loans are backed by issuance of receivables-based, securitized warrants. These receivables already benefited from a rapid process set up to exercise real-estate liens in case of default. Similar systems were set up in other countries (e.g., Crédit Foncier in France).

As for savings and loan (S&L) financial institutions, one of the critiques levelled against them has related to accounting issues. While maintaining their books at historical value levels, S&L institutions regularly failed to post the depreciation of receivables in due time – that is, within a sufficiently prompt timeline so that consideration of the debtor's default risk and potential systemic depreciation of the underlying assets could be alerted to and acted upon.

Of course, homogenous and/or numerous debts in high amounts do not generate a problem, as long as a real-estate crisis does not jeopardize the value of the assets. However, regardless of the eligibility or non-eligibility of their sale to chartered agencies (Freddy Mac or Fanny Mae), mortgage-backed securities are just another category of debt instruments. Ultimately, therefore, debt offered through secondary securitization mechanisms has become highly diversified in duration and scope (i.e., balloons without reimbursement, tax holiday effects, variable rates, capping and multiple combinations of characteristics), alongside the emergence of an increasingly diverse spectrum of financing (even credit cards, etc.).

These patterns have enabled US citizens to further reduce savings ratios by virtue of a mere microeconomic consequence – specifically, as asset values increased at a rate corresponding to the inflated rise in real-estate prices of uncertain character and backing, the debt of US homeowners also increased massively, along with a determinant and protracted impact on the real-estate, insurance and credit sectors. Predictably, the financial community's overall view of the real-estate debt securitization model proved hopelessly simplistic – that is, in case of difficulty, the homeowner could put up the property for sale.

Notwithstanding that the possibility of many million properties defaulting in a short period of time was not widely anticipated, neither were threshold effects that could be triggered by market changes as diffuse as variations in interest forecasts. Other issues that escaped projections included the fact that the legal sale of backing assets could accelerate a broad decrease in values, which in turn might jeopardize notation levels in a given securitization environment. Rather, it might have been expected that mortgage-backed securities' prices would decline as a result (mirroring the price behaviour of assets that no longer commanded instant value), thereby triggering buyer abstinence in anticipation of market collapse.

EXTENDING THE FIELD OF DEBTS AND GUARANTEES

Even if they do not share the same debtor, household, enterprise and government debts may merge, in a manner such that respective governments must act as a final recourse. Of course, this was precisely the direction of economic history in 2008, when the FED in the USA or other central banks had to intervene to re-establish the solvency of the banking systems,

---

[57] Fannie Mae (Federal National Mortgage Association) was created in 1938, as part of the New Deal programme. For 2007, it had a total balance sheet of $882bn for a net equity of $44bn. Fannie Mae was placed under the umbrella of the Federal Housing Finance Agency (FHFA) in September 2008, when the sub-prime crisis broke out. Freddie Mac (Federal Home Loan Mortgage Corporation) is under the same Federal Agency umbrella, but remains traded on the stock exchange. Both institutions hold or guarantee half of the US mortgage market of $14.5tn (Q2 2009, source FED), nearly equivalent to US global GDP.

through: (1) purchasing defaulted assets via TARP (Troubled Assets Recovery Program); (2) guaranteeing new issuances; and (3) providing increases in capital (Royal Bank of Scotland "RBS", ING, DEXIA, BPCE, etc.).

DEVIATIONS FROM EFFECTIVE RISK CONTROL: THE CDS CASE

The *credit default swap* (CDS) – a swap of default risk – allows two players to transfer the default risk attached to an asset or to a group of assets (in general bonds or other types of instruments). Even though one format is dominant (ISDA), such contracts are not standardized and multiple variations exist. In general, CDS contracts are exchanged with a commission expressed in basic points, which protects the buyer against a debtor's or issuer's default. In the case of default, the CDS seller pays the holder of the contract. As may be vividly recalled, the 2008 Lehman bankruptcy gave rise to legal and moral disputes involving contractual consideration for this genre of market contracts. Despite these new trends, however, the CDS market has remained without oversight for some time but is now narrowly regulated with respect to the clearing process.[58]

European Regulation (European Market Infrastructure Regulation "EMIR" 648/2012 of ESMA origin), as a result of the G20 decision made at the September 2009 summit in Pittsburgh, now requires that central counterparties and a trade repository be organized, where derivative instruments will have to be recorded and cleared. The US Dodd–Frank Act provides for the same requirements. We immediately understand that this will bring about the currently missing transparency and knowledge on carried risk of derivative instruments; on the contrary, such centralization increases the systemic character of default risk, which is no longer spread between a previously unknown number of market participants. Nevertheless, to give some flexibility to the requirements, the Council of the European Union has also delegated the implementation (June 6, 2013 10611 and July 22, 2013 published on July 24).

In the USA,[59] the same flexible approach has been adopted by the CFTC and SEC. The list of derivative contracts to be traded on a registered central trading and clearing platform is decided by those agencies; small banks and "end users" that use swaps to cover their commercial operations have been exempt from such obligation. Entities that trade over the counter are to declare the existence of the trade and why they aren't going through a CCP. Issuers and listed companies have to go through their governance committees to have their hedging process approved.

Despite this new regulation, the CDS contract remains independent of the underlying asset class – thereby explaining the extraordinary amounts of affected assets, and the brutal reduction of their inventory in the recent past. Until now, no final resolution has been provided as to the total amount of impacted inventory, especially the equivalent value that should have materialized to meet outstanding warrants during clearance of CDS instruments on the $240 billion Lehman debt. In fact, the final claimed amount seems to have accounted for only $10 billion. One of the explanations provided to date is that the players (buyers and sellers) concurrently showed only the net amount of CDS value, but this point remains to be analysed.

---

[58] European Market Infrastructure Regulation (EMIR): nude CDS instruments issued on sovereign debt, but released without a hedging basis, are now prohibited on regulated markets in part to avoid speculation. The US equivalent is Title VII of the Dodd–Frank Act adopted on May 20, 2010 with similar approaches. Nevertheless, the allocation of surveillance is different in the USA and EU.

[59] Visit the Financial Regulatory Reform Center.

It is also possible that some issuers bought back their own paper but beneficiaries disappeared, in part because of the massively contracted amounts of value remaining to be recovered and by virtue of the unknown origin of some of the underlying funds.

Given this type of uncertainty, how can these types of instrument-based debts be correctly appraised on the balance sheets of concerned entities? Although balance sheets designed for posting such values may be set up with the best and clearest of intentions, they may inevitably raise doubts. It is not the "conduits" of value which are at stake, but the value of CDS instruments' guarantees, and especially the identity and collateral validation of the debtor's counterparty. For instance, managers of some European banks convened for crisis meetings when the validity of the CDS instruments sold by AIG on Lehman Brothers' debt was disputed, albeit for a fortuitously short period of time.

Both the under-appraisal of risk and the time lag between premium payments and the occurrence of default events (including uncertainty about their definition) were identified as the cause of huge speculative movements on all financial markets during the autumn 2008 crisis – the resulting volatility was then linked to a rapid liquidity crisis that emerged concurrently, alongside other risks predictably associated with such market events.

A significant number of sovereign CDS contracts carry a quotation that remains independent of underlying assets. Following the Libor scandal, and given the concentration of the CDS market among only a few major banking hands, a question therefore arose with regard to how the insurance premium (that the CDS quote is deemed to represent) and attendant interest rate fluctuations interacted with the actual sovereign debt instrument that applicable CDS instruments were designed to hedge against. However, because of national tax policies, sovereign debt-based financial markets did not show sensible interest rates – at least of the range that in any eventuality could cover the default risk that made issuance and trading of CDS instruments necessary in the first place.

Even in the absence of suspicion about the role of market makers, if the underlying CDS debt is issued by a financially troubled country then it is axiomatic that the corresponding CDS market for such debt may shrink, and in the process may generate a precipitous rise in interest rates on that debt. By issuing guarantees on sovereign debt in this manner, the CDS system remains a predominant driver for producing capital liquidity, and thus a misleadingly attractive trap for impacted governments. As one example, both the Lehman Brothers and AIG events demonstrated that governments would have to step in and externally monetize their stressed banking and insurance institutions, for instance in case of the latter's impending collapse.

The CDS and other swap markets, where quotes are self-assembled by observation and "modelling" (as if this market were to represent a quotation basis worthy of trust), is in fact a fake construction that supports the issuance of fake sovereign money. CDS instruments and their market constitute a timing game that simply increases the actual risk of sovereign defaults. In the final equation, however, tangible commissions generated by the financial sector organizers are not a fake – as such parties have benefited handsomely from the past absence of regulation, budget discipline and governmental leadership.

TOWARDS THE FULL LIBERATION OF MONEY FROM ANY REFERENTIAL

As highlighted in the preceding discussion, the recent historical period has seen metal currencies become marginalized, while banks no longer exert control over script money – the latter trend occurring despite outdated regulations that, in some countries, maintain banking monopolies over credit distribution activities. In the uncommon instances where banks have maintained such a monopoly, it is either because they provide some specific guarantee or because they benefit from some interest cost advantages or legal structures enabling them to issue loans to individuals, for instance to be used for housing investments. Throughout history, the capability to issue money (in different forms) also represents a capability for various types of entities operating on a wider basis than a single territory or a defined monetary zone. This precedent is largely antiquated – for instance, such a privilege was repealed in Britain (1844) by UK Chancellor Robert Peel, who championed the Bank Charter Act that revoked private banks' privilege to issue money.

The spurious excess dollar liquidity maintained through a number of such mechanisms has been a major factor in reducing the role of the classical credit multiplier, by allowing refinancing from loans produced "outside the system". Banks could not sequentially derive income from such transactions, and thus preferred to cash-out in the form of one-time commissions (see the later section on shadow and parallel banking systems, including a reference to the Gary B. Gorton report of February 2010[60] noting the differences in volume between refinancing by non-banking institutions and the resulting parallel system of supporting figures).

As a consequence of these types of phenomena, and driven by the fair market value system of accounting, the "full service spectrum" reality of operations conducted in the financial sector is inadequately reflected by current statistical systems (that function only within respective national legal frameworks) and is no longer appropriately translated by existing accounting operations. As we have already described, one prime example of this can be found in the phenomenon involving issuance of different forms of money outside the traditional banking system.

With the digital information age, a new form of posting transactions is also developing. These postings are no longer backed by classical monetary references (dollar, euro and yen) but are often based on other metrics (carbon credits, indices, computer use or storing units, frequent miles, etc.), or involve the corollary development of increasingly novel electronic exchange-specialized platforms (electronic compensation networks, ECNs). The possible permutations in this regard are only limited by imagination. The resulting instruments have a transactional component and are liquid assets that have totally escaped from any oversight by central banks. This, in part, explains the total disarray of applicable regulatory oversight, for instance when considering flash trading phenomena or fractionation risks observed throughout financial markets.

This manner of reporting exchange activity through electronic platforms simply reflects a new way of refurbishing ancestral barter structures, but is differentiated from historical models by the manner in which the initial barter is not followed by a physical exchange but is simply recorded on ledgers as fact. Furthermore, with traditional barter it was still possible for a Regent or Prince (sovereign) to serve as a "last-recourse warrantor", an approach that is no longer applicable for electronic trading environments devoid of the now-extinct trading floor specialists. For instance, and on a practical scale, it is not an uncommon occurrence for today's sea or airlift containers to change ownership several times before arriving at a final destination. The coinage to satisfy the payment of delivered goods could be guaranteed. The changes in property of new trading generate postings and balances until clearing. It is money, but private money. Only the unit can be guaranteed by the sovereign – being attached to a financial instrument, it cannot be guaranteed whether it will fail either in its legal existence or possibility of collection. The new money has to be secured separately and what is called "securitization", a legal set-up, is intended to satisfy such a goal.

---

[60] Already quoted – see References.

Analogically drawing another example from the contemporary securitization environment, it is not uncommon to observe multiplication factors on the rise for a number of information technology-enabled transactions, independent of any physical exchange but involving software platforms and interconnected networks. In addition, transactions can be balanced between two or more clearings before they are posted, raising the widely acknowledged issue of whether accounting knowledge on the magnitude of outstanding balances in the pipeline is sufficient – for instance, in case of failure by one or more counterparties. These markets finalize with the digitalization-induced dematerialization of money, and thus the impact of these trends is very substantial. For instance, for the raw material index markets (Dow Jones, Standard & Poor's) alone, amounts traded increased from $13 trillion at the end of 2003 to $260 trillion recorded in March 2008.

We also note that the city banking cores have been created by industrial or market trading needs (London – colonial and industrial need for raw materials; Chicago – agricultural production and resulting crop prices coverage markets; Paris – industry and colonial goods; New York – capital for industry; Venice – oriental trade; Amsterdam – flowers; etc.). Because of the importance of extended money and the economic contributions of the financial sectors in such cities when they are key to nations, when there is a decline and because of the liberation of money from basic trade, governments usually design the appropriate legislation to keep them alive. This is, for instance, the case with London and Hong Kong as well as Luxembourg, Singapore or Switzerland as a whole. The legislation usually takes the path of better protection of hosted capital and trade but may include secrecy and tax incentives, with an essentially territorial system regarding taxation (London and Singapore with limited tax liability on local income only or specially agreed-upon individual tax assessments like in Belgium or Switzerland).

GUARANTEES AND THE EXTENSION OF MONETARY INSTRUMENTS LIBERATED FROM UNIFIED BACKING AND ISSUANCE CONSTRAINTS

In the preceding discussion, we introduced and described the classic and historic seignorage privilege that originally did not include the concept of legal tender. Usually the sovereign or bank (called a chartered bank) which had been granted the privilege to issue money was also accorded the authority to force the citizenry's acceptance of officially issued money as legal tender – thereby in most successful cases contributing to the widespread acceptance of fiat money. However, centuries of experience demonstrated that such imposed currency acceptance by society needs to be backed by voluntary means as well, otherwise goods to be sold will disappear from open markets where currency acceptance is enforced – and the appearance of black market structures will ensue, as sellers seek competing avenues to obtain alternative reliable currency value against real goods. Such examples have been seen in the late Soviet Union or some 1950s Latin American and Caribbean economies, where back-door dollar economies competed with state-enforced currency systems, or in the former East German Democratic Republic where western Deutschmarks competed with the communist era's currency.

In this context, guarantees and their coupled financial instruments erode the legal distinctions and separations between central bank tenders and guaranteed financial instruments. Further consideration of such trends includes the concept of extended money (including M5 and M5's monetary equivalents, which were described in our previous book and will be discussed extensively here, in subsequent chapters) – a concept that is increasingly recognized in the financial community as a topic of discussion no longer to be avoided.

Monetary Effects of Guarantees

Finally, owing to CDS and other guaranteed securitization contracts, debt instruments issued by governments, as well as the digitally invoiced receivables or debits issued by enterprises, all share characteristics similar to those of scripted money and thus may be categorized as fiduciary currency instruments. In addition to the intended purpose of such securitization contracts, namely the acceleration of monetary rotation (monetary velocity), these are a modulating source driving speculation, systemic risk and volatility in the hands of a small and specialized fraction of financial community players. As a consequence, it is of paramount importance that central banks or other supervisory bodies maintain updated knowledge on the functionality and status of securitized instruments, specifically for the purpose of implementing appropriate measures to ensure proper transactional flow, execution and safe clearing mechanisms.

Our preceding discussion reinforces the universal concepts that underlie the definitions for a broad spectrum of monetary diversity, ranging from limited monetary forms to coinage, paper bills and a range of state-guaranteed monetary instruments that can be extended to any issuer, platform or means of exchange. The entire post-Bretton Woods financial system, including the global network of central banks, has forfeited complete command of knowledge with regard to every detail of the evolution of the contemporary economy. Dated and non-modernized regulatory regimes instituted in the context of this New World environment cannot be expected to function in an effective and efficient manner.

SHADOW OR PARALLEL BANKING SYSTEMS

There is no universal definition of the phenomenon known as "shadow banking", which was described in a recent paper issued by the National Bureau of Economic Research.[61] This report introduced and defined the term "shadow banking" as denoting "traditional banking funding via the parallel banking system".[62] Thus, the term "shadow banking" can also denote

---

[61] NBER. Paul Allen McCulley, General Manager for PIMCO, notes that he first saw this shadow banking terminology used at the Federal Reserve Bank of Kansas City Symposium of August 2007 held in Jacksons Hole. McCulley missed one document. The most sensitive document and the first known one dates back to 1993. It is published in J.W. d'Arista and T. Schlesinger, "The parallel banking system", Economic Policy Institute Briefing Paper Series 202/775-8810, p. 2. Over the past few decades, the US system has been reshaped by the spread of multifunctional financial conglomerates and the emergence of an unregulated parallel banking system. Along with this powerful trend, like securitization, these events have broken down the carefully compartmentalized credit and capital marketplace established by New Deal legislation 60 years ago. This document nevertheless has been written in the context of the US 1991 banking crisis and the US set-up of monetary mutual funds and specialized financing conglomerates such as GE and GM subsidiaries, at that time non-banks. It does not apprehend, like later papers, the international functioning of shadow banking and the tax implications that we raise, which at that time were refinanced by Japan's balance of payments surplus. A paper of March 2012 by Viral V. Acharya of NY Stern School of Business, "The growth of a shadow banking system in emerging markets: Evidence from India", adds very little to the analysis. M. Acharya writes more wisely on a wide range of topics and is more knowledgeable on Korean issues.

[62] Working paper 15787, dated February 2010, nber.org/papers/w15787, see graphic on p. 9.

a "parallel banking system", as well as a "securitized banking system".[63] Within Gary B. Gorton's report to the US Financial Crisis Commission in Congress (previously noted in this chapter), such parallel banking is defined as a bank refinancing system derived from pension plans, hedge funds and investment trusts. The early supporting financial instruments for this "shadow-banking" system were the securitization mechanisms already described above, including ABS instruments. The report cites a listed cumulative value for these instruments approaching $14 trillion, while also quoting an uncertain figure of $71 trillion in terms of insertion of capital into this system by US investors alone.

The European definitions for tracking this sector differ, with various reports citing intermediaries and credit distribution hubs outside the banking system. In a March 19, 2012 Green Book presented on April 24, 2012, the European Commission quotes a figure for this secondary securitization market of EU 21 trillion in 2002, growing to a value of EU 46 trillion in 2010. Finally, in its November 18, 2012 report on "shadow-banking" statistics, the European Commission's Financial Stability Board (FSB) published a consultative document entitled "Initial Integrated Set of Recommendations to Strengthen Oversight and Regulation of Shadow Banking".[64] In this report, the FSB describes "shadow banking" as "credit intermediation involving entities and activities (fully or partially) outside the regular banking system" or "non-bank credit intermediation". The report underscores the FSB's incapacity to conceptually handle the matter, merely by categorizing in terms of two definitions: "regular" and "non-regular", the further frontiers of which were left to regulators.

After a data collection effort across 25 jurisdictions representing 90% of world GDP, the FSB reported the 2011 National Flow of Funds (calculated by adding up the assets detained by OFIs (other financial institutions): MMFs[65] and NBFIs[66]) as equalling a total of EU 66.614 trillion; equivalent to 111% of global GDP. In this total the USA, with EU 23 trillion, represents 35%; Europe, with EU 22 trillion, represents 33%; the UK, with EU 9 trillion, reaches 13%; Japan, with EU 4 trillion, clocks in at 6%. The FSB notes a decline in the US share, down from 44% in 2002 to EU 23 trillion (35%) in 2011 – a share replaced by the UK, Switzerland and Hong Kong, all harbouring major international financial centres. The report critiqued the consistency of data between jurisdictions, including the approximation of global volumes based on that data, the impact of which on analysis of the financial system remained unclear. For instance, the FSB notes that, depending on jurisdiction and compared with other "shadow-banking" actors, NBFIs have highly varied share types and are more dependent on refinancing from bank credits than any inherent proclivity to acquire bank assets.

As if knowledge of practices required for regulation would reduce risks that have been under discussion for countless years (and that were already described by Gorton in February of 2010), the FSB nevertheless recommends further widening the scope of granular data analysis. Its Standing Committee on Assessment of Vulnerability (SCAV) also clearly identified the major processes that may be a risk – and goes on to repeat common knowledge, namely that monetary funds may run off the regulatory axis, and that securitization and REPO systems create external risks to the broader banking system.

---

[63] Working paper 15787 on p. 7 asks: "What is this new banking system, the 'parallel banking system' or 'shadow banking system' or 'securitized banking system'?"

[64] Document to be found on the FSB website.

[65] Monetary mutual funds (MMFs).

[66] Non-bank financial institutions (NBFIs).

Whatever the definition of the scope of the so-called "shadow banking" (as discussed at a conference held in Paris in 2013 at the initiative of the European Institute for Financial Research (EIFR)), all authoritative bodies (including the EU Commission FSB, the European Systemic Risk Board (ESRB), the US Federal Oversight Stability Committee (FOSC) and the SCAV) confirm that extra-regulatory "shadow banking" now provides financing for 50–75% of the real US economy, and 25–30% in the EU.

Since the Seoul G20 meeting, a broad expectation has taken root that systemic risk must be addressed definitively. At present, the European Commission is awaiting comments on how to regulate and reduce the risk. Three approaches are being considered: (1) regulating through banking mechanisms, (2) an increase in the scope of current regulations on instruments and markets (MIFID – 2011/61/EC and AIFMD – "Alternative Investments Fund Manager Directive"), or (3) direct regulation of refinancing entities (MMFs).

In our opinion, there are virtually insurmountable difficulties inherent in defining "shadow-banking" actors and their respective scope, as well as in setting up the required interdisciplinary committees. Such bodies would need to integrate experts in the fields of banking, instruments and processes (including securitization and REPO agreements), all for the purpose of defining the playing field and scope. The scale of difficulty involved is so daunting, and the proposed approach so reliant on overly generalized concepts, that the effort would prove unmanageable if not entirely inconclusive. Being inadequately conceptualized, such an approach would unmask loopholes that can be controlled only by excessive regulation, which in turn challenges legal principles of individual liberty accepted in most stable or even evolving democracies.

The manner in which the FSB has been engaged represents a dead end. In its last report, dated November 14, 2013, it recommends a two-step analysis after macro mapping the risk focus. In reality, it is an admittance that macro mapping is not sufficient to follow up on money flows. It is the consequence of denying, wrongly, the existence of new forms of monies. To quote this last report: "For 2013 shadow banking monitoring exercise, data and information were collected from 25 jurisdictions and the euro area as a whole from the following sources:

 (i) Flow of funds data at the end of 2012…
 (ii) A short analysis of national trends…
(iii) Additional information on self-securitization and non-bank financial entities prudentially consolidated into a banking group for jurisdictions in which this is relevant."

The report, as a note, explains what self-securitization is: "(retain securitization) is defined as those securitization transactions done solely for the purpose of using the securities created as collateral with the central bank in order to obtain funding, with no intent to sell them to third-party investors. All securities issued by the structured finance vehicles (SFVs) for all tranches are owned by the originating bank and remain on its balance sheet." By explaining the existence of such a process, the FSB is saying that there is no longer much difference, aside from a legal one, between central bank money and other money. This REPO system aimed at justifying the use of central bank new money to support quantitative easing (QE) leads to a detailed analysis we will consider later about stamped warranties and nominal values combined with speed rotation and time.

The target of reducing non-bank intermediation that was set first will not be achieved and makes no sense. The FSB 2013 report on 2012 figures gives, for 20 jurisdictions, an intermediation by non-banks including the Eurozone and the USA of 125% of GDP, 6 percentage points higher than in 2012.

In the USA, the established approach entitles the FOSC to regulate "shadow-banking" entities (which present significant systemic risk) under its jurisdiction, on a case-by-case basis. Viewed in a broader sense, it is an understatement to contend that processes and entities outside the system should be regulated, specifically by requiring identical processes to those mandated by the Basel Committee on Banking Regulation (BCBS) or Dodd–Frank statutes in the USA. Either pathway would result in regulations leading to increased prudential ratio requirements, while reducing the banking system's financing leverage (for instance by inducing so-called undercover narrowing of "refinancing pipe capacities").

In considering the foregoing discussion, one may need to understand that "shadow banking" has been fed by deficits and international macroeconomic imbalances – on the heels of a 1980s concept favouring banking deregulation, along with an intent to foster competition in order to reduce margin-generated income from banking activity. For the same reasons that drove the refinancing of imbalances through money issuance, both governments and private economic sectors require a combined dynamic between traditional banking and the emerging "shadow-banking" sector. Reminiscent of morphine dependency, the addiction to this dual system cannot be cut instantaneously. Moreover, attempting to impose regulatory regimes without adequate knowledge as to the resulting dynamics will only serve to further decelerate monetary rotation (velocity), and as a consequence reduce economic growth. Although data collection at more granulation-dependent levels is interesting for students and academic bankers, it is likely to yield ineffective or dangerous conclusions if taken too seriously, not to mention prompting consideration of inappropriate drivers that lead in the direction of a centralized financial sector economy. Fortunately, the future of such a track seems remote, as more than 70% of the post-2008 US economy has already been refinanced through the new dual "shadow-banking" system. Already declining Basel III guidelines, it appears unlikely that any US government will head in this direction, at least in the near future.

Of substantial and broader concern are the conclusions presented in a study on economic and financial sector "interconnectedness" that is attached to the FSB-issued document entitled "Global Shadow Monitoring – Institutional Results Report 2012", dated November 18, 2012.[67] In this report, the context of "interconnectedness" denotes the dependency of the banking system on "shadow banking"-driven refinancing, and vice versa. As illuminated in this report, the underlying paradox is that one sector (mainstream banking) is being subjected to detailed regulation, whereas "shadow banking" remains virtually unregulated. As for the notion that the indirect financing of "shadow banking" by the mainstream banking sector will channel regulatory oversight into the "shadow-banking" world, this has proven to be but a mere dream. Since the collapse of Lehman Brothers, it is openly evident that the double-entry accounting system remains a legally credible reality, and that the precedent of fair-market valuation generates a continuing mirage that places the entire world fiscal system at risk.

During the historical timeline and development of this dual-sector financial environment, deviations from exchange values initially appeared comforting, in part because these facilitated ample margins for placating issuers as well as the multitude of instrument-trading

---

[67] See reports on the FSB website http://www.financialstabilityboard.org/list/fsb_publications/index. htm. The last report entitled "Global Shadow Banking Monitoring" is dated November 14, 2013.

financial players who would eventually need to be compensated (although the source of that eventual compensation remained unknown). Yet another way to view the pattern of "interconnectedness", as reported by the aforementioned 2012 FSB report, presents more frightening implications than provided in the report's analysis. If, throughout many jurisdictions (mostly European), the assets held by NBFIs represent a value below even 20% of overall bank holdings, then one may erroneously conclude that the level of risk is relatively low. However, history confirms that the contrary is in fact true: coupled with rapid contraction of associated instruments, a runoff from ostensibly manageable levels of REPO lending enveloped the US financial sector in a matter of days, leaving the US banking system short of $2 billion[68] and rapidly impacting associated transactional activity (the ultimate "short-circuit" event for any banking system).

Notwithstanding its role as a risk factor, speed is not a standalone parameter and cannot simply be obviated in the absence of eliminating the runner – an option which is not on the world financial system's agenda. In the report mentioned, we observe that the pressure on banks has reduced refinancing activity in the US system. However, we also note that the magnitude of global "shadow-banking" activity has increased concurrently to a substantial degree. The primary reason for this involves the continuation and propagation of macroeconomic imbalances that have to be repositioned somewhere in the financial system – and with progressive ease in the face of greater liquidity in the fiscal environment. The reduction of bank-driven refinancing within the present economy merely demonstrates the reduction of banking's participatory share in this activity, along with its rapid decline in Europe (largely due to the anticipation of Basel III).

However, the fact remains that the overall economy continues to urgently require refinancing. Reminiscent of the effects following the 1933 enactment of the Glass–Steagall Act, ongoing reductions in private equity refinancing by banks do not reduce this need, which continues to grow as holding companies now enter the refinancing subsector. Moreover, any boundary frontier that the FSB attempts to implement (so as to firewall the interface between non-banking financial institutions and banks themselves, stopping contagion of failures) will always be "leaky" in nature. If that were not the case, and if either type of financial institution was severely constrained by regulatory regimes that failed to first deal with applicable monetary reform issues, then significant economic damage would occur within both subsectors of the financial community.

In conclusion, we may say that if "shadow banking", defined as non-bank credit intermediation, is now accepted as a necessity for modern economies, its analysis should be organized functionally as such and by instruments and sectors. It is fed by imbalances but carries the risks of any monetary flow, disappearance and change in traded values of both the instruments used and the underlying assets. The FSB reports on this topic might have contributed to such understanding of global money, even if they do still use this verbiage of "shadow money" that was used to cover the refusal of modern realities.[69]

---

[68] Gary B. Gorton working paper report no. 15787, February 2010.

[69] Note 1 of the FSB 2013 report: "some authorities or market participants prefer to use other terms such as 'market based financing' instead of 'shadow banking'. The use of the term 'shadow banking' is not intended to cast a pejorative tone on this system of credit intermediation. However, the FSB is using the term 'shadow banking' as this is the most commonly employed and, in particular, has been used in earlier G20 communication."

BEFORE ACCOUNTING FOR ANY TRANSACTION – THE SAMPLING TOPIC. THE MIX UP BETWEEN NUMBERS AND FORMULAE[70]

We have explored the reasons for metals such as gold, silver or bronze being the basis for clearing a transaction. We have seen that, as many authors recognized and de Gaulle advocated, metals are transcendental. It is a physical reality that humans cannot change. As such, the definition of metal cannot be changed by the debtor of an obligation and, when available, can constitute a fixed guarantee for a transaction to be paid in the future. Being transcendental, it was deemed to comply with the monetary definition of not only being accepted by two parties, but by an undefined number of parties whatever language they speak and write; the constituents of a monetary circle. We have seen the evolution from metal ingots to stamped coinage with a face value or weightage guarantee, and script money (Chapters 1 and 2). We have also seen the limits of metal's use for monetary purposes. Now, before going into the sociologically modern use of monetary language that is stampage, and its generalization in accounting, we discuss a key issue – the roles of the number and the figure. Gold has disappeared as a practical means of payment. Contrary to what one may think, there is a need for an icon in the monetary world. We agree to the fact that trust, the basis of any flowing monetary system, is similar to belief, and is necessary. The universality of metals and weight has now been transferred to numbers, as the heterogeneity of guarantees cannot replace metals if there is no other general layer of guarantees by a government to cover them all rising again. The question is, who should be responsible at last recourse for such a monetary set-up? Guarantees are not numbers, nor are they stamping, prices or necessarily values.

We note that sampling will consist of stamping a face value on an instrument, making a number of units correspond to a referential unit (a monetary unit such as dollar, euro or British pound, etc.). Only the monetary unit definition is, in essence, a sovereign privilege, not the sampling of, for example, a bank bill or a T-bond. The associated number will be given by the issuer and, at issuance, will correspond to a price. Further on the instrument, until redemption, may be exchanged at another number of units corresponding to the price of the instrument. It will not be stamped and the original sampling will remain. It may differ from the sampled original number due to the changes in the status of the receivable (standing of the issuer, interest rate and remaining duration) until redemption at the original sampled value, and supply and demand on the markets. We also understand that it will only be exchangeable in the same way that public issuances would be when the budget is in deficit.

Figure 3.2 attempts to show that traded prices for financial instruments tend to move back towards the nominal issuance price over time, except when the instrument is not redeemable. Among the stress factors are the velocity, the interest rates and the volume lag between amounts redeemed and new issuances. Exchangeability between instruments when volumes are not in balance will also play a key role. It is an interconnected system that we will describe further.

Numbers have superior, unchangeable qualities. Two plus two, in whatever language or with whatever basis, will always derive the same reality and reverse from the same reality the same numbers. The operating factors are the realities to which it may apply. The basis for a calculation is not going to change its realities. Not being of human origin, or being outside its sphere of control, it may also be looked at as proof of the existence of a creator outside our human space – but that is imposed on us.

---

[70] Here a formula may also be a standard if the formula is not to vary.

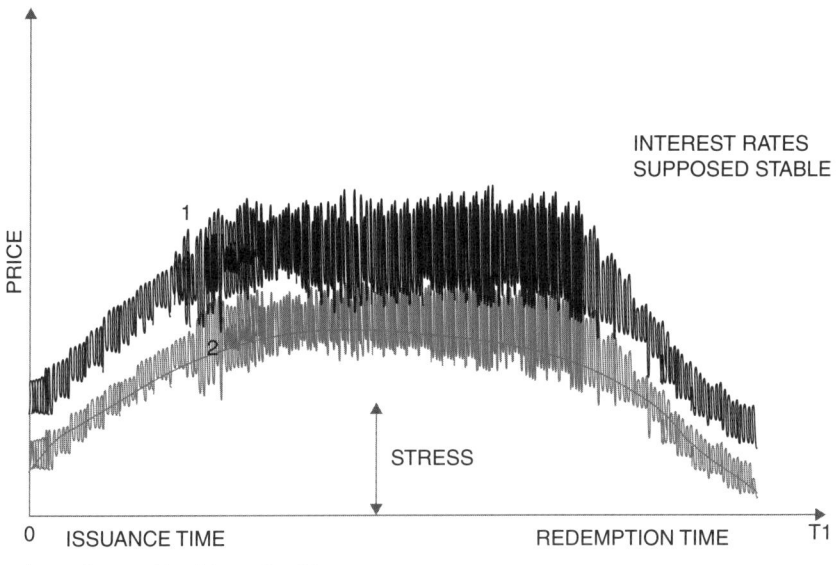

FIGURE 3.2   Tentative evolution in value of a financial instrument over time

Why can we not answer this question of how, since Rousseau and Kant,[71] French and Prussian thinkers knew how to push towards the great developments in relativity of H. Poincaré and Einstein. In our new context of open marketplaces, numbers used to post transactions are replacing gold, and users as well as witnesses believe in what is shown as a valuation figure or a transaction price or a calculated numbered diagnostic. The referential units the numbers apply to are not relevant, in a wider context. The unit is just a legal aspect, but the expression is deemed to be dollars in the US zone and euros in the Eurozone. Being implied from the marketplace used, it may often not even be quoted. The numbers will determine an exchange ratio. It may also have perverse effects. Applying a number to a formula that may or may not be transparent, relevant to realities at a particular time and not in the past or future, can mislead. The public may worship numbers as they appear mixed up with human behaviour and rulings, and without knowledge they may become idolatry due to faith, easiness or worst, compliance and a lack of courage needed to challenge formulas that, by construction, are not of physical nature as they include values like time and speed and therefore they never perfectly represent realities and dimensions. This is the reason for the next chapter; the need for universal monetary language and the mix up with set standards.

Numbers are universal; equations, as standards, are volatile and different from both numbers and accounting, while the unification of language is an over-simplifying process that requires constant reconsideration. This topic raises questions. First, we need to fundamentally explain why the system suddenly failed in an atmosphere which appeared quiet until liquidity vanished from the markets. No individual would challenge a reassuring set-up; the supervisors, the rating agencies and the regulators were each fed with numbers

---

[71] Jean-Jacques Rousseau (1712–1778); Emmanuel Kant (1724–1804).

and certitudes, allowing all possible financial extravagances without any means of escape except the fast reduction of interest rates to neutralize the effect of excessive debt in the global system.

Second, this diagnostic comes to the conclusion that the point of view from which economies are looked at has to change. The famous dispute between Maynard Keynes and Freidrich Hayek about systems is no longer appropriate, and none of the answers correspond to what they would consider analysing today (if ever they have been correctly understood). They addressed the topics of the time; the never-ending US economic crisis for Keynes with the tools he had, and for Hayek the worst moral deviances that humanity had ever faced. In ranking the importance of their respective analyses from a human perspective, Hayek's approach was far more relevant but Keynes never knew what was to happen in the Germanic world and the communist world. The latter was never directly exposed to it, and Keynes lacked modesty about what was important to him and what was just a mechanism to be used to address US issues. Von Mises and his successor Hayek knew, through their own circumstances, the fatal link between successive events. Coming from the most advanced society in terms of philosophers, they could neither be understood nor believed if their English was not good enough to communicate, which was the case at least for Hayek. It was not like Einstein dealing with science, with little competition.

In today's time, another frontier has to be drawn in conceiving monetary reform. It is about what should be totally regulated (such as money definition and uses), what is real (such as numbers), and what information and physical realities are created by the mix up of definitions and human behaviour, as well as how observation should be organized for transparency and compliance with morals. Nothing should be final, and the border between what should be of centralized governance and what should remain individual liberty is relevant to various circles, which are themselves very much dependent on principles and education. Having a single general tool for fulfilling the sampling role of money is again of paramount importance. Having a system that can be both neutral and not modifiable by users and issuers will bring the trust that central bank money might have lost because of their proximity of central banks to governments and the public debt issuance. The surprising success of bitcoin, despite its lack of identification rule, is there for holders. It is the undecipherable issuance formula with a commitment to limited quantities. The criticism will get us nowhere if it is not focused on realities. The bitcoin is the result of excessive quantity and distrust in the unit and its use as a better reserve. It should not hide the need for electronic money to be policed. Anyone who is going to propose a guaranteed mechanism for sampling will be successful, including if they bring some mysticism, as bitcoin does, with a formula that the public cannot understand, like the chemical formula of gold.[72]

QUESTIONS AND ANSWERS

Past and 21st-Century Money Analysis

How can modern money be defined?
  Money can only be defined through its functions as it is a functional tool.

---

[72] See Bank of France Focus no. 10, December 5, 2013 on the dangers of virtual monies: the bitcoin example.

What are these functions?
  They are still the classical ones:

  – price setting
  – payment and trading instrument
  – a reserve of value.

Can money be defined in other ways?
  Yes, intrinsically.

How can money carry value intrinsically?
  Metallic content, with gold being one of the most common in the past, along with silver.

Why is gold iconic?
  As we have seen, it is practical, stable and universal as to its chemical definition. It is the same formula and weight for all market participants whatever language they use. Humans cannot change the formula.

Why did gold disappear as a monetary reference?
  Because it works as a brake when money needs are flexible and depend on flows and prices. If gold is accumulated, there are shortages. If gold is abundant, it interacts with the prices of goods independently from the needs for these goods, missing the goal of being an adjustment mechanism.

How could gold or other precious metals be replaced?
  Gold has intrinsic value. It can be replaced by books and records, in essence "figures". If accepted by a market participant. The money instrument (receivable or debt) with the figure attached to it and recorded as proof of existence and acceptance will play the same role as weight did for metals. Commercial laws on collection, bankruptcies and accounting standards under control of courts become the stamping.

Are dollars or euros defined intrinsically as monetary units?
  The dollar, since August 1971, has no link and no measurement referential to anything. The euro, a new currency resulting from a treaty, never had. There is no commitment from their issuing central bank to peg them to any price. Their evolution, nevertheless, can be followed by comparison with inflation indexes on their domestic markets and by exchange rates between currencies; X dollars being worth Y euros. Despite a general commitment not to intervene in foreign exchange markets, there are limits to the clear understanding of the set-up. As the dollar is a key currency on international markets, it happens that with limiting regulations (Basel III or US equivalent) there are shortages in this currency for banks to satisfy their needs and consequently to provide long-term financing. To override that situation, the FED has concluded swap commitments with other central banks such as the European Central Bank, Swiss Central, Bank of England, Bank of Japan, etc.). These swaps are at fixed exchange rates, creating an artificial link between fiat moneys.

What is today's seignorage privilege?
  Owing to its strategic functions in the economy that we have reviewed, the sovereign has, in theory, monopoly over issuing money and fixing its face value by stamping the monetary unit and a figure. From this power to set the currency in a country derives the associated power for the issuer to receive remuneration by means of withholding taxes. For a coin,

there would be the possibility to reduce the metal content compared with an unchanged face value. In modern times, the equivalent would be a tax on transactions (sales tax, Tobin tax on some financial transactions, issuing financial papers with no support). Taxes are a specific, organized and set-by-law category of seignorage, in the same way that the authorization given by parliament to government or central bank to issue new money or debt is another.

What is the limit to seignorage power?
The power for its issuer to impose this issued money to satisfy an obligation.

What is legal tender?
Legal tender is a money instrument issued by a government which, within a certain jurisdiction, must be accepted to satisfy a claim.

What are examples of legal tenders?
A bank bill is legal tender. However, since a European directive regarding services of payments, electronic money is also to be considered as such.

Why did the traditional concepts of money disappear?
Because stamping is no longer a centralized or fixed function with the innovation of securitization. Financial instruments may now carry similar and attached guarantees to those a centralized issuer like a central bank may have issued by signature or precious metal. By marginal tax rates on individual reduction, disintermediation of the refinancing of the economy is expended.

How is the guarantee on a security grounded?
By taking leans on assets that are legally attached to the instrument and may be executed against by the debtor or another holder of the original debt. The reserve function, which was required from traditional money by its convertibility into gold at the central bank, is now privatized and therefore decentralized. Rating agencies are becoming a mix of the verification and control functions of the old metal weight of a coin, and the officers of the king who helped control markets.

What is the result of this transformation from paper bills to other financial instruments to finance the economy and answer its needs?
Securitization was the answer to the growth of exchanges, where precious metal availability was limited and not linked to exchanges, variable in volume, and represented by resulting receivables and debts.

What is the drawback of securitization and other guaranteeing mechanisms?
There are few, if any, limitations to issuances and exchanges, which may be totally independent – books or records, it is immaterial. Figures showing on financials are only guided by regulation standards if under a particular jurisdiction. The value of the instrument becomes disconnected from its nominal value at issuance, but it is not claimable, only exchangeable, linked to the status of the guarantees. With no other safeguards, the value of the guarantee is not always visible and, being intangible, may also be volatile.

What are the key results of this transformation?
The total dematerialization of money. The traditional multiplier of money limited through banks by surveillance ratios exploded figures. The credit distribution banking function

limited by charters disappeared, and was replaced by intermediation. The real financing went to those holding the balances on a worldwide scale. Shadow banking has appeared.

What is the origin of the 2007 crisis?

The origin of the 2007 crisis came from the contraction of banks' refinancing by non-banks, because of the shrinking value of guarantees granted to them.

What is shadow or parallel banking?

Shadow banking has a legal definition due to governmental statistical standards. It is the lending function of any entity not registered as a bank: hedge funds, monetary mutual funds, insurance companies and retirement funds. Being of legal essence it is a limited definition, looked at from a banking point of view. Only money lent to banks is considered in the definition.

Why this limited definition?

It is historical, and the result of the monopoly previously granted to banks to distribute financing. Before the 1980s, in an inflationary environment, all surveillance was based on the volume of credit distribution exercised by central banks over their legal scope of competence; the banking sector. In this set-up, central banks could only see what was in their jurisdiction, monetary zone and what commercial banks were doing.

Why do we propose another definition?

Because the refinancing of the economy is globalized through financial markets, and the divide between what a bank is and what it is not is artificial. Corporations are able to carry out their business without a bank, and need only a payment system that they may also integrate. The second reason is that any legal definition is limited to a territory. With the development of "private" money and trade deficits or surpluses, that is to say imbalances, it is a very limited view – many corporations are no longer national and mostly international. We look at corporations, including banks refinanced by individuals personally or through governments, being the providers and clients.

Are we far from that view?

No, the FED may at any time consider a corporation as a systemic risk and have it submitted to regulation.

How may governments support their financial centres?

When the domestic business that created them is no longer sufficient to justify their size and employment, governments use better protection and flexibility arguments and tax arguments to locate executives with high income and transactions.

What are the possible consequences of our analysis segregation between nominal value of a financial monetary instrument, price, stamping and sampling compared with value?

As these concepts are different but all are to be used for book and records, choosing which accounting standards will refer to and decide who should operate them raises disputes. All being realities, using them simultaneously may allow a better analysis of monetary flows and consistency of financial statements.

What are the consequences of the distinction between, nominal value of a monetary instrument, a price, a sampling and a stamping?

As books and records will follow up and determine financial statements, all these concepts can be used for the posting.

CHAPTER 4

The Contemporary Basis for Money Expression: Accounting Ledgers

"Money calculation reaches its full perfection in capital accounting. It establishes the money price of the available means and confronts the total with the changes brought about by action and by the operation of other factors"[1]

— **L. Von Mises**

BOOK BALANCES ARE EITHER MONEY OR POTENTIAL MONEY

In describing the evolutionary changes surrounding "today's money" (see Chapter 3), we implicitly found that the expansion of its functional role across all layers of society had changed in nature, and now encompassed diverse financial instruments – including those packaged in specialized legal vehicles. Within this ensuing chapter, we will see that the actors in today's financial sector no longer refer to disappearing metal coinage or scripted money on the balance sheets of banks, but rather to financial instruments and comprehensive accounting statements[2] that reflect their implementation. The resulting balances of each of the postings on the accounts relevant to monetary elements become the crosshairs of their legally defined intersection. The importance of the relationship between these elements on the way they are posted and the financial statements disclosed is such that we need to discuss their origin and importance – as well as the manner in which their functional interplay is set.

---

[1] Von Mises, L., *Human Action*, ch. XIII, p. 231. See References.

[2] Multiple papers that did not exist, or were disregarded at the time we published our previous book, now refer to the role of "balance sheets". Among these sources are Ruscher, E. and Wolf, G. (2012), "Corporate balance sheet adjustments stylized facts, clauses and consequences", European Economy, Economic Papers no. 449 and McRosenberg, A., Keller, C., Setser, B. and Rubini, N. (2002), "A balance sheet approach to the financial crisis", IMF Working Papers no. WP/02/210. Already previously quoted by the authors is the OECD yearly 81st 2009–2010 annual report that is also quite meaningful, and which states that: "large mismatches in international balance sheets also create risks" (p. 43).

A SINGLE WORLDWIDE LANGUAGE; ACCOUNTING AND FINANCIAL STATEMENTS

Without the support of a tangible precious metal, but merely based on a figure that is inappropriately termed a *par value*, today's monetary instruments require a substitute reference. Thus, any figure appearing on transaction ledgers must correspond to a measurement unit. So far, this remains a virtual measurement, but based on the precepts of Von Mises' economic doctrine, such a virtual representation is not a physical measurement unit. The unit in question is, in fact, the transactional exchange *par value* that routinely appears on financial statements – including standards that govern this set-up, and which find their source in transfer laws and accepted practices set by authoritative bodies and not by physical realities. Although not denominated in gold, the transactional counterparts of such figures appearing on accounting records are monetary instruments, and thus real enough in today's terms. Given this recognition, and so as to develop our analysis, we need to explore details about the "determinant rules" that underpin our contemporary monetary system.

The mix-up that Von Mises complained about comes from the fact that over time, some accounting practices which were used for centuries became an integral matter of law admitted wrongly as equivalent to realities. As such, accounting regimes were designed to ensure the safety, regulation and verification of transactional exchanges; a basis for potential judicial recourse in the event that disputes arose. Resulting legal disputes invariably dealt with matters that involved requests pertaining to discovery and/or demonstrations of proof required in order to support the claims and briefs of either plaintiff or defendant; usually with regard to the transactional occurrence in question. With the development of a financial society, the matter of financial statements and their comparability became the cause of the need for unification and generalization of practices. They triggered the creation of independent authoritative bodies to develop the standard to be used to keep the books and close the financials.

Moreover, statutory laws and associated operational regulations were used to organize the manner in which the accounting system and its components should operate together. Depending on the country[3] and, as an accessory or a basis, books and financials became used for tax reporting needs.

There are two universal accounting precepts that accountants should comply with so as not to have their books and financial statements rejected; consistency and double entry or double posting.

The Consistency-Based Principle of Bookkeeping

At the outset, one basic principle requires emphasis, namely: every monetary transaction within an enterprise needs to be fully recorded. In accounting practice, this is referred to as the "consistency principle". We will see that it is a principle of law with all its consequences for evidence. As a derivative of this principle, accountants have set a rule that forbids any cancelling of posted data. If a posting is wrong, which may happen, the posting has to be reversed, and not wiped off the ledgers. It is also a matter of internal control and audit track.

---

[3] In continental European countries the principle is of having "a single balance sheet" and "system of accounting" for tax and business purposes. This is not the case in the USA. Everywhere, tax authorities set rules about the way the transactions should be followed and the software organized to comply with the request for evidence.

Accounting became, long ago, a matter of law to ensure the safety of exchanges and the potential recourse to judicial courts when a dispute was arising. These legal disputes requested matters of investigation and proven demonstrations of what occurred for the plaintiff. Regulations and laws had to organize the way evidence could be brought to the attention of the judges.

Discoveries and evidence can only be pertinent if the consistency principle has been complied with. If there are missing postings, the consistency principle is breached and not all of the truth has been told.

The "Double-Posting" Principle

Based on long historical precedents, both property and contract/tort law have established the basic precepts for "reporting" the transfer of ownership and "contractual consideration" rights between one or more counterparties. Without statutory and/or precedent-driven bodies of both property and contract/tort law that define ownership and transfer principles – and an accompanying judicial system designed to ensure their implementation – accounting practice and transactional flow could not exist. Conversely, without an accounting regime, such laws could not operate effectively in regulating transactional flow. The double-entry or double-posting system originates from both the legal facts of property transfer and the need for evidence.

Ever since Luca Pacioli, a priest serving the Lombardian bankers, wrote *La Suma* – a seminal work on how to properly keep accounting ledgers – the need to keep track of transactions has been recognized as a basic prerequisite of sound management. The legendary Lombardian bankers financed 15th-century transnational and international trade throughout Western Europe and Oriental Mediterranean. As the financial sector experts of their time, the Lombards needed to keep track of credit or debit balances against corresponding counterparties in commerce. This meant commanding and retaining detailed information such as *"they owe me or I owe them* a specific amount of given money at a defined time".

This double-posting principle is simple and logical. It derives from the transfer of property when trading and transacting, that is any acquired asset shown on the assets side of the balance sheet must be matched with a corresponding debit entered on the liability side of the balance sheet. That debt entry reflects the debt incurred for the price paid on the asset, and can be recorded either as a cash reduction or as a credit on the liability side. By definition, the price being the same for the seller and the buyer, the debited and credited amounts are equal for the same transaction – this is the so-called "accounting identity". By convention, it was decided that debits would show on the left column of ledgers, and credits on the right column. If each of the postings reflects this accounting identity, the totals of the ledgers' debits and credits are equal.

Which established transactional categories are accounting procedures applicable to? Without qualification, they include all of them: buy/sell transactions, a range of wholesale and retail sales, hiring processes, as well as cash and contractual commitments other than those already enumerated – for instance, renting, leasing, investments, larger fixed goods or asset transactions, etc.

In examining a range of standard transactional ledgers, it is readily apparent that some debits represent a universal property right: for instance, buildings and machinery (whether recorded as debts or receivables) often involve a legal link to a third party. In recording the activities and contributions of primary debtors and creditors as well as third parties, in some settings it may be elected to offset balances against each other – for equal amounts, complying with the accounting identity precept, for instance as many current account recording approaches prefer. In other cases and depending on applicable law, balancing may or may not be authorized. In the financial sector, the impact of this issue is of paramount importance

– and specifically with regard to the prudential ratios and balance sheet structures utilized by banking institutions.[4]

Even when utilizing comparable accounting standards, differences between applicable property and commercial laws between various countries can present challenges when comparing financial statements; and particularly when this involves the rights to collect receivables and sales of existing liens on underlying assets. It is also necessary to point out that an enterprise may change the intrinsic make-up of its assets and liabilities through transactional exchanges (sales of a company's receivables for instance), thereby generating levels of compensation that would otherwise not be possible. Furthermore, the time basis used for recording transactional clearing may need to be evaluated over a time period. For instance, when a debtor is in a financially troubled situation, a balancing of debts and credits for a troubled enterprise is rarely authorized; for them, debts remain on the books as due and payable while credits accumulate during legal proceedings (examples include Chapter 11, i.e. suspending payment to creditors while a recovery plan is submitted to the bankruptcy court). We will subsequently revisit this technical issue and its transparent as well as opaque representation in aberrant market valuations that played a major role in the 2008 financial crisis.

The double-entry system manifests other less obvious qualities that help ground any audit process, and thereby reinforce the thesis that "posted values" should not be amended. Upon introduction of an error in even a single posted item for a transaction, the resulting debit/credit summation on the balance sheet and profit/loss ledgers will not equalize, simply because a specific account with the wrong balance was posted on. The accounting identity will only be respected if an equivalent error – or several entries whose sum is equal to the error in question – is also made on the opposite side of the ledger. Especially if the sourcing of data is organized so as to be presented separately, the foregoing type of scenario is a statistically unrealistic occurrence. Regardless, the localization of such errors on the ledger or account records will be very helpful in auditing the comprehensive books.

When cash accounts are justified by reconciliation (arithmetical explanation of differences) against third-party statements – for instance by explaining differences between bank account balances in one set of books versus statements issued by the bank – any unexplained discrepancy indicates a mistake in the counterpart account. In every such case, the original source of the error needs to be identified, a process that is facilitated by the advantages of the double-entry system. It may be explained either by a mistake attracting attention from the auditors (internal or independent) or a fraud shown by the disappearance of cash from the bank account. Reconciliation with IRS will follow the same pattern. The accounting identity works as proof, as for any arithmetical operation.

CONSEQUENCES OF THE BASIC ACCOUNTING PRINCIPLES

Taking these principles forward into the context of the financial system, any issuance of money must be posted beginning at the level of a central bank, but also in a manner reflecting all intermediate downstream players in the banking system – and, as a result, across the entire economic system of enterprises with whom individual holders of monetary instruments will deal. This consequence is the fundamental grounding of all the following developments.

---

[4] Balancing debit and credit will reduce gross categorical amounts and consequently the balance sheet total.

From a managerial perspective, accounting procedures and standards also became an integral component of tax regulation – especially following WWI, when the financial appetite of cash-hungry governments ensured that the levy of taxes was broadened beyond agriculture, to include industry and commerce. Where not directly set up by governments themselves (for instance during wars or in the immediate period thereafter and in Europe for tax collection purposes), accounting standards were established by specialized independent authoritative bodies.

These included the FASB (USA), the IASB (an international private and independent standard setter which attempted to be the successor of national agencies for Europe and other countries' private sectors[5]) and the IPSASB (for the public sector with the same geographic scope[6]). Beyond a large and still growing body of systemic procedures used to regulate accounting practice by such bodies, standard setters have inherited the general rules which were already observed, grounded for centuries in the requirement for the entrepreneur to follow up on their business and to identify errors and combat fraud. To us, the whole monetary system can only be explained using legal set-ups such as the ownership concept and accounting principles to report transactions and consequent results. On the basis of these general principles, briefly described above, standards setters are now continuously developing new rules in addition to the already quoted ones in order to make financial statements comparable and usable by investors of whatever category they belong to (households, financial institutions, non-financial institutions, government, etc.).

CONCEPTS AND RULES TO REPORT EXCHANGES AND DETERMINE THE IMAGE OF FINANCIAL STATEMENTS

As already discussed, accounting ledgers (books) and the resulting financial statements are to record any and all transactions that occurred between one enterprise and another, a person acting as a corporate proprietor or an individual ("household" is the standard administrative wording). Governments and non-profit organizations are also subject to the duty to keep books and records and only persons acting privately are exempt.

The maintenance of accounting books and records is a legal obligation for any commercial person in any country in the world. As noted in French legal statutes: "any person or corporation having the qualification of a commercial person has to post any transaction influencing their enterprise's belongings. These transactions have to be chronologically posted in the books. They have to take an inventory at least once every 12 months, including the existence and the value of the enterprise's belongings, and provisions for setting up financial statements at the end of the business year" (French law article L123-12 of the commercial code).

Of key importance is the consequence resulting from posting any transaction – namely, the appearance of exchanges showing on both the debit and credit sides of the P&L (profit and loss account) will be compulsory, and the resultant recording of all sales and purchases

---

[5] European Union Member countries kept their own agencies to adapt when necessary and implement accounting regulation decided by the Commission after IASB standard adoptions. There is a filtering process. A special committee "EFRAG" advises the Commission, but the initiative power remains mainly with the IASB. The Commission may not adopt a standard proposed by the IASB.

[6] A convergence project has been launched under the umbrella of the IMF, World Bank and ECB to promote a convergence between IFRS and IPSAS to have "integrated accounts for the public sector and also reduce differences with the US public sector system".

involving counterparties will generate a debt or receivable entry in the balance sheet, along with entries reflected in updating the balance. In the same manner, any type of expense or sale of services will show on the P&L, until cleared by a corresponding payment on the balance sheet. Speed of money flows will impact the balances of each of the accounts with a third party.

If the rate at which balance sheet postings are generated exceeds the speed of the clearing process, then artificial changes in the acceleration of transactional exchange rates may indicate expansion in global transactional volume – a pattern that does not necessarily correlate with underlying economic growth. In other words, if representations of the money lent across the economy and shown on the books are driven purely by acceleration in monetary rotation (and merely reflect artificial growth in transactional volume), then such trends are largely irrelevant from an economic perspective – unless underlying transactions are coupled with tangible physical exchanges for products and/or services. Any decline in the speed of the payment process – either due to the psychological attitude of entrepreneurs or because of liquidity shortages – will further inflate figures showing transactional volume. Moreover, any additional issuance of debt (including monetary issues or buyouts of monetary instruments by central financial institutions) will also generate further balance sheet expansion, including for central financial institutions.

It should also be noted that P&L ledgers represent an annual statement reporting on transactions that occurred during a preceding period of time, usually one calendar year. This is not the case for balance sheets that track and reflect ownership of assets and debt commitments at the closing date. Even when usually closed on a yearly basis if not more frequently, these records reflect the status of ownership (which constitutes an everlasting right), until legal modifications are transacted and cleared via a sale or on the basis of "commitment satisfaction" (usually based on amounts accumulated). Not surprisingly in this setting, any analysis that seeks to explain the underlying causes for expansion or contraction of balance values can be approached only by linking transactional exchanges reported on P&Ls with balance sheets themselves.

To effectively accomplish the ever-extending purposes of financial statements – to record ownership, be evidence of ownership, inform the entrepreneur of their achievements, fight against fraud for all participants in the economy, and make financials comparable for investors or managers to appraise the enterprise's performance – many extra principles have had to be added.

General mandatory principles

- *The "financial year" principle.* So as to accurately measure and reflect financial performance, all financial statements should correspond to a clearly defined time period, usually designated as the financial or fiscal year.
- *Parallel accounting of revenues and expenses.* The accounting record should reflect clear parallelism between revenues and expenses in the P&L account reported for all years, that is corresponding to any revenue reported and generated, and respective correlating accruals and expenses should be recorded and tracked in parallel. Also, parallelism of expenses or accruals is required to validate and finalize revenues. This correlation between revenues and expenses is to determine the margin and net profits of the operations.
- *Principle of "independence between financial years".* The above-noted principle of parallelism raises difficulties when a contract recorded on the ledger lacks a linear implementation period, and when it straddles a closing date for books (in constructive operational accounting reality, this will frequently be the case). This paradox is referred to as the "principle of independence between financial years".

- *Reference currency.* Books should be kept in a currency set by law. In the USA, the dollar and in the EU, the euro (for the 18 out of 28 EU countries that comprise the Eurozone).

In summary, accounting report periods should be annualized and issued independently from each other, with strict yearly cut-offs. The accounting process is intended to produce financial statements that, at a minimum, include: a balance sheet and a P&L accounting statement issued at a pre-set or compulsory frequency, with 12 months being standard. Transactions should be posted in the year to which they relate, and their influence on the previous and subsequent years' profit and loss should be reflected in corresponding accounting reports.

Besides the general principles that we have quickly reviewed, and that are deemed to be included in the general framework, standards setters elaborate on the prevailing rules that accountants commit to apply – such as, for the USA, in concert with adoption of their professional statute by CPAs (mandate). In addition to other authoritative regulatory bodies (such as the SEC or its worldwide equivalents), the accounting standard setters' organizations drive the existing regulatory set-up. In Europe, after being proposed by standard setters, standards are set by regulation. Businesses are to use the standards and accountants to verify their appropriate implementation. To fill the gap left by regulation, only interpretations, opinions and determination of applicability can be decided by other authoritative bodies. They are, for instance, National Securities and Exchange Commissions, accounting profession, or advisory committees to the European Commission. As we will see further on in Chapter 7 (Figures 7.3 and 7.5) about regulation, US SEC role in standard setting is with the European banking union taken over by ESMA a coordinating surveillance agency for financial markets. As Member States of the Union have kept their own SEC equivalent National Agencies a coordination was in need and taken over by ESMA. Because SEC only regulates what is public the space left by regulation to professional organizations as the AICPA (American Institute of CPAs) is wider than it is in Europe where accounting standards when adopted are applicable to any existing enterprise. This is often called "soft regulation". On both sides of the Atlantic, independent auditors may use their professional judgment to implement regulation and interpretations complement them in order that financial statements give a fair view of the financial situation and financial performance of the relevant business.

Accounting standards may allow some options; some compulsory standards are disputed and are discussed inside the arenas where the standards are elaborated, and some are rejected. We note that accounting standard setters have decided to work together to achieve standard convergence, but as is now the case with many topics, the trend stopped at the end of 2012 – the US SEC has issued a release stating that it is not appropriate for it to adopt IAS standards (those of the EU and other countries) and that it will stay with US FAS standards.

With the need to analyse what happened with the 2007 financial crisis, all regulators and political leaders are calling for a single set of financial reporting standards and comparability of financial standards across the world, with IFRS standards being referential. However, the limit to this convergence is the sovereignty of each monetary zone and the risk surveillance duty of national authorities. The EU opted for IFRS, but as for the IFRS to be used for public listings in the USA, the same questions arise. In November 2013 a report was issued by the Special Counsellor to the Internal Market Commissioner, entitled "Should IFRS Standards be more European?" This report raises the real issue of the legitimacy of the so-called independent bodies such as EFRAG (European Financial Reporting Advisory Group) to comment on IFRS proposals and reinforce the European Commission role at the early stages of preparation of standards, either by restructuring EFRAG, transferring its advising duties to one of the European surveillance authorities or even creating a specialized new agency within the European system. In our opinion, the issue which has so far been avoided is to have major countries decide about governance criteria at international level. Should the decision process be the European system of one member state having one vote, or should it be based on the importance of the financial world in each country? The outcome would be totally different. The topic is similar for each international monetary body, and is the financial world easy to valuate? Is the size of the economy perhaps a better criterion? How should adjustments be made for size differences? What is ultimately at stake is the supervision of the financial system which cannot wait and, practically, can ultimately only go to the existing authorities with a bilateral coordination.

The 2007 crisis, where the IASB was not able to suspend IFRS 39 (when financial instruments in portfolios could no longer be valuated) as the FASB did in due time, was a warning and justifies the new report on IFRS, questioning its governance. The sharing of sovereignty and the urgent request for clarification about this matter is at stake. Specific standards – those we will briefly describe – created by human beings, are not the laws of physics and are able to adapt to social realities where lobbyist pressures and dogmas can be destructive. The disputes between the USA and the EU on accounting topics should not be overstated. They relate to sovereignty, which is hard or impossible to remove constitutionally, and also to the interests of different sectors because of different set-ups in the financial industries and diverging priorities. For instance, putting aside the difficulties about fair market value that are necessarily dependent on the set-up of financial industries, financial markets, governmental debts and retirement benefits system realities are essentially the same. On November 6, 2013 the FASB voted to move forward with preparing a final standard on revenue recognition. It is based on a substantial approach, for instance for a complex transaction with a client linking several contractual performance obligations together such as the immediate delivering of a telephone set with the carrying of telecommunication over time. In such cases, the revenue recognition, the first and usually the most important line of a P & L will apprehend over time as one the various contracts and allocate its obligations to perform after being priced economically parallel to the costs. The remaining issue of this convergence and unification of methodology is the larger leeway left to professionals for interpretation. It was adopted jointly by FASB (as Accounting Standard Update 'ASU' no. 2014-9 topic 609) and IASB (IFRS no. 15) on May 28, 2014. It will take effect in 2017 for public companies and in 2018 for private ones. As joint project between FASB and the IASB showing that convergence is possible and a joint transition resource group for revenue recognition was decided on June 3, 2014. Revenue recognition is a major item for the issuance of financial instruments and the collection of substantiated data. We will see this further at several stages of our analysis.

Some principles may, in limited scope, be optional if they don't contradict the fair image when required.

Optional principles

- *Cash versus accrual accounting.* One can opt for either a "cash accounting" or an "accrual accounting"-based reporting system. In the case of cash accounting, transactions are posted only when a cash collection, bank collection or disbursement occurs. This method is only applicable to independent professions and small enterprises (within certain limits). The cash accounting option is not considered for major enterprises, as books should fairly represent the situation and therefore include all "certain commitments" (purchases to be delivered or already delivered but not paid, or expenses to be paid following use or consumption, etc.). In the case of accrual accounting, transactions are posted as soon as a contractual commitment exists or is verified. A sale is posted as it occurs – meaning the point at which parties to a transaction agree on what property is transferred, and for what price – rather than contingent on payment having been made. Neither of the two major recognized accounting standards systems recognize cash accounting for use by corporations.

■ We notice that the two methodologies differ in terms of the timing difference between the occurrence of key elements of a transaction, but not by substance. Books are said to be kept on an accrual basis or so-called "commitment accounting" (as opposed to cash accounting) in settings where transactions are posted before the resulting cash disbursement or collection from a transaction occurs. The resulting spread in the accounting process reflects the gap in the books between the time of posting the transfer of property (as a confirmation of the transactional agreement) and the subsequent receipt by the seller of the receivable due and the actual corresponding incursion of equivalent debt by the buyer.

Disputed issues

■ *Contractual or substantive approach to postings.* There is a disputed bidirectional issue equally representing the triumph of form over substance and at times the reverse. A "contractual approach to postings" involves the posting of transactions, as they are legally defined, on a contract. The obvious drawback of this approach is that taxation, legal and regulatory considerations may lead to the adoption of contractual language that appears to diverge from the intended financial reality of the contractually driven transaction itself. The most common examples are commercial financing and leasing contracts. Long the oligopolistic purview of banks, classic lending activity is subject to a bank's internal limitations on volume, rates and guarantees. However, such limits do not always apply to contracts involving commercial financing or leases. In the essence of lending practice, there is little practical difference between lending and leasing. A company in need of capital equipment may purchase the latter with lending-generated money or rent it (being committed to pay a rent over a similar period of time as the loan would have been reimbursed).

The process of adhering to the letter of "contractual language" while posting a transaction can give rise to divergent posting regimens that correspond to different types of contracts. In cases involving equipment-based assets and loans made as debts with interest on those assets, these may be posted as a P&L expense entry. In other cases, a property lien will remain under ownership of a leasing institution (without entry of a classic debt), but a lease's commitment to the lessor will be confirmed in the form of notes attached to the financials. As such, a rental obligation will appear in the P&L and not as accrued interest on behalf of the landlord, etc.

Despite the existence of a range of different contracts governing an inherently similar body of substance, it has long been recognized that the mechanics of a financing arrangement will determine the movement of funds and the impact of that process. Naturally, financing agreements are subject to tax effects that are primarily attributable to depreciation rules. For instance, at the lessor's side of the transaction pipeline, this impacts the general accounting policies and tax rules that govern the financial institution. Conversely, at the user's side of the pipeline, the impact will be on user-specific accounting practice and a different set of tax rules.

In the interests of transparency, the objective of choice would point towards favouring a substance-driven rather than a contractual-centred approach, but this stratagem will encounter two categories of challenge:[7]

---

[7] See European Directive 2013/34/EU on annual financial statements, consolidated financial statements and related reports; also texts EEDRL SEC/2011/1289 and 1290.

- *The first challenge* confronts accounting teams that represent many small and medium-sized companies. A substantive approach would disregard contractual consideration in favour of actuarial calculations coupled to a monetary "cost-of-financing" approach. The latter would also need to take into account the resulting tax differentials, compared with merely following the course of contractual execution and receipt of stipulated payments as these are processed. This is a more complicated approach for small and medium-sized companies to handle bookkeeping-wise than just posting in the books the collections and payments.
- *The second challenge* takes into account the potential of evolving difficulties in the relationship between two parties to a contract. One example would involve a tenant-leasing issue, where posting of transactional events at the corporate tenant level would have no value in the eyes of the leasing institution (whose representatives view only the terms of the contract as being enforceable). If the substantive approach were to have been adopted in this setting, then the entire balance sheet of a tenant company encountering financial distress (alongside the potential risk of disruption in operations) would need to be reconsidered.[8]

Ultimately, these differences primarily reflect time synchronization issues, actuarial factors and distortion effects – the latter attributable to various systems of taxation. Regardless, the choice of specific accounting options selected may lead to significant impact on the appearance of selected financial reports generated on behalf of capital-intensive industries.

Adopted principles and rules subject to implementation challenges or rejection

- *Prudence principle.* This approach considers the comprehensive risk of loss-associated factors that can be attached to a transaction or an intangible asset, specifically after the transactional event occurs or is shown on the books. Examples include, among many others, social commitments that an employer has reached with staff. Statistics show that some employees in this setting would inevitably ask for indemnification and predictably litigate when quitting a company, depending on the prevailing conditions at the time of severance. As the risk of this type of occurrence is indeterminate, it is not to be posted. As a consequence of challenging the prudence principle, or setting a precise definition of what prudence is, two matters raise disputes about the timing to post reserves for depreciation. Firstly, when they have to be considered. Also, regarding the change of value of fixed assets if they have to be considered, and when they should be posted depending on whether a sale is considered and whether the asset is exploited or not.
- *Reserves mitigating against hypothetically expected loss.* In comparison, a matter more closely financial in nature relates to the maintenance of reserves for the purpose of potentially mitigating against future losses in the portfolios of receivables. For instance, even if payments by a series of debtors are current when averaged over time, some of them will be in default at any one moment. This is a statistical factor that will vary over

---

[8] Obligating the use of substance over form in arriving at accounting decisions, a draft directive on financial statements has been submitted to the IFRS and FASB, and will be issued in 2014. The directive is expected to provide a substance-driven accounting option to small companies, while not for larger private equity-owned and publicly listed companies.

time, among other factors depending on the general economic situation. Ongoing discussions continue among standard setters as to when and how the risk of such transient defaults (defined only as a certain risk but not as an occurrence) should be posted, and in what amounts.

- *Capital gains or losses.* Another example of a controversial rule involves accounting procedures designed to address potential capital gains or losses on an asset. Assets in general are submitted to an impairment valuation test at closing. If the value is under the historical posted value, a reserve may be accrued if the loss is durable, but when the asset is being used there is controversy. In cases of possible gain, due to the fact that an asset's potential sale value exceeds that of the posted value, and when the asset is being operated, such circumstances will be disregarded and no posting of profit will be made prior to its realization. If it even corresponds to a fixed asset available for sale, the posting of the potential capital gain before realization is controversial and suggests a degree of certainty that the sale will happen soon after closing. When considering only negative factors, current accounting referees reject this principle if it does not relate to an asset available for sale, and when it corresponds to a fixed asset being operated.

- *Historical value.* This principle involves posting balance sheet elements at their real cost (termed "cost accounting"). The opposing accounting principles are "inflation accounting" and "fair value" (before called "fair Market value"), the latter applicable only to some liquid types of balance sheet elements such as financial portfolios. In an inflationary monetary context, determining the rise in prices for fixed assets, or for any reason such as interest rate decline, the "historical value" doctrine is also not coherent with the previously noted rejection of the "prudence principle". In other words, prevailing practice insists that either all potential profits and losses are taken into account, or none at all if they do not correspond to liquidities.

As may be seen from the foregoing discussion, the functional scope and impact of today's money is closely linked to accounting practices presently operant on a global scale. The general interest and public domain expectations of performance criteria applicable to the accounting profession should be as homogenous as practical, so as to allow for: (1) performance assessments over time and (2) comparison with alternative operational service-sector investments, including their reliability and transparency. The public will also expect independent guarantees that their constituency expectations are met (opinions provided by independent auditors evaluating other auditors) and that sanctions are available if needed – and capable of being implemented by specialized authoritative bodies such as the SEC or the judiciary.

In short, books and records are not intended only for the entrepreneur. Rather, today's books are largely in the public domain, given that they express the functional activity of today's currency base and the results of how money in all its forms operates and modulates transactional exchanges that impact contemporary society. Accordingly, the durability of accounting standards is also an essential prerequisite that supports the need for comparison of accounting standards and their effectiveness over time – particularly given the fact that repetitive changes in accounting concepts may result from either financial innovation or excessive creativity of standard setters engaged in self-justification. Such serial changes may render some evolving accounting regimes as ineffective guarantors of future world monetary stability. Arguing against that premise, however, is the historical survival of accounting principles that, by today's standards, are ancient[9] and have stood the test of time, in terms of both reliability and effectiveness.

THE IMAGE PRESENTED BY FINANCIAL STATEMENTS INFLUENCES THE ANALYSIS OF ECONOMIC DATA AND TRANSACTIONAL EXCHANGES

No longer used as a reference for monetary valuation, and with gold ranked at the front, precious metals represent only a fraction of contemporary currency instruments, pegged at less than $1 trillion in commodity market-defined metal value – compared with an annual global world GDP of $73.9 trillion (2013 source IMF). As already stated, the nominal values stamped on the face of coins, printed on bills issued by central banks and shown on private instruments (notes, cheques, etc.) are now associated with accounting standards that standardize their recognition and relative numerical value denominations.

The role of accounting, as well as the worldwide corporate-centred enterprise of issuing bank financials and current account statements, has reached the scale of major trading economies. Today's monetary instruments and virtual money constitute the only remaining observable image of currency expression, raising the question of the required stability of the monetary unit being used (besides, in South America, inflation accounting to address the high inflation context was never really developed and has never been shown to be a realistic answer to the negative effects volatile currencies have on the economy). As such, individuals, as well as enterprises and corporations, can only comprehend their capacity to trade by using books that record nominal values corresponding to the "price" of transactions. Ledgers showing these transactional exchanges and their prices constitute decisive monetary and financial evidence – the balances depicted and reflecting the occurrence and results of deposits, loans, revenues, expenditures and withdrawals serve to determine the owner's capabilities to collect or withdraw money.

Other major operational consequences have resulted recently from the generalization of the following accounting rules:

- *Fair value*. Fair value is defined as "The price that would be received to sell an asset or paid to transfer a liability in an orderly transaction between market participants at the measurement date (i.e. an exit price)" (extract from IFRS Foundation, technical summary) on IFRS 13 (not yet fully adopted and delayed for full implementation, if ever, until 2017). The fair value standard, when applicable, obliges the replacement of historical value by "fair value" grounded on a market-based measurement referential. As a result, an entity's intention to hold an asset or to settle or otherwise fulfil a liability is not

---

[9] Imprinted on clay tablets recovered from archeological sites in the Middle East (NYC Metropolitan Museum and the Louvre Museum), some accounting formats may be found without however understanding either the precise language or the meaning of the accompanying figures. These tablets date back to the same period as the origin of written script, or around 3000 years ago. As they are known in the modern world, "origin formats" of accounting date back to banking transactions developed by the Lombards (also the name of a population settled in northeast Italy after the final fall of the Western Roman Empire (410–476)), who settled in what is today known as the Lombardia Province in the northeast pre-alpine region of Italy and adjoining the Swiss Canton of Ticino. The regional capital of Bellinzona houses the innumerable fortress remnants of multi-generational Lombardian civil wars.

relevant when measuring fair value.[10] Consequently, a change in value for an already post-ed transaction (for instance representing a receivable, a debt or other assets) will generate uncertainty as regards a resulting determination of balances (see our previous comments on the double-posting rule and accounting identity). In theory, if recorded as directed for financial instruments using the fair value[11] standard in the P&L account, either a profit or loss will be generated (depending on whether a rise or decline of value is involved).

- *Balancing.* A very important topic is the offset of hedging instruments or debit balances from credit balances of similar nature, or reverse. This is, in Europe, the topic of IFRS 7, which has been applicable since January 1, 2013, and the revised IFRS 32. Simply because of the fair valuation standard now appraising counterparty risk, and the fact that the valuation method-ology may differ and follow three different patterns depending on whether a reference fluid market exists (level one method), some markets exist that may be used as reference for valu-ation (level two method) or no market exists (and a modelling approach should be found – level three method), there is a problem in balancing. Balancing is an attraction for a lot of insti-tutions, especially the financial ones submitted to prudential regulations, as it will change their ratios and balance sheet image as well as their profitability ratios. This topic is still under fierce discussion and the only exit found was to make detailed exhibits compulsory (IFRS 13). It is a major topic for the determination of M5 and M6. Moreover, any change in value should logi-cally generate a corresponding equivalent potential gain or loss in the counterparty's section of his own balance sheet. Even disputed by standard setters, the issue at stake is to decide if changes in value are to be posted as a gain or loss in the P & L, or directly posted on the balance sheet as a change in equity. Nevertheless with IFRS 9 being adopted[12] one of the major dyfunc-tions of the fair value standard, the total lack of transparency about what in the P & L is or not deriving from value variations and what comes from transactions as well as the reconciliation

---

[10] Extract from IFRS Foundation, summary of IFRS 13 release.

[11] See IFRS 13 measurement to apply to IFRS that require or permit fair value measurements or disclo-sures, and provide a single IFRS framework for measuring fair value and requiring disclosures about fair value measurement. IFRS 13 does not apply to share-based payment transactions, leasing transactions and when impairment is the standard to apply. IFRS 39, the standard which will be replaced by now adopted IFRS 9, addresses the matter of classification of financial instruments. The standard defines fair value as the concept of cost price notion at the time of the transaction or measurement. The concept of fair value that causes changes in value for many posted financial instruments has been adopted by both international standards setters; the FASB and IASB, however, totally disagree on the implementation and model to be used by private-sector companies (IAS no. 9). The new standard provides for an exemp-tion to instruments to be kept until maturation that may be valued at amortized cost (to be recorded in the "banking book" as opposed to the "trading book" for trading transactions). Both institutions differ on when to account for loss expectancy (from the beginning for FASB's current position) or when the solvency status of the issuer changes (loss given approach); IASB and Basel III's current position with a prospective reserve for losses within the 12 months following closing. The new standard also adds a new category of portfolios; the ones that are to be hold until maturity but might be sold as they are to be "reserve of liquidities". For implicitly or legally being guaranteed by governments, regulated loans are excluded from the reserve determination system provided. This system is based on the accepted clas-sification between performing, underperforming, nonperforming originally determined by the number of days there has been a default. The related amounts are important (may be 900 billion) but far less than the Fanny May and Freddy Mac US Agencies amounts of guarantees ranking in trillion that are different but in essence similar.

[12] As of May 2014 waiting to be endorsed by the European Commission.

with the equity variation over an accounting period has been fixed. Through "other comprehensive income" value variations may not go directly into the profits or losses but be recycled later on after closings. Therefore variation in net equity for a period can be reconciled with profit and losses and nature of the value variations in outstanding assets and liabilities.

- *Impairment tests*. Both international standards setters adopted the concept of impairment testing. The methodologies to assess values for both non-financial and financial assets are well developed when not referring to financial instruments as we define them (see Chapter 5). However, for financial instruments, if they do not fall under fair market, the topic is still disputed.

In both situations, if the change involves a decline in value, then – even if not posted as losses – it will trigger a notion in the analyst's mind that the indebted entity may not be able to repay its debts (if profits are insufficient to cover the unrealized loss). The idea that a debt may be worth less than its nominal commitment if financially demonstrated is the admittance at macroeconomic level when spread that the financial system has failed and that the ultimate holder of the debt will, when it has matured, not be reimbursed. It also carries the underlying idea that at such a level the government or the central bank will have to pay for the default and the currency to be wiped off as public debt. Either it will be a tax payers' expense or a monetary collapse or sequences of both. Anyway at the end of a cycle when the level of debt is too high compared with potential flows it means that the debts won't be claimable any longer especially its central (central bank and governmental) component and by interconnection with holders (for instance, long term insurance savings and banking reserves to comply with surveillance regulation) the entire system. It is a redistribution process threatening private property showing a kind of collusion between standard accounting setters and investors' powers. As the holders may not be knowledgeable and the reciprocity rule in accounting translating the law that a debtor owes the same amount as the corresponding creditor it is unfair. The matters will be out before the collapse if macroeconomic imbalances are not fixed. The change of values on books to market values is just misleading about the commitments. In the absence of inflation it is a mere lie. The knowledge of the discrepancy on the balance sheets between nominal values for debts or historical values for equity and the market values is, of course, necessary. It is a mark-up of the monetary risks. We will see that in Chapter 8.

Almost all monetary flow transactions are now processed through electronic exchanges, and their evidentiary proof is confirmed by book postings that in turn characterize the ownership rights of each individual or enterprise. Notwithstanding, private individuals are not expected to maintain books and records that are sensitive to changes caused by electronic exchanges; whereas financial statements that are delivered to individuals (bank statements, card statements, automatic wire transfers and withholdings, etc.) are expected to remain relatively stable in the face of outside market-driven change caused by the flow of monetary transactions.

Indisputably a transnational financial sector player in its present-day scope, accounting has become the universal language of currency and monetary exchange. It should not be falsified, it should be recognizable, and financial statements resulting from its standardized implementation should be comparable across markets, financial institutions, international monetary systems, regional economies and national borders. Serious and widespread doubt as to the quality of bank statements or financial statements would trigger immediate defiance from concerned economic agents, and could have a devastating effect on both transactional dynamics and economic stability. Amplifying even limited doubts about the soundness of the financial sector or either micro- or macroeconomic conditions, random financial rumours can develop without control on financial markets – a major origin point for refinancing of our economies. With rumours driving any market, serious agents would abstain from participation, leading to suppression of monetary velocity in conjunction with freezing of transactional flow and subsequent risk of recession or full-scale participatory regression from economic participation. Constituting a potential direct threat to social stability, such potential scenarios remain a major challenge for modern economies on the world stage. Ultimately, however, when all is said and done, the recording and analysis of financial statements has emerged as the primary factor determining whether today's financial transactions will be conducted and successfully closed. It is unlikely that such a determination will be impacted by the opinion or intervention of rating agencies.

DIRECT SYSTEMATIC IMPACT OF ACCOUNTING STANDARDS

Double-Entry Consequence

The double-entry system operates like a virus in the air. Because double entry is the obvious legal consequence of an exchange, any outstanding to any receivable in one balance sheet relates to a debt in another one. If the debtor fails, they will contaminate the creditor. Independently from the posted reciprocal amount, the value will change. However, we note again that the values will be different from the committed nominal value of the instrument, and sometimes from the price the instrument has been acquired at. The bankruptcy legal environment of companies will differ, depending on which jurisdiction they are located in. Collection will be an uncertain process as to the ultimate proceeds, and the counterparties may play different games on portfolios. Without any event of default, the balance sheet and profit situation of the issuer will vary and, independently from accounting standards, these variations will propagate vibrations or changes in values – the limit being failure, where the debtor's default can affect the creditor. The accounting standard brings volatility when having to post traded values different from the legal commitment and varying by factors external to the entity holding the portfolios concerned.

Value Consequence

Changes in value exist independently from use (for a building or equipment) or recoverability (for a receivable). When posted like any profit or loss deriving from operations, these changes have a systemic influence, as they will affect the net equity of an enterprise. As a consequence to the change in equity or wealth, it will interact with credit. Going up, it will allow more credit. Going down, it will slow down borrowing capabilities. This is the story of the Japanese long stagnation and of any deflation process. There again, value accounting as fair value interacts and adds to volatility.

WHERE MISLEADING STANDARDS GENERATE DISTORTED IMAGES

Valuation Incertitude in Accounting Standards

The above developments about accounting standards and values are to determine macroeconomic consequences and also regulatory consequences. The real experience was the appraisal of Greek debt at the financial institutions level. There was no doubt that depreciation had to be posted. However, as entrepreneurial liberty allows, depending on their individual views, many of them depreciated the values differently from commercial banks. The regulator had to intervene to impose a general depreciation ratio for banks in the absence of any kind of knowledge about the risk of default, before a governmental agreement was adopted which itself had no more rationale.

The Appraisal Spark Plug that Drives a Continued "Fair Value" Crisis

In our previous book, we described the origin and effect of a "fair value rule" (issued by accounting standard setters) that obliges the accounting profession to assess financial instruments, bonds and equity stock portfolios by comparing their historical posted cost price with their measured value in terms of fair value with the observed difference to be posted in the P&L statement. The "appraisal rule" is general in scope and applies to the entirety of financial instrument portfolios, inclusive of their coverage spectrum and the estimation of volume represented in terms of comparable markets for similar financial instruments. In considering the combined effect of ongoing financial market development (alongside a global slowdown in monetary velocity), it becomes apparent that the accurate determination of fair value is infeasible in the absence of a deeply liquid market, rationally linked to the warrantees attached to the traded instrument when it corresponds to an equity title, when warrantee values for bonds or receivable are unknown or too volatile, or when default rates and interest rates are artificial. Interest rates, especially on long-term collectable instruments, are of key importance and may be influenced by regulation, especially tax and prudential regulation, but also the uncertainties which drive money flows to such instruments. This is, for instance, the case for tax-free and sovereign issuances. The accounting vocabulary has removed the word "market" from its original wording of "fair market value", but the meaning of "fair" remains questionable due to either the intellectual honesty of standard setters or their understanding of the financial world.[13]

A practical image of the issues can be found by reading the last McKinsey Global Institute (MGI) report of March 2013 on financial globalization (based on 2011 statistics reported to the BIS). In the growth to 325% of financial depth to GDP, it is stated that 25% comes from changes in instrument values. As there is very limited growth in GDPs and very limited inflation, we again see here the disconnection between tangible flows and financials flows, for sure a risk for the financial stability that our system triggers.

This observation raises three issues. The first issue refers to immediate doubts about the soundness of balance sheets in the present financial environment – for example, if portfolios were to be appraised at less than the posted value, then the resulting negative margin would consume outstanding equity, resulting in a destabilized balance sheet profile. A second source of doubt arises when financial markets enter a slowdown phase with contracted liquidity, and the question of "real marketability" for financial instruments arises – including their transaction at sufficient volumes. As we have seen from the euro's past crisis, it immediately raises the question of the capacity of central banks to intervene in the markets to bail them out as the US FED does. A third issue relates to the backing behind financial instruments. If the underlying guarantee value is known to have declined, then the intrinsic value of the instrument is jeopardized. As seen during 2007, in such an eventuality the flow of capital may go into syncope – that is, a marked reduction of transactional turnaround.[14]

In this multifactorial setting, the potential for propagation of financial instrument failures will depend on the degree to which the financial system succumbs to major uncertainty, as opposed to a simple atmosphere of prudence in not relying on short- and mid-term economic forecasts.

---

[13] It is the limit to their independence that has now been reduced with the presence within their board of representatives of the administration for the FASB, and before with the European process requiring the European Commission to adopt the proposed accounting standards before they became applicable in the EU.

[14] Shin, H.-S., Sapra, H., and Plantin, G., "Marking to market: Panacea or Pandora's box?", *Journal of Accounting Research*, Princeton University, August 12, 2007, 46: 435–460 (2008).

Moreover, if even a single but sizable publicly listed company fails or a government is in default, all other entities holding some of its counterparty balances will be affected. This is a historically classic paradigm known to impact banking system entities that cross-hold each other's debt obligations on a range of primary financial instruments, as well as their secondary and tertiary derivatives. Clearly, this was one major reason for the contraction of liquidity affecting money markets during the 2007–2008 crises. One example points to banks who declined to invest in sovereign debt instruments of their own jurisdiction (even when in cash surplus), and who instead preferred to refinance by resorting to central bank mechanisms.

The preceding seems obvious when recalling that one trigger of recent financial market failures involved a deficiency in available cash – needed to satisfy both cash creditors and vendors who are vulnerable to non-payment cascades that generate propagating chains of failure. Surprisingly today, prevailing accounting standards do not directly impose requirements to immediately post any uncertainty of unrealized profits from "market price"-level sales. A second drawback is that by mixing "certain"/realized as well as "uncertain"/unrealized profits and losses on the books, existing accounting procedures tend to obscure the monetary velocity factor, thereby superimposing a major layer of otherwise unrecognized opacity on financial statements. Specifically in this regard, there are many sound reasons for initiating the reform of relevant accounting standards, if not sanctioning the rule setters and authors of such procedures themselves.[15] Certitude should be a universal criterion required in all financial statements. Certitude in payments should be distinguished from value, time and flows that are other appraisal factors to be disclosed separately and analysed depending on the underlying attached guarantees. It is immediately a monetary issue, as facts have shown since 2007, and we have to go into it.

MONETARY ASPECTS OF FINANCIAL STATEMENTS

We have seen that accounting standards differ from reality, in the same manner that in physics, calendars differ from the time that actually elapses. Because of prevailing standards, it is a fact that at the time of issuance, a receivable on one side of an accounting ledger is reflected as a debt in another party's ledger. No consideration is given to the real-world impact of such a representation. Such a sequence of postings, which is necessary, is also risk contagious, regardless of whether auditors and legal institutions attest with security to the reciprocity of books that meet international accounting standards. A clear area of controversy is the potential for exuberance in the representation of value, a parameter that may be different for the holder of an instrument than for the issuer, or with respect to the instrument's intrinsic value. There are no immediate solutions to this problem – other than mitigation by organizing guarantees to promote stabilization of apparent posted values, and by allowing accountants latitude to maintain these values in normal and stable conditions, meaning the absence of default or known risk of default.

From the foregoing discussion, we again see the validity in raising the issue of a precipitous link between any "determined" or "stamped" value, and a corresponding monetary equivalent. The reasons for this are clear, but the solution is not necessarily found in an

---

[15] Severinson, C. and Yermo, J., OECD no. 2/12/12. The effect of solvency regulations and accounting standards on long-term investments; implications for insurers and pension funds. This paper calls for extreme prudence with regard to FMV standards.

ultimate system of guarantees, such as we discussed previously with regard to CDS instruments. The speed of transactional exchanges and corresponding clearings is also a phenomenon of importance. Regardless, portrayed reality or its correct analytical perception does not necessarily result in a major impact on financial statements, as seen for 2007–2008 – with sudden collapse and recessionary contraction resulting from pent-up inflation of false economic value, and the resulting value destruction attributable to sudden decompression of the system by knowledge of the actors themselves, mostly banks, that the system was wrong by the mere fact that the goals given to teams were to sell the bad stuff by wrapping them well, and to keep the good.

As issued and implemented, the prevailing accounting standards can contribute to value destruction following an artificial build-up of market value. As such, accounting standards need to consider patterns of cash liquidity flow, if market valuation is deemed insufficient. For instance, discounted cash flow (DCF) is a recommended substitute methodology for fair market evaluation, if the latter is deemed non-existent. Thus, there are alternative approaches for the determination of the basis of asset valuation or for designing and implementing impairment tests[16] for asset integrity. The above illuminates the volatility risk of utilizing "stamped market values" or synthetic substitutes at the financial statement level, with such volatility then resulting from the combined effects of:

1. Accounting standards evaluation instead of sampled cost values.
2. Trust effects of interpreting balance sheet integrity and representation.
3. Variations in transactional exchange speeds.
4. Issuance of guarantees not appearing directly in the monetary sampling for instruments on the balance sheet.
5. As already quoted, using interest rates for discounting based only on extraordinary circumstances, and regulations to address them that are subject to changes and international competition on the monetary playing field.

These effects can all combine and generate contagion through the required legal double-entry reciprocity. Nevertheless, we note that governments are linked to continuity trends in their own policies; like drugs, any sudden disorderly change or cut in their current interventions would trigger a collapse in the balance sheets' net equities and obscure the results in the balance P&L accounts.

These cumulative factors interact in a manner which is not controlled by any centralized authority, and not understandable for either managers or entrepreneurs who need to derive solid forecasts both from financials as well as respective operational models. If the potential instability threat is not effectively mitigated and becomes dominant, then financial sector capital sources will either stop investing or disinvest. A major question thus arises: how can sufficient stability best be achieved, without suppressing credit distribution or demand for loans, slowing transactional exchange flow and monetary velocity, and thereby depressing the economy as a whole? This broader question will need to be addressed in any future global monetary reform regime. The latter part of the question also diverts our attention to the evolving

---

[16] The impairment test is performed on an asset other than a financial instrument. The rationale for this is to determine the depreciation to be taken, for instance if the asset's usable value is expected to be less than its book value.

transnational regulatory regime, where we see additional direct and indirect impact as regards monetary flow – and with respect to public perception of both the representational integrity and reliability of financial statements.

This combined impact is the key reason why the posting of synthetic component valuations should not be intermixed on balance sheets (i.e., following the legal commitment of money to transactions); this should preclude a significant impact on financial statements that in and of themselves exert a profound impact on perceived financial image. Also, all elements that enter into the preparation of financial statements should be similarly constructed, including allowance for time and risk variations that empower observers to properly analyse the image presented in diverse financial statements – prepared on behalf of private/public enterprises and governments alike.

It remains a reality that the existing system is self-determinant, in that the will of any major outside player (beyond accountants and independent auditors) to control the elements that go into formulating the financial statement image, which is presented to the open world, can be distorted through a maze of analytical mirrors.

Statistical bodies were knowledgeable of such a reality and risk of image distortion, despite being engaged in the process of building "integrated economic and financial accounts by institutional sectors".[17] Economic agents have decided not to take into account "changes in value" that do not result from real transactions.

In the end-run, the analysis of publicly presented images and the reading of financials should be left to the public – notwithstanding professional analysts and rating agencies, who will be subject to regulatory oversight in terms of presentation, accuracy, weighting and interpretation of the information provided. Recognition of the latter duality is why standard setters and authorities operating in the post 2007–2008 crisis environment concluded that rating agencies should now also be regulated. This regulatory process is presently underway.

THE NECESSARY APPROACH IN ACCOUNTING: A HIERARCHY OF DANGEROUSNESS

Accounting is to report transactions, properties and commitments. Transparency relating to accounting is not only a legal requirement but also a prerequisite to achieve the best allocation of financial resources, as it brings comparability. However, the posting processes of transactions carry and determine combined risk factors. Line by line, assets and liabilities, without unlimited guarantees to be claimable at their full posted sampled values, will have varied posted value amounts over the time they show on the books. They will vary intrinsically because of the stamping quality, but also due to supply and demand, and finally from counterpart risk status. It is the simple and justified result of a free market economy. As a whole, the image of financial statements for users and viewers is static. Users and viewers will have to operate their own individual corrections just as rating agencies, credit committees and investors will. With variable individual volatility of assets' values taken by line and globally, with the image of financial statements, there are several ways to look at assets and liabilities from a contagious, conveying risk appraisal point of view.

---

[17] Eurostat ECB schedule 3.1, online data: note "general concepts".

Degrees of Contagion ("Interconnection")

Neutral Assets

These are the ones with no counterpart, such as real-estate property, equipment or machinery. Being operated, they may generate profit or losses but are not intrinsically contagious as a receivable being also a debt.

Contagious Assets

These are assets with counterparts, such as receivables and debts. They are contagious to the commitment reciprocal positions debtors and creditors have on their respective books. The current literature calls these commitments "interconnections".

Some assets, like directly posted receivables and debts, are 100% contagious in case of failure or change in their counterparty carrying risk until term. At term, the risk is precisely known; either the commitment is fully satisfied or it is not, or partially for a known amount and conditions. They are the first line of contagion factor.

As we know, some assets may be modified by being carried through a financial vehicle. The interconnection is then cut off and only operates through parties other than those who originated the underlying instruments. Owing to financial market guarantees, the contagion factor (until term) operates because of variation in pricing of the instrument if posted. This is a second line of contagion factors.

Within this second line, some contagious assets are governmental ones. These are guaranteed by governments and the problems they may carry have a special substance that cannot be mixed with others because of such a guarantee. This raises a question for the stress tests of banks and other financial institutions, which are now carried out on both sides of the Atlantic.

Some assets are short term, and then they may have either only a private status as a commercial receivable, or carry with them some statutory guarantees such as commercial papers and some securitized instruments or asset-backed or mortgage-backed securities. This is an undercover line of contagion. Market liquidity and duration will be the approach for contagion appraisal of instruments.

For short-term financial instruments, the volume involved will be a determinant of the associated risk. In special environments, the risk will decline with the size of the market where traded. Because of the systemic accompanying risk of loss of market liquidity, there will be an implicit guarantee that the central bank will need to intervene to keep it sufficient.

Long term is a different matter, because of the amounts involved, like in real estate. Governments are obliged to bring guarantees either on the instruments through special institutions (such as Freddy Mac and Fanny Mae) or directly to the banks holding such instruments. Then the topic becomes a macroeconomic one.

We have already suggested, in 2006 at the European Commission, that staff (internal market) should come back to legal commitments, keeping all the impairment tests going as a system within the standards, and providing information about the values of instruments according to a classification frame with differentials appearing when liquid in the short term in other comprehensive income (OCI).

In our opinion, only short-term liquid instruments should be put at fair value, as their valuation corresponds to a guaranteed market. This suggestion does not prevent information about valuation risks of other financial assets. The current IFRS draft exposure of IFRS 13, allowing model accounting and categories, brings us back to the standards prevailing in the USA at the time of the S&L crisis, which cost $170 billion at that time's dollar value, and triggered, on a different basis, the increase in the "fair market value" for portfolios of mortgage-backed securities; a rather homogenous category of receivables.

The Fair Value Conceptual Mistake Contributes to Instability and Distrust

The wrongness of the fair market value on which accounting standard setters are still working (exposure draft for IFRS no. 9 and 13), despite other instructions from the G20 (see Pittsburgh press release limiting the approach to very liquid instruments), can further be easily demonstrated. Users of financial instruments – both those designated for which financials are set but also those other, more numerous real actors involved in the exchanges creating values in the production and distribution sectors balance sheets – are analysing the balance sheets. As water in the desert (Von Mises' example), assets do not have the same values for each of them depending on who the actors are and what their goals are. The substitution of imperfect market values – set by standard priority choice for finding the fair value – for the only certain indicator, which is the stamped value of the legal commitment to pay, not only brings deceit to those who are remote from the marketplace but also brings confusion as liquidity and warrantees are not general. This is the reason for the standard setter orientation towards fair value (last IAS 13 and 9 exposure drafts), which had to be corrected by governments when the markets failed (IAS 39 implementation had to be suspended at the end of 2008) as they are still failing due to lack of liquidity when not helped by QE or LTRO. To keep the financial system floating, governments, through their central banks, had and still have to intervene at the expense of citizens to bring the liquidity guarantee, and also to support values on government and financial institution balance sheets by bringing down interest rates.

Low interest rates are no more than a means of redistributing an asset's values and savings' rewards. It disqualifies the risk criteria for the use of financial resources as governmental guarantees because the seignorage overrides industrial risk taking. Worse, the general implementation of the fair market value is an incentive to service and industrial actors to speculate when they should not; when hedged financial commitments, carried because of their operations, do not change in value with the financial markets. Only financial institutions should be impacted on, and both should be followed up as to the spread between price values, nominal values and trade values. Any discrepancy between these values constitutes a first-row risk. The following, as we will see further on, should be organized. The difference between the nominal value of an instrument and its traded value should be looked at carefully. The implementation of market values to non-rotating instruments should be looked at even more carefully. The spreads appearing as a result are only of limited duration as commitments have a clearing term, and if the instrument is renewable because of being exchangeable, we are in the presence of money issuance or destruction by both changes in values when traded and exchanged, or artificial creation when only applicable to portfolio valuations. Overall, the FMV brings an inappropriate allocation of roles detrimental to the economy. Industrial and service producers should not be allocated a monetary role and risk not directly deriving from their own operations. Only financial institutions with monetary duties or under the monetary control of central banks or surveillance should.

There is no basis to democratically ground these compulsory accounting standard interventions corresponding to money issuance, a seignorage privilege in which the ultimate burden bearer is not determined and will only be so in the long term. Owing to inflation, will it be the holders of fixed income, and then whom precisely, probably in the retirement benefits systems? Will it be, by default like in Cyprus and Greece, at the expense of over €100,000 depositors? Will it be the taxpayers who reimburse the debt instruments that were acquired? In any case, it is certainly unfair as these policies have to last long enough to have the systems fixed, and in between traders can operate to disengage, while central ones are just discussing when and how they could disengage. One can believe that the ordinary citizen with little free money, and who has to organize their retirement benefits, will not be the winner because they are tied to a monetary zone with exit tax and to a system – the exit tax is paid when a tax resident quits this status by transferring domicile to another country; a system such as a retirement benefit can only be vested after a number of years of contributions, quitting would generate an abandonment and consequent loss of what had already been contributed.

Supporting their fate would bring other sovereign issues, as it did in Cyprus. However, the Cyprus case, putting aside the important fact that there are individuals everywhere, was rather simple as the Cypriot tax system and their accumulated big money deposits may not have been from day-to-day savings. The matter would be different for big governmental refinancing. Fixing the matter would hit sovereignty. One has to remember the dispute about war damages after WWI. Fixing did happen by default, and the German monetary problem was fixed by H. Schacht. However, at the end of an uncontrolled succession of events, including German recovery and the revival of the German economy, was the war, and almost the needs of civilization, and at least of the most brilliant civilization ever created, were not renewed by refuge in the USA or UK.

The second reason for the falsity is conceptual, and is the basis for what will follow in our developments. Accounting is a language intended to translate a system; the monetary system of exchanges. This system is characterized by a dynamic instability, without which it does not exist, and we would all disappear as would happen if there was no interest or actors in a transaction. In short, this is the reason why price control and centralized economies failed.

A Need for Mathematical Approaches

Minsky and Douady were the theorists who made the most important contributions in comprehending mathematical instability. As already pointed out by Hyman Minsky, markets are unstable by construction, and because we must use a monetary unit to operate and commit to orders, surveillance is necessary to guarantee soundness of the monetary unit, and have values appearing in transactions which can be understood by each party. The market cannot exist without a monetary unit, or it would be reduced to barter. Looking after systemic risks and taking action when necessary requires some knowledge of the engagements between financial actors. We have already noted that this information will vanish if market prices (and not values) are used and qualified as "fair", and then if these prices replace, in financial statements, legal sampled commitments or posted historical cost. This game sleight is done by virtue of a compulsory accounting standard that applies fair value principles to some financial instruments, or even worse, the mixed and fuzzy concepts of the last IFRS exposure draft which is meant to replace the existing one.[18]

Referring to recent works by major mathematicians, such as Raphaël Douady, about financial crisis dynamics,[19] the universe is represented by variables $(X_1,...,X_n)$ evolving through time $(X_1(t),...,X_n(t))$ in an orderly or disorderly manner ("deterministic" or "stochastic") with

---

[18] A new adopted IFRS no. 9 proposes a new classification of financial instruments that may be appraised or not, depending on the model and intents of the one issuing the financials, which is totally disconnected from the instrument itself.

[19] Choi, Y. and Douady, R. Financial crisis dynamics: Attempt to define a market instability indicator. *Quantitative Finance* 12, 2012, 1351–1365.

various degrees of uncertainty. Mathematicians trying to map their models on this complicated jungle would be surprised by economists' and accountants' certitudes about values. In the end, we could say that accountants' efforts to convey certitude just seem a desperate attempt to hide their incapability and lack of understanding of what money is.

This lack of understanding brings anxiety to the public and the regulator, who must admit the failure of forecasts based on the limited scope of M1 and M2, and on financials. Even diagnostics based on static financial statements are wrong more than half of the time, as evidenced by some grading published by rating agencies in the recent past. The origin of this factual failure lies in the limited scope of observed phenomena, and in the restricted definition of model input values. The fair value accounting standard is just aggravating the phenomena and bringing disorder and distrust to the financials of portfolios' holders such as banks and financial institutions.

We expect models to be able to raise warnings about "noises" made by increased instabilities in the systems. These noises may allow regulators to take appropriate measures before collapse or before central banks are obliged to intervene with indistinguishable measures to restore liquidity and allow preferable specific actions.

QUESTIONS AND ANSWERS

The Contemporary Basis for Currency Expression: Accounting and Records

What is accounting today?
  A single language with two main standard setters: the FASB for the USA and the IASB for most of the world except the USA.

What are the main principles used in accounting?
  Consistency, which requires that all transactions be recorded, the double-posting principle and the independence of accounting periods.

Why is double posting important?
  Double posting is the legal representation of a transaction. A buyer corresponds to each seller, and they have set a price that, if both are keeping books, will show on their respective ledgers for the same amount until being paid (the debt being satisfied by a monetary exchange). For this reason, double posting is the grounding for what auditors call the audit trail. The audit trail will allow us to check, via the ledgers, with the supposed counterparty whether balances for both buyer and seller reconcile. If not, there is a problem – fraud (the postings have been tampered with) or a mistake (a posting is wrong or missing).

What key consequences can we see from the use of a universal language?
  First, it supports the fact that receivables and debts being recorded are, or potentially will become, money. One has to remember that the universality of accounting standards is a recent phenomenon and that the disclosure of financial statements only expanded after WWI with tax collection needs and after WWII with the addition of requests from financial markets.

What is a financial statement?
  Being intangible, it is an image of monetary essence that uses numbers associated with a single currency unit for its basis. The image determining several financial ratios – such as

equity, debt, liquidity, etc. – is of the same nature as the struck figure on a coin or paper bill. It is not the value or the weight; it is a mere description system.

What are the consequences?

From the double-entry principle and universality results contagion in cases where a debtor or warrantor fails. Accounting-wise, in cases where the debtor defaults, the creditor will have to cancel or depreciate the collectable balance. In doing so, they also generate losses and impact their equity. The second consequence is that a value may be attributed to the exchangeability (including reimbursement of debts) of the items showing on the books. The resulting financial statements, independently from the item itself, will be impacted without connection with double posting. The balance sheets will be more or less volatile over time, depending on the exchangeability factor linked to speed.

Is double entry necessary?

Yes. It's first the proof of reconnaissance of a performance or a delivery and second the image of a debt or receivable. Together it is the legal set up on which our society relies.

What is the problem?

The problem of the independence and interaction of factors (guarantees, figures, value and prices and time) is that the deriving complication is, at best, not accessible to immediate understanding by the witnesses or actors of exchanges using the financial. Each instrument has its own character, and may have its own life separate from financial statements as a whole. The adding of figures and the meaning of this new stamping process is at stake with an affect on exchanges.

Do all instruments equally carry contagious viruses through double entry?

No; the ones with no counterpart as an asset are not directly contagious. Nevertheless, they may become contagious when values go down. Then the impairment tests will bring down values on other financials, not to mention real transaction prices. However, overall, guarantees given on refinancing by being down-valued will reduce this refinancing. It is the haircut phenomenon.

Why did the fair value accounting standard for financial instruments contribute to distrust?

Fair value is a concept based on pretending that market values are the most significant ones, and therefore the fairest for being shown on financials. The problem is that market values and trading values are both disconnected from legal commitments. Even if markets were transparent and liquid, which is not the general situation, the difference between such hypothetical values and legal commitments constitutes a volatile stress. Volatility is contrary to what is needed for a monetary instrument. When the spread is high, any change in the speed of money rotation or interest rate level with trend dynamics will bring collapse, as there is a cap on time because of the limited duration of any instrument. To simplify the picture, values are capped when on the uptrend, but may fall to nothing on the downtrend.

The exception is a worse scenario. It is when debts are not reimbursed and constantly renewed as the economy is unbalanced (for instance, when the budget is in deficit). The economy is in indebting mode when associated with no saving. This operating mode has limits, due to anticipation that the economy needs imbalances to progress, and that nothing is going to remain equal. At some point one agent stops refinancing and the model fails.

What are the already known consequences of the Fair Values concept?

Indirectly, the fair value concept is vicious just by jeopardizing the concept that a debt, being a legal commitment, has a fixed value at term. Challenging this concept is attacking the property right on which free economies are built. It brings distrust by itself and by allowing hiding of determined reality, the due amounts during a period of time often aggravates imbalances and the ultimate catastrophe will be the one we were warned about with the CDSs issued by AIG, a difficult contagion to stop.

If free markets are the most efficient way of exchanging they have to be open and transparent. The linkage of books with them is just an incentive to manipulate them and bring distortion to tax systems and exchange prices, just the contrary to what should be aimed at.

Furthermore the confusion follows the economy by comparing traded values and commitments.

Who are the mathematicians who gave us the tools to comprehend instability?

Minsky and Douady (see Chapter 8).

The Regulation and Observation Limits Already Accepted, Compared with the Realities of Modern Exchanges

"Don't become angry with our politicians. They are the best ones to divert us with regulations that they revise time and time again, despite being aware of their inability to eliminate the abuses found in conventions or other things we were speaking of; and without understanding that they are only cutting off a few of the Hydra's many heads."

— **Plato, writing in *The Republic*, Book IV**

MONETARY REGULATION AND FOLLOW-UP

Given recognition that neither existing central bank regulations nor a gold standard provide adequate monetary regulation in today's world, a clear need exists for an updated oversight regime. To understand the likely requirements for designing new monetary regulations, one first needs to understand how such regulatory systems were developed in the past – including their purpose, goals and partially relevant roots in Keynesian theory or otherwise outdated approaches. Although some applicable models and institutions still exist (such as central banks and the banking system's monopoly on deposits), today's new patterns of monetary flow determine what additional requirements for monetary regulation need to be considered in the future. A good starting point is to evaluate how the evolution of money's role in society renders traditional observations, operational requirements and existing regulatory systems obsolete. The basis for any new regulatory design should be viewed primarily from a statistical and regulatory viewpoint – and one that takes into account today's information technology-driven transactional environment.

A RETROSPECTIVE ANALYSIS OF CLASSIC MONEY IN OPERATION

Notwithstanding significant changes in the nature, design and execution of contemporary transactions – the definition of a primary exchange objective, the process of property transfer and required credit – these basic transactional elements remain intact. Drawing on an

8000-year history of commercial activity, human society has developed an intimate understanding of transactional processes and regulations. Some recent changes in theories and models have been integrated into society's transactional culture, while other traditional elements remain an integral part of enduring and time-proven transactional environments. Changes in our financial environment do not invalidate the basics. Quite the contrary – basic elements actually require occasional reinforcement, in a manner analogous to the field of physics, where established theories and formulae periodically require adaptation, reconfiguration and even reconstruction to fit changing external realities and knowledge. To best appreciate this concept, we need to initially return to classically rooted concepts.

GOVERNMENTAL AND CENTRAL BANK MONETARY OPERATIONS

Inception, Monopolies and Measurement Aggregates as Classical Mechanisms for Issuing Money

As discussed in previous chapters, the concept of financing has evolved alongside economically driven change. Despite several banking failures, including an 18th-century debacle instigated by the notorious "John Law",[1] the innovation of scripted money facilitated two centuries of banking system expansion and the emergence of the industrial revolution. As defined by the ECB, contemporary scripted money represents between 80% and 90% of the currency pool value equivalent for western countries, and operationally enables money transfers (cards, cheques, wires, automatic payments, etc.) that even today, disputed by the service of payment providers, remain a privilege accorded to bankers and exercised on behalf of their clients.

The existing scripted money issuance mechanism is initiated by commercial banks, entitled to use deposited money as a driver of lending activity (Figure 5.1). As we will see in a closed system where economic agents can only use banks, money allocated for lending will ultimately return to the originating bank. Even if disbursed across several other financial agents in the interim, the funds can eventually be channelled only down a pathway that results in their return to the primary issuing bank.

For instance, what happens when a bank lends one dollar to a client? The originating bank issues a one-dollar note posted as assets, and one dollar (on behalf of the borrower) posted as liabilities. The bank has thereby increased its assets and liabilities by one dollar (through an *ex nihilo* or "out of nothing" transaction). These posted dollar values will progressively disappear from ledgers, when the issuing bank receives the corresponding reimbursement from the primary debtor or a secondary buyer in possession of the note. If our contemporary banks ceased lending, such implementations of script money would decline.

It is clear that any issuance of scripted money fundamentally relies on confidence – as the amount of funds loaned and recorded on the bank's balance sheets is a multiple of that bank's equity, which in turn could not be maintained in the face of a general public withdrawal of clients' deposits from the bank. The collective panic phenomenon seen during the 1929 crisis was again observed in 2008, for the Northern Rock case (a UK bank specializing in real-estate

---

[1] John Law de Lauriston (1671–1729), a Scottish adventurer who settled in France and was supported by the Regent after Louis XIV passed away, issued a large quantity of paper bills through a "Royal Bank" (that had been granted the Royal privilege to issue currency). In 1720, following a harsh run of speculation, the bank failed and entered bankruptcy. As a result, sovereign debt was reduced and the economy recovered at the expense of fixed income. See Chapter 1.

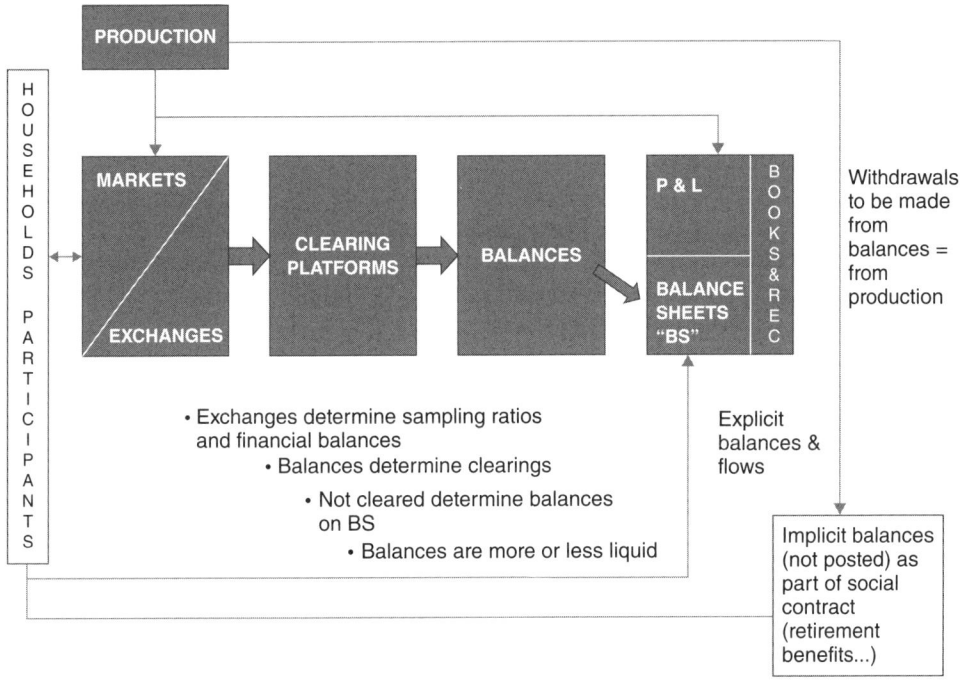

Note: Central government issues stamped currency (constitutional) through its central bank, which is granted a money issuance monopoly. Central banks lend to commercial banks and government. Usually constitutional set-ups limit the amount to be lent to the government. Commercial banks have a lending monopoly for individuals, enterprises and other private sectors. Commercial banks also have an exclusive right to receive deposits from the public. Consequently, subject to home savings, currency cannot escape from the system and determines a "multiplier", depending on the speed at which the lent money goes back into the commercial banks.

FIGURE 5.1   The actual money issuance process

finance). In response to the latter crisis, the British government attempted to limit money issuance through an arsenal of measures, the main one being a credit limitation framework that resulted in the system fractionating banking reserve requirements.

One might also recall that the classical scripted monetary set-up is based on regulations traced back to the 18th century, where central banks exercised a monopoly to issue money, but also established regulations for granting a limited oligopoly of commercial banks conditional rights to lend money. Without such an operational financial system infrastructure utilizing scripted money, the following discussion of money aggregates and multiplier concepts would have little meaning – because there would be no mechanism for managing the flow of money between issuance, payments and deposits.

TRADITIONAL MONETARY AGGREGATES

To effectively meet their responsibilities, central banks have been obliged to conceive and implement execution and measurement tools that their infrastructure generated and categorize the latter for the purpose of surveying the respective effects of utilizing such tools. These tools include "money aggregates". Grounded and justified by economic theories developed over the centuries and beginning in the 1970s, the traditional form of monetary aggregates was deployed by most central banks in the 1970s. The primary role of such aggregates has been to contain inflation (rising at a concerning level in the 1970s) through stricter controls on monetary supply. These controls served a triple purpose,[2] namely: (1) to provide meaningful information, (2) to create indicators for economic policies, and (3) to define strategies destined to be established as monetary policies. Various forms of monetary aggregates have been developed to fit with the monetary organization and institutions, as existed in each respective country at the time of their inception. As a result, every central bank maintains its own definition for each individual aggregate.[3] Historically, the designation of each aggregate did not correspond to the same operational and legal realities across the structure of a single central bank, or between different central banks. This in turn introduced complexity into any attempt at comparative analysis. Nevertheless, the role of monetary aggregates is common throughout the global financial sector. Recently, the EU has attempted to introduce standardization.

Monetary Aggregates in Central Banks

At present, the definitions of monetary aggregates are not converged or identical – that is, they are not based strictly on a bilateral system between different pairs of central banks, but rather are now structured to be more broadly consistent within monetary zones (the USA, as reported by the Federal System of Central Banks or the Eurozone, as specifically reported to Eurostat by the Member Central Banks for the Eurozone).[4]

The existing definitions of monetary aggregates are as follows.

M0 (or MR): The total of an individual central bank's physical currency and other account assets that are available to be exchanged against physical currency.

M1: The total of M0 (MR) plus a component of the central bank's reserves, plus active demand accounts (including cheque and current accounts); it is also called "money stock currency". M1 A includes cheque accounts as well.

M2: The total of M1 plus most savings accounts, money market accounts, retail money market mutual funds and small (under $100,000) denomination time account deposits.

M3: The total of M2 plus all other CDSs, including large time deposits, deposits of Eurodollars and repurchase agreements.

M4: The sum of M1 plus M2, in addition to medium-term CDSs. M4 is presently not used by either the FED or the ECB.

The US monetary base, seasonally adjusted (FED source), reached $13.325 trillion on September 2013, with M1 at $2.555 trillion and M2 at $10.770 trillion showing a small variation over the last two years (M1 at $2.127 trillion and M2 at $9.515 trillion at October 2011). Components not posted in a given monetary zone are unknown to the relevant central bank (not shown as foreign deposits).

---

[2] According to Frederic Mishkin, Research Director of the New York FED from 1994 to 1997.

[3] For the Eurozone, see Eurosystem: Banque de France. For the FED definitions, see Board of Directors of the Federal Bank System.

[4] Source: Banque de France and Documentation Française for M4.

For the Eurozone (18), the figures are listed below in trillions of euros (ECB source):

31.12	M1	M2	M3
2010	4.708	8.386	9.525
2011	4.782	8.573	9.724
2012	5.086	8.970	9.741
2013	5.396	9.207	9.831

See also Figure 5.2.

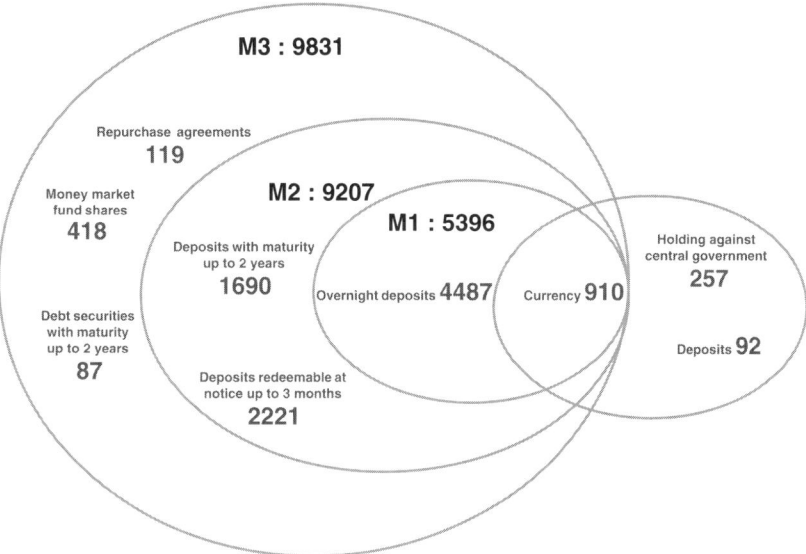

in billion euros (Dec 2013)

FIGURE 5.2   Euro system: components supporting monetary aggregates – June 2012

ACCEPTED CONCEPTS THAT COMPLEMENT TRADITIONAL MONETARY ANALYSIS – LIMITS AND EVOLUTION

From the Known Money Multiplier through the Banking System to a New Perspective

When an individual or corporate client makes a deposit at a bank, the latter can utilize the value of the deposit at will, but within regulatory limitations imposed by supervisory agencies and designed to ensure that a fraction ([*f*] in banking parlance, for instance 10% of a $1000 deposit, or $100) is kept available to cover potential withdrawals from the bank's depository. In the instance portrayed, the bank will now be able to utilize the remaining balance of $900 for lending or other activities, in the service of one or more clients.

With a given transactional case, for instance a lending activity, the process will similarly generate a bank deposit – such that a lending operation involving the $900 would only allow $810 to be disbursed for a loan, the remaining $90 being kept in regulatory reserve. By repeating the process, calculations would show that the bank is free to distribute a total of loans in the amount of $[1000(1 – f/f)]$ – for our case $1710, while the initial deposit was $1000! In the case example above, with only one loan following the original deposit of $1000, the bank would have placed $190 into discretionary reserves. With the remaining $810, the bank can again grant a new loan of $729, then of $646, etc. If, because of the administrative process, each loan is separated by a two-month time lag per year, at the sixth loan, $6582 will have been distributed including the original $1000 deposit. This phenomenon is called the credit multiplier.[5]

Further comments will be made about the "multiplier"; about the motivation for the banks to distribute credits, and the risks attached besides the first one – the credit risk that they are supposed to be qualified to handle as professionals. For each movement of funds, the bank transforms deposits into loan transactions – a process termed "conversion". In this manner, banks earn money through the differential effect of the credit rate as applied to internal deposits, and the additional external rate applied when making loans to clients. However, at the same time loans (such as real-estate ones) will have a longer duration than the deposits that usually can be withdrawn at will. The conversion process thus generates a liquidity risk for the bank, explaining the regulatory reserve we have talked about above. Aside from the limited velocity of transactions, this multiplier may have an almost unlimited effect if the bank did not keep some of its funds available as disbursement liquidity, or if the central bank did not implement some limitation measures on the commercial bank to ensure execution of two requirements: (1) that some of the funds be kept available as open liquidity and (2) that some of the funds be delivered back as deposits into banking reserves. Understanding its mechanism, we notice that the multiplier is a reality not limited to banks, but banks on the contrary were an arm to limit its effect as long as only bank financing was the ordinary money stream for the economy and its refinancing. As long as fractional reserves were regulated conditional on the volume of money to be recycled within the system, correctly or not, it was under possible control. Since bank refinancing is no longer the main source of financing for the economy, the multiplier factor can be analysed more generally as the rotation of money, but should encompass all actors keeping books and records and more than tender money. A growing exchange platform linking market participants, producers and consumers, if not the same, is a money issuer to the extent that its balances are accepted; new money has escaped from its traditional frame and limitations that the multiplier had set, either by regulation through banks or by physical means. Only the latter remains, but cannot be looked at in the same way depending on the nature and legal statute of the balances.

---

[5] In 1811 England, in the case *Carr vs. Carr*, Sir William Grant concluded that if money deposited at the bank was not identified as belonging to the depositor, then it belonged to the bank. In other words, a deposit (gold) is treated as a loan to the bank. Accepted as precedent-driven law in the British legal system and never subsequently challenged, this court decision constitutes the historical basis for lending as a bank function, and for characterizing and regulating the risk taken on public deposits (inclusive limits on liability imposed by central banks or governmental agencies, i.e. the present deposit insurance and restitution liability for European banks is capped at €100,000). In the USA, the deposit insurance has been raised to a $250,000 cap per account. The deposits with US banks have been estimated in September 2013 at $10 trillion being insured.

TRADITIONAL REGULATORY MEASURES TO ENSURE BANKS' STABILITY LIMITS

To ensure the safety of the banking system, but also the fluidity of the monetary system and the fight against inflation, monetary authoritative bodies have developed, based on quantitative money theories, an arsenal of control measures. These include prudential ratios and other metrics that regulatory bodies impose on banks. These control measures include: (1) minimum equity levels available for loan distributions (leverage limits); (2) daily amounts available for clearing of international payment balances between commercial banks and expressed in central bank currency equivalents; (3) maintenance of multiplier rates applied to deposits; (4) options for central bank intervention to ensure refinancing market liquidity; (5) discount policies involving a rate basis applied by the central bank on pre-term financial instruments (notes provided by commercial banks to the central bank prior to respective due dates of the instruments). Regulators also endeavour to equalize the leverage limitations between the equity used by banks and the debts that banks themselves carry. By issuing regulation and operating surveillance, the monetary agencies may achieve the protection of the payment systems (reinforced recently on both sides of the Atlantic). They don't cover what is outside the banking system and, for the banking system including the guarantees on public deposits, they don't ensure that globally the system will survive a macroeconomic crisis in a free economy environment. The current system relies on the idea that central banks will provide the money needed to maintain the required liquidity for exchanges to happen in the absence of players. We will see that these accepted policies and technical tools have not been able to sustain banking stability when money flows from imbalances came into play to destroy posted values in balance sheets or mere traded values and financial markets liquidity dried up. They were contrary to the pre-eminent philosophy of having independent central banks and market superiority. The concepts, the tools and their wrap-up have been revisited (see further the banking resolution and Chapter 7).

MONEY ISSUANCE THROUGH CENTRAL BANK INTERVENTIONS

The ultimate first players entitled to create and issue direct money are the central banks. They can intervene in three ways, namely: (1) by buying instruments from banks and posting them; (2) by lending to the treasury (or buying T-bonds); and (3) by buying foreign currencies collateralized against a quantity of the respective national currency that is generated (created), issued or printed specifically for the purpose of leveraging in a foreign currency. Another example involves situations where a central bank assumes control over currency transferred to the central bank by commercial banks, which in turn receive respective funds from client deposits delivered into their respective accounts.

To summarize, the money creation mechanism is a central bank action that links a financial player (including individuals or companies, public bodies, even chartered government entities) to an institution with monetary power (money received by law in the capacity of a registered bank). Such a receiver is, in essence, issuing a receivable against itself, namely one that will be accepted as a means of payment. This mechanism involves: (1) an ongoing creation process (granting of loans, purchase of tangible assets and financial instruments by banks, movement of currency surplus into the country), as well as (2) a process of monetary destruction (debited loan reimbursements and sale of assets by banks, in addition to outgoing national currency flow). The German 1919–1925 monetary crisis showed that there are limits to central bank interventions, which are the social behaviour towards a currency, mostly meaning the trust and anticipation of holders. BIS papers also refer to sound fiscal policies, a link to warranties that a government has to provide to its own currency if it is to be legal tender for a future exchange.

THE INVESTMENT MULTIPLIER

Different from the credit multiplier, the investment multiplier phenomenon has been widely discussed by Keynes and was adopted by Franklin D. Roosevelt as a cornerstone of the monetary policy associated with the "New Deal". This policy was devised to fight the US economic slowdown after the 1929 economic crisis, and was based on the following facts. When investing in infrastructures on behalf of the USA – as in building a plant or a hydroelectric power dam to produce electricity – the government will not only provide work for the contracting company, but also to countless subcontractors and public works agencies as well. The jobs created by providing salaries to all resulting new employees will stimulate consumption, and will re-stimulate the consumer goods industry and retail markets.

However, in the surrounding environment where factories were not used to their full capacity, due to excess inventory during the Great Depression for instance, it was clear that channelling "easy money" to consumers would generate fewer new jobs than investing in infrastructure. Rather, the key question at the time was to determine what amount of money was needed to generate a sufficient number of jobs, in comparison with prevailing and projected unemployment rates.

Considering the above, we immediately accept that an "offer policy" will oppose a "demand policy", and that their respective efficiencies need to be estimated prior to implementing any type of "monetary easing" policy. Efficiency will depend not only on available in-house means of production, but also on foreign trade exchange that may generate imports required to feed newly available money outwards, and which in turn will depend on currency exchange rates. Keynes and the then FED Chairman Eccles believed in the virtues of a policy designed to stimulate demand. But theories are theory, and even Keynesian ones have proven insufficient.

The inflation-generating effects of an excess monetary surplus are widely known, in part recalling the German crisis and accompanying hyperinflation statistics of the early 1920s. Alongside the US Department of Commerce, Simon Kuznets[6] and the National Bureau of Economic Research provided the Federal government with the required data to avoid a similar episode in the USA. Also, given the distinct nature of US history and its Federal structures, the prevailing culture in the US government harboured an innate prejudice against allowing a monarch or source of semi-independent governmental authority (e.g., the US FED) to issue new money at will, and potentially against the will of the central government. As the Federal government itself integrated that reality, history recalls that most economists (especially traditionalists) opposed Keynes' general theory, most notably when his books arrived stateside in 1936. Notwithstanding this opposition, and given that unemployment figures were intolerable (25% in 1933, and still 17% in 1935), the capability to demonstrate theory based on facts proved quickly convincing but not in its effectiveness.

[6] Simon Kuznets, Professor of Economics and Statistics at the University of Pennsylvania.

FOLLOWING UP ON REGULATING MONEY ISSUANCE IN A CHANGED ECONOMIC ENVIRONMENT. MONETARY SUPERVISION: AN ANCIENT QUESTION

The question of how to regulate and control an unstable banking and financial system was broadly already at stake in the period from 1929 to 1930, particularly when analysing the causes of that ongoing 1929 financial crisis and intervening in the various financial improprieties and scandals of the day. See Figure 5.3. The 1934–1935 banking and financial reforms only partially addressed these needs. If the economists of that time developed the necessary theories, history would prove that no long-term regulation was possible without the type of statistical basis that ultimately emerged as a result of the Bretton Woods Accord, at war's end. Only the war changed matters, as well as the victory of the USA and dollar domination. Things have changed again, but no new theory has been set up.

The traditional monetary oversight

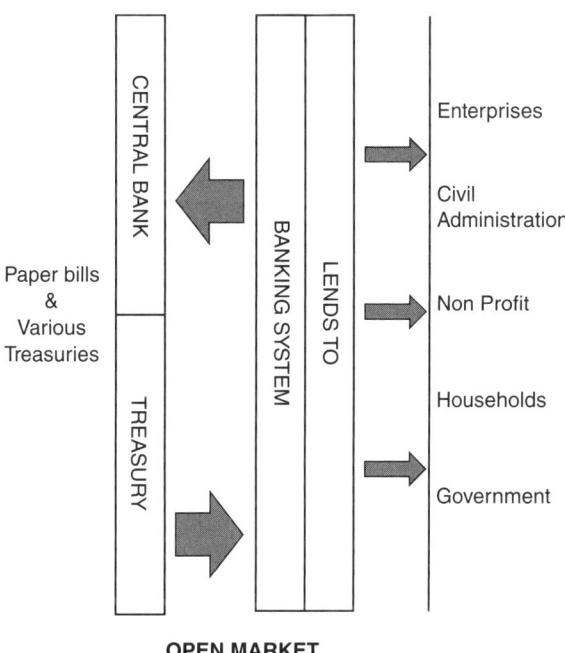

OPEN MARKET AND LIQUIDITY

THE CONTROLLING SYSTEM

o The central bank provides liquities to banks by buying or selling financial instruments
o Specialized agencies regulate limits or favour lending by banks through:
   o Accepting financial instruments created by banks when lending
   o Warranting some loans (enhancing long-term lending & prioritized investments)
   o Accepting treasuries

THE MISSING TRANSACTIONS

o Intercompany lending
o Direct financing reversing the FLOWS

➡ Half of the financing or more done the other way round • Arrows are reversed

FIGURE 5.3   Monetary regulation and follow-up

THE PRESENT-DAY NON-UTILITY OF CLASSICAL AGGREGATES

We were reminded above that such classical analyses have traditionally been grounded in the thinking of centralized monetary and banking set-ups – institutional organizations and their networks that are equipped and mandated to enable monopolistic control over the right to issue money and lend capital. Following the historically more recent outburst of modern money in its novel expanding forms and functionality, the meaningful role of these institutions has come into question, and thus requires broad reform and redesign.

Considering what is known about changes in the nature of diverse financial instruments used to clear primary transactional exchanges, and the very real expanding role for such new instruments (including associated refinancing within a parallel "shadow banking" sector active in refinancing), virtually no sense of surprise is justified when looking at prevailing trends and projections. Central banks can access the most comprehensive data in this regard. Yet, due to their internal set-up under present conditions, central banks are ill-equipped to meaningfully determine true monetary velocity in the external financial sector and overall economy. Today, with the disintermediation of financing throughout our economy, and the limited jurisdiction of legal systems in this regard, available data can only provide a general picture of assets and liabilities held by holding agents (administration, financial institutions, households, enterprises). Analogous to representing asset values in the absence of linkage to measurements of mobile monetary flow, such data provides insight into concepts of limited relevance and thus a window only into the past.

In an overall context, and particularly when considering both monetary injections made since 2007 and the very weak evolution of GDP (for the already developed industrialized nations) during the intervening period, it is clear that monetary velocity is slowing to a concerning degree when not supported by non-conventional monetary policies. It is as if masses of expanding and available real (currency) and virtual (derivative instruments) money are frozen with government help – that is, in the form of savings instruments. This includes pension plans, life insurance policies and tax exemption mechanisms (no withholding tax); all designed to favour the issuance of sovereign debt and the maintenance of low interest rate policies that artificially subsidize disposable income. It may also be considered that today's increasingly draconian "prudential policies" are also pushing many existing banking institutions to use their equity ratio requirements in the direction of supporting sovereign debt – a practice that will significantly enhance overall systemic risk.

At the end of 2009, M3 was 1.6 trillion euros for France, only a fraction of the nation's 12.5 trillion euros net worth that represents the difference between 32.5 trillion euros in assets and 20 trillion euros in liabilities. 6.8 trillion euros comprised the French financial sector assets (consisting of shares, instruments and mutual funds), thereby distinguishing M3 only by the solvency of the issuers – financial organizations (MFIs and monetary institutions) on the one hand and enterprises on the other. Despite a 1-to-4 ratio in both categories, M3 represents mostly liquid financial instruments that are destined to be assimilated into currency. Economic agents can easily change their asset allocation between each category, and that fact alone has resulted in a near total loss of meaning for the M3 designation; which also includes pensions, as well as instruments deposited at or by banks (that by definition remain the property of their owner while not being shown on the books). These financial subsectors and instrument categories were not tracked closely as the 2007–2008 financial crises erupted in the USA.

Central bankers did try to follow up on the appearance of new types of monetary representation and financial instruments, in part by creating new categories with which to represent them (M2 for small short-term deposits, M3 to add for savings, etc.). In doing so, central bankers and regulators rapidly encountered a vexing issue: nothing can prevent an agent from purchasing M2 assets in lieu of real money. Some economists are stating that in applying Goodhart's law,[7] only publication of the money supply index will induce behaviour that seeks to escape from constraints that the supply index is tied to. Using this discovery,[8] since 2000 the FED has no longer provided information on M2 targets, and in 2006 ceased publishing M3 data. Three years prior to that point, the FED had already abandoned issuing M3 data as an internal tool for assessing monetary policy. Professor Congton[9] from International Money Research has provided an interesting but partial analysis of the FED's decision. This occurred when the FED directly confronted the difficulty of precisely measuring aggregates and their impact – including the dynamics of the monetary system associated with migration away from simple script money to complex financial instruments and savings mechanisms, new forms of which continue to emerge today.

Viewed retrospectively, fiduciary money was a simple and easy category of monetary data to describe and measure. Script money was already more complicated, and presented a wider field for research – while still remaining within defined boundaries set by financial institutions and subject to regulation. In contrast, the ongoing transition to an entirely new generation of derivative financial instruments presents significant uncertainties for our economic system.

Alongside the disappearance of significant currency exchange restrictions (other than those involving China), the advent of globalization and the concurrent loss of financial institutions' respective monopolies served to markedly transform the global financial environment. Within this new economic universe, electronic systems obviate the "delivery and transfer" of currency, and the clearing of transactions can be executed via an additional set of secondary or even tertiary transaction derivatives. Such financial engineering creativity has liberated currency exchange, with the resulting flux in monetary velocity varying in accordance with the mood of brokers (who are engaged in appraising the environment). In the absence of regulatory constraints, financial agents are free to operate with stocks and other financial instruments, in part by opportunistically tracking the accumulation of sovereign debts and trade deficits.

Many research papers tried to overtake the limitations set by the classical aggregates and definition of banks or non-bank financial institutions, but were unable to break their walls. Either they consider the non-bank financial intermediaries and focus on balance sheets, and try then to discover by empirical observation a link between values, rates and liquidity, or they focus on explaining bubbles caused by excess liquidity provided by excess resources or collateral values. They fail to be conclusive as they cannot provide a global image of the money

---

[7] Goodhart's law (chief economist at the Bank of England in 1975) says that, as soon as an economic or social indicator becomes a goal for policies, it loses all its potential informative value.

[8] Between 1975 and 2000, the FED reached its objective for M2 growth in only 11 years out of an expected 26.

[9] Tim Congton, British economist, member of the shadow monetary policy committee and author of *Keynes, the Keynesians and Monetarism* as well as author of the article "A decision following Federal reserve decision to discontinue publication of M3 data".

transformation inside their classical analytical system or they lose most of the interconnectivity with the global economy, not considering that most exchanges are made outside of it directly between enterprises that may or may not be considered financial.[10]

Despite the correct reasoning of all these papers triggered by the 2007 financial crisis and the wide enquiry led by the Commission on the cause of the financial crisis,[11] it is now generally accepted that agencies and international financial institutions cannot wisely ground the policies they would be in charge of conducting if they had determined as a target more than the financial stability. With only stability in sight they favour imposed stabilizing regulation instead of economic development through monetary policies to favour velocity.

At the centre of surveillance protocols set up in its 2010–2011 81st annual report, and after considering an epidemic of balance sheet mismatches and potentially deleterious international financial system interconnectivity, the BIS concludes: "The recent financial crisis highlighted shortcomings in policy makers' ability to measure systemic risk gaps, and are evident in both analytical frameworks and the available financial firm-level and aggregate data that policy makers and market participants use in making decisions. These gaps hinder market participants in pricing and managing risk, and policy makers in monitoring and responding to vulnerabilities. This experience should prompt improvements in macro-surveillance and data collection."[12]

NEW FORMS OF MONETARY EXCHANGE

To illustrate the topic, we provide three figures giving an overview of operations for the global financial system, considered in today's context. They incorporate three vantage points from which to consider these issues.

Figure 5.4 summarizes the categories of players who produce trading activity, and depicts various actors employed as individual persons versus enterprises and/or administrative agents that initiate transactional exchanges and generate or move monetary instruments through the financial system. The arrows indicate patterns of flow and direction, although some are bi-directional. These flows are measured in monetary units, even if they are not measured within a certain time frame – hence, all flows have individual velocities that vary at given points in time. In this figure we can appreciate that flows intersect at the level of both "service payment platforms" (for clearings) and financial markets (handling exchanges of equity, lending instruments of all kinds or guarantees).

---

[10] Shin, H.-S. and Tobias, A., Liquidity, monetary policy and financial cycles, *Economics & Finance* Vol. 14, Federal Reserve Bank of New York, Jan/Feb 2008. Extract: "Our findings suggest a need to rehabilitate balance sheet quantities as a relevant measure in the conduct of monetary policy, but with one twist. Rather than reaffirming the conventional monetarist identification of the money stock as an indicator of liquidity our analysis assigns this role to the stock of collateralized borrowings." On a parallel topic, also from Shin: "Procyclality and monetary aggregates", February 2011 and "Monetary aggregates and the central financial stability model", March 2012.

[11] With US Congress. Already quoted.

[12] BIS 2010/2012 81st annual report. The 2011/2012 82nd report emphasized the dependency of the entire system on US$ credit lent to the rest of the world, and which "has tended to grow much faster than credit to US residents – a gap that has widened substantially, following the crisis".

The Modern Finance System

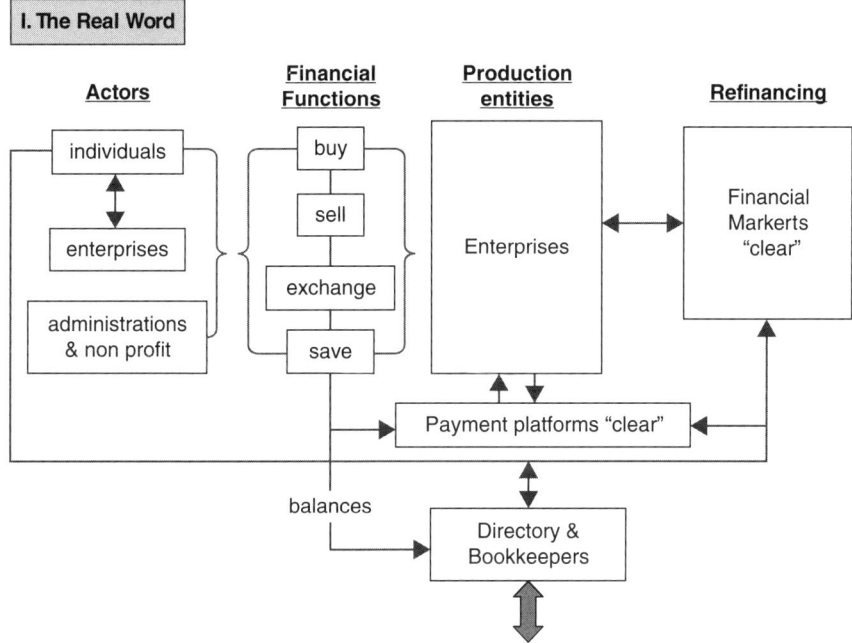

FIGURE 5.4   The Modern Finance System: The Real World

Figure 5.5 depicts categories of financial institutions that service various flows, through intervention at different points in the system and over time. These include: (1) banks and lending institutions that trade the flows; (2) pension plans and other retirement benefits institutions that store excess flow contents; or (3) withdrawal from flows to store assets or instruments on behalf of actors. Ultimately deriving revenue from "commissions" or other legal forms of compensation, these intervening financial institutions are supposed to adjust flows with the goal of maintaining balance in the system. In reality, as with fish in an aquarium, all actors in this system – whether active or not – randomly maintain and act on both needs and imprecise notions. Thus, governments, regulatory agencies and central financial institutions will regulate

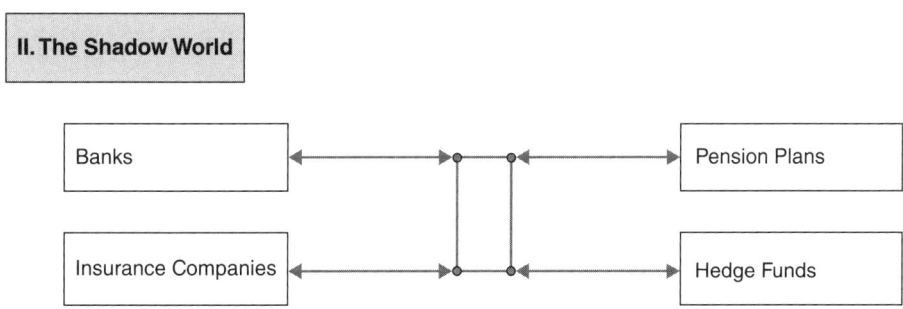

FIGURE 5.5   The Modern Finance System: The Shadow World

> ### III. THE LINKAGES-Money instruments through financial market & clearing

Financial instruments, whatever legal form they have, create links when traded on financial markets. Being transferable between categories, they allow clearing, meaning the satisfaction of debt commitments corresponding to exchanges and property transfers. Any financial instrument being potential "money", between them they can be exchanged at sampled values different from the original transactions that created them (see Figure 3.2).

FIGURE 5.6 The Modern Finance System: Linkages

the system so as to assign goals, and at times will introduce or provide financial instruments – in an attempt to gauge the appropriate capital endowment level required.

Figure 5.6 is merely intended to underscore that a matrix of links exists between all actors in the system, namely those identified on payment platforms and using a range of financial instruments. Whether regulated or not, financial markets intersect, and their interaction points are exposed to interplay between a volume of actors who function as intermediaries.

It is at this point in our analytical overview that the concept of a "social link" emerges. The term "link" here does not imply a link in the way we mean it, the latter requiring a universal ID number attributed separately to individual actors and traded instruments (and at times financial marketplaces). A true link can exist in concert with at least two parties who accept the conditions of a financial transaction, and exercise the will to execute (alternatives such as barter exchange are not considered here). This sequence of conditions in turn generates a transactional contract that is governed by laws and regulations.

It goes without saying that the conditions underlying such a concept have been conceptually analysed and regulated, and that their evolution occurs in tandem with changes: (1) in the nature of transactional exchanges, (2) in the accompanying tools utilized and (3) in the financial instruments or tangibles exchanged. From a bi-Atlantic perspective, our understanding of underlying concepts remains similar, and at times convergent or even replicated. An open matter relates to the allocation or assignment of jurisdictions, where international transactions are concerned. Although applicable rules exist, they remain inadequate for addressing all issues raised by the globalization of financial markets. Nevertheless, additional international regulation through *Exequatur* mechanisms is in the process of being implemented, for example for the purpose of implementing judicial decisions and "The Hague" treaties.[13]

In considering the preceding three figures together, we ascertain that the banking sector is not organized in a specific fashion as regards patterns of flows, monetary functions and social goals. Moreover, the preceding figures likely gloss over many realities, including the complexity of flow patterns inside the pipes (represented by respective arrows), their flow speeds,

---

[13] *Exequatur* is a legal process by which a court decision may be implemented in a country different from the jurisdiction where the decision was rendered. With respect to financial matters, this process is usually fluid in the western world, provided that: (1) concepts forming the groundwork of the decision are similar, (2) sovereignty issues are taken into account and (3) there has been no fraud with regard to establishing accurate forums of jurisdiction. The Hague conventions relate to a transnational regime, in existence since the 1893 Hague Conference on Private International Law. In 1971, the Hague Conference addressed foreign judgments in civil and commercial matters; in 2006, a convention on securities transactions was signed by the USA, but remains unratified.

density and pressures – and most importantly, time factors that influence the entire system, including its many actors.

The inadequacy of the financial sector's design infrastructure supports our thesis about a necessary and reasoned reform of the monetary system, beginning with the means for measurement of flows – in particular with reference to the shadow banking and virtual money compartments of the financial sector. As for traditional institutional banking itself, attempts at regulation of its flow patterns will have limited overall impact – since banking handles only a small percentage of overall transactional flow (compared with shadow banking and virtual money, where insufficient levels of observation also present additional limits).

Proper and effective measurement of flow patterns would allow for regulation focused on services linked to payment platforms, markets and instruments. By regulating the points of intersection between these elements, greater levels of transparency would be accessible to the public – specifically with regard to metrics that track the issuance of all forms of money. Additionally, rapid sanctioning of breaches would be rendered more feasible, and overall regulatory processes would be less expensive. The historic pattern of intermittent fraud and financial collapse calls for a change in the existing approaches, and for a new direction in monitoring and oversight.

As opposed to constraints on the printing and use of banks bills, an unprecedented degree of near-absolute freedom of foreign currency exchange (with the exception of China) – combined with disintermediation and globalization of international trade in currencies and monetary instruments – has spurred financial sector creativity. The latter supports expansion of the search for new trades to generate commissions, most notably in a consumption-driven society eager to amass even greater levels of debt. This pattern transpires in parallel to: (1) the unregulated and legally unfettered multiplication of financial instruments, (2) the unprecedented increase in trading volumes across financial markets and (3) the exponential growth of "virtual money" in the forms of secondary and tertiary instruments (derivatives), which in turn are backed by ill-defined assets. Acting in parallel with the above-noted trends, innovations in information and telecommunication technologies, financial mathematics and computer science have enabled a revolution in the monetary landscape – inclusive irreversible changes in the nature of money itself.

As we have seen, currency and monetary instrument transactions are no longer limited by rules that have traditionally applied to traders or the content of transactions. Rather, the measurement unit in which the monetary instrument trade is operated, its purpose and the identity of transactional counterparties are all assigned to the trader's judgment in the selection process – that is, if not subject to contractual regulation or market governance rules on the market where they are traded. In general, there are no general restrictions on direct trading between economic agents.

Laws and jurisprudence applicable to currency and transaction exchanges have undergone centuries of evolution, and a progressive increase in their depth and complexity. This includes addressing the elements that characterize a sale; how the wills of transactional players converge, how agreement is reached and terms structured, at what instant the sale is concluded, as well as the consequences and/or complications of the transaction. This evolutionary process will also continue to require resolution of the many resulting legal debates that consider applicable reference to the statutory as well as the precedent-driven basis of law. Thus, little can be added from an academic point of view.

Owing to the technological revolution, another major change has been in the identity and venue for the transactional point of sale, the meeting place if you will – and which today is increasingly found in virtual space. Other rapid changes have involved the tangible flow of exchange goods and services, the volume of transactions and overall speed of trades, as well as the resulting acceleration of monetary rotation. The use of money and the consequences of transactional exchanges have been altered drastically in our time.

Emerging alongside this revolution in trade processes are other remarkable changes in the means and process of payment.[14] These changes impact not only the transactional trading environment, but also the clearing process. As transactions route to any number of clearing systems, importance is attached not only to the price expressed (in the currency of the applicable central bank[s]), but also to currency exchange ratios that will determine the balances attributable to each market participant. Such measurements are recognized as significant only when they refer to free balances – namely, balances shown on the books as "accumulations allocated over time", and respectively assigned to each exchange participant (not subject to any requirements for meeting in person).

As prices and transactional exchange activity emerge as independent variables, their resulting importance is underscored by the impact of registration requirements for operating in today's trading arena – where participants are submitted to identification (reconnaissance) and solvency checks. Usually, most transactional exchanges are constrained by commitments of variable duration (rents, loan instalments, food, heating, insurance premiums, etc.), where only the applicable balance is available. In settings where excess accumulated money or conversely, consolidation, is concentrated in a limited number of hands, however, the options and choices for independently selecting the purpose and design of transactional exchange mechanisms are expanded. For instance, investment fund managers are subject to regulatory limitations determined in large part by their own choice of options; for instance, as regards the "governance rules and exemptions" available to them.

Owing to the emergence of banking-independent payment platforms and the accelerated digitalization of payment methods as well as the unification of identification conduits (smart debit/credit cards, smartphones), the profile of individuals engaging in transactions is now known as well as the profiles of enterprises – whose openly released financial statements already provide significant public transparency. Such levels of open disclosure cannot proceed without downstream consequences.

THE DRIVING ROLE OF MONETARY VELOCITY

Our prior discussion on the role of the "money multiplier" (monetary credit multiplier) illuminated the manner in which monetary velocity is an important metric for assessing economic health. The monetary credit and investment multipliers are analogous representations of monetary velocity. The speed with which money flows through the economy is a determinant variable, all efforts having been made to consistently increase its value – *receivables securitization* being one example. With the "accessible fraction" of monetary supply being defined by respective central banks, the velocity at which that access is granted in turn determines the volume and cumulative value of loans (or other debt) ultimately issued. In a closed banking system, it is easy to follow changing credit volumes via balance sheets, especially in the case of real-estate financing – where large balances with long duration allow for facile oversight and fine-tuning of both refinancing rates and compulsory reserve requirements. Of course, it remains self-evident that the money multiplier factor is merely one approach for representing

---

[14] EU regulation no. 260/2012 modifying regulation no. 924/2009 on transfers and withdrawals in euros.

monetary velocity, since the flow of money can operate in more than one fashion. The classical definition of money velocity GDP/M2 is too aggregate a formula to be anything but a limited meaning indicator of economic and financial health or sickness.[15] It only deals with the narrow scope of M2 showing the face of money but not with exchanges, growing outstanding balances and derivatives that change the face of what guarantees are in volume.

Today's transactional spectrum reflects various types and intensities of economic activity, including the association with absence or dependence on credit – ranging all the way down to mechanisms for offering very short-term credit (e.g., daily clearance of financial transactions, or those with monthly turnover such as credit cards). Novel securitization instruments and their design have altered the conceptual basis of modern currency, by blurring the traditional boundaries between tangible or liquid assets versus newer financial instruments and virtual derivative assets. The appearance of new structural forms of monetary transactions has transformed the concept of "operative value", which can be triggered by mere interaction with a range of economic agents (of differing asset bases with varied statutory roles). Attempts to better comprehend these new monetary forms have been made, in part by seeking to define broader and more encompassing concepts (e.g., broad money). However, even if necessity forced statisticians to modify balance sheets – so as to show aggregates for debts, equity and assets ownership – such efforts would represent research efforts[16] rather than any concrete basis for designing a new monetary system. A range of potential approaches require further development and scrutiny before they can be expanded on as a potential analytic basis, for proposing policy improvements and eventual monetary reform.

Systemic fragmentation between banking and non-banking compartments of the financial sector[17] prompt the following paraphrased observation: "Some lend or borrow from others without limitations, using accounting rules constructed around a non-adaptive global vantage point that inappropriately seek independence from the transformation of practices, that are targeted to follow globally legitimized regimes for governing transnational collections and sales of underlying assets." According to an official report[18] issued by the Commission, on underlying causes of financial crisis (Financial Crisis Inquiry Commission (FCIC)), refinancing by "investors" from non-banking subsectors reached a level of $73 trillion, equivalent to a 5× multiple of annual US GDP. Although these "REPO" patterns (the mechanism of which we will examine later in this book) have widely disappeared from the statistical repertoire of central banks, the ultimate origin of applicable borrowers still in existence remains unchanged. See Figure 5.7.

We also have to mention that the new pattern of distribution directly from a logistic platform receiving tangible goods from manufacturers, as well as the distribution of digital productions as a growing segment of the consumption of individuals and the online systems of payments, add up to the financial set-up factors (securitization) making money rotation structurally potentially faster compared with the previous environment.

---

[15] See Federal Reserve Bank of St. Louis Research Center. The October 2013 release gives a 1.55 ratio for the M2 velocity of the third quarter, still going down from the 2000 peak.

[16] Lim, E. and Subramanian, S., Factors underlying the definition of 'broad money'. An examination of current US monetary statistics and practices of other countries, IMF, March 2003.

[17] Investment funds, pension plans, insurance companies, etc.

[18] Gary B. Gorton Report 15787, February 2010: presented to the US Commission on the Causes of the Financial Crisis – National Bureau of Economic Research, *Questions and Answers about the Financial Crisis*, p. 7, www.nber.org/paper/w15787.

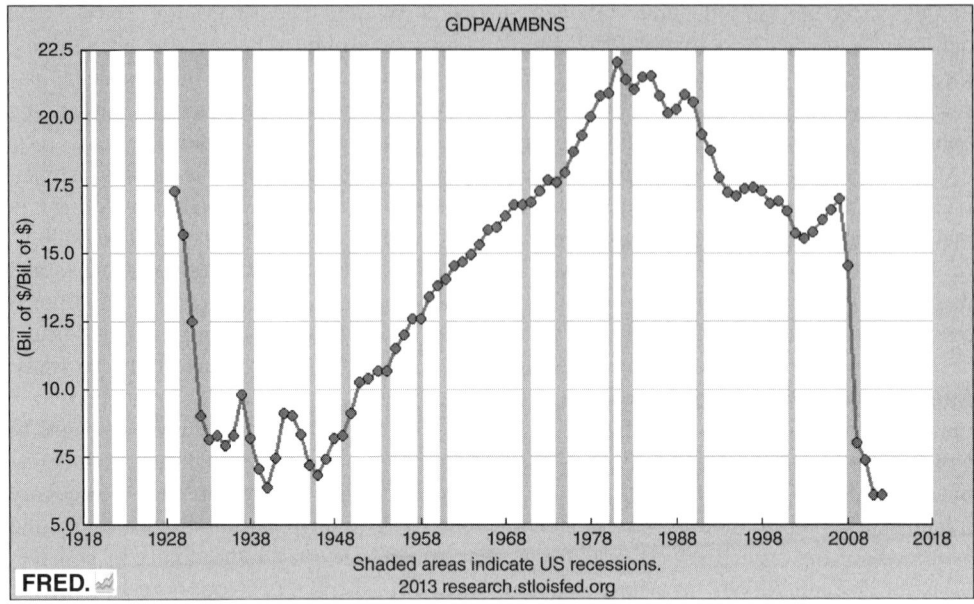

Gross domestic product (GDPA)/St. Louis adjusted monetary base (AMBNS).

FIGURE 5.7   Contraction of US monetary circulation

For this reason, the method of looking at money rotation should be adapted. It should comprehend all kinds of money, but also segregate between markets (financial and non-financial), retail and gross, and instruments' and actors' behaviour reconciled with them.

ARE CENTRAL BANKS PREREQUISITE INSTITUTIONS THAT SHOULD REMAIN INDEPENDENT FROM SOVEREIGN AUTHORITY?

The moment one challenges the contention that banks were originally granted a monopoly to issue money, and thereby vested with a responsibility to provide the economy with sufficient means of payment (when not fighting inflation and pursuing other mandated objectives), one invariably confronts the question as to whether there is a need for the existence of central banks. The precept was always questioned by the libertarian wing of economics (i.e., the 19th to mid-20th-century Austrian School of Economics), and recently endorsed by US Congressman Ron Paul.

Two questions are raised. The first one is the need itself for the existence of a central bank because of its sovereign role of issuing the nation's common means of payment and having a regulatory role in the value of its stamping. We have to remember that the US constitution only provides Congress with the right to set the exchange rate of the nation's currency and not to issue money. The second question is, since it was ultimately decided in all modern countries that a central bank should be granted the right to issue the currency, what should its goals and governance be?

If the global monetary pool were to be backed up by gold, then some might argue against the need for the type of centralized regulation provided by the existing worldwide system of central banks. However, only a limited volume of "above-ground" gold repositories and geologically proven "below-ground" gold ore reserves are known to exist. At today's market prices for gold, the potential amount of available gold on the planet represents only a fraction of the world GDP, and an exponentially smaller fraction when additionally considering both the estimated value for the entire global currency pool and the paper value of derivative monetary instruments.

Although competition between private issuers might create a sound metal currency (albeit insufficient in weight/volume to provide a reserve value equivalent to even world GDP), governments themselves have always been accused of using money to satisfy their own needs. Reviewing history back to antiquity, even if a nation's money management design separates a sovereign's (private) assets from the collective assets of the people, then the sovereign (say government) remains frequently accused of misusing power to mint money with the intent of satisfying the private needs of two social elements. These expenses include the governing oligarchy's daily expenses taken from national budgets (called the civil list in democracies) as well as the collective power of constituencies that represent issues of national self-interest (e.g., war or investments in infrastructure). Setting limits to split the difference in interests can also facilitate abuses, on the basis of arguing for the public interest. In more modern times, parliamentary control over government expenses, tax collections and spending has been a slowly progressive process. At times, such processes emerged too late – as may be seen in the call to convene the French *Etats Généraux* in 1787[19] by the monarch, then under the threat of treasury bankruptcy that had resulted from the failure to enact tax reforms.

Many authors reject the governmental right to issue money, including in the name of the people.[20] Such critics consider the absence of a central bank system as being feasible, particularly on an independent basis, so as to limit the government to the role of an economic agent whose credit can still be challenged by creditors. In contrast, a central bank would largely be immune from financial sector creditors, except on the basis of transnational geopolitical critique or conflict and even economic retaliation by governments and other central banks – for instance, through pressure exerted on the currency, commodity and equity markets or via a range of international trade nation-state mechanisms. The potential for encountering challenges, mounted by creditors against a government, was known to Madison and Jefferson – among the most brilliant of US Presidents. The latter was a close friend of Samuel DuPont and travelled, for a long period, to 18th-century France – thereby explaining the delayed creation of a central bank in the USA,[21] first on a privatized basis, and then government controlled. The underlying economic reasoning (and more precisely the positive contribution of a single

---

[19] The *Etats Généraux* were called on December 29, 1786 for a plenary meeting initially scheduled on January 29, 1787 and finally convened on February 22, 1787. Among the memoranda presented was one focused on provincial representation – in essence a copy of a paper originally prepared by Samuel DuPont. That document had proposed a suffrage system accessible to all who commanded an economic capacity and ending privilege assigned by class. A second memorandum submitted to the *Etats Généraux* centred on proposing tax reform.

[20] Presented on May 14, 1787 and adopted on September 17, 1787, the US Constitution, in part, revisited the November 1777 Charter of Confederated States, that aimed to accord the Federation – and subsequently the Constitutional member states (13 originally) – a privilege and right to mint currency and levy taxes.

[21] As Benjamin Franklin and Jefferson did, and were witnesses to rich France and its monarchy's financial difficulties. We briefly describe the failure of bank Law (Royal Bank), explaining the US attitude against any kind of central bank until the beginning of the 20th century.

currency to the development of modern financial transactions and market exchanges), progressively allowed this model to be further disseminated. At the time, it also had to be decided which institution would issue the national currency, and what the specific institutional mandate and governing statutes for a US central bank would be. In a broader sense, we note that – outside the USA – the 19th-century design for the set-up of central banks generally followed an initial private path, with subsequent transition to government ownership, thereby grounding confidence in the currency issued via an initial period of independence from the sovereign. The US FED ultimately straddled a pathway between these extremes. Today, the central bank statutes still ensure a neutral position for the US FED, whose financial operations and assets remain separate from the budgetary books of the US Treasury.

We have already discussed (in Chapter 2) why the attribute of trust in sampling and its stability over time require the existence of central regulation and supervision, explaining the existence of central banks. The current environment, with the FED buying MBS and treasuries at \$85 billion a month, show both the extension of money and the need for these purchases. The independence of a central bank as to its policies is a different topic from its mere existence, due to the need for harmonized, guaranteed stamping and stability.

The independence of a central bank may refer to two separate concepts. The first is the independence of its Board and President. When appointed, as is the rule in western countries, they are not to be dismissed by the government until the terms of their mandate. They may be deemed independent. The second concept is the operational independence within the Constitution. The constitution and the byelaws, besides giving the central bank its currency function, set its goals. For instance, the central banks are to fight a prevalent disease affecting currencies – the decline in value due to inflation. The drawing of goals is the limit to internal independence of central banks that may limit their ability to buy governmental issuances or lend money to the government. It may also, on the contrary, drive policies such as quantitative easing – referring to the absence of inflation and a slowing economic environment. The central banks not being under control of parliamentary bodies do still report to them for their monetary policies. When acting as regulator their decisions are also subject to judiciary control. What are "independence" or "commitments" and how can these concepts be translated by independent governance bodies are the questions.

Even if constitutionally authorized, such institutional independence cannot be absolute. For instance, the central bank (e.g., US FED) cannot detach itself from the US economy in an abstract fashion – ostensibly based on the intent of purely ensuring the best interests and optimal functional performance of the banking system. When banking liquidity disappears alongside the attendant risk of systemic bank failures, or when prices decline or rise as a consequence of governmental policies that disrupt macroeconomic equilibrium (government deficits, trade deficits, inflation, etc.), the central bank is then chartered to intervene. In these uncommon instances, when financial instruments prices decline as well as their liquidity, internal governance rules must be breached. The FED will purchase assets for the purpose of supporting asset valuation, much as a major bulge bracket commercial bank would.

The preceding examples of "non-conventional" policies for a central bank can also include purchasing governmental debts, for example for the purpose of managing price volatility and/or issuance prices. Policies of quantitative easing fall into the latter category.[22] Some

---

[22] Introduced during the 2000s in Japan, quantitative fiscal easing (FE) was subsequently adopted and continued in both the UK and the USA. Nevertheless, the contexts of the USA and Japan are totally different. During the period in the USA beginning for Q1 FE on December 14, 2008 and ending on March 30, 2010, the policy consisted of purchasing \$300 billion of treasury bonds, \$175 billion in Fanny Mae

(continued)

experts seek to distinguish QE from the printing of paper monetary bills, because associated purchases by the US FED are placed on the secondary market, rather than direct budgetary deficit-driven purchase of US treasury bonds. However, this technical distinction does not alter the underlying facts. The truth remains that the US FED is ultimately not dependent on the government, but rather that the US Treasury (government) becomes dependent in reverse. In essence, need drives legal evolution – despite the fact that economic recovery is not a legally grounded or guaranteed process.

Total central bank balance sheets (million $; euro = $1.35)

	FED	ECB
24/07/13 (FED) or 25/10/13 (ECB)	3575	3129

Sources: FED bulletin and monthly ECB bulletin.

We have already illuminated the contention that gold can no longer practically serve as the sole guarantee that backs a monetary system, despite its superficial "short to mid-term" capability for instilling temporary market confidence. However, this role for gold is based largely on its putative function as a value-based convergence driver for supporting price adjustments – that in turn allow for the appropriate volume of money to be made available to the economy. Naturally, for this sequence of events to occur in a stable and reproducible fashion, the dynamics of price adjustment require both a measurement-based method of determination, as well as agreement between involved parties such as governments and central banks. Of course, gold's cyclical phases of market behaviour underscore the limits of gold's potential role in this set of contexts.

Since WWII, the worldwide expansion of commercial trading and the role of the World Trade Organization (WTO) have contributed substantially to progress in raising humanity's standard of living. In a general sense, trade is facilitated by the process of extension, and through the impact of monetary unification and the use of money as a "price-setting" tool – the Eurozone being a prime example. The converse option – that of permitting a number of nation-state players to individually issue new currencies through a process of competitive devaluation – represents a choice that would have driven European society back to the Dark Ages. It did not happen. Monetary consolidation was pushing competition in the field of innovation and gains in productivity, as well as bringing scale economies with a larger market of consumers and investors.

Naturally, the major issue in our time is the status of central banks as an institutional mechanism in the world financial economy – including their coordination role and the objectives that would be democratically assigned to them within a new monetary environment. Ultimately, we believe that there is a need for central banks in setting measurement standards, in lieu of a return to the gold standard that we do not support. Given the need for unification

---

instruments and $125 billion in mortgage-backed securities (see savings and loan crisis). Q2 FE started when Q1 was finished, concluded on June 30, 2011 and comprised the purchase of $600 billion in US long-term securities. Q3 committed $85 billion each month, $40 billion for MBS and $45 billion for treasuries. ECB issued in 2011 $1 billion of 3-year LTRO (long-term refinancing operation) to ensure the liquidity of the European banking system, which is now in the process of being reimbursed. The Bank of Japan is also to administrate a new wide quantitative easing under pressure of the new government issued from the 2012 elections. With the exception of ECB, all balance sheets of central banks have been multiplied by more than three in 5 years. The FED balance sheet now exceeds $3 trillion.

of standards, as well as some centralized and orderly control, it is clear that a central financial authority established by democratic institutions needs to assume such functions.

Markets will not do so in and of themselves, and the short life of MIFID[23] confirms the latter conclusion. There is also the issue of the integral link between measurement standards and the crucial warrantee function to consider. If markets are to remain operationally free, then the basic mechanisms of monetary supply should remain unencumbered by the impact of speculation, and the power to sanction must rest within a democratically accepted and central-ized institutional base.

In the era of globalization, the foregoing conclusions do not imply that central banks, or their equivalent, should be dependent on governments. Given the absence of a unified global political leadership and in the face of the high-technology revolution transforming societies worldwide, tomorrow's policies must be formulated and conducted over time, and in a non-dogmatic fashion. The G20 system of ongoing negotiations – structured to allow for the insertion of time and unfolding geopolitical evolution – appears to be the most appropriate forum from which to set and implement guidelines for budgetary discipline and monetary reform. Subject to the G20's existing policy of inclusive representation extended to key nations, all political and monetary unions, as well as both the IMF and the BIS, an exten-sive range of technical requirements and economic topics are periodically compiled for consideration. The highest stakes of this process involve granting to the directorial boards of major international institutions the foundation of cross-consultation, advice and consent responses, continuity of shared political leadership and a clear mandate for addressing the key issues at hand.

The current set-up of legal independence, both in factual terms and goals, has no sus-tainability. The banks' governance implies that they can do what they want inside their constitutional framework. However, at the same time their goal is to maintain stability, if not the fight against inflation. In a general environment of deflation and monetary retrenchment, they can only maintain their fellow citizens' economic survival. Because of the slowdown in money velocity and budget deficits, it is an obligation for them to monetize debts and replace money which is stored – and it is stored somewhere – and to follow on quantitative easing policies. Without the necessary granular analysis, we can illustrate the needs by just witnessing the growth of their total balance sheets, which are currently keeping economies afloat. The theory would be that as soon as monetary velocity accelerates, the balance sheets shrink. The reason for this is that clearings accelerate and as a result, the book balances reduce when paid transactions are stable in volume and posted prices. We can also see a transfer of privately held balances towards central bank balance sheets when obliged to buy instruments produced by the system – governmental bonds or regulated securities – to keep the system flowing. In doing so, central banks reduce the pressure from slowing velocity on private balance sheets, but grow their own. This seems to be the case in Europe but not in the USA, raising questions about the real situation of the US economy and the validity of its statistics. Nevertheless, the share of these money injections corresponding to budget deficits and not needs resulting from velocity reduction, compared with the greater needs from bigger nominal value transactions, will never disappear. The amounts accumulated by counterparties give to them a liberty that central banks, through circumstances and limiting regulations, have lost. This liberty is without doubt a threat only limited by the regulations

---

[23] European directive addressing markets for financial instruments and derivatives – now under current revision.

on prudential ratios and taxation constraint. They will not survive because they are destructive of any kind of long-term industrial growth that requires trust in a wide refinancing of investments at the entrepreneurial level, instead of the refinancing of deficits. This limited independence of central banks, transferred to financial entities outside their jurisdiction will inevitably create disorders or an unsustainable situation for those who have sunk to such flexibility where others have not. As facts are even more inescapable, this independence will not lead to inflation as many writers not aware of the changes in the world have suggested but to a change in the stamping of currencies after a monetary war. Gods will have nothing to do with that, as the monetary history between the two world wars already showed.[24]

New Policies to Stabilize the Banking System

In a conceptual environment, where central banks were supposed to be independent and not to interfere with markets, their intervention processes as known for decades could no longer be unlimited when faced with huge monetary flows. Letting a systemically important bank fail, as in the Lehman Brothers case, is not acceptable when considering the consequences. The FSB answer was to call for banking resolution systems to be set (see Chapter 7). For Europe, a banking recovery and resolution directive (BRRD) for the banking industry is intended to anticipate the difficulties with a surveillance system and require banks to build up a plan in case such difficulties arise. In essence, what happens if a portfolio's value goes down or if deposits go away, or a crisis appears in a sector of the economy or with public debts. This is the purpose of stress testing, which banks are submitted to on both sides of the Atlantic. When these difficulties do appear, the resolution system will take over to impose either a recovery or a liquidation process without contagion effects. In essence, it gives power to the central banks to impose cross-nation or monetary zone solutions. With the aim of avoiding what happened with Lehman Brothers, the intention is to disconnect the bank from central bank money and taxpayer's money. Among the tools are the request for sufficient equity and limited leverage after the assets have been risk weight appraised. At that stage the central bank will require additional equity (if this is deemed to be insufficient) or, if the failure is obvious, impose an orderly process of partial or total liquidation with the maintenance of support functions. To insure the financing the authority will impose an equity and long-term non-claimable financing instrument haircut. This is called the "bail in". If no sufficient resolution fund comes through the banking system from contributions over time, the sale of assets and/or a bridge bank might also be imposed before the central bank or a bail-out process intervenes.

THE INSUFFICIENCIES OF THE CURRENT SYSTEM FOR SATISFYING INFORMATION NEEDS

Statistics, as available through the described current system of aggregates and banking surveillance, do not provide the necessary information to ascertain a monetary policy without risks. The value effect of transactions, a dynamic phenomenon compared with classical analysis, is just approached through the sectorial "bubble concept" and mostly when looking at real-estate transactions and stock exchanges. There is no direct global view on books

---

[24] This has already been discussed in our previous book.

and records of financial institutions, where the quality of numbers has only been looked at through stress testing piece by piece portfolios missing the outside of system counterparties' risks and what is totally outside but nevertheless interconnected through values as opposed to numbers.

QUESTIONS AND ANSWERS

The Accepted Regulation and Observation Limits Compared with the Realities of Modern Times

What is the basis for the traditional monetary organization of countries?
The basis is the monopoly of issuing money, sometimes chartered to private banks, and since the fractional reserve system appeared, the control of credit distribution granted with monopoly to commercial banks.

What is the basis for the surveillance system?
Owing to the set-up, the surveillance system has been organized with the follow-up of aggregates, the issued money amounts M1 and M2 and credit distribution by banks. Nevertheless, there is further statistical follow-up at national accounting levels, but not directly at the central banks' level with action powers.

What is missing in the current surveillance system?
Intercompany financing (vendors' credit to clients) is the main supply of refinancing for the economy. Direct economy financing, independent of tangible goods or service delivery transactions, reverses the traditional flow. Instead of having the banks financing the economy, the banks need refinancing from the economy, which has produced new money derived from transactions and imbalances.

Do the traditional money credit or investment multiplier processes still make sense in terms of explaining a monetary mechanism? Are classical aggregates still valid?
No. Today everything is a matter of derivative extending money from legal tenders to mere receivables, and by transformation of these to any kind of claimable instrument. The regulated world of banks no longer provides the majority of refinancing. Providing the necessary guarantees to ensure they fall under the monetary definition of being claimable receivables and flows is the key reference. The topic to comprehend is the matter of velocity that interacts with a reduction of necessary masses, and brings instability because of being more transferable and convertible. Speed is known as a concept but not to be calculated, while it should be.

What are the key questions about money issuance today?
There are only three interlinked questions. The first one, still furiously debated, is who should be granted, by the citizen, the right to issue money? This is the question of the central bank and its independence. With this question comes that of how to organize independence. The second topic is determining the most appropriate volume to have in the pipeline and the third, the goals to be assigned to monetary policies.

With what concept is the question of goals linked to the second topic?
This question is not only linked to the determination of the volume of money issuance and debt to flow through the economy, but also to its stamping and value.

Who should be in charge of determining the relevant goals for a monetary policy to be followed, and in what time frame?

It is a social and democratic issue. Constitutions should be updated regarding what the national currency is, how its stamping is determined and how its relative value should be set against foreign currencies. International treaties should complete the set-up when participating in a monetary zone, and for coherence within the international monetary system. Within constitutions, implementation should be left to governments under the control of elected chambers. Central banks and civil agencies should regulate systemic participants within the framework.

Redefining the Monetary System and Measurements of Monetary Flow – Towards M5 and M6

"Economic calculation can comprehend everything that is exchanged"[1]

— **L. Von Mises**

As previous chapters have argued, both the intrinsic nature of money and its uses have undergone a major transformation, pointing away from applicable definitions that were previously established over millennia. Alongside updated approaches for observing and measuring its flows and balances, a new definition of today's money is required.

In the present chapter, we propose a new model for characterizing the full spectrum of money-driven transactional exchanges and balances, which is as varied as the diverse array of monetary receivables and debt instruments presently floating on world markets. By better defining such financial instruments and their regulated markets, the respective tasks of legislators and regulators will be streamlined – particularly in drafting reset parameters for accounting standards and value maintenance guarantees that can conform to real-world conditions, while still retaining the flexibility required to address inevitable deviations from norms that might arise in the future.

Economists usually command only a limited degree of "real power".[2] In Europe, as in the USA, economists author many articles and books as indicators of their academic standing. By convention, the trend is to work within existing regulatory and conceptual regimes, rather than in advancing novel concepts that would promote changes in the established world monetary and financial system. The work of such economists also presents a quasi-guarantee of acceptance, which in turn provides the necessary stability for existing institutional systems. Although engaged in active solicitation of support from various camps of economists, politicians and

---

[1] Von Mises, L., *Human Action*, ch. XII, p. 213. See References.

[2] This was the situation for Keynes, who – in his time – confronted the process of convincing European "old-school" economists of his theories, and thus left the LSE to emigrate to Harvard and the New World.

political leaders have little time to engage in independent thinking and thus do not independently offer a plethora of new options.

With the resulting common deficit of vision, one cannot be surprised by the absence of "acknowledged anticipation of crisis" that preceded the recent 2007–2008 financial collapse. This prescriptive failure was not primarily attributable to the nature of existing information sources or follow-on tools. For instance, the opinions of contemporary 21st-century economists would not have been improved upon if the work of mostly European 20th-century economists (who dealt with an entirely different environment in their time) had offered an alternative foundation of economic thought and innovation in our time. Rather, we would argue that the leadership failure of modern economists in the recent crisis involved a general refusal to drastically refine their knowledge and views on the evolving status of world financial and monetary markets.[3] Beyond this observation, leading economists pursue academic careers linked to research centres that are either directly or indirectly funded by government entities – one consequence of which includes the tendency not to pursue efforts that would disturb the basis of existing, and frequently conventional, ideas.

Despite a responsibility to carry out generally accepted oversight mandates, we note that the world's independent central banks also failed to prospectively anticipate and pre-emptively address the real-world consequences of recent economic crisis – the evolution of which could be overlooked only if viewing the environment through blinkers. It is acknowledged that the FED massively intervened in an *a posteriori* fashion, by growing its balance sheet via purchases of "failing value" assets (i.e., as of April 9, 2009, liquidity injections for the banking system had reached $2.1 trillion on balance sheets). The government also massively intervened in the context of allowing mortgage-backed security-specialized "enhancing agencies" (that had granted additional guarantees of their own to improve marketability and price, i.e. Fanny Mae and Freddie Mac, AIG Natexis and Dexia) to keep markets in operating conditions, specifically by accumulating portfolios – the posting of losses for which remain incomplete. Other central banks fortunately followed suit. On that occasion, none of the central banks or governments back-purchased their own currencies, but rather opted to acquire various financial assets.

The above-noted historical incidents demonstrate the present-day limitations of defining money solely in the context of hard currency and liquid bank deposits. Owing to the direct availability of money and the overall deregulation of our economies it is, at times, difficult to clearly distinguish fundamental differences in the functions of "central bank currency" from those provided by other exchange instruments. Increasingly, therefore, many monetary instruments are considered to share some functional attributes with universal debt instruments, such as convertible treasury bonds. As a consequence of recent crises, central banks now

---

[3] Hayek discussed the matter of the need for a central bank in *Constitution of Liberty*. At the start of his chapter on the monetary framework, he concluded that there was no choice other than having banks in place. His arguments are interesting to consider and quote: "Perhaps, if governments had never interfered, a kind of monetary arrangement might have evolved, which would not have required deliberate control; in particular, if men had not come to extensively use credit instrument as money or as close substitutes for money, we might have been able to rely on some self-regulating mechanism." (In making this statement, he quotes his mentor, Ludwig Von Mises.) *Human Action*, pp. 429–445 (Library Fund edition, vol. 2, pp. 432–448). See References.

appreciate that value does not necessarily correspond to any of the following parameters: solvency, operational aspects of transactional exchange or flow patterns for trading of monetary instruments. Once again, governmental and non-governmental guarantees have obscured the realities underlying corresponding financial instruments, such as mortgage-backed securities and others, where discrepancies are monetized either through interaction of the instruments on markets or by way of relevant supporting (enhancing) agencies, as noted above. At the same time, central banks have intervened with regard to real-estate bubbles and equity market bubbles, notwithstanding their poor record in anticipating the occurrence of such anomalies, particularly since the global impact of limits is rarely taken into consideration (in contrast to bond market bubbles that are global in nature and related to interest rates, but do not reflect solvency risk at a microeconomic level).

Shaped by contemporary tools of direct finance, many contemporary transactional exchanges rely more on the mechanism of balance than face value. Examples of this trend include the concept of "deposits" on the purchase of shares and a range of paradigms from the field of real estate: for example, aside from first-time buyers, the buyers responding to the resale of a relatively new house will be more concerned with the differential between the purchase and likely resale price of a pre-owned property than by the price of its intended acquisition. Buyers will also indirectly assess real-estate market liquidity, by considering the average number of months required to sell a comparable property at a given price.

The parameter of absolute value is now secondary to the concept of balance. However, in cases where there is a decline in asset value, the balance is influenced more by the leverage effect of the debt, and can exceed the reimbursement capabilities of the borrower. Even worse, during a crisis one will observe a freeze in transactions and a cessation of currency flow – that is, exchangeable assets and liabilities are involved, and these are functionally equivalent to money. Naturally, when linking these types of monetary equivalents to gross income, the category-by-category visibility of money supply becomes an issue. For instance, and as we have already observed, individuals' asset valuations have grown out of proportion with their income, leading to doubt as regards their value – at least in the absence of a coherent evolution in GDP and its allocation; a process that did not occur in recent history.[4]

Such an emerging concept of monetary supply should be expanded to include all contractual assets and liabilities issued by any enterprise, including those of central banks – who institutionally lend to commercial banks (not distinguished from non-registered banks or other financial institutions) in an analogous fashion to a holding company interacting with its "special sector subsidiaries". Studies on this theme have begun to appear – one example is an article in *The Guardian* published in early 2009, listing different categories assets which provides an interesting insight into what further studies on this issue might expose. Data in this regard is not published by central banks, even though it would provide a fairly accurate image of how the "multiplier effect" impacts bank reserves (debt leverage), as well as a good view of how the multiplier operates through intermediaries of central banks – including the role of "carried risk" with central banks' client companies (e.g., commercial banks that they lend to).

---

[4] Despite clear statistics from the US Bureau of Economic Analysis, with regard to the share of real-estate assets represented within the net wealth of householders, one will see the growth of this category and the recent brutal contraction in value – revealing a drastic decline of households' net worth.

AT THE CORE OF THE ISSUE: THE DEFINITION OF CURRENCY

To formulate an idea of the issue at hand, it is interesting to consider some pertinent figures (expressed in USD trillion – 2012), regardless of their underlying consistency.

A global financial pyramid

1. Central bank gold reserves	0.8 T
2. Cash and bank currency reserves (MO)	3.9 T
3. Value of assets owned by banks (BRI source)	39.0 T
4. Shadow banking system linked to CDS (ISDA source)	62.0 T
5. Asset bubbles, including real estate (est. P. Allen 2007)	290.0 T

In comparison, a sensitive issue relates to public injections of liquidity through "direct expenses or guarantees", a process pathway whose value was estimated to reach $1.9 trillion. This is not on the same scale as the 2007 bubble bursting (average 40% on shares, other financial instruments and real estate). The role of securitization instruments not only led to an increase of monetary supply, but also drove increases in monetary velocity of transactional exchanges (with various types of securitization instruments, it is not exceptional to witness an exchange of existing volumes). According to the Fisher formula (held applicable at the first level of approximation), the inter-crisis freeze on transactional exchanges and the resulting brutal collapse of the interbank money market (credit crunch) immediately triggered a violent recessionary effect:

$$M + V = P + Q$$

with M and V declining, and determining a decreasing Q (GDP) value.

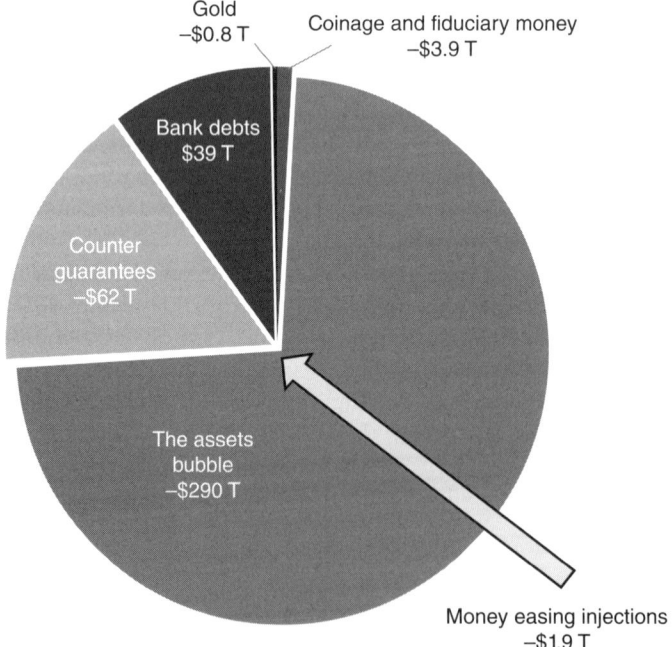

FIGURE 6.1   Allocation of global money supply (trillion $, 2012)

The above figures are not published by central banks but by various international monetary institutions. Figure 6.1 is taken from an article by Paddy Allen published in *The Guardian* on January 29, 2009. This bubble amount is not defined as the tool and definition, for it does not exist. We believe it has to be read as the amounts in excess of M1 and M2 with high volatility characterizing a bubble.

The results illustrate a fair view of the "multiplier effect" on bank reserves (leverage effect) and of the associated "incurred risk" involved. We will come back later (in Chapter 8) to the notion of a bubble that, to us, is related to the values covered by flows at certain levels of interest rates for each market, combined with rotation speed. If either the rotation and/or the flows slow down, values will go down despite recorded prices remaining stable. However, if the spread becomes too high we have a balloon that may burst. This is the reason for QE buying MBS and sovereign bonds to keep these markets fluid at a microeconomic level, and considering issuers because of balancing their respective budgets, which they may be unable to reimburse when the amounts issued are too high. Then they either have to play on regulation or interest rates to oblige issued money to ask for exchange at the reimbursement date.

THE NEW ENVIRONMENT: BROADENING THE DEFINITION OF CURRENCY

Today's central banks present definitions that are no longer adaptively matched to the realities of the "new money" of today.[5] If one accepts the huge phenomena of disintermediation and globalization of the economy, the degree of whose impact had previously not been forecasted, democratic principles of central bank surveillance are no longer operationally adequate at the level of comprehension required when considering the issuance of notes by central banks or the issuance of script money by commercial banks. Rather, to facilitate the survival of market economies in our time, the sum of all financial instruments that facilitate transactional exchanges needs to be considered, as well as convertibility between instruments. To do so at the outset, we need to summate the financial statements of all private economies and compare the resulting amount with the monetary base of one or more central banks.

Owing to the unfolding trend of global financialization, transactional exchanges exerting economic impact are posted at the corporate level, even if applicable transactions are concluded with individual (not institutional) counterparties. Already in place, the implementation of the European Automatic Payment Area (SEPA[6]) will provide for "real-time" aggregate data for clearing procedures executed through the ECB. In addition, the implementation of the Legal Identifier for Financial Markets (LEI),[7] as well as the protocol for unification of market

---

[5] Most professionals in finance, since they analysed the 2008 crisis, seem to be converging on this diagnostic. George Soros correctly denies the general equilibrium in the new paradigm of financial markets and opposes his reflexibility approach. Richard Duncan, an experienced long-time equity analyst specialist, set a theory he calls "the quantity theory of credit" to substitute for the quantity theory of money. "In recent decades, the usefulness of the quantity of money as a tool for analyzing changes in the economy has broken down because the extraordinary expansion of credit has made money irrelevant in comparison. The money supply is no longer the most important factor affecting economic change. It is the credit supply that matters now. Revise the quantity of money theory in a way that makes it applicable to the fiat money based economic system that has evolved since 1968."

[6] Single European Payment Area.

[7] FSB release June 8, 2012.

clearing principles (PFMI), disclosed in April 2012, are both aimed at the same systemic target(s) and thus support our description of how one should view today's monetary system.

As has been suggested, the disintermediation of conventional bank refinancing versus non-bank-mediated industry financing also reflects the necessity of redefining money in a broader context that transforms its identity and use in terms of a more diverse range of assets or liabilities. Such innovative trends are not subject to challenge, but rather the extension of tender money across any jurisdictions (if any) is questionable, including such money's virtually limitless use, purpose and amounts of denomination. Maurice Allais underscores this observation, namely: "The entire difficulties met (referring to the 1997 crisis) result from the fundamentally unrecognized fact that no decentralized market-based economic system can operate normally if the uncontrolled *ex nihilo* creation of notes and instruments [that constitute *'means of payment'*] can for a time escape the imperative of needed adjustments."[8] Thus, Allais justifies a monetary approach that he himself considers more global than conventional approaches based on regulatory compliant definitions preferred by central banks. Arising from this argument, we see the emergence of the concept that the more broadly defined monetary base actually exchanged during transactions continues to expand – compared with the more narrowly defined type of "liquid monetary base" which continues to contract as a result of prudential regulation implemented in the aftermath of recent financial crises.

Along these lines, an interesting paper was issued by OECD[9] that, remarkably, escaped attention, or was at least disregarded in contrast to the dominant monodimensional thinking of Alan Greenspan and other central bankers (with the notable exception of Canada) – who appear adept at following the type of uniformed thinking that is best reserved for publication in "unhealthy" academic reviews that they sponsor. Backed up by a strong statistical base, this important document concludes: "Rapid growth of financial activity and increasing fluidity flows between different types of institutions indicate that the usefulness of traditional monetary and financial indicators has increasingly degraded, to a point where monetary aggregates have emerged as unreliable metrics that tend to place increasing emphasis on exchange rate stability, while focusing on a wider range of indicators – in a manner designed to steer monetary policy to its ultimate goals." This key diagnostic conclusion, presented in our previous book, was similarly ignored, notwithstanding that our warning should have highlighted the dubious success of unrestrained "debt issuance" and accompanying disintermediation – also statistically described to a substantial extent in the aforementioned OECD paper. Regardless, such warnings have not prompted politicians to reform a "superficially happy" system where, on a daily basis, extrinsic levels of value grow for the benefit of portfolio owners and managers; growing every day for the benefit of portfolio holders – not understanding the pitfalls of burst-out phenomena and the premonition value of initial sentinels of impending crisis appearing as early as 2000 (i.e., seminal corporate scandals such as Enron, WorldCom, etc.). This first indicator of downstream instability called for reform, rather than regulation; the latter pathway being adopted at the time.

---

[8] Maurice Allais, Nobel Prize. *La crise Mondiale d'aujourd'hui : pour de profondes réformes des institutions bancaires et financières*, Editions Clément Juglar, 1999.

[9] Edey, M.L. and Hviding, K., OCDE/6D(95) Economics Department Working Paper no. 154, Economic Studies no. 25, "An assessment of financial reforms in OCDE countries", Paris, 1995.

NEW MONETARY AGGREGATES DEFINE EXTENDED CONCEPTS OF MONEY

As already discussed above, the authors recommend an extended form of monetary aggregates that allow for instantaneous ("real-time") observations of transactional velocity categorized by different types of assets and liabilities – and that provide an advanced system of monetary metrics in the absence of which "value-setting" methods, such as the "fair value" appraisals recommended by accounting standard setters, have limited meaning or validity.

Defining New Classes of Monetary Aggregates: M5 and M6

Facing the failure of macroeconomic deregulation and accounting standards that prevailed at the time of the 2007 crisis, a new MFI microeconomic regulatory regime is being developed. Without a general framework in place, however, the new regime may not provide better efficiency than its predecessor; specifically, as the field of monetary players that needs to be accounted for no longer presents precisely defined functional and geographical[10] boundaries.

The question at hand is to determine the feasibility of defining a "new monetary universe" that encompasses the entire global transactional space where economic quasi-monetary agents operate – and by observing that field to characterize component actions and ensure that individual sets of transactions do not generate collective risks. This field (global transactional space) that we propose to call M5 and M6 should: (1) sensibly consider most financial assets presently utilized for transactional exchanges and (2) provide the necessary follow-up on M5 and M6, including (3) monitoring their underlying asset base. M5 would correspond to all liquid assets and liabilities of enterprises, while M6 would represent the total asset values for all enterprises. The difference between the two aggregates (M5 vs. M6) would then represent assets and liabilities without counterparts (fixed assets, physical money, equity balances). These definitions should also allow for identifying the economic status of the holders and that of their counterparties, in a manner and with a scope that corresponds to contemporary reality and that does not stop at the boundaries of the traditional banking sector (and includes shadow finance, as well). In such a system, banks and other MFIs would stand among "other enterprises", whereas households and civil administrations would be deemed to own the entire value of their enterprises, in addition to their "private" holdings.

Solely by virtue of this approach, it would be practically feasible to avoid a burdensome level of microeconomic surveillance from impacting all enterprises – in particular because such a concept would be designed to draw present-day currencies and other forms of money back under the control of the existing economic and financial framework. The Napoleonic monetary world of the Germinal franc accomplished an analogous objective in the form of a return to metal currency. By today's standards, this would represent a comeback to coinage and fiat money,[11] including a return to the internal institutional use of scripted money, issued and operated by regulated entities – for example, via suppression of (and specific limits placed on) unrestrained securitization.

---

[10] The overlapping jurisdiction of the USA and Basel III adopted by the EU regulations and applying to foreign branches and subsidiaries is a supporting argument that, being irrational, it leads to a fractured financial world (Europlace Convention of January 2013 at the NYSE in New York). See minutes of round table on convergence organized by EIFR.

[11] The political impact of the July financial bankruptcy of the monarchy and the John Law banking system failure provide a historical reminder. See Chapter 1.

Given their unique institutional experience, central banks have a decent shot at effectively controlling the framework within which they have been set up. Through regulation, and driven by the institutional need to survive, central banks will generally utilize regulation to regain or maintain control. Attempts to reverse this tendency, for instance by utilizing means drawn from an idealized past model that is outside the scope of central banks' origin, is likely to fail. Much like the adage that toothpaste will not go back into the tube, the only consequence of such attempts would involve a return to centralized monetary management, thereby limiting monetary supply and its free use. A certain outcome would emerge: economic stagnation linked to insufficiencies in the nature, quantity, velocity and allocation of all forms of money. Although phrasing the basic question is fundamental, answering it in depth is far more complex.

An analysis focused on the "first-tier" consequences of a free currency supply faces at least three technical obstacles: (1) the capacity to collect very diverse information (instruments issued by all kinds of enterprises and non-regulated financial institutions – themselves required, or in some instances not required, to submit annualized financials to public and civil authorities); (2) territorial currency control (for instance, issuance of notes with dollar counterparts in tax haven countries) without regulatory oversight by the central bank of the denominated currency; and finally (3) an accounting focus concentrated on all the assets of the economy (these can in theory include securitized instruments, for instance in the form of a "substitutive category"). Because of the potential conversion of assets and liabilities from one category to another, including the potentially artificial transformation of an illiquid asset into a quasi-liquid financial asset, beyond the range specified by M5, the entire group of assets and liabilities (as well as balance sheet totals) should define M6, the global space for transactional exchange.

Analytical and Representational Tracks for Determining M5 and M6

For the determination of M5, an enterprise's balance sheet and P&L account is positioned at the optimal level of data collection, as most enterprises sort their assets and liabilities by nature or category, and thus provide a metric of enterprise activity via amounts of revenue that reflect rates of transactional rotation – for instance, when linked with sales to third-party clients or vendors – and the resulting receivables. From such data, it is then possible to determine a monetary aggregate, defined as "any asset item having a counterpart and thus having either the nature of receivable, debt or equity". The input for such a monetary aggregate will comprise any liquid asset or liability (each of them determining a ratio with the revenues and fixed assets and liabilities). On the contrary, assets considered today as being liquid (e.g., cash money) and corresponding to M1 would not be included in M5.

The ratio between M5 and M6 (the two aggregates that reflect "liquid vs. fixed" assets and liabilities) will indicate liquidity, a key factor in determining the sustainability of values. Bubble generation will be highlighted through consolidation, for instance by neutralization of investment values that would appear in those portfolios with values that are no longer coherent with profit flows and posted goodwill and/or intangibles. Forecasting burst-out phenomena will also be possible by observing a slowdown in the transactional speed (velocity) ratio. In an adaptive consolidation of financial statements, it will also be possible to determine inter-company financing, by separating receivables and revenues – depending on whether this manoeuvre is implemented with households or other enterprises that are, by law, required to keep books and records.

As surprising at it might seem to accountants and civil servants in general, or to central bankers specifically, the foregoing approach maintains an accessible synthetic knowledge of assets and liabilities. Concurrently, corresponding values remain readily available within financial statement totals – for example, prior to accounting consolidation that would cancel them by reciprocity (i.e., a receivable is an equal debt) – specifically, since such values reflect an appropriate measurement of "carried risks" similar to those defined during analyses conducted as a consequence of debates on the prudential set-up (Basel II and Solvency II). These analyses led to a consensus that determination of a leverage measurement was necessary. Furthermore, these totals, corresponding to what we define as M6, allow for the realistic measurement of a decentralized monetary supply, as long as receivables and debts are not immediately sold, and provided that the standards for balancing debts and receivables remain uniform from an accounting standpoint.

M5 and M6 correspond to a rupture within the make-up of classical monetary aggregates, particularly as the latter have limited applicability – as demonstrated by the fact that central banks and other institutions recognize an obligation to complement their aggregates with data and studies derived from national accounting systems. Moreover, it remains a given that the inventory approach (the base) cannot be appraised without information on exchange turnover (monetary transaction velocity). Accordingly, the bi-millenary concept relating to the volume of financing has become no more than a calculation trick, and a device of some utility in reconciling the legal qualification of commitments. In contrast, the transformation of assets and liabilities into corresponding categories has become a visible phenomenon that cannot be hidden from required observation. Owing to the progress in setting up-to-date accounting standards, it is important to establish workable limits to the double-entry concept (see Chapter 4), such that these remain operative only within certain thresholds of values and liquidity. When additionally considering "off-balance sheet" commitments – as they would be defined – we could then include two additional aggregates, designated M5′ and M6′.

Nothing, as regards this project, mounted in the common interest actually breaches the sovereign power of nations, and there is no obstacle that would prevent all nations from remaining within such a proposed system – with the exception of China (as long as its leadership opts for a non-convertible currency). Adopting the proposed approach may also allow for a debate, in that the current system is impeded by virtue of a variety of interfering factors.

M5/M6 and their Derivatives M5′/M6′: Determining Definitions and Uses

The purpose of M5 and M6 monetary aggregates is to detect contractual linkages that may emerge after inception of potential new categories of financial instruments (see Figure 6.2). In doing so, follow-up on any new monetary issuances is assured, as is effective tracking of ongoing transformation of transactional contracts and enhanced monitoring of economic dynamics. To actually achieve these purposes and objectives, it is necessary to monitor the original nature, functional design and flow of transactional contracts that generate both receivables and debts, including attached guarantees. By starting from inception to destruction, one can apprehend upward models as well as downward models both from legal (the legal nature of the instrument set by law, regulation and jurisprudence) and monetary unit standpoints.

Definition of M5

If it looks like what are called "financial assets", M5 is viewed in a more granular analysis, excluding anything and any appraisal that is not the result of a transaction and the resulting contract. An M5 component is a contract, a receivable, a debt or an equity contract set by commercial laws. M5 is defined as "any belonging with a counterpart having as a consequence the characteristic of a receivable, debt or equity". Among these are included the aforementioned liquid elements of assets and liabilities that are found in a corresponding balance sheet. It also comprises (in a segregated category) all the items that are defined within first-generation M1 and M2 monetary aggregate categories, including cash liquidity, bank accounts and bank loans or deposits.

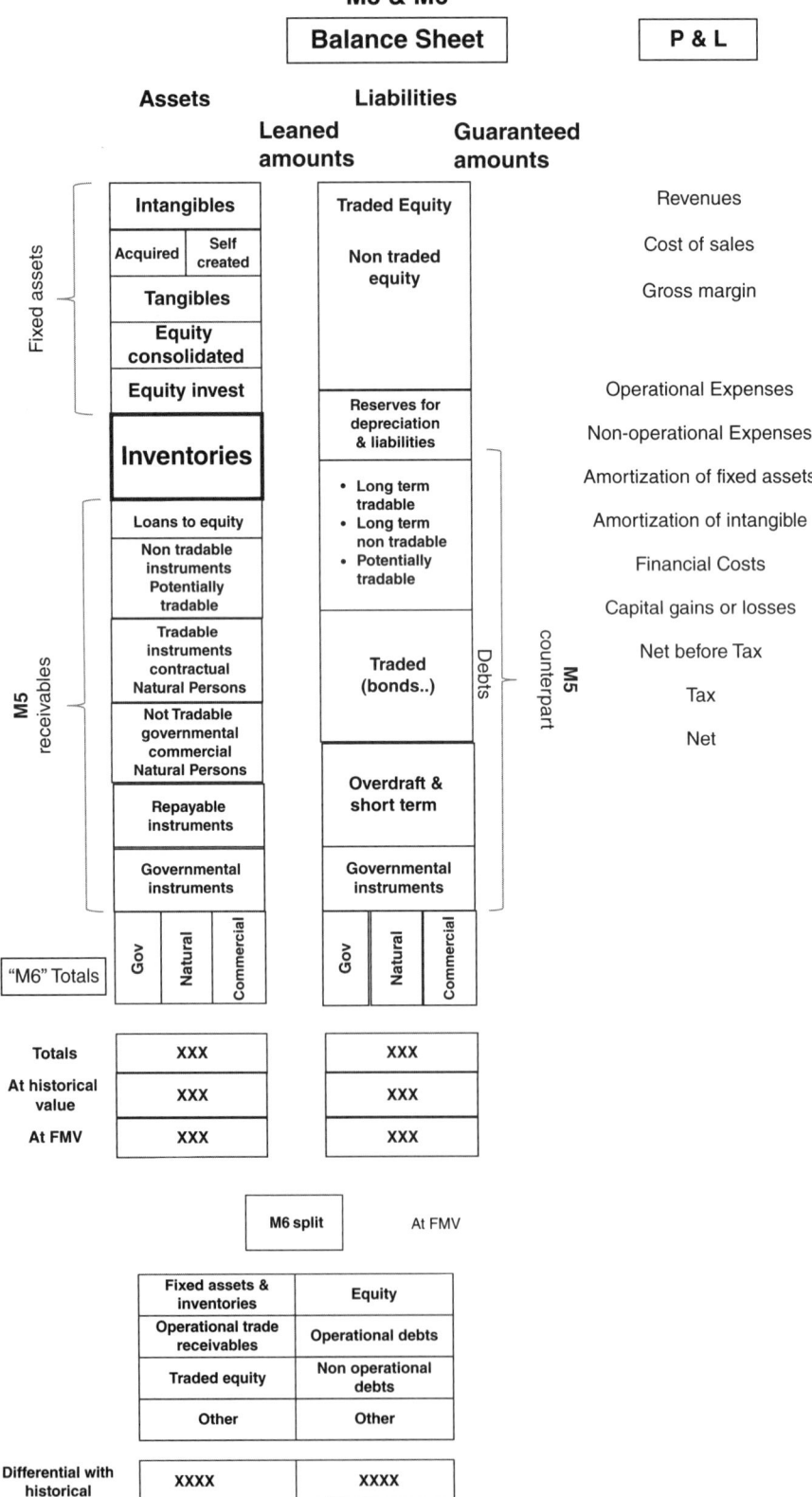

FIGURE 6.2   M5 and M6

The contractual terms that define an M5 instrument are always considered as being subject to revision, but only accepted as such under the following limited circumstances:

- The conditions at the beginning of the contract were fraudulent or unrealistic and the contract is therefore subject to breach or renegotiation if not simple default.
- The circumstances that emerged during the life of the contract were subsequently non-compliant with the entry circumstances that were contemplated when signed and the contract implementation is doubtful.
- The clearing process at termination becomes impossible (e.g., the goods to be delivered do not exist).

Laws and jurisprudence are the determinant of the analysis.

Conceptually, the measurements are no longer fixed in time and final at a given date, but rather are examined in serial fashion, with the underlying purpose of understanding monetary flows. To generate appropriate analytical lenses as tools, two "moments in time" and the transactional purpose are analysed:

- The moment at which the contract is concluded (generation of the client's receivable or applicable vendor accounts and other financial debits or loans).
- The lifetime duration – longer or shorter – of the contract.
- The purpose of the transaction – either financial in nature or producing tangible/intangible goods and services in the course of executing the contract.

Within M5, we then define various categories that identify potential or existing monetary instruments:

- Established M1 and M2 instruments (see Chapter 5).
- Receivables to be categorized, depending on whether there are private receivables (a client/vendor receivable) or regulated receivables (asset-backed securities).
- Receivables that are registered with a regulated market, if not hosted by an equity instrument.
- Traded equity instruments.
- Non-traded equity instruments.

All of M5 elements show a nominal value and a due date (cashable for M1 or infinite for perpetual). The difference between the nominal value and the posted value would have to be tracked as virtual.

If compliant with applicable regulations, a defined type of instrument can migrate and transform into another type of instrument. The instruments are viewed in terms of their attached transferability in addition to their above marketability (we have already discussed the conditions and attributes requested for an instrument to be money in Chapter 3).

By implementing such a categorization system, legal and regulatory systems can easily be developed and implemented, if not already in widespread existence (for instance, as is the case for maintaining metrics on receivables). One open issue is the significant progress made in market regulation (i.e., since the outbreak of the recent economic crisis). Regarding the role of new financial instruments, it is a renewable issue that comes under automatic review and control – in recognition that the components of instruments are fluid – but generally remains grouped via the original category in force at inception of the instrument, assuming this covers all required elements for component analysis and assigning a given type designation for the original instrument in question. We will see in Chapter 7 how our theory reconciles with the effort deployed to set a more resilient financial system.

One exception involves non-recognized instruments that would otherwise not be listed on a regulated market or recognized by law – these will not be accorded the same privileges or recognition when being posted (assuming that this is even allowed). For instance, the sale of real-estate properties is subject to licensing formalities in most countries – when such formalities are not satisfied, the sale cannot be opposed to third parties and cannot be posted on financial statements.

Definition of M6

M6 is a representation of the global space for transactional exchange, and is defined as the total of the relevant balance sheets of enterprises, administrations and non-profit entities. As noted, the difference between M5 and M6 represents assets and liabilities without counterparts (fixed assets, physical money, equity balances).

Segregation and Derived Aggregates: M5′ and M6′

We have seen that the M5 components needed to be segregated between elements registered as tradable on regulated markets versus instruments in other marketplaces. Laws governing instruments and markets (including marketplace governance and trading rules) will provide the definitions required for segregating traders, markets and instruments. Collection and clearing, default consequences and trading volume/velocity will be disclosed factors that facilitate classification.

M5′ and M6′ are equivalent to the basic M5 and M6 aggregates, but also incorporate associated derivatives and guarantees, thus adding or reducing the resulting excess in value or insufficiency generated by the latter's inclusion. Guarantees will also have to be segregated between those attached to the instruments (leans; when not shown in the analysed balance sheet, those attributable to a third party, the markets where traded and finally the guarantee mechanism). The guarantees granted will also have to show separately if they are attached to an asset or generally from the balance sheet and P&L.

Data collection requirements

- *Applicable data must originate from yearly financial statements.* This means that each country much have a financial statement collection system, a requirement that is implemented in most countries, at least through tax filing.[12]
- *Financial statements must conform to a predetermined scope of observation.* Enterprises keep books and records as legal entities, but in doing so they may consider several entities reported as being one entity under the control of one centre of management. In such cases, multiple coupled entities may produce consolidated financial statements. Subject to the rule that the financial statements of a single enterprise cannot be counted twice by two consolidating entities, the proposed "new monetary aggregate"-supporting data

---

[12] In all European countries, yearly financial statements of corporations are deposited with a trade registration board or equivalent. Not for SMEs under certain thresholds. Tax filing requirements are not completely identical between countries, but nevertheless very close within Western Europe. Convergence of standards is on the table of economic government in Europe, if not about tax rates at least about determining the basis.

collection system should be based on consolidated financials, so as to neutralize the potential effects of non-existent exposure to intra-group vendor and client balances.

- *Territorial and perspective scope of observation.* Enterprises are often registered to operate over a nationwide territory, both on a stand-alone as well as a consolidated basis. Enterprises that are included in both a domestic and foreign territory will have to be segregated with precision, regarding the relevant monetary zones – both with respect to their balance sheets and exchange transactions. This separation will allow for the amendment of current estimates of international exposures – it should be understood that these are inaccurate when viewed from the internal context of a single monetary zone. The reason for this is that a significant percentage of banking activities are subject to balances recorded as "exposures", when in fact such values are merely client/vendor accounts, such as is the case for an automotive manufacturer providing its vehicles to a local distribution subsidiary – in this instance, as a matter of fact there is no exposure, as the inventory shown in the export position is in fact the manufacturer's own inventory. The value added per company – a transnational approach – conducted by the WTO in its last report (2013), and all comments about where the value is located, is of course more meaningful than the data of gross exchanges that are of limited use when considering, as is necessary, who the beneficial owners of profits and resulting monetary surpluses are. With high balances due to gross in trade, monetary issuances and full exchangeability, this is the only possible approach but, like the speed measurement of M2 conducted by the Federal Bank of St. Louis, data for a comprehensive analysis requires M5 and M6.

A special remark has to be made about derivatives for which the accounting standards for reporting the off-balance sheet data are not sufficient and will have to be developed further. One of the disputed matters is the contradiction between the concept of independence between closings imposing a parallel treatment between revenues and expenses and linking them with the period of time covered by the financial statements under review and the hedging of future operational periods which are to exist; this is relevant to post-period operations. Companies' operations do not stop at year-end. Hedging of these future operations may have to be made.

The segregation of nude derivatives or of derivatives not linked to an instrument or which have a duration in excess of the instrument's is a key issue. They will either be tradable on a regulated market or not because of being traded between companies. The volume of derivatives pertaining to the first category will be known under the regulation currently implemented for derivative financial markets. The second category will not, and will have to be aggregated separately and linked to an organized category of issuers. These derivatives contribute to the stability of companies hedging their investments, assets and operations – for instance, a food company would commit deliveries of poultry to a chain of restaurants or a retail distributor at a set price, while the production is not achieved and will depend, for its cost, on the price of soya beans. Such a company has to hedge the cost of soya beans at an appropriate price. This example, where nothing is yet posted in the financials, is one of thousands. Indirectly, the derivatives are also at the same time a guarantee attached to what we have classified as monetary instruments.

However, these last assessments are only true up to certain thresholds, and lead us to again analyse the link between the microeconomy and macroeconomy. Over such a threshold, nude hedging generates a systemic risk that has to be monitored with the exchangeability of instruments' measurements and available free equity levels. It will be a concern for the surveillance modelling that we will see in Chapter 8.

Other aggregates (derived from analysis of financial statements)

- All revenues (as defined by accounting standard setters – bills and accounts receivables should reconcile with tax filing in some jurisdictions, but will be uncertain to some extent because of "cash-basis accounting" which is differentiated from the "accrued accounting method").
- The global output of an entity (production): in the aggregate, this value should recoup GNP – defined as the sum of all added values.
- The value-added factor – that is the difference between "billed production" and in-sourced subcontracting activity.

The Utility of M5 and M6 Aggregates

The financial conditions for monetary or financial instrument holders or their delegates can vary, for instance if the quantitative measurement of consolidated contracts leads to a potential impact on the clearing of balances and particularly if analysis of such quantitative measurements is significantly modulated from either a macroeconomic or microeconomic perspective. (*Example*: A given contract is valid, but revenue accumulation creates a concentration factor that enables bargaining against the counterparty, such that the latter may pay less or be paid more than the instrument's nominal value.) One analytical advantage in the use of M5 and M6 aggregates would be added stability.

FROM A PRACTICAL POINT OF VIEW, WHAT ARE THE DATA LIMITATIONS FOR DETERMINING THE VALUES OF NEW MONETARY AGGREGATES?

The data collection of balance-sheet information is currently at stake in the USA – where the only available data are the IRS files for corporate taxes and the SEC files for all listed companies. In Europe, companies are required to file, and deemed compliant when they do so, with the Registrar of Commerce. What information is currently legally available, how it is currently dealt with and by whom are questions to be explored further – however, such data is increasingly available in Europe, given data exchange standards defined by various taxation administrations.

What Information Will These New Aggregates Yield?

First and foremost, one impact of these new monetary aggregates would be to improve the existing statistical base: at present, both the Bureau of Economic Analysis[13] and Eurostat[14] issue "net worth" schedules by institutional sector (Households, Non-Financial Corporations, MFIs, Financial Intermediaries, Other Financial Vehicles, Governments, Insurance and major Foreign Corporate Entities). European statistics data repositories rely mostly on data streams fed by Europe's central banks. This data is categorized based on asset type, distinguishing tangible assets from both financial assets and liabilities – in doing so, this helps determine net financial

---

[13] Based on NIPA chapter 7.
[14] ECB 2005/5 Guideline and ESA 95.

worth. The requisite financial assets are classified only in terms of their legal nature and may be entered in a separate line intended for receivables that are not instruments. This European set-up complies with intrinsic European regulations, and its system of operation is quite interesting as it converges conceptually with our own views. For instance, it disregards gold, as well as special drawing rights (SDR), which, by definition, are not designated as liabilities. As we have already noted, the above set-up disregards any changes in value that are not generated by "real transactions". In doing so, the results generated may be compared accurately with GDP.

Nevertheless, all papers[15] complain about insufficient data. As they are compiled from lower-level sources of collection, existing statistics are based on accounting classification rules and cannot be linked to exchanges. As a result, such statistics will not show the causes of possible shocks – and even obvious ones (e.g., the sub-prime crisis) resulting from the decline in value of real estate as transmitted through instability in financial instruments. This weakness in present data systems, which fails to illuminate major crisis trends, reflects the fact that inherent links are basically not macroeconomic. Rather, they are impacted by market volatility and the speed of monetary rotation (monetary velocity), a phenomenon that differs from one financial market and one instrument to the next, in part depending on government-associated guarantees. Such statistics also largely miss the impact and status of foreign instruments holders, and their ultimate beneficiaries – who cannot be tracked and followed from one jurisdiction to another without specific transnational agreements.

A New Aggregated Conceptual Approach Allowing Operational Transactions and Financial Ones to be Reconciled

M5 assets are distinguished from M5 liabilities as well as from trans-territorial consolidations, which would now yield a consolidated trial balance with foreign subsidiaries. So as to ensure consistency and combat fraud, each balance sheet composition is at historical value. M5 assets will be analysed on a monetary basis. Out of this base, tradable instruments from M5 + M1 and M2 elements will define *total liquidity*. All the usual financial ratios (i.e., debt to equity) will be available.

When analysing M5′ and M6′, we evidence the nature of the link and its flexibility between realized operational transactions (commercial exchanges) and the financial world of money. This link is only analysed (if useful) by sector. For instance, for the construction sector because of its contribution to GDP – usually between 60% and 80% – and the duration of the associated financing, with MBS going up to 30 years and burdening the balance sheets or because of securitization, agencies and hedge funds outside the banking system. The global analysis was missing in the USA in 2007. Because of a change in the size of jurisdictions, because of globalization and the overall exchangeability of instruments (see later), such analysis is needed and will be allowed.

The Resulting Breakthrough

Better knowledge. Because the M5, M6 aggregates and their derivatives (M5′ and M6′) "comprehend and assess" the entire scope of the monetary landscape, this capability resolves both

---

[15] The FSB April 18, 2012 report and OECD annual report complain about the need to improve the data by making it more detailed.

the issue of risk surveillance versus unachievable surveillance and the regulatory requirements to monitor patterns of "shadow monetary movement". Being inside the perimeter, there is no longer any shadow money per se (see prior definition). Any price-denominated contract is potentially money, if not already monetized. By introducing and using the future M5/M6 monetary aggregate system described here, the entire securitization process that almost destroyed the monetary system in 2007 now becomes hypothetically controllable. The difference between original historical values when underlying instruments were issued and the traded price of the newly structured instrument that was issued in substitution or exchange becomes visible. It is transparent and the price lag can be appraised. Spread risk linked to both the original debtor's quality and slowdown in rotation is measurable.

Enhanced security. By considering that any price-denominated contract is *actual money*, the door is now open to general regulation that protects the democratic rights of individuals and enterprises. Instruments which are clearly defined from a legal aspect (in terms of their attached guarantees) can be registered with a regulated market (as was originally expected but did not materialize with CDSs). Such next-generation instruments may now also receive a recognizable, attached guarantee either from the marketplace (alongside clearing insurance funds) or, in addition, from government agencies. Besides sanctioning representational fraud, there is no further need to regulate players when they don't operate with individuals. There has been resistance to the views already described in our previous book *Virtual Money*, but the FSB-supported LEI project[16] demonstrates *de facto* recognition of the need for a globalized aggregate system.

Additional breakthroughs that would also prove advantageous

- Measurements of *monetary velocity* would result from a comparison of production with receivables and vendor balances. Even if not a physical measurement, these would nevertheless provide a necessary indicator of economic health and performance. Thresholds are to be determined as *possible versus artificial* (e.g., by comparing workforce capacities with revenues, or number of lunches with number of existing people, or oil consumption with number of engines, etc.).

- The evolution of balance sheet totals by asset classes, compared with revenues and production, would provide several forward indicators of bubble creation or advance signals of upcoming burst activity risk.

- New indicators will be developed that allow horizontal and points over time to be compared. For instance, we show the difference between M5 and M6 at historical traded values and market values of the same category of M5 financial assets. This will give information to market surveillance authorities. Further, we will see that system stability indicators would be possible (after Chapter 4).

Change of paradigm. The use of the credit multiplier ratio as informative data makes no sense, since many non-bank entities can issue money by granting the authorization to open an account in their books with an open balance authorization. Being tough, the multiplier concept is misleading for students. The multiplier is simply a reduced measurement of velocity of flows in the banking system.

---

[16] FSB press release of June 8, 2012, "A global legal entity identifier for financial markets".

However, the overall paradigm is just the social contract of money acceptance or rejection with a sampling instrument. It has always existed, but there was no data collection system to comprehend it. Explanations were only made when a failure happened (and was treated, or was the cause of a rupture by revolution or war). We will come back to that later. M5 and M6 show the difference between effectively posted prices and values, exerting the effect of speed and masses.

DEFINING NEW MONEY – THE DIFFERENCE BETWEEN SHADOW BANKING MONEY, VIRTUAL MONEY AND THE NEW AGGREGATES

Legal Segregation between Different Types of Money, Depending on Underlying Guarantees and Transferability

Although shadow banking exists conceptually, it fails to meet the quality of precision for acceptable regulatory thresholds and judicial validation, by virtue of the fact that "shadow banking" processes involve complementary overlap between the monetarily regulated banking versus non-banking space. In the first reports issued in response to the Seoul G20 request for investigation and systemic risk control of shadow banking, the required precision is lacking. In the USA, the scope and definition of banks functioning inside the FRS is historically determined – some legitimate banks are in the system, while others are not. Being differentiated in this manner, not all US banks are subject to the same type and level of regulation, a frontier that is not finalized and which may vary in proportion to the size evolution of respective banks. On the other side of this spectrum, there is no ongoing attempt to define what instruments may be used as money equivalents and along what electronic frontiers, new means of communication or direct private clearing routes money may be used without foreseeable limits. In such an environment, the democratic impetus for protection of the individual requires that laws be stable and intelligible – in this context, there is no sound regulation to be considered.

Monetary instruments differ, depending on the practicality of their non-restricted transferability and/or intrinsic guarantees. The latter is similar to the consistent intrinsic exchangeability between monetary dollar bills (old for new) or, to provide an externalized example, a warrantor guaranteeing asset liquidity (mortgage-backed securities) or backing up that liquidity via leans (ABS and MBS). In the latter case, if liquidity proves to be absent, evolution is still possible. The market values subtending such different categories will vary over time, but not the commitment that their sampling is likely to confirm until renegotiation. The difficulty with inventorying guarantees for detailed analysis of M5 is their diversity and the fact that they overlap with different events and amounts. This is why, for clarity, they need to be defined precisely and kept segregated before being looked at.

Given the reality of different monetary instrument types, the unlimited possibility of financial innovation and the latitude for transformation that a free economy requires to be efficient, one approach aimed at also considering the M5 monetary aggregate design includes the need for a detailed analysis regarding the nature and velocity of monetary flow. In this regard, the border between shadow and non-shadow money is entirely artificial and should be jettisoned. As the reader will note, we detailed the link between shadow and non-shadow monetary flows in Chapter 3 (i.e., when commenting on the associated connectivity between shadow money and the banking system on the one hand, and the FSB report that covered this issue on the other hand).

SHADOW BANKING IS DIFFERENT FROM VIRTUAL MONEY

Shadow banking differs from virtual money, the latter being defined as M5 and M6 aggregates with subcategories M5' and M6'. The M6 aggregate is required because it allows for reconciliation between countries that permit the offsetting of balances, and those whose bankruptcy laws do not. This constitutes a major difference between Europe and the USA, with major consequences as to "book content" and "prudential ratios". As noted (Chapter 3) in the previous discussion on shadow banking, we consider that the conceptual border should be defined precisely as regards tangible or intangible goods to be detained or evaluated for transactional exchange versus money – or extended money fitting the dynamic M5 definition, namely money that will be needed to clear the exchange. Using such an approach, gold is not money but a mere asset. Money itself is a sampled contractual instrument deemed acceptable by a market participant.

With such an approach (M5 and M6), everything that is monetary in nature will override the phenomenon of shadow banking, causing the latter to dissipate. The "connected refinancing" that the FSB considers is of the same nature as any other form of financing, and as derived from accepted accounting practice follows the rule that balances are individually equal. Only negotiations and the judiciary can change the reality that a monetary framework is an organized world with rules that constitute a social contract. The shadow banking approach is just an attempt to extend the banking scope to analyse the latter's operational process of refinancing.

With the M5/M6 system, boundaries are set by institutions that receive monetary deposits, whatever their nature. These institutions are directly responsible, and the prior artificial distinctions between the definition of M1 money, bank account deposits and cash financial instruments also dissipate. By adopting such an approach (M5/M6), we adhere to the legally defined reality of risk, namely the legal failure resulting from the transit between good standing and failed standing. Debts are due for their nominal amounts, as are collections.[17] Systemic deposits of financial instruments make the depositor responsible not merely for their value, but for their post-deposit existence.

QUESTIONS AND ANSWERS

Redefining the Monetary System and Measurement of Monetary Flows

What is money?
   Von Mises said: "Can economic calculation comprehend everything that is exchanged?" When he wrote, gold and the metallic system was still the base for money but he already understood that "his" money could not represent an image of the exchanges for economic calculation. We concur totally with what Von Mises said a century ago.

How do we define money?
   We distinguish between potential money and money. Potential money is any asset used to satisfy a debt. The most common and practical ones for insurance purposes are receivables. As soon as they are accepted by more than the issuer and the debtor, we have a potential monetary instrument, if its stamping is recognizable and the term defined. Is being claimable for exchange by a third-party holder the criterion?

---

[17] Shearman and Sterling papers, December 2012 (see Argentina's public bond issues).

*What do we witness about the monetary classical aggregates and the use of money? What
are we witness to when looking at the facts and what writers say in general? (See "At the
Core of the Issue: The Definition of Currency".)*

Central bank money is no longer significant amount-wise. M1 and M2 are limited. The
assets of banks are 10 times what the traditional money of M1 and M2 is, giving a sensible
idea of the way the credit multiplier functions. However, assets that would be considered
as being inside an asset bubble – a value expression – show three times the value of M2.

What do we propose to replace classical monetary aggregates?

We propose M5 and M6. M5 counts for all receivables and debts on balance sheets
totals, meaning those with counterparts. M6 consists of the balance sheet totals which,
in comparison with M5, provide the value of what are owned assets with no counterpart.
M6 combined with M5 and P&L provides a value variation of asset classes subject to the
non-use of fair market values in the way which is currently standard. More M5 and M6
comparison with revenues provides the currency velocity.

What will the velocity indicator and variation of amounts provide?

They are key indicators when analysed by type of instrument, and with markets, to address
problems of slowdown or bubbles.

What are the difficulties in determining new aggregates?

The first one that has to be resolved is the definition of what a group is consisting of
a single economic entity. Inter-company receivables and debts that are not limited to
a national territory should be balances as well as transaction values showing on their
individual P&Ls for consolidation. Definitions already exist to address this difficulty.
There are issues, especially in the USA, about financial statement information being
provided other than to the tax administration, and not being only a statistical sample.

CHAPTER 7

The Monetary System

"The one who aims at becoming knowledgeable, has to deal with money regulation"[1]

— **Bata batra 175b**

INTERNATIONAL EXCHANGES – INTERACTIONS AND MONETARY ZONE COHERENCE

There is no possible monetary system set-up without a regulatory system that guarantees the link, meaning the measurement language between posted numbers and exchanges, to ensure acceptance from users and to pursue social goals. Money requires a sufficient space of use that can only result from trust and jurisdictional authority, usually both intricately mixed. Logic leads us to start from where we stand in terms of regulation. We think we have sufficiently explored money as a concept to cover our general needs. We are still missing international exchanges, though. Having tried to comprehend what money is, the issue of looking at the international monetary system that, not surprisingly, has changed since WWII is now to be analysed.

Even if still formally or implicitly existing as set after Bretton Woods, it has been deprived of its post-war purpose, and moreover in 1971, as we have already seen, of its mechanisms to ensure a currency basis. More recently, it has been reconsidered and completed to give face to the 2007–2008 financial crisis that hit the entire world with, until now, no definitive answers and international decisions. With consolidation of political entities, the jurisdiction where money is in use and its optimization are also at stake as a question for the international forums that may be able to find a way and decide on a new system: the G20, the IMF or any forum where major countries can convene.

---

[1] Babylon Talmud, 1st century AD. This recommendation underscores the overall function of money as a topic restricted to the best people (think rabbis).

GENERAL FRAMEWORK

As its ideogram indicates,[2] meaning both danger and opportunity at the same time, the crisis can also be used as a new start. The threat of a systemic collapse that prevailed during a few weeks during the autumn of 2007 determined some analysis about what is grounding the market economy and liberalism, of which a few points emerged. To start with, the crisis never caused sufficiently harm to justify, for the most part, challenging the fundamentals of the market economy openly. Despite the financial, industrial and social disequilibrium generated by the delocalization of the production means to optimize the use of resources, the improvement in standard of living of the populations who were parties to exchanges seemed to remain the referential economic criterion.

Nevertheless, the limits to the system justify corrective actions in the course of an international coordination, which allowed the G20 to set up a new meeting place associating young emerging nations with economically mature countries for better worldwide economic regulation. The success of corrective measures in the monetary field, but also regulatory and tax set-ups in an open system, is subject to strong coordination. Without such coordination, no fight against monetary dumping or derivative instrument deviance effects with regard to economic responsibilities and tax havens is possible. For the time being, the G20 has only demonstrated its efficiency in the financial field during the peak of the crisis. Since the calm down and bank refinancing, the system has been insured again in most western countries and the sense of urgency has disappeared from the scene. Convergence on regulation and accounting standards that were set as goals at the Pittsburgh September 2009 summit have now vanished. The SEC is not considering the use of IFRS standards for the time being, and the Basel regulation will not be joined by the USA in the foreseeable future. The slowdown of the economy that is being experienced by western economies, including the USA, when putting aside the effects of stock exchange prices on GDP seems to suggest that the result of QE is not sufficient for governments in terms of the very high rates of unemployment hitting countries either with little independent voice (like those of Southern Europe) or that are used to such a situation. Either way, political risk is disregarded like it was after WWI, or considered as no one's responsibility in the absence of international leadership.[3]

The blindness or absence of action will not resolve the matter of restoring growth and facing the challenges of societies that have changed – with longer life expectancies, low demography and pollution in a world that has double the number of inhabitants since WWII. One may wish that the G20 could take hold of the other important matters regarding the finality of the necessary new system and its durability. The outcome of the Copenhagen summit in December 2009 on climate change and the absence of financial help measures for the planet's poorest countries at the level of expectation (they were expecting 100 billion dollars – less than a few per cent of the recovery plans), clearly illustrates the preference of big countries under budget constraints for national expenses. The following G20 meetings confirmed the loss of speed in reforms that followed the Pittsburgh September 2009 meeting. The USA will no longer launch a Marshall Plan to benefit industry, as a big chunk of this industry has been transferred to countries with low labour costs. Without the contribution of major countries such as China, what progress can be expected on these key matters? The launch of a new international order is more than ever on the agenda, despite the obstacles, and due to today's

---

[2] 危机

[3] Chancellor Angela Merkel from Germany raised concerns about the situation in Spain at a G20 summit at the end of 2012.

absence of conversion of this ambition into tangible realities, the G20's creation can only be considered as the first (and only) political step towards achieving something. Its goals regarding the handling of the risk to the monetary system, and the agenda which has already been set to deal with technical questions, should involve an agreement on common economic aspirations, the fields of regulation and surveillance, that could be shared or designed together.

Over the political matter of the sharing of sovereignty and the philosophy grounding the accepted model, if we remain on the monetary issue, common surveillance should allow homogenous regulation.

Both regulation and surveillance have to aim at several targets. The first is to fix an appropriate framework to ensure the coherence of instruments, the operation and efficiency of financial markets, and the reality of risk control. By nature, this framework should be flexible and should consider two main elements:

- First, the induced effects of a risk control system that may generate worse systemic dangers than none (this was the case when the 2007 crisis started triggering massive sales orders on financial markets).
- Second, the classical perverse effect of any regulation on traders themselves who are able to get around any imposed processes by engineering, including changing the jurisdiction in which their markets and instruments are dealt with. Even managed money, for significant amounts are subject to a global world where the liberty of transferring domiciles is a principle in the same way as the liberty of individuals.

Only a shared general philosophy can address these two issues. It has still to be designed, taught and understood – as guidance for the judges and courts that need to have a similar philosophy.

If we had to list the matters to be dealt with in this environment, we would have the following basic items: improvement of surveillance and regulation through efficient agencies, revisiting the accounting standards (with the idea that standards are the basis for the information system that is needed for the markets, the traders but also for all economic agents – employees, vendors, customers, civil agencies as IRS, etc. and not only the investors), the reform of the monetary system, with reforms of the banking system and tax system, the reform of the laws setting the statute of instruments and the liability of actors of the financial chain, the reform of the independent auditors' duties and the framework of the auditors' profession, and ultimately a shared concept of household protection and moral behaviour for the market. We are far from that system, legal set-ups still being national, and have favoured financial market fragmentation that makes the interests of market participants in opposition to those of their clients. For instance, the self-limitation of bonuses is not going to have any effect on independent brokers who are usually former bank executives and experts at getting the margins. Worse, being hidden, it will slowly convince the public of a mafia system between a professional being in or out of the system and being linked by a common carrier interest.

DESCRIPTION OF THE CURRENT OPERATIONAL SYSTEM: DISTINCTION BETWEEN NATIONAL AND INTERNATIONAL SYSTEMS

The current system distinguishes between the national system, usually headed by a central bank and using a national currency, and the international monetary system, which links most of them as a global layer. This distinction goes back, at least, to ancient Greece. Plato (*The Republic* and *The Laws*, describing his ideal city and political set-up) considers the domestic money used between free citizens and the international (foreign) currencies that the Republic will take care of by changing the coins, melting them or using them in international trade.[4] In *The Republic*, Plato recommended a "law that would forbid any individual to hold either gold or silver".[5] It was a currency control system. Money, at that time, already had all the attributes of the money that we knew up to the 20th century. The new international monetary system is framed by the fact that national currencies are almost totally freely convertible – with the major exception of the Chinese currency. Nevertheless, we note that to have a statistical follow-up, regulation provides that effective payments between monetary zones are usually to be conducted either through the central bank or a bank delegated to centralize the currency international exchanges. We hereafter concentrate on the international system, not without a glimpse at the ongoing process of European integration and what the boundaries of a monetary zone are, as well as the boundaries (if any) between micro-surveillance and macro-surveillance, a coordination issue.

THE CURRENT INTERNATIONAL SYSTEM

The International Set-up

Despite changes in their goals due to the 1971 breach of the link between the dollar and gold, and a change in philosophy, all the international institutions that were created in the 1944 Bretton Woods agreements – the IMF, World Bank and BIS – are still in existence. Some, such as WTO, were added to follow up on the change in economic philosophy from an internationally controlled one towards free trade.

Since the final unilateral fall in August 1971, triggered by the USA, of the July 1944 Bretton Woods agreements influenced almost totally by the end of dollar convertibility at a fixed rate into gold, we live under a system of moral understanding with the 1976 Jamaica agreements where participating countries[6] agree to let currency exchange rates float. Since the Milton Friedman era[7] and the fall of the Iron Curtain in 1990, the free market economy with free trade has become an accepted religion. Europe was and still is (in 2013) in trade surplus, the USA in trade deficit.[8] The idea was that if the Chinese currency was undervalued and left free to fluctuate (which is still not the case), it would adjust to give relief to the US economy. The missing understanding of participants is that China, while keeping its Communist political organization, adopted the free market economy competitive system with the extraordinary success that we know (again, see the statistics in our previous book), keeping full control at the same time over their currency. The diplomatic efforts put into China to let its currency float

---

[4] *The Laws*, book V notes also Plato's concept: "From there the need for a market place and of a currency sign of value of exchanged goods" (French translation by Victor Cousin) and the distinction between merchants standing to exchange in the "Agora" (the central meeting place of the city) and traders who would travel to get the goods to be exchanged.

[5] *The Laws*, book II, paragraph XII.

[6] See www.cvce.eu. Interim Committee of the Board of Governors of the IMF.

[7] Milton Friedman (1912–2006) – economist and leader of the Chicago School of Economics Nobel Prize in economic sciences – was an advisor to President Reagan. He inspired the FED's monetary policy to answer the 2007–2012 crisis.

[8] See US Bureau of Census – US Bureau of Economic Analysis and Eurostat.

never achieved anything. Religions, even if philosophically sensible in being as dogmatic as laws, will never adapt to the real world and convince anyone against their own interest. Self-interest will usually win against undefined and remote common interest.

Besides the new regulatory set-up in each of the monetary zones, and the G20, there is little to say about the current international system. Since the Jamaica agreements of 1976, the current system relies on the IMF byelaws. By itself, the system, which is no longer based on gold, has switched to an ongoing negotiation system through the informal G20 we have been talking about and that gathers at least twice a year with an agenda of general goals summarized in a press release.[9] However, the G20, as a result of the 2007 crisis, is not an agreement on how the monetary system should operate but a mere forum. It aims to cure the causes of this crisis by better regulating financial markets and the financial system's surveillance. From a monetary perspective, putting aside the regulatory absence of direct power, the agreement is simply to let the currency exchange markets live out their life with a commitment from member states not to intervene. The agreement is really below the level of what member states would agree to, as one can guess that in the case of erratic variations the board of the IMF would convene and call for interventions. Negotiations are, in reality, ongoing between the major monetary zones over how to converge in the field of accounting and surveillance standards but not on the topic of monetary issues.

Where there is an agreement in the form of an understanding is on how to operate to salvage a financially troubled country. The set-up of intervening forces will depend on which country is being treated – small ones are to go to the IMF, medium-sized members of the EU to what is called the Troika gathering of experts from the IMF, the EU and the ECB. The ESM and IMF are to give financial support to the limit their respective equity allows. There is also a convergence and similarities about the surveillance system and the need to have a resolution process for troubled banks.

Nevertheless, even if the IMF lost its core mission and was reduced to being a kind of consulting firm and a surveillance institution without authoritative power, and a lending institution, all of the international institutions that were created with the Bretton Woods agreements would remain in existence.

What is called the international monetary system as such comprises today the following transnational leading institutions, gathering most of the world's countries to handle currency-based international functionalities, and to facilitate a globalized trade of goods and services within the underlying concept of a global free market economy:

- The International Monetary Fund (IMF).
- The Bank for International Settlements (BIS).
- The World Bank Group (WBG).
- The World Trade Organization (WTO).
- The nations' various gatherings of heads of state and/or finance ministers plus the IMF, G20, Troika and Ecofin.

The International Monetary Fund

The IMF, with 187 member countries and the WBG, with 188 member countries have kept the general goals and organizations they were designed with.

---

[9] The last meeting was in Melbourne, Australia on June 6, 2014.

Purpose

The IMF's duties are set in the updated article 1 "purpose" of its byelaws:

(i) To promote international cooperation through a permanent institution.

(ii) To facilitate the expansion and balance growth of international trade and to contribute thereby to the promotion and maintenance of a high level of employment and real income, and to the development of the productive resources of the members as a primary object of economic policy.

(iii) To promote exchange stability, to maintain orderly exchange arrangements among members and to avoid competitive exchange depreciation.

(iv) To assist in the establishment of a multilateral system of payments in respect of current transactions between members and the elimination of foreign exchange restrictions, which hamper the growth of world trade.

(v) To give confidence to members by making the general resources of the Fund temporarily available to them under adequate safeguards, thus providing them with the opportunity to correct maladjustments in their balance of payments without resorting to measures destructive to national or international prosperity.

The main reason for the IMF is set out in (iii) above; the ultimate goal assigned to it was to avoid repetition of the vicious circle of competitive devaluation. However, behind this goal was the reality of the gold reserves of both the USA and the IMF itself coming from its member states. After decades of war (Korea and then Vietnam being the main ones), implicit conflicts such as the Cold War and inflation in the exchange rate, these gold reserves were no longer either adapted to the nominal value of circulating money if claimable or to the expansion of the world trade and financial development that was to take place after.[10] Therefore, the international community decided to create a new international reserve asset under the auspices of the IMF – special drawing rights.

In 1969, SDR appeared to complement national currencies and support the fixed exchange system. The purpose was to allow loans to those countries that needed to refinance their external exchange deficits. The SDR are claim rights against the freely usable currency of IMF members. 21.4 billion was originally issued, but after the last increase in 2009 the issued amount is now 204 trillion (equivalent to US$311 billion). The purpose of this money is to be used between countries with an external trade surplus to support those in need. The money is determined by volume in proportion to dollars, euros, British pounds and Japanese yen in theory, based on their respective share of the international trade and central bank reserves.[11] As a consequence of the grounding concept, this proportion has to be revisited from time to time and this is done through a board. The last revision was in 2010 and the next one is due in 2015. In October 2011, the Board of the IMF was submitted a debate on the possibility of revision before that date, but this was rejected. The value of the SDR results as a set proportion of the various referential currencies above evaluated at market price. It is also a unit of account for the IMF and some other international organizations. The drawing rights are available to each member country in proportion to their capital stake in the IMF. Up to this proportion there is no interest charged between members.

---

[10] Originally, 0.888671 grams of fine gold equalled 1 dollar.

[11] US$0.666, €0.423, Y12.1, £0.111.

As opposed to any receivable created against a transaction, SDR are not money but more of a clearing process of countries – those in balance of payment surpluses and those with payment deficits. It does affect directly the national currencies and the books of the economic agents in these countries, but may add up to guarantees given to the issuers of debts through national central banks that will be able to buy currency-denominated instruments and therefore take action on the currency markets. We note immediately that the system as designed (and there is no surprise in this) is in opposition to the philosophy that dominated the world after the USA abandoned the gold reference of "no intervention" in the currency exchange market. It was created in 1969 to support the system that ended in August 1971.

What is interesting in the SDR system is the value determination decided by a special executive board of the IMF that is supposed to convene at least every 5 years, if not before as a case of urgency. The value is determined in dollars and published every day on the IMF website. It results from a mix of euros, yen, British pounds and US dollars. The proportion of each currency expressed in dollars will be determined by microeconomic aggregates to ensure that it reflects the relative importance of such currencies in the world's trading and financial system. With effect as of January 2011, it was reassessed so as to fairly represent the value of exports and reserves.

Staff

The IMF has a staff of around 2670 coming from 154 different countries, half of them economists based at its headquarters.

Governance

With 188 member countries, the IMF has kept its general goals and organizations. With a new capital structure extended to emerging countries and through its board of governors representing 24 member countries, it is still a key gathering place to be taken into account as an international governance body. In addition to its General Manager, Mrs Christine Lagarde of France, there is now a First Deputy Managing Director from the USA and three Deputy Managing Directors – one from China, one from Egypt and one from Japan. Two important committees operate to advise the Board, the IMF, the Financial Committee and the Development Committee.

Because of its still influential role, quotas in the IMF capital and voting rights are important topics as well as its governance. The allocation is deemed to reflect the position of each member country in the global economy.[12] A reform was decided in April 2010 (under the 14th general review of quotas). The proposed reform included an amendment to reform the Executive Board, also with 24 members, to move to an all-elected Executive Board. This reform has still not been achieved, the required quorum having not been reached.[13] The Executive Board is composed of eight directors representing the major countries – USA, Japan, Germany, France, UK and China – and 16 directors in constituencies representing between 4 and 22 countries.

---

[12] Looked at through GDP and blended GDP, meaning directly for 60% and PPI adjustment for 40%.

[13] Press releases no. 12/499 and 13/127 on reforming the Board; the required quorum is 3/5th of the 188 members representing 85% of the Fund's total voting power. In April 2013 only 71.3% of the total voting power has approved the Board reform. The quota increase approval only requests a quorum of 70% of the total voting rights, which was reached but still has to be completed.

The Executive Board's duties are to set new members' quotas and quota increases, SDR allocations and to propose amendments to byelaws and articles of agreement. After that, and with this last unachieved revision of quotas and voting rights, the USA will remain the dominant country in the institution.

Quota share (after revision still to be enforced)

USA	17.4
Japan	6.5
Germany	5.6
UK	4.2
France	4.2
China	6.7
Russian Federation	2.7
India	2.7

Source: IMF website, June 2013.

The IMF's revised duties are[14] to promote international cooperation through a permanent institution. To summarize according to its byelaws (see the IMF website release of August 2013), the IMF is to provide loans to its member countries experiencing balance of payment problems and to provide advice to troubled countries with economic policy advice. To fulfil its lending role, the IMF has several loan structures depending on need and a country's issues (Extended Credit Facility (ECF), Standby Credit Facility (SCF), Rapid Credit Facility (RCF) with no interest, Stand By Arrangements (SBA), Flexible Credit Line (FCL), Precautionary and Liquidity Line (PLL), and Extended Fund Facility (EFF) for longer-term needs where interest is charged). This financial assistance is deemed to enable countries to rebuild their international reserves, stabilize their currencies, continue paying for imports and restore conditions for strong economic growth while undertaking policies to correct underlying problems. The IMF distinguishes between the poorest countries that are granted concessional terms (meaning charging no interest to them) and non-concessional terms where interest is charged. The access limit is typically a multiple of the country's IMF quota.

It should be noted that in 1969, before the formal abandonment of the Bretton Woods agreements, there was an attempt to fix the matter of providing money to those countries in

---

[14] Set out in the article 1 "purpose" of its updated byelaws:

(i) To facilitate the expansion and balance growth of international trade and to contribute thereby to the promotion and maintenance of a high level of employment and real income, and to the development of the productive resources of the members as a primary object of economic policy.

(ii) To promote exchange stability to maintain orderly exchange arrangements among members and to avoid competitive exchange depreciation.

(iii) To assist in the establishment of a multilateral system of payments in respect of current transactions between members and the elimination of foreign exchange restrictions which hamper the growth of world trade.

(iv) To give confidence to members by making the general resources of the Fund temporarily available to them under adequate safeguards, thus providing them with the opportunity to correct maladjustments in their balance of payments without resorting to measures destructive to national or international prosperity.

need. This was the design of the SDR complementary reserve money for national currencies. It was created to support the fixed exchange system. The purpose was to allow loans to those countries in need, to refinance their external exchange deficits. The SDR are claim rights against the freely usable currency of IMF members. They survived the official abandonment of the fixed exchange system and the Jamaica agreements with free currency exchanges that could not mean a total loss of control – not acceptable for the simple reason that exports and imports are dependent on exchange rates and the world, the troubled country for its imports and its counterparts for their exports are immediately concerned when the trade volume is significant. Being contagious, political unrest that results from or causes an economic failure is also at stake. Article (ii) (see footnote 14) remained in the IMF byelaws as a general goal, and so the SDR came about.

Issues

As an existing international agency the IMF is, so far, the only organized forum where nations can gather to issue new money if needed. The factual influence of the IMF is linked to the fact that in borrowing money from the IMF the troubled country becomes committed to following its economic and tax policy recommendations, and that when split into tranches, loan transfers are subject to reaching the set economic goal achievements.

Because of its lending and economic analysis competences, the IMF overlaps with some of the World Bank's duties and capacities. Both institutions coordinate through the IMF World Bank Development Committees (see below). This role – the sharing of duties with other international institutions – is certainly to be debated, as well as the governance of the IMF when dealing with separate matters if in the future extended like SDR.

The Bank for International Settlements

Conceived to manage the payment of damages after WWI, BIS was definitely established in 1930. Since then, after the troubled period of WWII, it has continued to operate as a clearing house between central banks. After Bretton Woods and the decision to keep it alive adding to that settlement function, it became a support centre for central banks. Besides helping to stabilize some currencies in the 1970s (the French franc and the UK pound), and contributing to some IMF actions, it helped in the creation of the European Monetary Union that later became the European Monetary System. Also in its support function a statistical centre, the Irving Fisher Committee on Central Banks Statistics (IFC) was created as an economic research centre. To fulfil its support and coordination functions between banks, BIS sat, among others, on two committees: one for prudential surveillance – the Basel Committee for Banking Supervision (BCBS), called the Basel Committee; and the Solvency Committee for the Insurance Sector (International Association of Insurance Supervisors (IAIS)). The BCBS received a mandate to identify sources of stress in global financial markets. It comprises representatives of 27 member countries. BIS also has a committee on payment and settlement systems (for depositary and settlement infrastructures). All of these committees issue standards to become regulations when endorsed by nations. The whole system relies on commitments from member states. When not endorsed, they have no transnational legal value.

With no hierarchic link but technical resources, BIS also became the home for the FSB, which is now the central body for the international surveillance scheme. The capital is 600,000 shares, 400,000 having so far been issued, representing 3000 million SDR as defined by the IMF. They have been allocated to the 60 member states through their respective national central banks. The majority stake of the issued capital is owned by Belgium, France, Germany, Italy, the UK and the USA. A board of 20, usually the governors of the central banks, manages the institution. It currently employs a staff of around 650 from 54 countries.

Through the G20 forum of heads of state, the Basel and Solvency committees of no legal grounding have gained reconnaissance. The G20 countries have committed to adopt a regulation programme with goals including the commitment to adopt Basel's and Solvency's committee recommendations. BIS is very much the place of expertise and bank representatives.

An informal committee of experts factually representing the most important private financial institution is operated by BIS. With the paramount importance of the Basel and Solvency committees, BIS gives an important contribution to surveillance and regulation for banks and insurance providers. It also provides a statistical collection tool for international clearings and prudential ratios.

The World Bank Group

Along with the IMF, the WBG is one of the international institutions created by the Bretton Woods agreements. With a staff of employees and consultants of around 10,000 scattered in 130 countries, the WBG comprises the Internal Bank for Reconstruction and Development (IBRD) and the associated International Development Association (IDA), as well as the International Finance Corporation (IFC). The IBRD, IDA and their subsidiaries aim to reduce poverty in the middle-income and creditworthy poorer countries. IDA focuses on the poorest countries. They assist these countries by providing both technicians and monies in a project-based approach. Credit support is made through loans and guarantees. The IFC provides credit to the private sector in poor countries and also finances infrastructure projects in any country if private finance is lacking. In 2011, $46.9 billion was lent for 303 new projects. The total of ongoing projects was 1800. In 2012, $35 billion was lent for new projects while the Multilateral International Guarantee Agency (MIGA), created in 1988, was revived to provide guarantees including political risk insurance for the financing of long-term heavy infrastructures which are difficult to finance with the banking system.

To illustrate what international monetary institutions and their financing arms have to address in terms of development, we provide in Table 7.1 a schedule of life expectancies in some major countries.

TABLE 7.1 Life expectancy in major countries

	Age	Rank		Age	Rank
Japan	83.91	1	United Kingdom	80.17	9
Italy	81.86	2	European Union	79.76 (2010 estimate)	36
Canada	81.48	3	United States	78.49	50
France	81.46	4	China	74.80 (source China)	69
Spain	81.27	5	Brazil	72.79	123
Switzerland	81.17	6	India	67.14	160
Netherlands	80.91	7	Russia	66.46	163
Germany	80.18	8			

Source: CIA with exceptions (China).

The World Trade Organization

The WTO is a more recent multilateral international institution. It resulted in 1995 from the GATT (General Agreement on Tariff and Trade) and governed the execution of the 60 agreements that concluded the Uruguay round in 1994. With 159 member countries or custom unions – the latest countries joining being the Russian Federation on August 28, 2012 and in the first quarter of 2013, Laos and Tajikistan – its primary purpose is to open trade for the benefit of all. See Figure 7.1.

All WTO members may participate in all councils, committees, etc., except Appellate Body, Dispute Settlement panels, and plural-lateral committees.

To achieve its purpose, it has a statistical follow-up on international trade, conducts studies on the obstacles met and also operates on disputes.

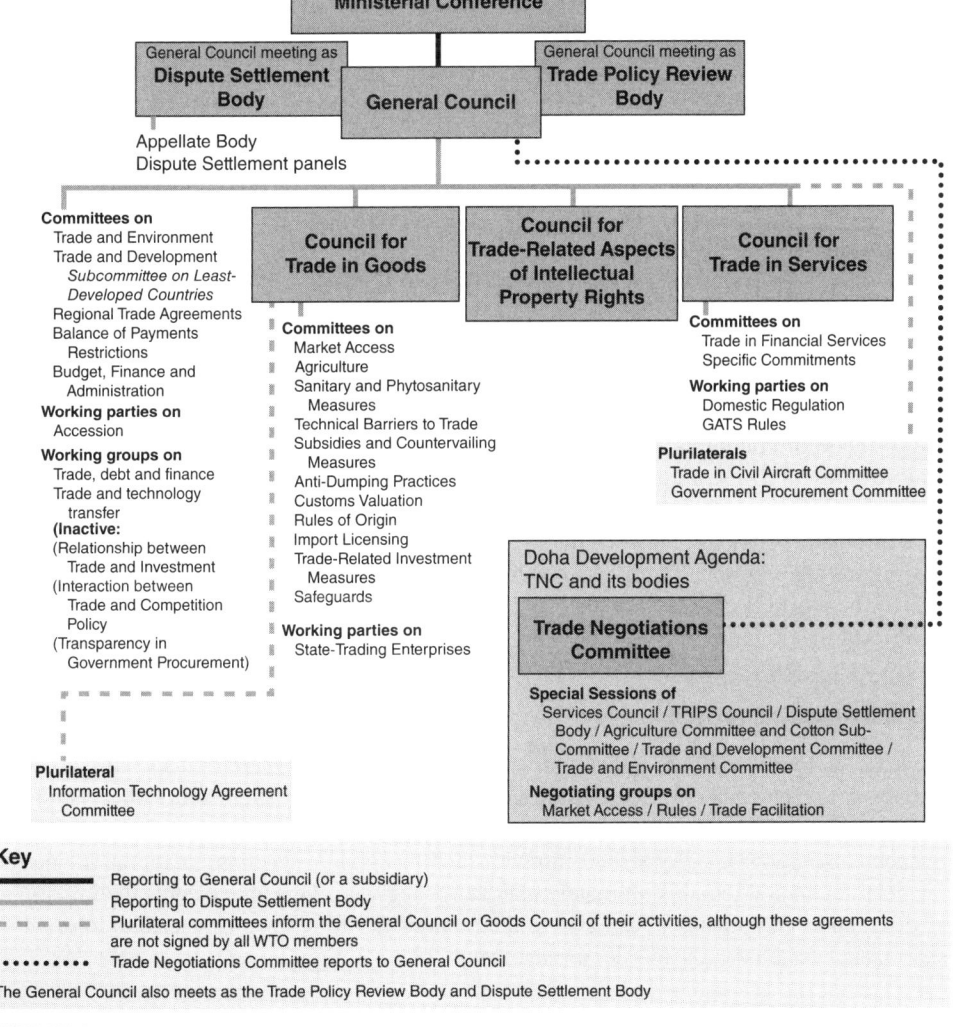

FIGURE 7.1 WTO structure
Source: WTO website.

Major disputes creating obstacles to a level playing field are often raised at the WTO by major industries. An emblematic example is disputes about the governmental subsidies or loans to aircraft projects for aircraft manufacturers. This is the dispute between Boeing and Airbus. Currently, there are 182 dispute cases before the WTO arbitration. 27 new disputes were filed in 2012 and a big one, the "banana dispute", was settled. The WTO also tries to assist the 30 non-member countries in meeting the conditions to join.

INTERNATIONAL COORDINATION

G5 to G20

After the USA put an end to the convertibility of the dollar, and with the dollar crisis of the 1970s, there was a need for coordination to stabilize exchange rates while the IMF could no longer reach its purpose of a stable exchange system, and where the United Nations' multi-lateral system with other humanitarian and cultural roles was inefficient. Also, countries such as Japan and Germany, now again great industrial powers, had to participate in inter-national cooperation. In Rambouillet, France in 1975 the G7 met – France, Germany, the UK, Italy, Japan and the USA; Canada joined one year later, the G7 becoming the G8. The idea was to set an informal system gathering together the key economic western powers and Russia as the USA could no longer be the only one on which the stability of the monetary system could rely.

In September 1999, it appeared that restricting this informal committee to the G8 was no longer possible and that other key countries had to be present, such as China, India, Brazil, Pakistan and Mexico among others. In 2008, with the new financial global crisis and with the initiative of the French President, the G20 became institutional despite the absence of a treaty to set its purpose and powers. Nevertheless, the G20 created a multi-lateral mode of communication that allows progress and may allow negotiations between senior representatives of countries and international organizations that know each other. It has an agenda of what to achieve and issues press releases. The most recent press releases have often been common between the IMF, the G20, ECB and EU.[15] As a matter of fact, the institutions are reciprocally represented to each other. The General Manager for the IMF as well as the World Bank sits in on the G20's meetings. Actions like country reviews are often conducted in common.

The G20's Reasons to Exist

The reasons for the G20 are rather simple. We are reminded of them by its Chairman, Mark Carney, in a September 5, 2013 letter to the G20 leaders for their September summit in St. Petersburg: "To further complicate matters, financial markets and many of the largest financial institutions are global, but – notwithstanding agreements on international standards – financial regulation remains ultimately national or regional. This underscores the importance of the support G20 members can give to their authorities to remove obstacles to information sharing and establish cross-border arrangements for resolution."

---

[15] Los Cabos, June 18–19, 2012 on the IMF and its relationship with the G20. Press release and common press release on Greece with the EU, ECB of October 17, 2012.

The Coordination of Goals Assigned to the G20

In the Washington 2008 meeting, leaders committed on behalf of the countries they represented to fundamental reform the global financial system: "The objectives were to correct the fault lines that led to the global financial crisis and to build a safer, more resilient source of finance to serve better the needs of the real economy. At that and subsequent Summits, the G20 called on the Financial Stability Board FSB to develop and coordinate a comprehensive framework of reforms. By reducing the risk of future financial crises and the consequences of financial instability, these reforms are an essential contribution to the G20's primary objective of strong, sustainable and balanced growth."

We will add one comment to the FSB Chairman's letter. The logorrhoea of phrases about the progress that has been made since Pittsburgh in each of the successive reports to the G20, and the need for "strengthening the FSB capacity" (title I of the September 5, 2013 report to the G20, St. Petersburg meeting), besides being usual for that kind of institution, may jeopardize its own credibility. Nevertheless, it should not hide the capacity of some of the BIS teams subject to coordination needs to handle projects. BIS, for instance, adding to its ongoing previous projects that failed to prevent the crisis, such as Basel II and Solvency, is to follow up several specific projects. One of them relates to improving data collection (data gap initiative DGI of November 2009 due to the gap in economic and financial statistics) – an inter-agency group of the G20 and a specific one on counterparts in banks' refinancing through a projected template. If this template were to cover the entire scope of money instruments, which is not the case, or at least encounter shadow banking, it would be going in the right direction. Also, a subcommittee, the cross-border cooperation committee on crisis management, may become useful at any point in time if placed under the political leadership that only today G20 may represent.

Troika

Troika is an informal gathering of experts issuing from the IMF, and two constitutional bodies of the EU (the ECB and the Commission), created to follow up on the decisions taken in May 2010 to support the Greek financial crisis and lend it money. With the infliction on Greece of a strong corrective therapy for its budget imbalances, it raised a lot of resentment from the Greek population, and they asked for it to be dismantled. In between, to the contrary, lending entities such as the IMF, EU bodies and so on were not and could not give up oversight of public money. The role of this gathering was to be reinforced with Portugal, Ireland and Cyprus crisis follow-up that needed coordinated action between international bodies. The IMF's participation in lending to some European countries with expert support inside a monetary zone is at stake. In the future, it may be replaced by the ESM that we will see later, and that will have the legal power to lend money as the ECB did not because of its byelaws. Nevertheless, Troika was set up as a consulting and governance surveillance informal gathering but was approved by its initiators, which is interesting. The fact that the ESM could replace the IMF for interventions inside the Eurozone of the EU does not remove the need for international cooperation between monetary zones. It also raises interest in distinguishing between areas of expertise, lending capacities and voting rights inside international monetary institutions. Permanent evolutions of the economy and the impossibility of agreeing upon optimum criteria to measure such evolutions because of its political national implications make changes to voting rights difficult and necessarily slow. This does not mean that participants don't agree regarding the quality of the expertise and the goals of action; that is at stake when considering international monetary reform. Sometimes, moral authority is more efficient than a factual legal power to impose. It gives more flexibility in appraising a situation and for the corrective actions which would follow.

MICRO- AND MACRO-PRUDENTIAL SURVEILLANCE AGENCIES' FRAMEWORK[16]

It seems a sociological rule by which societies, and more specifically their institutions, cannot self-reform. Reforms can only happen when triggered by external negative events. We have to distinguish between macro-prudential financial supervision and micro-prudential supervision. Micro-surveillance, even if it failed, already existed in both the dollar area and in Europe. What was missing was macro-prudential surveillance, which was addressed internationally through the creation of the FSB and, in each zone, by its equivalent. The European issues were different from the US ones as, besides the ECB, no transnational agencies existed and a full reorganization was needed. In the USA, it was more a matter of filling the gaps and addressing the failures that the 2007 crisis showed.

The setting up or reorganization of existing agencies decided in the USA (law restoring American financial stability of July 10, 2010), known as the Dodd–Frank Act (DFA), and in the EU with several European Council's decisions[17] and international trans-European treaties, are the first steps. The EU is an unaccomplished political structure that is still on its way to integration. The early stages allowed for speculations, so that even if slow, speed of action does not necessarily mean ineffectiveness when goals are clearly being set. Nevertheless, the different political set-ups between the USA and its European counterparts cannot hide their general failure to anticipate what happened in 2007, and the fact that there have been unanswered or wrongly answered warnings before. In 2000, what was attributed to financial scandals (WorldCom, Enron) should have raised attention other than simply attributing the scandals to insufficient regulation which needed to be modified or completed. What was said to be caused by a bubble and wrong-doings was just a symptom of the monetary crisis.

The diagnostics were done at the national level as well as some regulatory (SOX law and equivalent) answers mostly implemented at country level, with limited international coordination.

The structural monetary issues at the international level were not addressed and had to wait until the crisis broke out in 2007 just to be analysed; the persistent incapacity to address them is still there in 2014.

The lack of perception by central banks, often subject to very restrictive constitutional frameworks, of the very strong evolutions of the financial system and of the risks generated by asset inflation, bubbles and debts had to be dealt with. Institutions when created are always justified – they hire, they exist and as any human body they compete and try to achieve goals

---

[16] From the European Council release on June 9, 2009 recommending the set-up of a European risk agency that was, thereafter, agreed.

[17] The EU's system of government is very different from the US one, with a much longer legislative process that cannot be overridden by a central government to push legislation directly to the European Parliament, as none exists, and each country keeps its own legislative rights until a European Directive is adopted that it can always complement.

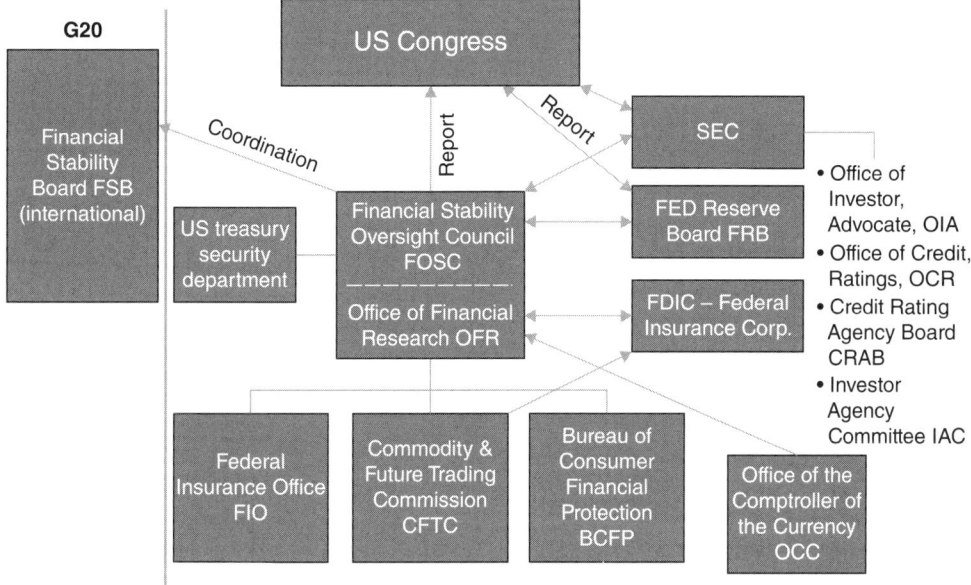

FIGURE 7.2 The US macro- and micro-surveillance set-up

and survive. On the reverse, they are not easy to self-reform and certainly not just by the virtue of multiple voices requiring them to do so.

To answer these insufficiencies, the G20 at the international level decided on a global agency – the "Financial Stability Forum"[18] – that will succeed a pre-existing but non-operating body, the "Forum of Financial Stability". Without any corresponding legal statute, this new forum will only have an alert role and no sanctioning power.

The corresponding US set-up is complex and not systematic. It distinguishes between banks depending on their size (less than 10 billion in assets, more than 10 billion, more than 50 billion in assets) and between Federal and State jurisdiction to split the duties by sector and purpose between multiple agencies (new agency to protect the consumer of financial invest-ments outside the SEC). Without reconsidering it the USA created, to mirror the international set-up, the Financial Stability Oversight Council (FSOC) that gathers 10 of the financial regu-lators to follow up on systemic risks missing during the crisis. It also extended the fields and powers of existing agencies such as the FED and SEC and created new ones such as the Office of Financial Research with a new data centre and both a research and analysis centre (OFR) within the treasury department and a new agency – the Bureau of Consumer Financial Protec-tion (BCFP) – as well as an authority for the resolution of financial institutions which was missing during the crisis. See Figure 7.2.

---

[18] It gathers the member states' supervisory and regulation bodies in the fields of banking, insurance and markets as well as international concerned institutions (OCDE, BIS, IMF, Basel Committee, IASB, IOSCO, IAIS). Besides the European Commission it comprises the following countries: Argentina, Australia, Brazil, Canada, China, France, Germany, Hong Kong, India, Indonesia, Italy, Japan, Korea, Mexico, the Netherlands, Russia, Saudi Arabia, Singapore, South Africa, Spain, Switzerland, Turkey, the UK and the USA.

The EU on its side has created the equivalent counsel to the FSOC – the European System of Financial Supervision (ESFS) – which is part of the European Stability Board (ESB).

These new bodies have their heads. Unfortunately, they are not backed up by global analysis or political leadership and, for the European ones, are striking inside the limited European budget to get their financing while the US ones are financed within existing agencies.

The key and pre-emptive issue of national strategies is not to regulate with set goals but to know how they will determine enterprises to invest, innovate and manufacture the products their fellow citizens want to consume or provide the services they expect in a globalized world.

The goal of these agencies could first be to suppress the excessive and perverse regulations that characterize the financial information and the financial and judicial system to operate in unified and simplified principles. The extension of a general law (for financial instruments and accountability of all agents of the financial chain) of tools and information concepts (of which accounting is just one element) should become the lead road map for these agencies to reduce the field of necessary regulation. Transparent concepts should allow actors to know what their duties and obligations are to commit their liability.

This creation of agencies to survey the systemic risk is further justified as no common agreement exists over the functioning of surveillance and regulation, and their respective field of competence or statute, with financial professions having different risk exposures and time cycles: ones regulating and ones overseeing, ones dealing with insurance and ones dealing with banks. Should they be separated or unique?

The obvious answer was to coordinate both inside each of the monetary zones and internationally. However, again, coordination does not mean the capability for action and sanction. The FSB has been established to coordinate at the international level the work of national financial authorities and international standard-setting bodies and to develop and promote the implementation of effective regulatory, supervisory and other financial sector policies in the interests of financial stability. It brings together national authorities responsible for financial stability in 24 countries and jurisdictions, international financial institutions, sector-specific international groupings of regulators and committees of central bank experts. We also note that the FSB reports to the G20 on the progress achieved in the deployment of the decided scheme of surveillance and regulation (see Figure 7.3).[19]

The EU – with its recent Eurozone component and smaller financial markets than the USA and the UK – mostly dealing with non-UK money, was totally missing a global surveillance system. The European Commission sat in October 2008 to discuss the "High Level Group on Financial Regulation". The Group, headed by Jacques de Larosière,[20] delivered a report in February 2009. This report, with 29 recommendations, grounded the new European surveillance system as since developed. It first distinguishes between two levels: the macro-prudential level with the ESRC and the micro-prudential level with the ESFS. In reality, de Larosière had a deep knowledge of the issues relating to the crisis, as a conference he gave at Columbia University in February 2010 shows. In this report we not only see what we have said about fair market value but also the question he develops even more in his speech of the connection between asset prices and leverage, with a lack of surveillance of central banks and a need to reconsider the entire system and its goals.

---

[19] September 2013 report to the G20, available on the FSB website.

[20] Former Governor of the Banque de France and former General Manager of the IMF. See also his sharp analysis on the causes of the 2007 crisis in a conference given at Columbia University in December 2010.

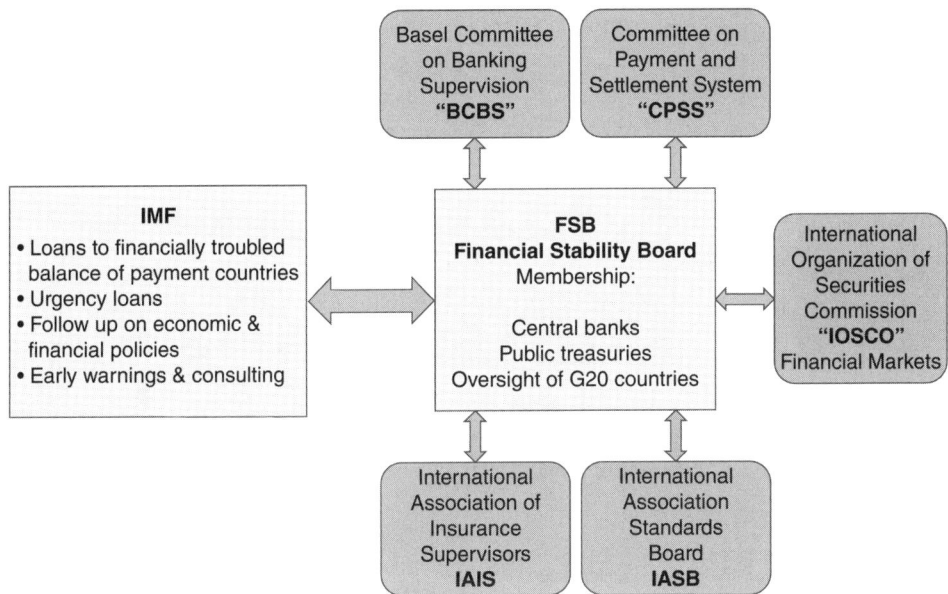

FIGURE 7.3   G20 decided international surveillance system chart

The solution ultimately adopted by the EU for the ESFS is to have three agencies: the EBA (European Banking Authority) for banks, the EIOPA (European Insurance and Occupational Pension Authority) for insurance companies and pension funds and the ESMA (European Securities and Market Authority) for markets. This is different from the pre-existing set-up prevailing in the USA, which keeps the framework of surveillance agencies specialized per objective as they are already defined and adds one (the SEC) for protection of the financial consumer. The general organization of these European agencies has been revisited in the course of establishing the Banking Union. Grouped as the European Supervisory Authorities (ESAs) of the ESFS, they are now[21] under the authority of the European Central Bank (ECB). See Figure 7.4.

The Transnational Coordination Goals

With Washington and the meetings that followed, the G20 leaders, considering the reasons for the crisis, self-assigned four goals: (1) to increase the resilience of their banking system against crises; (2) to suppress the "too-big-to-fail" criterion used to decide whether to support a bank at the taxpayers' expense; (3) to regulate the derivative markets' handling commitments of such unknown values that they cannot be faced; (4) to reduce shadow banking.

An FSB report dated September 5, 2013 was issued to the G20 leaders in the process of implementing global financial regulations to achieve these goals. With Basel III, the resilience topic is addressed with member countries committed at term (2019) to follow on common set cushion standards. The report raises two issues – the first is the calculation of capital needs.

---

[21] The European Council adopted this proposal on 9/12/2012. As we will see below, from the Banking Union agreement of December 2013 the ECB's authority over the globally systemically important banks (G-SIBs) and transnational banks will become effective on November 4, 2014.

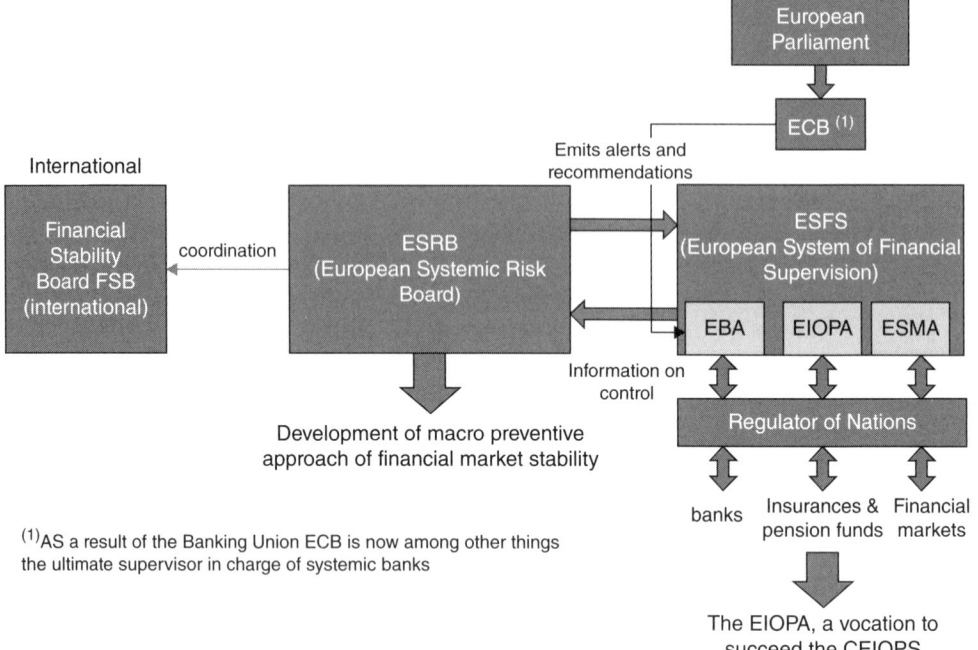

FIGURE 7.4   European surveillance frameworks
Reinforcement of net equity: Which harmonization of game rules? Future frame of European regulation

It is noted that the way monetary zones and countries calculate their capital needs to comply with the debt ratio shows worryingly large differences. The second issue is that the leverage ratio has not been agreed upon.

We know and further see that the resolution of financial institutions is almost organized, as well as the clearing of derivative markets, but that the market regulation arbitrage chasing capital from regulated spaces to less regulation is not, and then there is the matter of shadow banking. In our opinion, these last two matters make the goals self-assigned to G20 members inefficient for achieving their ultimate purpose of guaranteeing financial stability. To us, the reason is that they are missing a global approach that a common reporting template for banks and all systemic institutions, if one day achieved, will not replace. The means and methodology followed by G20 members is just wrong. In our opinion, this comment doesn't reduce the need for the G20 forum. We will elaborate on this topic following a dead-end road with the combination of excessive debt, more stringent prudential ratio requirements and appropriate scaling of interest rates to let the economy decentralize its decisions (policies to increase equity on both sides of the Atlantic are a dead end).

With the Solvency II directive on November 13, 2013 (a European trilogue revision agreement),[22] the EU addressed the matter of a single set of prudential rules for insurance companies, mutual and pension funds within the new European political entity, with the goal of having a revised Directive adopted by March 2015 and for its implementation in January

---

[22] https://eiopa.europa.eu.

2016. For this sector falling under "shadow banking" there is no convergence goal between the two sides of the Atlantic.

We believe that the High-Level Group on Financial Supervision, headed by former IMF General Manager Jacques de Larosière[23] (that, of course, is restricted to EU weaknesses encountering global topics on rates and macroeconomic imbalances, as well as regulatory, supervisory and crisis management failures; see Chapter 1), should have been the basis for the reforms still to achieve. Only the regulatory aspect was dealt with, and global structural issues as well as imbalances are still a threat that regulation is not combating.

COORDINATION ISSUES INSIDE THE EUROZONE AS OPPOSED TO INTERNATIONAL

Despite the action of the FSB, competition and coordination between the new agencies is still a concern because of the basic obstacle of sovereignty that not all western countries will agree to give up, and also because of pre-existing systems of law and a long tradition of banking regulation which is consequently very different from what happens in Europe from one country to another. A revolution is being achieved with the banking Resolution and Recovery Directive to be implemented over two years with centralization of supervision by the ECB. Some topics are still in need of fine-tuning, including the need to know if the processes are organized with a single point of entry (SPE) giving the national authorities of the bank group holding the prevailing authority or with multiple entry points (MPE) depending on where the operations are located. Over time, cooperation between national authorities under the BCE umbrella will achieve this fine-tuning and keep the necessary flexibility to cope with diverse and unlimited operational realities. If significant progress (already noted in Chapter 6) has also been made in the matter of having a unified system of identification for markets (LEI) as well as for individuals and common Principles for Financial Market Infrastructures (PFMI), some key matters – if internally organized – are not going on the convergence track to deal with internationally. For instance, the convergence of accounting standards between the FASB and IFRS for financial instruments (despite the G20's Pittsburgh 2009 injunction) has made almost no progress. However, new hopes are given with the joint adoption by FASB and IFRS of a new accounting standard on revenue recognition. It will be of key importance in the path driving to a M5 monetary aggregate when implemented through the Joint Transition Group that they created as it does not allow companies to escape from legal realities of contracts.

The European Stability Mechanism and the European Central Bank

Because of its youth, the Eurozone faces specific problems of coordination that were discovered during the financial crisis to be specific, and not addressed or insufficiently addressed by the Maastricht Treaty. The byelaws of the ECB are similar to those of the Federal Reserve Bank. As a matter of fact, it is the indirect successor of the German Central Bank that was created after WWII under Allied occupation of Germany by copying the FED's byelaws.

It was decided that the ECB should be strictly independent of governments. Governments were to be, if necessary, unprivileged borrowers just like any bank. This is the basic reason why the ECB cannot buy public debts when issued. The objective, a democratic

---

[23] Brussels, 25 February 2009 report; "The high level Group on Financial Supervision" in the EU report commissioned by the President of the European Commission to Jacques de Larosière in October 2008.

one, is to make governments go to their democratic parliamentary institutions for expenses and when levying taxes to finance them. Also, to cap public debt, governments have to go to the public to issue debt if the central bank will not buy the new issuances. The concepts grounding the set-up were sensible, but not adapted to the diversity of the member states, even if less different than the US states. Speculation was quick to locate a loophole – when sovereign debt issuances came on the market, mechanisms such as the preference for safe assets came into play to their full extent as no currency issue was directly at stake. There was no moral hazard in selling Greek, Portuguese or other similar debts against German ones. Putting national budget policies first and intervening in the sovereign debt market was not considered, if not impossible. Worse, speculation was several months ahead before the loopholes could be fixed.

The conceptual independence of the ECB, with no specific mechanism and subject to the realities of respective member states' political forces and eagerness for consumption and debt, can no longer be operative as to its goals. The world trade deficits, even at the balance of payments level with incoming money flows, have sometimes created reserves that were free to operate in that context. Furthermore, while the Eurozone taken as a whole was balanced, limiting the currency exchange risk, the dollar domination makes it useful for denominating contracts (oil or aerospace industry contracts, for instance) that create potential flows to base forward purchases or sales of currency – of amounts such that they are not proportional to the capacities of the central bank to fight speculations, adding to the problems of member states in refinancing at sensible rates on debt markets independently too small to give liquidity to investors.

For this reason there was a need for an appropriate specific institutional instrument. Hence, the European Stability Mechanism (ESM) treaty was signed. A successor to the EFSF, with insufficient means and created as a provisional tool to end in 2013, the ESM was designed to operate like the IMF, as an intergovernmental institution with a subscribed capital of 700 billion euros, of which 80 billion is to be paid at start and the balance callable. With an initial capacity of 500 billion, it will lend money to member states to recapitalize their troubled banks; it will operate as a consultant. It will overall be able to buy sovereign bonds from member states both on issuance and the secondary market. It is managed by a board of governors that should be ministers with responsibility for finance. In case of urgency, an emergency procedure can be undertaken whereby a decision to grant financial assistance only requires an 85% majority of the vote cast. As a counterpart to its action, the ESM can require a "fiscal compact", meaning a commitment from the beneficiary state to implement measures to reach a balanced budget over time. As always, the detailed implementation of these new treaties and regulations is of paramount importance. Among the open matters is the cut off between the old system and the new one. Ranking first are the guidance about what correct-ive actions will be imposed on the member countries and their timing. Moreover, there is the matter of what kind of sovereign debt instruments will be acquired. The accumulation of debts is at stake, as we immediately understand that the perspective of "bail-outs" comes with the perspective of the ESM, and that the amounts at stake are such that the new participants do not want to be involved in past accumulation. In order to avoid deviances in appraising the situation of banks, the balancing of risks and rewards requires fine-tuning. The ESM is not to lend to banks before the ECB has taken over the supervision of the banking system, as already decided in 2014. In addition, through a specialized subsidiary and to ensure accountability of member states, no lending intervention will happen before the states have committed at least 13% of the amounts at stake.

THE BANKING UNION[24]

The other matter still open and different from the USA and for the same historical reasons is the structure of the banking systems. The European banking system until recently was national, while mainly using a single currency. Again, because of the independence concept, in case a bank was in trouble the ECB could not intervene. Despite better social integration than the USA and higher savings ratios, the EU was deemed to be weaker than other zones in not being able to prevent cash runs or merely constant retrieving of deposits from banks located in countries and depositing in other countries with a stronger reputation or bigger wealth (disregarding the effect on tax collection). No mechanism was set for intervention. The single-market advantages of scale economies would play out, and the weaker ones would disappear. The specificity of the banking system and its monetary role was not considered. This has been the story of Greece, with an economy mostly operating with banknotes and consequent tax collection difficulties. It also resulted in excessive interest rate differences for the refinancing of public debts but also of private enterprises between countries such as Germany and countries along the Mediterranean. The example given is a company operating cross-border between Italy and Germany, the Italian branch borrowing when possible in Italy at 200 basis points over that prevailing in Germany, the risk being of course the same.

To address this problem and complete the European monetary aspect of the Eurozone, it was proposed in June 2012 that a road map towards a banking union (http://www.consilium.europa.eu) should be followed that would establish a single supervisory mechanism (SSM) "allowing the ESM to have the possibility to recapitalize banks directly". This proposal, as a matter of fact, fits into existing ongoing processes as EU Regulation no. 1093/2010 that has created the EBA (see the general framework above) and CRD4, a proposal setting the regulatory prudential requirements for banks (derived from the Basel Committee proposals). In addition, the Commission called the Parliament and the Council for Directives[25] to address the deposit guarantee schemes (DGS) for protecting deposits at banks and improving the mechanism for increased efficiency of the already existing €100,000 per account guarantee, and finally the failed banks' resolution process. One of the difficulties of implementing a banking union inside the single market is allocating responsibilities appropriately between national supervisory bodies; the national central banks all have to be maintained and integrated in the general framework. The Commission is calling for a single rule-book[26] that would also address the matters arising from the fact that only 18 countries out of 28[27] in the EU are using the euro. The so-called "European Banking Union" transferring the ultimate say to the ECB was the answer to ensure that any bank failure would be taken care of, and that such failure would not become contagious to the entire system.

The initiative powers regarding bank supervision, when most of them operate across borders with a single authorization to do so (who is responsible for the proper information collection, where to audit them, who is responsible for giving instructions and sanctioning if there are issues to be taken care of, knowing that at least some small but numerous banks in Spain and Germany are fragile), needs to be organized and is about to be.

---

[24] For details, see http//ec.europ.eu/internal market/finances/banking-union/.

[25] A Directive is a general legal framework that, when adopted by parliament, will commit member states to adopt in their own legislation at minimum the corresponding regulation. It is called the transposition process.

[26] Press release from the European Commission COM/2012 510 (final).

[27] After Croatia joined the Union on July 1, 2013 and Latvia on January 1, 2014.

The European Banking Union was finally adopted on December 14, 2012 at a European Council held in Brussels. It is to address two topics: supervision and resolution. It has been decided that the ECB will be the single supervisor and authority for the banking system inside the Union. All banks with assets over 30 billion euros or 20% of the original member state GDP will be supervised and sanctioned, if needed, by the ECB. A provisional list of 177 banks or banking groups (130) of the 6200 EU banks was established to be under direct supervision of the ECB. Banks not under the ECB supervisory power will remain supervised by the member state supervision systems, leaving the ECB the power to take over in case of a problem at a bank. There was an issue about the fact that the ECB is only the central bank for the Eurozone – only 18 countries of the 28 having joined the Eurozone single-currency system, and the remainder not having access to the decision-making process of the new supervision.

For them, an intermediate oversight council with the ECB distinct from the board of governors has been set. However, the issue was the UK with its currency and large banking system outside the euro. The UK is part of the system but is protected from decisions imposed on it by a voting process that requires decisions to gather support from a majority of member states that are not part of the Eurozone.[28]

The Banking Union is currently finishing its governance rules and the levels at which the euro monetary system should be handled (short term and long term), who should bear the burden of past issued debts, how new debt should be pooled, how the banking system should be organized as to resolution, if central banks should or should not be separated from surveillance as the governor of the central bank of the Netherlands, M. Klaas Knot recommends, and how the new system should find its legitimacy, as discussed by M. Jacek Rostowski, the Polish Minister of Finance (a candidate for the Eurozone).[29]

A new formal SSM with its supervisory board and a resolution fund has been negotiated with the European Parliament within the Union mechanism. A new breakthrough and fine-tuning will still be needed for it to be totally effective to deal with the matter of bank resolution and treaties, or laws be taken to address the European Banking Union just being the general frame of the set-up with the ESM to allow recapitalization of banks. There are still topics to be worked out to decide how a bank would be closed in case the ECB refuses (as it can) to salvage a financial institution that would be in danger.[30] The financing of the ultimate

---

[28] At Entretiens du Trésor held on December 13, 2013, Governor Mark Carney from the Bank of England declared that the UK will faithfully comply with the EU regulation about banking supervision and that not being part of the Eurozone is not a problem.

[29] Entretiens du Trésor, November 30, 2012 at the Paris Ministry of Finance. Also present: Mario Draghi, President of the ECB; Mrs Christine Lagarde; Victorrio Grilli, Minister of Finance of Italy; Martin Hillwig, Director of the Max Planck Institute for Research on Collective Goods; Sylvie Goulard, from the European Parliament. Entretien du Trésor held at the Ministry of Finance on December 13, 2013 was more focused on financing the economy, especially SMEs in the context of a wider recourse to financial markets than to bank financing. M. Barnier, the European Commissioner, indicated that he will propose mechanisms for extended securitization of receivables.

[30] CAE Note no. 3, "Compléter l'Euro" (Complete the Euro) has been issued by Conseil d'Analyse Economique, France, which is an independent body set up alongside the French Prime Minister. This note recommends the creation of an independent budget committee. A speech he gave in Paris on April 9, 2013 comments on the note of Jean Tirolle, a member of this council, raising the issue of nationally sanctioning breaches in good governance or risk taking as opposed to having an independent European board. He also raises the topic of financing the guarantees (100,000) given by law to depositors and the difficulty for governments to deal transnationally with already troubled banks.

losses after bank failures through the single resolution fund to be organized before the ESM can be called upon. Besides the Cyprus crisis there are still constitutional issues over mechanisms to cancel equity and subordinated loans if, as we have seen with the Drexel[31] case in the USA, the resolution shows finally over time an *in bonis* position because of uncertainty about the valuation of portfolios when starting the process.

The new set-up includes the resolution process, both from a practical point of view as a requirement for finalizing the Eurozone – like the dollar US zone is already – but also from a theoretical point of view. As we stand, with money no longer the central banks' currency or commercial banks' credit money, financial market trust is at stake. The financial instruments that are systemic in the flows and guarantees have to be homogenous within a zone in terms of legal status, in case of failure of any of the handlers through their respective balance sheets – just as there are legal and resolution processes for failing enterprises (Chapter 10). However, the topic, being systemic, cannot be left just to private views from a creditor's perspective and suspended with the occurrence of failure. The instruments must be visible as to their underlying guarantees for them to be exchangeable throughout a zone, and internationally. They have to carry the universal acceptability that ancient precious metal coinage had. No longer being intrinsic but book and market matters, they need to be legally monitored by a central authority within the zone. The possibility of melting gold coinage had to be replaced, bookkeeper by bookkeeper and instrument by instrument. The general framework has been adopted by a June 26, 2013 Ecofin.[32] The general framework of banking resolution has been drawn. When losses result from a monetary failure (a bank or other financial institution), a hierarchy in the order they have to be bearded is set. The first losers will be the stockholders, the subordinated debt holders. Because of the legal system of leans, the amount such holders may get back from an investment's work out is dependent on what senior debt holders (covered bonds) with guarantees will get. Among the unsecured big companies, the SMEs and the private individual depositors over their guaranteed €100,000 will come last. In addition, some priorities and sanctuaries are set. Employees are privileged, but also debts that are key to the institution's activity in order to avoid uncontrollable disruption – as well as to operate, as a switch to contagion, any interbank lending with a maturity of less than 7 days. A mutualized resolution fund was already decided (see later) but as mentioned, and to avoid responsibility, it will not intervene before the bail-in resolution system has taken 8% of losses above 5% of banks' assets. In Europe the unsecured debt for Eurozone banks is at €1.40 trillion to 40% being considered as tier one (equivalent to equity) for Basel III regulation on prudential ratios. More or less, the process is similar to what was decided for Cyprus' banking system failure. We note the question of whether the new system will apply to pre-existing debts.

A political agreement was reached between the European Parliament and member states. The Directive will both progressively shorten to 7 years the repayment deadlines from the bail in, and organize financing by levying, over 10 years, a standard 0.8% of 1% of covered deposits to create ex ante funding. Bank contributions to DGS will reflect individual risk profiles, which means that more risky banks will have to pay more.[33]

The Bank Recovery and Resolution System (BRRS), designed by Ecofin, was finally adopted on December 17, 2013 through the trilogue EU decision process, but so far through

---

[31]Drexel Burnham Lambert bank failure – Journal of Financial Intermediation, Vol 3 No 1, 1994.

[32] Gathering of EU Finance Ministers – see Glossary.

[33] More details are available at http://ec.europa.eu/internal market/bank/guarantee.

the idea of intergovernmental treaties. The systematic resolution approach establishes several concepts that we have already proposed and will develop:

1. It classifies under the central authority of the ECB and the agencies the various kinds of debts depending on the guarantees attributed to each of them. By operating this classification it officializes the monetary nature of these debts. They become homogenized and therefore can be openly and widely traded.
2. Being widely accepted, it complies with the monetary attributes. Being under control of an authority, the (graded) claimable character is controlled and its seignorage power still there by up or downgrading the status of an issuance.
3. It reconciles with the analytical approach of balance sheets as we develop it further on with M5 and M6 analysis, where the underlying guarantees are considered.
4. It classifies the agents by the bail-in and bail-out process, which requires setting priorities. This is not a real novelty in commercial and social law but the concept is expanded to become applicable on a general worldwide basis.
5. It reconciles with the reality that economic agents, market participants or not, may choose what money they want as if they were using a currency and a referential coinage. There the issuer is free to issue, under the Basel prudential constraint when applicable, what kind of money he wants to sell. In doing so, he will be submitted to the market expectations of potential buyers.
6. We also note that if the new Directive only covers the territory of banking activities, the resulting wider financial markets with less disintermediation than in the USA will have a driver role for all monetary flows. The general organization of the ESFS has been revisited in the course of establishing the Banking Union. Grouped as the European supervisory authorities of the ESFS, they are now[34] under the authority of the European central bank. The ECB, as US financial agencies, has been under the FED. On November 4, 2014 the ECB will be in charge of directly supervising European systemic banks[35] in cooperation with national and European agencies (but with the last say). For instance, the quality asset review (QAR) being done, the stress tests of the around 128 European systemic banks is already conducted by the ECB with procurements given by the EBA and its colleges of national supervisors. The ECB now has the ultimate power over bank registration, surveillance and sanctioning.

The decision taking is organized through an already set Resolution Board[36] with wide powers, which has been fully operational since January 2014. It comprises for executive sessions: "the Executive Director, four other permanent members while the Commission and the ECB would be permanent observers. In addition, to ensure that the interests of all Member States on which the resolution has an impact were considered, further members would be part of that session according to the institution that was being resolved" (extract from European Commission memo dated December 19, 2013). To avoid a decision freeze, none of the participants in the deliberation would have a veto. The control or reporting of the ECB – which

---

[34] The European Council adopted this new proposal on 9/12/2012.

[35] EU Council Regulation no. 1024/2013 of October 15, 2013 conferring specific tasks on the ECB concerning policies relating to the prudential surveillance of credit institutions.

[36] "In its plenary session, the Board would take all decisions of a general nature and the decisions which involve the use of the single resolution fund above a certain threshold."

holds ultimate surveillance and regulation power, and is an independent entity to the European Parliament in the same way as the FED is in the USA to Congress – is still to be organized.

Subject to the above matters being resolved by spring of 2014 the new mechanism due to Michel Barnier, with high efficiency, will bring major improvements to the European financial set-up. The agreed-upon resolution process still misses completion of the single resolution fund, also already decided, that would be the equivalent of the US FDIC to fund the bail-out of banks after the bail-in process has been endorsed. The funding of this mechanism is still to be negotiated regarding its details, but it has already been agreed that it will be self-funded by the banking system as seen above. Eurozone member states were committed to having an intergovernmental agreement on the functioning of the fund by March 2014. National contributions to the fund were first to be mutualized over a period of 10 years, later (at March 2013 council-level agreement) reduced to 8 years. The topic in debate was how Federal it should be and how progressively it should be mutualized over time because of the different pre-existing debts in banks of each of the member states. At council level it was decided that the fund should be financed at 40% within 2 years, before being fully operational at the latest after 8 years with a targeted amount of 1% of covered deposits, a transitional bridge financing system with a backstop by national government has been agreed upon.

The final open issue is calibration of the prudential referential and how progressively the new Basel ratios (lending credit ratio (LCR)) should be enforced. The time schedule is to have the SRB operational by January 2015 and the new revisited deposit guarantee scheme and funding by May 2015, with the bail-in resolution system applicable as of January 2016.

THE FISCAL POLICY COORDINATION ISSUE COMPARED WITH THE USA

Having the necessary set-up with appropriate surveillance and intervention is one thing, the realities to deal with are another. The US taxation system is mostly Federal, and states must have balanced budgets. With tax-exempt bonds benefiting US residents, the refinancing of states' debts is mostly internal to the USA. The matter is the US Federal General Deficit that does not need to be developed here as a monetary issue as long as dollar-denominated instruments are accepted and the US budget blockage[37] having been widely discussed everywhere. The basic data for 2012 is: receipt tax collection $2.45 trillion, equivalent to 15.8% of GDP of $15.6 trillion expenses, $3.54 trillion determining a $1.327 trillion Federal deficit equal to 7% of GDP. Combined expenses (Federal and states) are $6.28 trillion, equal to 40.3% of US GDP.

The playing field in the EU (28 member countries) is completely different. The European budget is mostly limited to European common institutions cost supporting and specific development programmes (see later). For the period from 2007 to 2013 it is limited to 864 million euros, around 1.05–1.1% of global GNI (GDP plus or minus external exchanges); GDP stands at around 16–16.8 trillion (depending on the source of statistics – IMF, World Bank or CIA).

---

[37] Article 1, Section 9, Clause 7 of the US Constitution states: "No money shall be drawn from the Treasury but in consequence of appropriation made by law and a regular statement of accounts of receipts & expenditures of all public money shall be published from time to time. Budget & Accounting Act of 1921 and 31 U.S.C $1105 completes the set up. US budget goes from October 1st to September 30th and budget shall be submitted no later than the first Monday of February."

Consequently, the topic is not at a European level but at a national level; there is a need to limit the divergence of budget policies and public debt. Only general guidance exists, with no real sanctioning – like a limitation of the deficit at 3% of GDP and a debt ceiling of 60% (called the Stability and Growth Pact (SGP)) – soon to be overridden by key member states at the creation of the monetary union (January 1, 1994) and with the adoption of the euro (December 1998). With the crisis budget differences between member states, fiscal policies and macroeconomic imbalances rocketed with some – such as Greece, Ireland and Portugal – encountering major political and social challenges, including high unemployment (Spain 26%), and some others on the way to surpluses with low unemployment (4.5%) such as Germany. The grounds for financial speculation against debts were there, triggering higher refinancing costs to add to the stress.

To fix the topic, when the financial crisis broke out the EU first adopted, in March 2011 at an Ecofin Council, the Six-Pack regulations to reform[38] the SGP with new requirements for member states in terms of fiscal policy and for fixing macroeconomic imbalances to set progressive sanctions in case of non-compliance with commitments. Further, for the Euro-zone, the EU adopted the appropriate legislation based on article 136 of the EU treaty to set a coordination process for the last year budgetary cycle, and member states had to comply with the set rules included in the Treaty on Stability, Coordination and Governance (TSCG) adopted on March 2, 2012 (applicable since January 1, 2013). This reinforces the request for convergence of budgetary policies between member states. The TSCG also introduces financial sanctions in case of breach of the commitments taken to address imbalances detected by the Commission and the following recommendations. However, two pacts adopted on May 30, 2013 add to the set-up with a common budgetary process timeline, which is already applicable, imposing that member countries:

- By April, publish their medium-term fiscal plan (stability programmes), together with their policy priorities for growth and employment for the forthcoming 12 months (national reform programmes).
- By October 15, publish their draft budgets for the following year.
- By December, adopt their budgets for the following year.

The innovation is that the Commission (the executive arm of the Union), after examination, gives an opinion on each draft budget by November at the latest. If the Commission detects severe non-compliance with the obligations under the SGP, it will ask the concerned member state to submit a revised plan. For the Eurozone as a whole, the Commission will publish a comprehensive assessment of the budget outlook for the following years.

Importantly, the Six-Pack process will enhance the soundness of the national budgetary processes by obliging member states to base their draft budgets on independent microeconomic forecasts and ensure independent bodies are in place to monitor compliance with national fiscal rules. The Greek crisis showed a need to rely on better statistics than those available at the time.

---

[38] Five directives and one regulation: Regulation EC no. 1466/97 reinforcing the budget surveillance and the coordination; Regulation EC no. 1467/97 regarding speeding up of excessive deficit procedures; Regulation of the European Parliament and European Council on the effective enforcement of the budgetary stability; Council Directive 2011/85/24 on the requirement for the fiscal framework of the member states; Regulation on the prevention and correction of macroeconomic imbalances; Regulation on enforcement to correct excessive microeconomic imbalances in the euro area.

The new regulation gives power to the Commission to better monitor and address directly a recommendation to a member state in case it falls under the Excessive Deficit Procedure (EDP). When the budgetary situation of a member state is deemed troubled enough to have major adverse effects on the financial stability of the Eurozone, in such cases the Commission can call on the Council of Ministers. The Council of Ministers can then recommend the concerned member state to adopt corrective actions or put together a draft macroeconomic adjustment programme or precautionary assistance. Such a state will remain under new enhanced surveillance until it has paid back a minimum of 75% of the assistance received. A financial sanction is also to be contemplated in case of non-compliance (capped to 0.1% of GDP) and a reduction plan of the public debt when exceeding 60% of GDP at a minimum 1/20th% a year pace.

Finally, the Two-Pack process provides the available tools for an adjustment programme in case a member state is in need of financial support.

This new European-coordinated European budget process is to resolve the seams between member states – and even when they have adopted the golden rule of budget balancing they will still go through the experience to appraise its sustainability over time. Nevertheless, what was accomplished in a short period of time is encouraging, especially when considering the global situation of little or no deficit in the major countries, and a global surplus. The open topic is no longer a monetary one but a political one – sustainability. To what limit is sharing deficits and surpluses for the benefit of better integration within society understood and accepted by those who think they give more than they receive?

Article 13 of the March 2, 2012 treaty should be noted. It may draw the path for further evolution in coordination. "As foreseen in the title II of Protocol (N°1) on the role of national Parliaments in the European Union annexed to the European Union Treaties, the European Parliament and national Parliaments of Contracting Parties will together determine the organization and promotion of a conference of representatives of relevant committees of the National Parliaments and of representatives of relevant committees' commission of the European Parliament in order to discuss budgetary Policies and other issuers covered by this treaty." What is at stake here is a change between what, in tax collection, could be transferred to European level. Nevertheless, reading official declarations, it may be limited to specific taxes not yet organized – like the tax on financial transactions or the Ecotax which is collected, or will be collected, on trucks. These taxes are either directly connected to international matters, or specific to European territory organization.

THE GROWING ISSUES OF THE SIZE OF THE MONETARY ZONES – RESEARCH FOR OPTIMUM

If it is clear that widening the size of a monetary zone increases competition and therefore productivity and inventiveness, it also has some limiting effect on such progress. Economic and political coherence is at stake. Within the monetary zone, with its reserve function, money flows cause accumulations and the fractioning of financial markets and financial instruments with different rotation speeds. These phenomena, generated by rating agencies' gradings, cause obscurity instead of transparency as traded prices can be different depending on markets; they are not known by all of the players at the same time. Ultimately, the sustainability of the social contract that links a nation's citizens is not to be determined mathematically, and any other way is just guessing about costs. In terms of incomes and benefits, some believe that they are paying for others. The wider a zone is, the less homogenous and predictable it is. Historically, we know that at certain stages, profiles or categories of citizens with disparate circles operate as lobbyists and, to believers, pretend to obtain favours they think they deserve for their clients. At least they have an informative role on hidden problems to be addressed by regulators and constituents. They are paid to bring this information to light. Ultimately, they are the sign of insufficient agreement to a social contract – a need for change, the objective image that a limit has been reached. Morally reprehensible injustices can only bring dissatisfaction, social tension and speculation. Allowing speculation, they draw a limit to a market's efficiency.

Robert Mundell theorized the notion of an optimum currency area. He held this optimum as the territory wherein all of the productive factors can freely be moved from one place to another. For this reason, some have claimed that for such a condition to be satisfied requires a political unification. The key objective of the Rome Treaty (six countries creating the single market in Europe) was to commit member countries and impose such freedom inside the zone, later extended by different steps to 28 countries. Mundell's theory is not to be challenged. Nevertheless, there are obstacles to a free unified market that are not to be satisfied by a political union and are of a different nature. Over large territories, it is possible to adopt long-term transitional economic policies and, ultimately, populations attached to territories using a single currency with different price levels taking into account comparative competitive advantages, including the agreement to live in a certain environment. Liberty to move within a zone is a necessary concept and a required legal privilege but a restricted reality. High real-estate prices in some areas of California, London and Paris and lower ones elsewhere are different realities depending on geography and transportation infrastructures.

Braudel's views on society are pertinent here. Geography, including different climates, will play a role to reduce the fluidity of the means of production as well as pre-existing cultures and history. Over vast territories, laws will defer to history and culture. They do so in Europe as well as in the USA. Political unification is not a prerequisite if not similar to unique leadership. The Roman Empire operated for a long time with a different set-up, where each citizen until Emperor Caracalla (211 AD) kept their citizenship and, with it, the attached civil and jurisdictional rights and exemptions. In the 19th century, the French Kingdom and following Empire and Republic – inspired by the knowledge of the Roman civilization – copied the model with great success in countries such as Morocco, Tunisia and others, where native citizens kept their original civil rights. Single monetary institutions and harmonized money and financing rules are, on the contrary, a prerequisite – as well as leadership in case of difficulty – to address the resolution processes including the determination of each of the money endowments needed, depending on where the money is being used, and who is using it. In any case, we believe, contrary to what is too often said, that unification is not a solution, and now less than ever, as the increasing sophistication of monetary instruments requires specialized regulation and different endowments and reserves. The Roman Empire would never have survived without adaptation to realities, which explains the split into two parts achieved by Diocletian when trying to improve and unify the monetary system.[39] The recent German reunification was a political goal, but for a few years a

---

[39] It is interesting to note that oriental countries require more administration than western ones for the same efficiency in raising a cost issue for similar results. The Soviet Empire was a successor to the over-administrated Oriental Empire. Two thousand years later, the most recent Serbian/Croatian wars are still taking place along ancient borders.

difficult achievement because of the different levels of productivity and innovation. Because of this experience, the extension of the Union to other eastern countries was achieved without trying to level individual incomes and, to the contrary, keeping it as an advantage to have lower labour costs. For a monetary zone, such a structure will be a major advantage for global costs, but also by bringing competition between regions and resulting incentives to improve the structural efficiency of local governments.

Modern money has changed the topic, in a way. Without currency exchange restrictions on the transfer of huge book amounts, monetary zones are both legally possible and practically not surrounded by geographical fences.[40] The legal tender system no longer has significance in a free globalized economy as political and legal sovereignty stops at borders, and markets will freely push the currency exchange rate up or down. Also, the dollar has worldwide use and double nationality is common for business people – the notion of currency residency or non-residency for bank accounts no longer represents a controlling reality. For instance, the zone for some euro debts is much bigger than seen in the statistics, because of the history of France and its culturally wide universe consisting of many African and especially economically important countries' citizens – through geographical closeness and the importance of exchanges. If there are difficulties in their own countries, these citizens sometimes choose to appear as non-resident and sometimes as resident in a financial sense, and may switch between the two at any time. This is also true for the UK pound zone. On an ever wider basis, accounts for foreign-controlled companies appear as resident in the country where they have been incorporated, ignoring the controlling ownership. This is an effect of the development of international exchanges and companies we have already been discussing as a new reality, changing the meaning of statistics in analysis – for instance the monetary exposure risk analysis of the banking system per country. In reality, such risks do not really exist if they show the counterpart of an exporter's balances often representing inventories located in subsidiaries spread in different countries, as they will disappear when consolidating the financial statements of each one into the mother holding company (see Chapter 4). Because of the complexity of the matter and the inappropriateness of available statistics, markets have a leeway to speculations.

The Triffin paradox is a key issue, Europe being an example of a political set-up where finance people, politicians and citizens have contradictory perspectives. The strong macroeconomic data of the zone, combined with stable national political systems and a new unknown centralized governance system with the Banking Union, leads automatically to a strong euro that US critics push to reinforce. Suddenly, we have a pattern that, with the dollar still transnational, at least for transactions, leads to increased instability and erratic risk of speculation, which is unsustainable by the USA because of its smaller size compared with other zones. Everyone may, one day, have to reconvene as a case of urgency or collapse similar to what happened in 2007.

Money, as opposed to other matters, needs to be used as widely as possible to favour exchanges, and one has to remember that the harsh British devaluation of 1931 was only determined by the absence of recovery both in Europe and America. While there is no sign of convergence and of any strategy to converge as encouraged by the G20, there is a stringent requirement to achieve monetary global governance.

---

[40] The time required to transmit an instruction fell to 1 minute in 1850 when a cable was set on the Channel sea floor between France and Britain, and since then it has reduced constantly. The transatlantic liaison between the USA and the UK was inaugurated on August 5, 1858.

THE MONETARY INTERACTION OF SYSTEMS

General Interaction: Scale Economies Resulting from Monetary Integration and Political Obstacles

With exchanges requiring trust, there is a need for guarantees as to the measurement tool of prices and also the fairness of markets. Surveillance addresses the fairness, but still does not globally address the question of foreign exchange, measurement and aggregates even if the FSB is there to raise the issues. Markets not being perfect, there is a need for action and sanctioning over the available volume of money and its trading prices.

It has been said that there would be no history of monetary unification success where there was no political unity to drive a single or coordinated budget policy for governments. The given examples of success are Switzerland (Swiss franc, 1815) and Germany (1870). Europe evidently had an issue over, like the US Federation, having member states with totally different production and budget patterns but less (than the USA) political integration. The almost completed free market zone, like the US one, aggravates the problem of money flowing to the safest places and the safest institutions. The structural differences in economies and development stages that have been addressed by structural European funds to help less developed regions and countries have not addressed the fact of remaining structural production advantages that some regions have compared with others. In the absence of sufficient means and of a unified banking supervision and intervention tool, excess money existing all over the world and being free to speculate is a threat to the single currency, despite positive aggregates. The saying (Gresham law) that "bad money pushes good out" may be true. The above new oversight set-up is addressing the insufficiencies that appeared in the field after the 2007 crisis broke out. The banking union treaty, the new intervention set-up already decided on, is to address the issue of a centralized back-up for the single currency, like the dollar already has. Where the difference with the USA will remain is in the time elapsing. Because of the ongoing integration process with scale economies in an already achieved single market, all industries have to become bigger, meaning some have to become the consolidators and others the consolidated. Of course, companies becoming regional when they have been national, or becoming national after having been only regional, or just quitting, requires reorganization, adaptations and suffering. Productivity means fewer staff for the same production. It cannot be done in one day, and also favours centres with competitive advantages, meaning transfers at the expense of population. It is, on another scale, the whole debate about globalization.

Through balance sheets, risks are spreading with no limits. It is the counterpart of productivity.[41]

INTERNATIONAL MICROECONOMIC REGULATION COORDINATION SPECIFICS

In the framework of the G20 and the FSB, everyone calls for a convergence of both regulations and standards, but if the issues to be dealt with are similar – the playing field and resulting legal framework being different for historical reasons – reaching the goals will not

---

[41] Cotorelli, G. and Goldberger, C. (2012) Banking globalization and monetary transmission, *Journal of Finance*, vol. 67.

yet happen for the microeconomic world. That is the case for the IFRS accounting principles that the SEC declared not yet to be appropriate for US needs.[42] The prudential system to be adopted for banks, called Basel III, is so far known to have the support of US agencies, but they have not yet decided to comply.

Other topics, like the regulation of derivative markets and margin requirements for instance, that deal with billions, seem to us to show a lack of precision in what is required to have efficiency and therefore reliability. Agencies may not have sufficient knowledge of practices and figures and, if they have, they are not capable of placing this knowledge within a globally accepted picture of how these markets should operate and be regulated. The delaying of the projects in these fields shows the hesitation generated by the absence of clear rules. As a consequence, the all-supervisory system is going to be costly and may deter actors from operating, or otherwise increase consolidation and systemic risks. This all relates to who is in charge of interpreting a rule or principle. Who is in charge to trigger an action and who will sanction and, if there is need, bring a case to justice? This is a concern at the operational level but even more so at the monetary level. No detailed authoritative action will be of any use if the whole system is not structured with a sanctioning system. However, even more basically, the liquidity guarantee of what today's money is, meaning public issuances, is not organized. This topic, as we will see, has been resolved for some kinds of monetary instruments and markets but not for all of what covers M5, and certainly not systematically.

This is also the case when separating depositary activities from proprietary trading activities. The USA has adopted the so-called Volker rule, which is now part of section 13 of the Bank Holding Company Act (BHCA), setting restrictions on proprietary trading and investment activities. However, the 300-page regulation is not going to be operational before 2019, and in the UK the equivalent Vickers rule of "ring fencing", which was adopted on June 16, 2010, is rather flexible. The Basel III set-up to achieve the same purpose is of different essence, with prudential ratios and portfolio weightings.

The definition of the frontier between the surveillance of the financial sector, the systemic risks the latter carries and the surveillance of money (see M5 and M6) is still to be elaborated. As money-restricted bases, M1 and M2 should also belong to central banks' jurisdictions for the simple reason that these are constitutional institutions, and when the system was about to fall the governments had to intervene at the citizens' expense. Further than the delegated surveillance granted to specialized agencies, central banks have to act for the prevention of bubbles and also to take monetary corrective actions.[43] This being said, surveillance, regulation and today's currency in its intermediation role cannot coexist without a microeconomic information system compatible with the constitutional central banks' responsibilities. The current definitions splitting fiduciary money from script money and global money, as understood by central bankers, have to lose their dogmatic character. Again, M5 and M6 aggregates are needed.

The Solvency II Directive for the insurance companies, mutuals and pension funds sector was adopted in 2009, and its ongoing revision that we have mentioned regarding the prevention of crisis and consumers' protection by a single rule book for Europe under EIOPA European supervision is of no concern for the USA.

---

[42] SEC staff release, September 2012.

[43] Several pieces of legislation and programmes were adopted to allow debtors to extend their payment dates and remain in their own homes.

TRANSNATIONAL REALITIES ABOUT FINANCIAL INSTRUMENTS' MARKETS AND SYSTEMIC RISK MEASUREMENT

We know about the difficulties encountered in the stress-test process of the banks and the disputes between monetary surveillance agencies. We also stated that, with the lack of M5 and M6 information, agencies will again not be able to appraise systemic risks and will again be subject to failure as they were in 2007. Figures are not a jurisdictional or legal issue. They are first an information issue which attempts to be resolved, but overall are a political issue that agencies will never be able to deal with. This is the first issue leading to the conclusion that the FSB, conceptually the only possible forum, cannot be the solution without being supported by an international treaty that does not yet exist.

The second issue is that M5, M6 and their derivatives-only figure aggregates are not sufficient unless grounded by legal systems for the execution of instruments, resolution of bookkeepers and depository status precise accountability definitions (see Chapter 6 covering M5/M6 and M5′/M6′). This includes the allocation between nations of regulation and surveillance powers when not held by international bodies with such power. From the allocation of regulation and surveillance also derives the allocation of tax liability determination, especially in the intangible fields of digital and financial industries.

This allocation is not organized or, if organized, no longer effective and does not exist yet besides the special European set-up that we have discovered with the ongoing integration of the euro monetary zone. However, it is a national allocation within the EU and not an international one. Its relationship with the US dollar zone and other zones only goes through the FSB, with no legal power whatsoever. The postal treaties, sea or train transportation of past centuries are of limited scope compared with the scope of modern exchanges to be addressed in the financial sphere.

We believe that agency staff are in the same position, approaching classification and measurement of financial instruments. They try to give guidance about their valuation, but they operate within their jurisdiction, which is by nature a national one. By nature, financial markets are national, as instruments are. Financial markets being national, where registered, they are under the jurisdiction of one country's system of courts and surveillance. At the same time, legal execution processes of traded instruments are different for each country or monetary zone. However, with financial globalization, the markets' participants are either international or interconnected. That is the reason, with global systemic impacts, why the topic of markets being properly organized was raised by the G20 during its 2009 Pittsburgh meeting. The CDS and AIG issue of their London branch hit by Lehman Brothers' failure was on everyone's minds. The impact was absorbed by the US government rescue of AIG, but the underlying topic of international transactions and international players was not treated.

There is still a lot of research to be launched to develop unified standards on stamping, valuation of face value and guarantees that neither accounting standards nor laws have undertaken as yet. The efforts which need to be made are important to the efficiency of surveillance agencies, but above all to the allocation of seignorage rights between nations that should, in our minds, remain a constitutional privilege. This would also address, as we will see, the matter of excessive compensation in the financial sector. Orderly resolution processes of both financial institutions and market counterparties, if not achieved, are on the way, from an organizational point of view, on both sides of the Atlantic. Nevertheless, and we will come back to this later, no one knows with what funds a failure will be refinanced without opening the central banks' money printers. Being organized and becoming transparent also leads to a more systemic and more obvious image of macroeconomic international unbalances. The international character of marketplaces and instruments with their legal consequences has not been sufficiently addressed.

Handling the Social Obstacles of Monetary Unification

Social coherence, common ethical values and general goals implicate some coherence that is not natural over wide territories, because of different natural resources, different climates and also different populations and infrastructures. Central governments, Federal or not, are trying to reduce differences considering also the free movement of the population that has to be taken care of, and the free flow of money. The infrastructure seen in Roman times, having a single major road system, similar infrastructures and a postal service, is no longer sufficient. The modern question is, with high taxes and social charges, who would benefit from the economic integration resulting from increased productivity due to competition and larger amounts of units being produced, as well as the sharing of costly infrastructures, and who would be disadvantaged by bearing a higher burden than the real cost would be if independent? In the end, excessive stress has caused some political set-ups to break. This was the reason, for instance, for the Roman Empire quitting Brittany[44] when the cost of maintaining troops there exceeded the potential return from trade. Of course, there are also a lot of cultural matters and strategic issues about territory consistency that can hardly be valued, but that may override a monetary approach. Let's just try to cover the economic field – not to give answers, but quick descriptions.

The Answer to Heterogeneity[45]

The capability of individuals to live together within a territory is limited not only by distances or other geographical obstacles, but also by cultural differences and inequalities.[46] Peace, as social peace, is a condition for economic development as the necessary investors are easily frightened by any unrest, requiring higher returns to cover the resulting risks. These are the reasons for nations fighting against poverty and inequalities, especially in developed countries where welfare is supposed to be favourable to education; a condition for high productivity. We have discussed all the factors – geographical, cultural and sociological, and the price levels – but there are limits to sustainable differences within a zone requiring corrective actions after they have been measured. There is a need to soften the movement of populations, depending on their education and expertise, to accommodate migration but also to add to individual competition for education, for instance. The general goal is the same on both sides of the Atlantic, but the answers are different.

---

[44] Today's UK.

[45] We don't have to address Chinese structural answers as the population cannot so far freely move across the country.

[46] See Chapter 1 on the Ancient Greece Solon's law to cancel debts.

EUROPE AND THE USA

The US Answer to Inequalities

The USA faces the issue of wide differences in personal income between states per capita income (in thousand dollars) and other major aggregates (source: Bureau of Economic Analysis (BEA)). The US nominal GDP for 2012 was 16,224,000 for 313,914 million (estimated) inhabitants, equivalent to $51,682 per capita, but differences are important when looked at on regional and household levels. See Table 7.2.

These statistics include transfers made through social programmes. Out of a GDP of 13,362 billion (June 2012) transfers represented 2362 trillion, that is to say 17.68%, made up of social security 759.4 trillion, Medicare 556.9 trillion, Medicaid 410.7 trillion and others 433.8 trillion. The transfers are not allocated per state here, and also expenditures over 3 trillion (including social transfers) are not either. This means that the per capita net income, if giving a good sense of differences in standard of living, should be interpreted with care considering also that they are only an average.

Nevertheless, social programmes and grants by the Federal government are tools for coherence in the USA, each state and municipality keeping their own budgets and liabilities but somehow being subsidized by the capability of issuing tax-free bonds.

The EU Answer to Inequalities

The EU and the Eurozone being of more recent creation than the USA, culturally diverse and having been joined by many countries coming from a communist world with different individual economic behaviours, the matter of inequalities has been recognized from inception. The concepts result already from the Single European Act of 1987 that institutionalized the goal of completing the internal market unification with total borders opening by December 31, 1992. The fast speed of unification required mitigation of the effect of market unification that would, under competition, destroy some of the production that has been protected by physical borders and tariffs. The Union's budget is limited to 132.7 billion for 2013, mostly financed by contributions from member states based on their GDP capped at 1.23%, and custom duties as well as a share of VAT.

Structural Funds and Cohesion Funds

The December 13, 2007 Lisbon Treaty was enforced in December 2009, with political common structures aimed at reviving the entire European project that started just after the war

TABLE 7.2 Households' mean income in 2012 (000 $)

The richest		The poorest	
Connecticut	94.80	New Mexico	59.20
New Jersey	94.00	South California	59.00
Massachusetts	89.20	Idaho	58.70
Alaska	84.70	Alabama	57.30
New York	81.40	Arkansas	54.10
Minnesota	75.20	West Virginia	53.90
Delaware	74.50	Mississippi	52.70

Source: Extract from Bureau of Census schedule S1901.

(CECA Treaty). When determining the functioning of the EU (eur-lexeuropea.eu), negotiators had in mind going much further than the mere monetary and free trade zone already achieved. The monetary union with a single currency decided on at the Maastricht Treaty of February 7, 1992 was already fully enforced with the introduction in 2002 of cash euros for the member states' citizens. We have to remember that, after the fall of a military union project (European Defence Community (EDC)) in 1950, the "Fathers" already had in mind an economic and political union, but their heirs concentrated on economic goals.

To address the need to reduce economic and social differences inside the EU, the European Parliament and the Council of the European Union defined and prioritized objectives through the period January 1, 2007 to December 31, 2013. With a project approach, three funds were created, fed by European budget resources of €347 billion for the period. The European Regional Development Fund was granted €201 billion. The European Social Fund was granted €67 billion and the Cohesion Fund €70 billion. The first objective was to address convergence between European regions. The threshold was to finance projects in a region where the GDP per capita was under 75% of the EU average, and aimed at accelerating their development. The second objective, not limited to any region outside those already covered by the cohesion fund, was to reinforce competitiveness, employment and attractiveness with innovation, promotion of entrepreneurship and environment protection as motto. The third and last objective was to favour trans-territorial cooperation with the ultimate goal of strengthening the economic and social cohesion of the Union. Cities and regions are induced to work together by learning from each other and setting joint projects.

We can see that many of the European Fathers' objectives have been achieved, and that the integration of countries that have only recently joined is still at stake. The European GDP for 2012 ranks at 16.8 trillion dollars for 507.69 million inhabitants. In 2010, the average per capita income was 32,400 euros (source: CIA facts). As opposed to the USA because of its different history, there are very few EU budget transfers. All of the very developed social coverage systems are per country. Further, the EU budget is very limited at around 120 trillion per year. As a percentage of GDP this is not comparable to the US structure seen above, receipts are at 44.53% for the Euro 28 or 45.3% for the Eurozone 18, and expenses at respectively 49.1% and 49.4% determining an around 4% of GDP deficit (source: Eurostat). See Table 7.3.

TABLE 7.3   GDP per person in the 28 member states

The richest (per capita 000 $)		The poorest	
Luxembourg	62.5	Bulgaria	10.3
Netherlands	31.0	Romania	11.0
Ireland	30.0	Latvia	12.0
Austria	29.3	Lithuania	12.8
Denmark	28.9	Estonia	14.9
Sweden	28.1	Poland	14.3
Belgium	27.7	Hungary	15.2
Germany	27.2	Slovakia	17.0
Finland	26.9	Portugal	18.0
UK	26.0	Malta	19.2
France	25.4	Czech. Rep.	19.3

Source: Eurostat 2009.

Besides the case of Luxembourg, more or less a city of 600,000 inhabitants, we immediately note the rather concentrated figures of average personal income when considering that the poorest are just those who recently joined the Union. Inside each country (Eurostat producing per-region statistics), the dispersion is more or less one-to-two and in some cases one-to-three.

The General Monetary Policy on Both Sides: Reinforce Equity, Regulate Transparency – A Dead End

The regulator has a problem. They are appointed to deal with a limited field. Free markets and free currency exchanges are the conceptual operating rule they have to guard. As opposed to general law, regulation is designed to address some specific goals such as fair competition and risk control. Because the 2007 crisis was shown to be financial with the collapse of the banking system, and some related industries such as insurance-issuing CDSs (AIG), the regulators – the same ones who did not see anything coming – were put in charge to create a framework that would prevent a repetition of such events.

This was the G20 agenda since the Pittsburgh meeting of September 2009. The tools already existed. Civil agencies were reinforced with the Dodd–Frank Act in the USA and some added. The European scheme, just coming out from the recent single currency set-up (1989), compared with the US dollar and 1913 central bank creation, was accelerated and a global system drawn with a coordination system set-up. The BIS (see above and Glossary), with its committees – Basel and Solvency; the USA being a witness more than an actor – self-assigned its new horizons with the agencies resulting from Dodd–Frank. In reality, the USA first wanted to keep its seignorage privilege benefit and no one in the administration wanted to change anything and take the risk of jeopardizing some of the US sovereignty that would have, in any case, required Congress to concur. They did not want any change to their banking and insurance surveillance system on which they had shown they could operate with no restriction. This has changed since bank competition implied trust for depositors and liberty to operate MMFs and other shadow banking institutions who can agree, or not, to refinance banks and set the lending rates of the money resources coming directly from the retirement system, individuals and big corporations on an already globalized mechanism. Despite having some advance in developing a strong surveillance system since Dodd–Frank, the USA has agreed to comply with the Basel III EU-driven standards, while not having yet implemented Basel II standard requisites regarding direct leverage, portfolio-weighted leverage and liquidity. It is to be a long process; the topics at stake lie on very technical details leading to major differential effects.

The surveillance systems are based on property laws and execution laws as well as guarantee mechanisms, which are specific to each monetary zone if not to countries. Made up of layers after layers, they are complicated and so much mended to consider possible and discovered leaks that only specialists could be effective if no grand plan replaced the existing playing field. If one plan was to come out, the obstacle would be that the dismantling has to be operated in an orderly manner and cannot be done instantly. A transition process will be needed, with all of the risks that would accompany it. Some monetary instruments will have to be of general status and treatment; others, either specific to a zone or customized, will have to be dealt with using an equivalence approach.

The knowledge of the playing field is also limited field by field, while the underlying material is money, meaning it is totally interconnected, as we have seen. Touching one thing could make the building that had been hit collapse. The crisis was already a demonstration of the absence of knowledge, when very few realized that helping the citizen to acquire real estate would generate uncollectable loans even if warranted by Freddy Mac and Fanny Mae, which in turn would generate a price bubble and a collapse. The collapse, limited at a time to the lending industry and under control of the Federal Housing Administration, would degenerate and, through the fair value accounting standard and by contagion, hit investments banks' warrantors and the entire western world with the price contraction of assets – one loss obliging others to sell, while the concept is that debt at nominal value evidently has to be reimbursed at par, just because of trust requirements and also because of the laws. Otherwise, it would be a case of bankruptcy laws applying to another environment if they became general.

The only answer to the crisis on both sides of the Atlantic that could be found was to act on the aggregates that were available. The management of loan distribution standards to be required from portfolio managers, and the reinforcement of equity requirements to be linked to the kind of exposures, was the answer. Nothing is very new there. Hayek already wrote about "the fatal conceit" of the belief, derived from physics, that measurement is an essential foundation of all sciences. He also cited a German philosopher named Erhard Weigel, who strove to construct a universal science which he proposed to call Pantaometra based, as the name suggests, on measuring everything.[47] Jean-Pierre Aubin[48] adds: "Cognitive sciences do not sustain that rationality of human brains can be reduced to the maximization of utility functions", the existence of which was already questioned by Henri Poincaré in a letter to Léon Walras: "satisfaction is thus a magnitude, but not a measurable magnitude".

The policy to enhance transparency with better moral justification for making financial statements totally comparable and markets equal for participants, allowing a power to sanction breaches, will not bring any sensible answer to the risks. Financial instruments' price determination does not follow the same rules as for other tangible assets or services. Value and price are not in the same relationship. The contractual origin of money is going to create, with the trust factor, separate formulae. Few limits to the resulting price volatility explain bubbles. The image of the instrument improved by transparency rules may exacerbate the phenomenon. Like double posting, when a participant fails, a change in trust or in interest rates will spread automatic changes in value that only market breakers could stop, but will not treat. We will see in Chapter 8 the run-for-safe-assets outcome. There is no adjustment of supply to demand. On the contrary, investors will look for safety, meaning little debt for the issuer who is in a financially balanced pattern with no need to issue.

The prudential policy that is conducted, if reducing the ongoing immediate risk, is just a tree hiding in the forest. Worse, it is misleading as, like for price increases, it facilitates refinancing non-productive investments when public budgets are imbalanced in many countries. To give an example, solvency investing in private equity will cost 47% of capital requirement, 37% for private bands and nothing for public debts. The guidance designed just for handling surveillance is, by itself, like the Maginot line,[49] a factor for them to be overridden by smarter users while the operators, buried in their conviction of having covered everything, feel safe.

---

[47] Idea matheseos universae cum speciminibus inventionum mathematicarum.

[48] Already quoted: *Time and Money*.

[49] Named by the general who designed it, to protect France from any German invasion from the East. It was not built alongside the mountainous Vosges region as this was deemed to be impracticable for tanks. In June 1940 the Germans overrode the Maginot line and passed through the Vosges.

They are missing a major risk factor – they have no antidote for the risk of money disaster that a collapse in prices is to create, as well as a slowdown in market trading volumes if not artificial. The money and intellectual resources spent for that, instead of ethics sanctioning and moral guidance, is worse than a loss.

A structured reform of the legal and monetary system and firewall mechanisms between zones to give time for rescuers in case of a collapse, or erratic changes in values that could trigger a collapse, are now a prerequisite before anything else is conducted. The required equity ratios determined on both sides of the Atlantic are amusing tools for statisticians, but they will disappear within a matter of seconds, faster than the books can be closed and reported to agencies, and new monetary injections will be required for further stealing from those with fixed incomes. The general pattern of the system having not changed, one cannot imagine that the scenario will be different than it was during 2007–2008. It can already be forecasted. The only difference will be that, as the functioning of the aforementioned Gresham law[50] is known as reversal, one cannot say at what level of injections the crisis may devolve into a fatal collapse.

The increase of equity amounts is to give a cushion to absorb variation in the value of assets. It is not a system. It is a buffer for a car, but the passengers may die with indirect shock resulting from deceleration. The plethoric regulation (like Basel) to determine for banks and other institutions carrying systemic financial risk appraised by risk weighting the portfolios and putting limits on leverage (proportion between total balance sheet and equity) is not a system by itself, just as bumpers do not address the issue of having cars with good brakes and knowing the speed limit. In the current environment of very different regulations and practices (mortgage-backed securities, etc.) between both sides of the Atlantic it will just enhance the value of financial creativity that will always go faster than regulation. It also undervalues the capacity for lobbyists to push for any kind of balancing between credits and debits that would result in a diminishing of the balance sheet totals, and therefore reduce the leverage appearance. The cushion theory that regulators have adopted, if grounded, is contradictory to the mechanism created to increase money rotation; the securitization process. Regulators are doing their best, but cannot, as a whole, resist mechanisms that have been designed for contradictory purposes, even if some are pushing for restrictions by asking sellers to keep some of the risk. This absence of global concept to override and choice between contradictory goals is again in need but cannot be conceived in the limited field of each jurisdiction, while money is global and any increase in its rotation increases its availability in greater proportion than its mere issuance, which is already large because of macroeconomic imbalances.

The Disputed Strategy: Addressing Macroeconomic Imbalances

Of course, imbalances such as in the balance of trade, the balance of payments and the budget deficit are a problem, as they create money accumulation, a result of the money issuance to finance them. We have already demonstrated that any transaction which is not cleared will result in the creation of a potential financial instrument that is a receivable. It will show on the

---

[50] Sir Thomas Gresham (1519–1579), after Arisphonanes' *The Frog* in 405 BC and others, said: "bad money drives out good". We know that this assumption, if taken as a law, is wrong and that it depends on the environment. The mistake is demonstrated by facts. Gold francs superseded the silver bimetallic system in the Latin Union. We know what made the Macedonian stater, the florin, the Roman denarius, the British pound and the US dollar not be held as "bad money", to become universally in use. For all it was the quality of the issuer or the warrantees attached, if not both.

financial statements of at least two parties, if they are not individuals who are not submitted to the obligation of accounting. It will be possible to refinance it by selling it. It can also be accumulated by any new acquiring holder, then making the global picture disconnected from the growth or contraction of production output.

Only looking at financials and net equity, one may believe there is enrichment, especially when interest rates are on a downtrend and prices going up.[51] The cooking of books happens, and the fact that the accumulation of notes and other financial instruments outside a monetary zone is not really recorded does not change them, but through balances deriving from trade deficit and intercompany lending aggravate their consequences of distorting images. The facts are hidden if, for whatever reasons, the money flows, as there is a natural tendency for issued money to go back to the zone where it was issued. Nevertheless, imbalances are not sustainable in the long run. The more transparency in books, the less they will be sustainable because the witness will soon reconcile with the expectation for money guarantees and return. Money managers, with this longer life expectancy of their clients, have to report on how they protect the money they are handling and the expectation is there. The phenomenon now operates on both faces. If the transparency expectation is not satisfied, and others are providing it, money will flow away from the first to the second. Whichever face you look at, it is determined that macroeconomic imbalances will not survive in the long run. However, the question that comes next is how and how fast to address them. Here comes the dispute.

Regarding budget balancing, if a majority of economists agree to the fact that it is not sustainable, they differ on the solutions. Most of them, as is understandable, are against increased taxation and advise some European countries not to do so. Some believe that reducing expenses will resolve the imbalances, and that the liberated money will be more efficient when used by the private sector. IMF experts and ECB experts disagree on the topic of stopping money issuances by balancing budgets. The IMF is now for flexibility, while the EU – having to address the ESM and banking union (see Mundell's theory) – advocates balanced macroeconomic aggregates. It has committed each of the member countries to budget discipline and, with aging populations and high social benefits, to reforms of the labour market. With an existing trade surplus, the balancing of macroeconomic surplus is within reach for the Union. The matter then is only governmental debt, and the future budget discipline for some of the member states. For the USA the playing field is wider, because the international use of the dollar interacts with other currency zones. The speed of the treatments to be inflicted determining sociological resistance is also at stake, and cannot be forgotten. We believe again that, as everyone is deemed to be intellectually honest, the dispute is due to the lack of sound information on monetary functioning. One has to admit that, so far, money injections made through so-called quantitative easing have not been efficient. Out of necessity it only allowed, at a certain point in time, the survival of banking institutions and had a price effect on the balancing of balance sheets destroyed by the value contraction of posted assets with the fair market accounting standard linked to an imperfect market. As we know, perfection is not defined with regard to sustainability, and if it is not linked to the evolution of production and demand they are a threat to stability. Others believe that the issuance of money is just a result of the seignorage benefit, and should continue to let the markets decide when to adjust.

This strategy can only be destructive, as modern industries require the accumulation of intangible assets such as human resources gathered as teams. When destroyed, it does not regenerate like a field not cultivated for a while. It may be destroyed definitively, and

---

[51] See the play by the German author Bertolt Brecht: "The Fabrizi System".

be transferred elsewhere forever. "Laissez-faire" cannot be a sensible policy, and on that topic western governments under pressure of the crisis converged to take action. Now, while we are in an indecisive situation, deviant thinkers can again suggest that markets operate freely outside any recognizable frame. There is no hope in such a strategy, except if it is a rupture strategy that would give birth to a new world. But again, this new world will have to be regulated. The problem is that no one knows what the social casualties may be in cases of disruption, and if the new world will be a democratic one. Past history does not play out for such a dramatic policy. This is probably the reason why the FED Board decided not to take the risk of reducing its quantitative easing, consisting of non-conventional policies of buying public debts. Debt accumulation will be the next topic for monetary policy makers. With uncertainty about GDP growth, they are besieged between letting the rates and the debt costs rise and reducing the debt volume, a factor not under control of the central bank.

The US$ credit position to the rest of the world has tended to grow much faster than credit to US residents, "a gap that has widened substantially after the crisis"[52] – a risk to be shared by both lenders and borrowers. "Large financial links among globally dispersed balance sheets can quietly transmit shocks of which the locations are too hard to predict, in unexpected ways. For example, the severe stress experienced during the financial crisis limited the ability of internationally active banks to supply credit. One result was that the cross border banks' lending to various emerging market economies declined much more than could be explained by demand factors alone."(Extract from OECD annual report.) This true comment from the OECD that just recognizes the importance of balance sheets in a monetary approach does not comment on the wrongly competitive national policies intended to favour domestic banks refinancing at the expense of other banks, just as currency exchange rate competition would. It is a matter that will have to be discussed inside the international authoritative monetary bodies, which is linked to the dollar role.

ALLOCATED ROLES AND GOALS IN THE INTERNATIONAL MONETARY SET-UP

To summarize how the current international monetary set-up operates, we can say that since the 2007 crisis, immense work has been achieved on both sides of the Atlantic, both at macro-surveillance and micro-surveillance levels.

- The liberal philosophy that governed the international relationship since the Reagan era is still prevailing, despite the 2007 crisis and especially, even with suspicions about the non-intervention on currency exchange rates in the context of criticism against China from other countries. The advantages of a fully open trade universe are still prevailing among nations.
- Regarding the achieving of commonly accepted philosophic goals, the allocation of duties has changed with events such as the US monetary role reduction with its withdrawal as a warrantor, but also because of the 2007–2008 financial crisis that resulted in the setting up of new meeting forums.

---

[52] OECD annual report 2010–2011.

- Nevertheless, national surveillance agencies trying to reign in the risks carried by their respective banking systems and evasion from their regulations are trying to expand them overseas, implementing policies that constitute barriers to globalization and free financial markets.
- The European surveillance system has a constitutional issue not yet fully addressed, which is the reporting to an elected democratic body such as the European Parliament. For the same historical reasons there is no European equivalent to the SEC.
- A lot is still missing, but is about to be achieved by the existing agencies, especially in terms of functioning and coherence about the roles as many issues may be relevant to several agencies – especially in the USA (SEC and BCFP, for example).
- The monetary issues have not been addressed in Europe or in the USA, as if nations did not want to see what happened in 2007, but the topic of handling huge monetary masses in a free market world is still there. The emergence of alternative payment instruments with insufficient control over legitimate use is now there with electronic monies.

The IMF's role has been reduced as the FSF and its successor the FSB have taken over the warning function. If the IMF is doing the job of issuing comments on its per-country analysis of economic developments and monetary policies, as a matter of fact because of the removal of its power to administrate a non-existing agreement on currency exchange rates and on monetary policies with little means and certainly no direct and indirect seignorage power, it became essentially an independent consulting firm.

The role of the WTO has increased as a forum for trade dispute, just as a result of a more global world where bigger companies are in dispute (aircraft manufacturers, etc.). As opposed to the "G" gatherings, the IMF and WTO are both legally grounded at an international level. None of the member countries want to suppress these financial institutions in case they need them.

The need for the G20 results from the difficulty of adapting the IMF and other Bretton Woods institutions to both new needs and new balances of power. The changes in voting rights and veto rights blockages are signs of this adaptation impossibility. Nevertheless, as a single-chamber democratic system has shown itself not to be sustainable, we believe that the G20 system, with other informal systems of decision making, may be the right answer to international coordination, splitting technical processes from sociologic issues and giving progressive answers to different urgencies and natures of problems. The border between what is national and what is international for regulation is a concern if no one wants a breaking off between monetary zones.

Today's International Situation and Issues

In Kingston, Jamaica on January 7–8, 1976, in the context of the 1975 oil crisis, under the Presidency of Willy de Clercq, Belgian Minister of Finance, the IMF Intermediate Governors Committee convened. It approved the already decided[53] sale of gold reserves. It also increased the authorized drawing ratio to members in proportion to their quotas both globally to 75% and per annum to 50%, and the lending ratio to 145%.

The framework for a new version of article IV of the IMF bylaws was also adopted to reshape these and substitute SDRs with gold for central bank reserves and to determine the exchange value of the currency. This agreement, a follow-up from the Jamaica agreement (see

---

[53] Press release dated August 1, 1975 on previous meeting of the Committee.

Chapter 3), put a formal end to Bretton Woods' fixed exchange currency system. It aims for stability, but contemplates adjustments in parities more in the way of a recommendation that can always be vetoed by the relevant country. It also tries, with a sale programme and a sharing of the realized profit resulting from the rise in price, to suppress the role of gold. Member countries were also to adopt a sale programme (see Chapter 3). None of the pursued objectives were reached.

As we have described, gold rose in value after the unilateral withdrawing of the USA in the summer of 1971, which had already put an end to the Bretton Woods system. In opposition to the aims, gold remained as a reserve at central banks and, furthermore, emerging countries and China was now buying gold as reserves. SDRs, with limited amounts, did not replace gold as a reserve. The free market of gold already at $450 a troy ounce compared with the official price of $42.22 when the USA gave up, reached $1000 and in 2013 floated around $1250 after a sharp fall from a peak at $1900 in 2012 since India put a tax on gold imports to restrain them, meaning that the market price is no longer a free market price. At the same time, markets were deemed to be perfect and international institutions were pushed by their key member states to demonetize gold to regain credibility. For sure, the banks which sold some of their gold looked like idiots at the expense of their citizens.

The causes of the US monetary crisis took place with the Keynesian policy followed by Kennedy while the economy was on the eve of slowing down. The strong dollar policy that followed with Reagan in 1984 further deteriorated the industrial position of the USA while at the same time the free trade philosophy did not benefit America except for American consumption, as a matter of fact, of Asia's production and China's industrial investments. The Secretary of Treasury John Connally said:[54] "The dollar is our currency but your problem." It was doubly true. Neither the USA nor the IMF was to overcome the matter of structural changes in relative economic power and allowing credit between generations to be a non-considered issue. The hiding from the public of the real economic trends was intended because of their political consequences. It was much more comfortable to let an asset. The posting of social debts resulting from population aging was not even politically correct, as it depended widely on the standard of living and health systems. It was not and could not be the duty of anyone, of any international institution or any central bank to raise these existing issues. Leadership was needed to remind people of the realities. Structurally, it could not legitimately exist and if it did, would not have been listened to.

We have widely discussed, in our first book, the mechanism by which the 2007 crisis broke out, but the fact is that the international negotiations of the 1970s addressed topics that were no longer in existence and did not consider what would or may come.

QUESTIONS AND ANSWERS

International Exchanges and Monetary Zone Coherence

How should international money and international monetary set-ups be defined?
Money, being a receivable and universal claimable instrument with a specific referential stamp, has to meet with different other stamps – what we call today foreign currencies. For guarantee reasons and seignorage rights, stamps are national. When meeting, we are

---

[54] Nixon's Secretary of State speech to European leaders in 1971.

on the international playing field, today on the currency markets both financial and raw material. International monetary institutions are the gatherings where nations will try to organize their common concern about international monetary exchanges.

Is what international monetary institutions pursue only international and currency stamping?

Not any longer, since the Bretton Woods agreements are over. They will also deal with national issues when supporting a distressed or underdeveloped participant, but when doing so they are in the pattern of favouring exchanges or avoiding contagious failures in international trade. They are now also dealing with stability as with convertibility; many financial markets are global, and their participants from various countries as well as the instruments they trade and clear are used by international participants. They will also try to follow up on systemic risks and set common goals about surveillance and regulation.

What are the key international monetary institutions and forums?

IMF, BIS, WTO, forums such as G20 and set-ups such as Troika.

What are the issues?

The change in the environment has not been followed by a monetary reform. The environment has changed and outdated the IMF statutory role. The economic strengths are shared differently, with emerging countries underrepresented. Extended money masses are not available for central interventions in cases of value volatility and currency exchange crisis. There is no general understanding of what money should be and how nations could coordinate their rights to guarantee money and exchange rates from crisis. Stamped values are no longer proportional to country reserves, while money became exchangeable and can flow between zones. There is another issue, which is the changes in economic power of the participants in international exchanges that the lack of flexibility of formally created institutions cannot reflect. This is the reason for G20 and Troika.

What are the common goals of international monetary bodies?

Monetary stability and to be a warning body about instability risks. They favour development.

What are the key functions of monetary international institutions?

They gather statistical data, they survey, regulate, give advice and sometimes they are granted the power to act on the financial markets.

What is their toolbox?

They may have money to lend, reserves or credit to give guarantees, and have consulting experts.

Why do we have monetary zone interactions?

Because of exchanges and companies' consolidation to achieve scale economies irrelevant of frontiers, consolidated balance sheets are spreading risk over the borders. The AIG London branch failure is an example during the 2007 crisis, causing the US government to intervene in support of AIG.

Why is there a need for the G20 coordination forum?

Because financial regulation remains ultimately mainly national, despite converging standards, while the main financial markets and financial systemic institutions are global.

What is the new surveillance system?
In the absence of a global monetary reform that was not possible to achieve due to its urgency, one of the only steps taken after the crisis was to create a forum – the FSB – gathering central banks, public treasuries and national oversight authorities. In addition, monetary zones reinforced their surveillance and regulation systems of the financial industries by creating, when needed, new agencies, and increasing prudential constraints for financial institutions and improving surveillance. For Europe, to avoid heterogeneity and be comparable with the USA, the ultimate regulation power was granted to the ECB as it was to the US FED. The Eurozone and European Union also reinforced its internal coherence to better guarantee the functioning of the banking system and unity of currency and interest rates throughout the zone. The zone also had to comply with the need for an optimum monetary zone, which is to provide a levelled playing field for its economic actors.

What are the key points addressed by agencies?
They are prudential constraints to avoid as far as possible sudden failures and limit risk taking and a resolution process that would limit contagion in case of inevitable failure.

What is a currency zone?
A currency zone is a geographical and/or political perimeter where inhabitants, individuals, corporations or civil agencies use the same monetary unit to exchange goods and services. It may be a matter of fact or a legal situation when such a zone corresponds to the use of a legal tender.

Who invented the concept of an optimum currency zone?
Professor Robert Mundell.

What does Mundell attribute to an optimum monetary zone?
Mundell says that a currency zone is optimum when means of production and labour can flow freely through such a zone.

Why is it a dead end for monetary policy to aim at achieving better stability of the banking system by increasing equity?
Just because it does not address the fundamental issue of money velocity and price levels, meaning that equity can be eaten up in a matter of seconds or just become meaningless. On the contrary, equity seen as a cushion to absorb price variation is dangerous – it contributes to accumulations that are an opposite concept to money velocity.

What is the disputed topic about macroeconomic unbalances?
Unbalances have determined huge public debts in balance sheets. These balance sheets have grown faster than production, bringing a systemic risk rising with transparency. How to reduce these excesses is disputed. Should it be through increasing taxes or reducing governmental expenses, and at what speed?

CHAPTER 8

What is the Conceptual Essence of Contractual Money, Constraints and Implications?

"The realistic alternative to an impracticable general micro-economy is to directly apprehend aggregated dimensions. Chosen because of the lack of other possible approach, the alternative raises a lot of problems. Most often considering directly aggregated dimensions is a cause for uncertainty or mistakes one should appraise the extent."[1]

— **Edmond Malinvaud (translation from French)**

In analysing what constitutes money, how it is used and characterized, and how it is currently managed on an international scale, we have raised issues relating to the concept of money. Among these varied issues, we first have to look at where new money stands and fits with a non-disrupted environment. Our conclusion as witness is that money became essentially of contractual nature with the deregulation that started with the Reagan era. Money is exchangeable receivables accepted by economic agents and regulated. M5, M6 and derivatives are its fairest real representation.

THE INTRINSIC NEW CONCEPTUAL VIEWS ON MONEY

Once we have treated the practical questions, how should money be viewed today from a philosophical point of view when considered as contractual and escaping strict traditional unity?

1. The contractual approach is not antagonistic to regulation, or to the development of markets. Regulation guarantees, and marketplaces are guaranteed by, general laws and jurisprudence for the contracts that financial instruments are. Specific laws and regulations are attached to them by internally set procurements for marketplaces. What is at stake is the

---

[1] Malinvaud, E., *Macroeconomic Research Paths*, ch. 6, p. 151. See References.

internationalization of both the law and the markets. Europe, as well as previous legal systems since the Roman Empire, has shown that a distinction can be made between rights attached to individuals and the rules related to commercial law. The law of money and financial instruments can become international (we already have international treaties establishing legal processes governing postal services, air transportation, sea transportation, etc.) by treaty and by law. The law defines the limits of liberty in continuation of the ideas of French philosophers and Locke, who set the foundations for our civilization. The current situation of the absence of a general international law governing key tradable financial instruments is not only a hassle for the economy, it is also a source of individual and collective risk – in particular as a limitation on economic growth but to the contrary by setting limits it opens new spaces for exchange. The existence of a general law is the necessary frame for contractual flexibility.

2. The contractual approach is mistakenly seen as personal liberty and opposed to social constraints.

This mistaken view misconstrues the evolution of our society when, in the 17th century, the first legal norms were created allowing the joining together by contract of several individuals into a corporation for a joint economic purpose. Contract law allowed these entities, after a simple registration and after obtaining the sovereign's approval, to become parties to contracts as natural persons could. The company, or corporation, was born. While this development recognized freedom of contract, it also recognized the need to take into account the rights of third parties. The contract setting up a partnership or corporation and giving it fiduciary duties that are not always yet fully recognized in some legislation in the western world provides broadened guarantees to the individuals dealing with these partnerships and corporations. Each time the law and the courts create a new kind of legal entity, or use such an entity creatively for special purposes, fiduciary duties are attached as a singular principle, demonstrating the importance of being accorded trust. Countries with judicial systems sanctioning severely the breach of fiduciary duties have more developed marketplaces (London in the UK, New York in the USA). The trust institution often used to support retirement benefits developed from the Roman institutions (Fiducia) has seen significant development.

3. The contractual approach does not prevent the consideration of social constraints.

A healthy regulatory system takes into account social constraints, and this is certainly a major issue for our modern societies. In many countries, this is a dual issue. First, it is a question of the time of retirement and the necessary associated benefits when life expectancy has increased compared with the productive period of life when contributions can be made. This question also covers issues related to healthcare coverage increasing costs when individuals are aging. Second, it is a question of how to organize and quantify the transfers of bargaining power between active people or enterprises and retired or ill people. These important matters have nothing to do with money concepts except for the fact that money is the intermediate tool to achieve whatever is decided by society about them. Again, money is required to post on books or to collect and transfer the needed bargaining power between contributors and benefactors. The more the periods to cover are extended, the more money has to be used both to measure the obligations and to record them on books. These societal concerns will influence national monetary policies since long life expectancies will lead governments to support stable money to protect the rights of retired citizens from inflation or from changes in the exchange ratios deriving from government action. The trend to reduce the benefits of idle citizens in order to give incentives to productive ones is thus at stake.

4. The contractual approach implies the need for regulation, justice and laws.

As opposed to what some of the authors cited herein (although not the majority) have written, it has not been demonstrated that money can exist as a totally private means of payment. The distinction between private and public is even subject to debate. A commonly accepted rule is private to the extent that it does not derive from a parliament. A rule deriving from parliament is a statutory rule. So what are we talking about here? In Chapter 4 we discovered some rules that are universally accepted. The trust's byelaws are the laws for its members, and this does not prevent the government through its agencies from getting involved. Because of the resulting diversity of individual and collective contractual liberty, which is a major advantage for flexibility and continuous adaption to environments, the problem of international coherence is raised, not with respect to what attaches to individuals, like culture, but with respect to financial markets. Again, this is a positive argument for pushing ahead with ongoing international negotiations.

5. Ultimately, the open issue is who, collectively, will have the right to intervene in global money measurement standards and money flows.

The extension of both monetary zones and monetary instruments has reduced the role of traditional script money to make the concept of legal tender almost irrelevant, not only inside such zones, but internationally. The credibility of guarantees linked to the value of tangible assets (such as real-estate assets for securitization, or solvent companies for commercial paper, or trading and payment platforms) has become a key factor for money credibility and thus for its rotation speed. Because financial markets are global, and if we accept the fact that globalization represents progress, there is a need for unification of legal structures and concepts to implement them. We argue that an international dialogue is needed to define the scope of international intervention as to the surveillance of money aggregates and exchange rates, to replace the Bretton Woods agreements and their failed successor, the Jamaica agreement. The issue of what should be centralized and what should be decentralized, which has already been analysed at the modern EU level, needs to be duplicated at the transatlantic level.

6. M5/M6 and the image effect.

As we have tried to demonstrate, today's money is the result of contracts, that is to say human economic activities. As a calendar is used to allow humans to meet at an agreed time, contracts imply a calendar, which is the time of delivery and payment. It is the legal image of the acceptance of a transfer of control or use of property. Financial statements are cut-outs of the image of explicit contracts (sales contracts, retirement benefits and other redistributions) and the implicit social contract of a society, its profile of consumption and sharing. Exchange ratios and sampled balances do not appear in this image. Ratings, values and prices, such as for gold and other raw materials or analysis through models, need to be looked at separately, as they sometimes impact the entire economy by contract (such as Libor and other interest rates). The provision of this information should be considered a monetary privilege of the same nature as seignorage was when stamping a coin and granting the coin a transferability right based on sovereignty. The correction of accounting standards (changing from a fair market value standard which was based on the mistaken, incomprehensible idea that markets represent a universally acceptable truth) and the clear identity and disclosure of who is in charge and what the purpose and effect of the image are, are of key importance in order to fulfil the expectation of the social contract that money represents. The self-realization that a rating, valuation or pricing creates is of the same effect as an indictment to the public, because the act of characterizing something or someone in fact impacts the reality of that thing or person. Like a judicial system, such a measurement must respect moral rules as a necessary component of the fair and transparent information necessary for the exercise of contractual liberty.

Those who manipulated Libor or Euribor have been sued. Those who set financial and accounting standards should also be liable in the event of wrongdoing with respect to influencing the presentation of information.

Resilient Open Questions in a New Environment

Understanding What Money Became; What Characterizes Money From Other Contracts Remains Unchanged

We have to focus our attention on sampling and the stability of sampling required for monetary exchange ratios, the trust resulting from guarantees backing both sampling and clearing. These aspects of money, when they work together, create the social contract that links all users of money, a social contract without which money would vanish. See Figure 8.1.

The definition of "extended money" described in previous chapters does not address the question of price sampling, as was already recognized by Hayek and Von Mises when they remarked that extended money is not a physical measurement. In order to flow freely, money must fulfil its role as a measurement tool and, it follows, if this role cannot be fulfilled, then parties to a transaction will not use it, and we will move outside the monetary realm to find them back in a barter exchange system. A new exchange basis therefore needs to be found to create trust in the stability of the measurement. This is an open issue, about which Robert A. Mundell had some ideas (conference at Pierre Mendes France Conference Centre in the Paris Ministry of Finance, Les Entretiens du Trésor, 2011). Mundell advocates the creation of a new currency in addition to the IMF's SDR system.

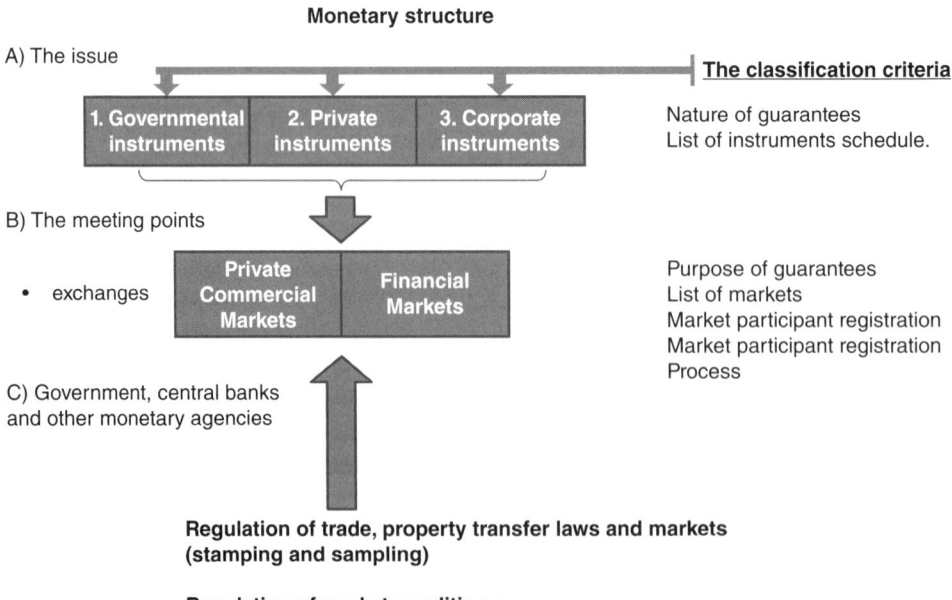

FIGURE 8.1   Monetary structure

How do we create guarantees that money does in fact exist and that it is indeed exchangeable? This question has two aspects. One is purely legal. Acting pursuant to a G20 decision, existing regulatory agencies have already pursued the goal of requiring most financial instruments to trade on regulated markets under appropriate worldwide coordination. Existing self-regulatory private markets have strengthened this process by allowing safe international trading of financial instruments without concentrating systemic risk in fewer markets and with fewer market players who are themselves subject to more prudential constraints. Central banks and regulatory agencies are raising this issue to no avail since they have no political power. In the meantime, regulatory agencies are trying to put the toothpaste of excess money back into the tube by issuing definitions and implementing new regulations or are trying to extend the tube's capacity to accommodate money. They define what a payment is, and what a clearing house is to provide, on a market-to-market basis and an instrument-by-instrument basis instead of establishing a general concept that market players and judges can follow up on. They will still have to decide what the consequences are, and to whom, of trading not listed on regulated marketplace financial instruments. Although they are doing their job, these regulatory agencies are beating around the bush by failing to deal with some very basic issues.

The first issue as to whether some monetary instruments should be redeemable, as currencies were in the past, and how that should be carried out, still needs to be raised. As does the question of what the nature of the guarantee should be and who should provide such a guarantee. On the contrary, what are being dealt with are the processes for unwinding – that is, how should the IMF organize a default when that becomes necessary, or, in essence, how can the funeral of dead institutions be organized without harming counterparties. The goal is achievable with lesser leverage of market participants and rules to allocate losses between bigger ones. However, it will result in a monetary contraction by virtue of the default of either particular financial instruments or the entire monetary system, with resultant, unknown social consequences. It is not the duty of these agencies, but rather that of the systemic risk surveillance oversight boards. These boards, however, cannot act legitimately since the issue of political leadership is at stake.

The second aspect of the issue of guarantees is what type of guarantee should be provided to holders after the instant of default to organize a resolution, and how should that guarantee be operated in order to be credible and to satisfy the expectation that the currency as a trading price is stable both during trading before the default, and after the market resumes operations. This question also raises the issue of the appropriate firewall mechanisms necessary for each market category if liquidity is disappearing or price variation too ample to be sustainable and how such a buffer should operate, whether automatically or by activation.

What kind of monetary instruments should be liquid, guaranteed in all circumstances like bank notes (meaning repayable on demand)? Which ones should be liquid because they are traded on financial markets, and not because of their maturity date, and in such a market, what should be the nature of the guarantee provided to participants, by whom, and to what extent? Where to set the boundaries is a key question.

The new understanding of money flows and the accumulation of recorded assets and liabilities that the extension of money aggregates will bring will, like any breakthrough, pose new questions. If we better understand flows and accumulation, logic demands that we find links between flows and standing open balances. In other words, we will have to expand our knowledge of processing and the reality of currency rotation.

This will open up an enormous field of discussion as to how to analyse the reasonable limits of aggregates and how to analyse the moving links between them. It will also open up the matter of a coherent taxation system and even the need to dismantle the tax systems that have developed over years and which no longer make sense.

Finally, it will raise the issue of why the new G20 meeting forum did not achieve what was expected of it as soon as the peak in the liquidity crisis was over – that is, an idea of how to create a process to approach all these matters, and what kind of conclusions can be expected.

STABILITY AND GUARANTEES

Several theoretical questions arise from the practical issues we have discussed in previous chapters. First is the question of money stability and the international money exchange stability target. Second, where will we find the necessary guarantees and trust in the new monetary system? Third, who wields seignorage power today? Finally, how is the new money to play its necessary social role?

Money as a Measurement Instrument: The Need for Stability

We have already seen that the role of money has changed. Now we will describe further several strategic structural changes, both political and technical.

As a technical matter, we have explained that the result of enlarged financial markets and limited disposable income is that the role of money is basically more of an exchange ratio than a means of payment relating to a transaction, and that such an exchange ratio relates to the balances resulting from a transaction if cleared and if not carried over indefinitely. However, within a unified monetary zone, meaning a single accounting system, the matter of the means of payment lost the role it had when payments were made by coins or paper bills. If all figures appearing on records and statements are multiplied or divided by a factor, nothing will change. This, in fact, happened on a single day in Europe on January 1, 2002, when national currencies were replaced by euros after the exchange rates between them had been stabilized for several years.

What is the impact of international currency exchange rate fluctuation? For external trade, fluctuation impacts countries trading between them with costs expressed in their respective currencies. Uncontrolled variations will prevent volume increases for such trade because of the risk of loss for either the exporting or the importing country. For the same reason, uncontrolled variations will be a deterrent to economic integration. Some countries import raw materials more than industrial finished products and vice versa, and there are an infinite variety of particular situations. Some countries have significant agricultural production, and some are more industrial than agricultural, as if they are compensating for their dependence on other countries for their basic needs. Some countries have significant raw material resources, and others have little or none. All of these countries will be impacted differently. Differences and specialization have already been described by Adam Smith as the basis for international exchanges. To allow long-term investments and knowledge of returns, as required for industrialized countries, and social peace for populations to be fed, there is an expectation of stable exchange rates in order to maintain stable internal prices and stable costs of production.

In modern times, and until WWII, the goal was clear and was reflected both in constitutions and in the creation of vast colonial empires by France and Britain to ensure their needs inside their unified monetary zones. Constitutions and central bank byelaws reflected the same concern for stable currency exchanges as a bastion against inflation. The 1929 US crisis – despite great efforts but successive competitive devaluations – reached Europe, especially Britain and Germany, in 1931, slowly leading with successive political failures to the devastation of WWII. The 1944 Bretton Woods IMF byelaws, meant to address the pre-war monetary problems, still reflected governments' concern with maintaining the general link to gold with stability. They failed.

The world has changed. Colonial empires and the big trading companies of the 17th century have disappeared. They have been replaced by free trade zones with a new kind of economic integration based on geographic proximity (such as ALENA in North America, Mercosur in South America and the EU in Europe) and by global, financially integrated companies, operating transnationally and beyond economic zones, as oil companies have been doing for decades and as most companies within the new economy are doing today (Google, Microsoft, Apple, etc.). The relative costs of raw materials and agricultural products in final products have been reduced drastically compared with intellectual contributions to costs, including R&D and marketing, and logistical costs, such as wrapping and storage, distribution and related activities and new businesses. A car may not cost more than $700 in raw materials, an Apple electronic product almost none and a digital music recording none at all if we disregard the electricity needed to have it transmitted to the listener. The fact that technological advances allow lighter and lighter products reinforces this trend. Carbon fibre, for example, has made car bodies lighter by 200 pounds in 5 years, while all electronic products are smaller and thinner. Coal is no longer the only available energy as it was in the 19th century, or as oil and coal were in the 20th. The issue is less a currency issue than a strategic issue, that is, the location and availability of rare earth elements. Exchange rate fluctuation will now influence when qualified labour is available, and peace ensures the place of production as well as taxation.

There is an impact on the international currency exchange from the allocation of various cash flows to pay for these factors of production, including determining the jurisdiction in which profits can be optimally located, since most of them can be located anywhere in the world when not constrained by local infrastructure requirements or legal protections. Because human resources are mobile, transport infrastructures and other logistic means are available and taxes and financial incentives exist, companies allocate operations as a function of their intangible assets, including patents and know-how, replacing an allocation model based on the location of natural resources. The optimization of scale economies through specialization is widely achieved as expected, with the dismantling of tariff barriers and other obstacles to international free trade that the WTO was assigned to monitor.

The issue of currency exchange to clear international trades has changed in such an environment. Since the only geographically immobile factor is the consumer, exchange rates are simply profit and means-of-production allocators. Since costs (taking into account exchange rates) include a lot of high-level human qualifications (research centres and taxable stockholder profits), again it is a flow matter with long-term impact on human education and qualifications. Here again speed of fluctuation (if fast) is the only monetary topic to the extent that it exceeds the hedged flow amounts by the operating companies and is faster than the possibilities of adaptation when needed and before they adjust. It is the reason why currency exchanges have to be stabilized. This stabilization can only derive from central banks' authorities and require political support. This question requires more than words to be transposed into a transparent system of responsibility shared between nations and entrepreneurs.

Having accepted the fact that currency requires a guarantor in order to fulfil its role as a sampling instrument allowing long-term investments and money rotation, currency analysts have considered several models. After the war, Mendes France,[2] in line with Keynes and his Bancor proposal (see Glossary), considered a guarantee and a price determination based on

---

[2] French statesman (1907–1982). Prime Minister only from second part of 1954 to very beginning of 1955. Left a major political heritage, freed Morocco from colonial status and concluded France's Indochina war.

the price of raw materials. The SDR as previously described is based on a basket of currencies with an agreement to reconsider the basket every 5 years. Starting from that assessment, there are two schools of thought. One school favours a measurement system free from any governmental or equivalent central bank intervention. This is the theory supported by a gold and raw materials basis. We have seen that a metallic measurement basis is no longer a price determinant. It may or may not achieve its goal as a guarantee, since only the countries with natural resources can ensure it. Its absence in a country may push that country to take possession of these resources, and we would naturally then return to colonial policies. Being reminded of this, the question of a measurement and governmental or equivalent central bank intervention remains, supported by a second school of thought wisely regarding a stable fixed sampling basis as required for a healthy economy. The leaders of the G20 declaration of February 17, 2013 discouraging the easing of money to push down currencies represents a variable of the second school. Nevertheless, recent Japanese events show that there may be a gap between declared intentions and facts.

It is probably a political issue to set these international exchange ratios and instead of falsely avoiding the problem just to face it, as it is a matter of relative economic strength and monetary discipline. Playing it collectively is the only way to decide what a measurement unit should be, as a practical and efficient way towards prosperity. At a conference delivered by him on the monetary system, Robert Mundell said: "Let us hope that the most important event of the 21st century will be that the dollar and the euro learn to live together."

Money Guarantees and Trust

In our tentative proposal to organize a system the safety of a financial instrument will be first evaluated from its holder's perspective, based on the guarantees granted to the balances it is linked to, such as:

- The nature of the instrument itself and the intrinsic legal and factual guarantees attached to it.
- The quality of the issuer of the instruments, that is to say their financial statements or financial flows for an individual.
- The quantity in which the issuer produces financial instrument units compared with needs and the adaptation, over time, of this quantity factor.
- The depository of the instrument, including the depository itself but also the jurisdiction in which it is created in terms of legal protection.
- The liquidity of the instrument that will create independence from its holder's balance sheet and that of the issuer it derives from. If an instrument can be traded easily on a market at fast speed, the holder escapes risk taking whatever the issuer's and holder's financial conditions.
- The currency sampling of the instrument that is needed for safe measurement.

We have noted that with electronic markets, the sampling instrument as a number or formula may be independent of the instrument itself or the issuer (see Figure 8.2). This key observation leads directly to undermining central banks' credibility in this respect or bringing a guarantee as old seignorage did and open competition about usable currencies.

We have already noted also (Chapters 6 and 7) that the directive on bank resolution and the stress-test process organized on both sides of the Atlantic deriving from Basel III go in the

The Scope: How to categorize instruments

1. by duration	2. by warranty	3. by traded instruments markets	4. by liquidly traded
Long term	Non guaranteed	Unregulated	Grading by trade volume compared with issued instruments amount
3 years	Guaranteed by assets		
24 months	Guaranteed by 3rd party liquidity	Regulated grade 1	
12 months	Guaranteed by 3rd party assets	Private markets grade 2	
6 months	Guaranteed by instruments		
3 months	Limited amount guarantee	Central banks markets	
cash	Direct gov or agencies		

Notes for columns 1 to 3:
Total and amounts by category are given by sector
of holders and jurisdiction which are located.
These amounts are reconciled with 4.

FIGURE 8.2 The scope: how to categorize instruments

same direction for the banking sector. We can now affirm that, if it needs to protect the global banking and payment system from contagion, it misses the sampling issue.

If the measurement reference system is commonly accepted, the question of the guarantee is only secondary, but important nevertheless. It derives immediately from the analysis. It is first a matter of firewall mechanism set up at the central banks or other central financial institutions for use of appropriate reserves necessary to fight speculation and regulate variations. It is second a matter of analysis of the financial markets and of the goals pursued in issuing the financial instruments, in order to evaluate, when appropriate, the sustainability of its limits and the point at which the entire economy is threatened by the withdrawal of refinancing for participants. This was the missing approach when housing financing became over-guaranteed by government programmes. The guarantee should not only cover the capacity to monitor the value of the currency but also ensure liquidity and stability during the time window of transactions and the average investment return period. The required amount can only be calculated by averaging. It should be determined by taking into account the kind of financial instrument contract in question on the one hand, and the capacity for potential speculation on the other. Since each financial instrument contract has a purpose, we should look at the potential of conversion of one instrument into an understanding, whether in the event of a threat to stability this conversion potential could be reduced or eliminated. The ultimate purpose of the market and goals of the refinancing should be monitoring in order to keep the moral hazard under control, to a volume to be determined, just like any money issuance.

This analysing leads to the diagnosis that an alternative synthetic currency, such as "bitcoin", which is of interest for analysing the missing monetary requirement of sampling is not compliant today with the needs of good money. Worse, its sampling monetary function is attractive because of its deemed neutrality and limited fixed issuance volume compared with central bank-manipulated monetary policies. However, this advantage, due to an outdated set-up, cannot hide that money has to be regulated for stability in sampling to become a reserve of value, which cannot be fulfilled with erratic changes, neutrality being better than partiality but still not sufficient. A currency needs wide acceptance from a sufficient number of users whose trust is dependent on visibility and stability over time for social redistribution (retirement benefits and others).

The risk appraisal approach, over time, is already used for the surveillance of banks when weighting their financial instruments' portfolios and setting the prudential ratios they should comply with. Banks themselves have their models to conduct risk policies. The weightage portfolio risk approach, Basel III, is also complementary to the leverage ratio global approach, which is given to banks. In line with what we say, that the banking regulations only deal partially with monetary issues, this granular approach has to apply to anyone using a financial instrument.

Is an independent warrantor as for weightage and measurements needed, or should it be left to each agent or to both the enterprise and the supervisor? As risk is to be evaluated permanently, would the solution be to both confront the results of the risk weightage and share the accountability?

It is a question of the credibility of the guarantor to resist and deter speculation through financial sanctions.[3] However, like a mirror, by attributing some extra virtues to a monetary instrument by just guaranteeing it, such a sponsor acquires a valuable seignorage right. This seignorage right changes the value of a standardized instrument operating as insurance, as the ultimate cost to the taxpayer should be placed under democratic surveillance if the instrument is being sufficiently traded to become a monetary instrument and submitted to the cost of regulation.

One Key Consequence of the New Set-up: The Final Trap

Once money is issued it is, in principle, in the system for ever – one party to it cannot unilaterally destroy it, so it is trapped until it is cleared. Once you create a financial instrument, it exists for ever if there is no default. Clearing is no more than a conversion from one instrument accepted for clearance into another instrument. This explains the phenomena we are experiencing today. If money is transferable depending on trust, money will move from risky instruments to safer ones and vice versa depending on the risk-taking appetite of the parties. This, along with the excess of money, explains the strangely low level of interest rewarding public debt instruments. Money has to go somewhere. When there is risk aversion somewhere in a system, the financial instruments' holders will try to escape the space where they are trapped by exchanging them for safer ones. Prices of exchanges will be pushed up for the safest ones with, consequently, returns down while the aforementioned riskier ones' prices will decline with return rates up.

---

[3] That approach is taken with IFRS 9, which is sanctioning the change in category of an instrument but is, to us, the wrong approach because again it mixes up the roles of the active agent with an interdiction to repeat such a change within a 2-year period for all instruments. To the contrary, even when used as hedging, the standardized instrument measurement should be unique in the context of making CCPs the place to trade them. If not the user, then the supervisor is the one to raise the appearance of new instruments or new set-ups showing new risks. The regulator should then be the one to ask for a change in the regulation of the instrument or the way it is traded. The change in weight should be regarded as dangerous when considering it has (under our concept of money) monetary effects. This concern was raised at a conference held at the Cnam on June 6, 2013 – Institute of France Quai Conti in Paris. Michel Pebereau, after presentations from Darvel Duffie (Professor of Finance, Stanford University) and Paul Glasserman (Professor of Business, Columbia University New York).

The total of debts in the monetary space is not correlated to this movement. It is because of the trap that exchanges operate according to this "safeness" pattern not similar to reality, but to the aim of sovereign financial instrument liquid exchange money – to be most visible in terms of warrantees. When there is too much debt, interest rates will no longer represent the risk/reward balance, but instead a balance between high risk and lower risks, and the scale is shattered. Negative interest rates are like renting a safe in a bank – you have to pay for the security.

The pattern we describe also shows that analysis cannot be global, but by category of instruments as we have seen for these governmental issuances. For instance, in the MGI analysis we note that the financial depth increase between 1995 and 2007 came at 25% from equity market valuation, of course a non-sustainable rate when compared with the evolutions in GDP. At the same time the MGI reveals that over the same period the financial institutions have funded their lending activities and asset activities by issuing new bonds and debt securities at the growing rate of 11% a year, reaching a stock of 39 trillion at the end of 2007. This 39 trillion is more than half the world GDP, showing the extent of the over-leverage of the financial activities and the correlation inside the trap and because of the trap of financial instrument issuances and asset values including equity in a non-inflationary environment.

We also note that this pattern "neutralizes" money as it did between the two world wars when gold became similar to the Holy Grail. Safer money will move more slowly and may be more attracted by sovereign debt than by risky industrial or just entrepreneurial investments. By a perverse phenomenon, the hierarchy of attention between flows and balance sheet appearances will change, favouring balance sheet totals and net equity with, most often, a false interpretation of inflated asset values as determining a better prudential ratio (Figure 8.3).

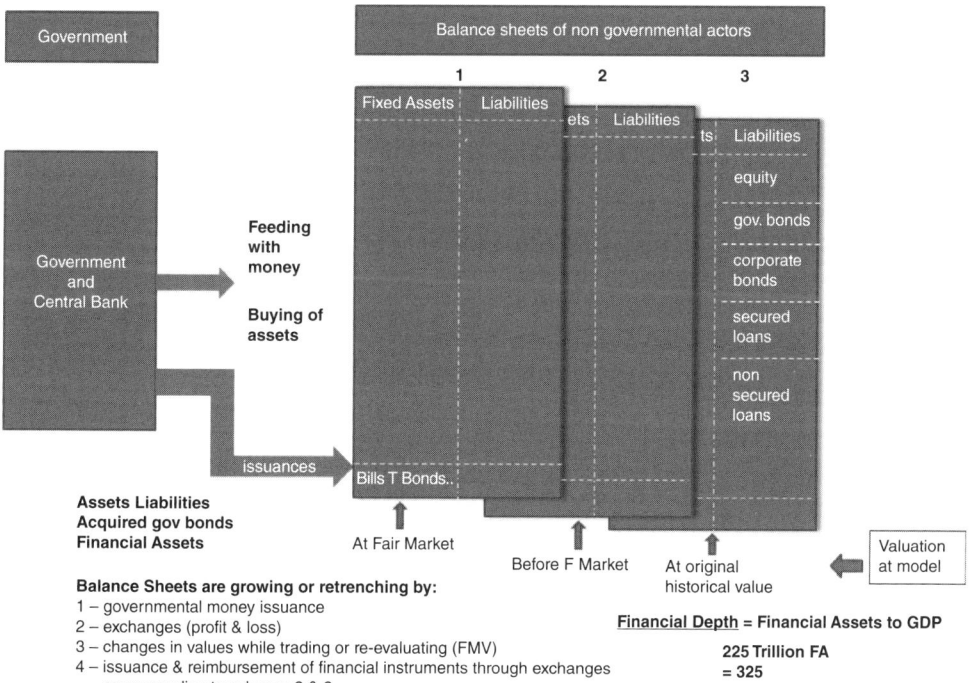

FIGURE 8.3 The money trap

THE EMERGENCE OF A NEW SEIGNORAGE

Spreading the Seignorage Rights between Chartered Financial Institutions Accepted to Trade Instruments and the Central Banks' Right to Drive Values

In Chapter 3 (21st-Century Money Analysis), we discussed three monetary functions[4] – one of which was the role of money as a reserve. We looked at the seignorage privilege and at one new aspect of it – the privilege of issuing currency when that currency is accepted outside its macroeconomic borders, called the "exorbitant privilege". We see that structures and fame have a strong resilience in the face of facts. This explains the return and mystic drive to gold, which is easy to understand as a single currency denominator and which is also reminiscent of a prosperous period when gold was available in large quantities, usually corresponding to military victories for the holding nation and to territorial expansion. The bargaining power of citizens during these periods of prosperity was on an upward slope. However, change for whatever reason – rise, decline or transformation of civilizations – are inevitable, and the economy and money must adapt. No privilege can survive for ever, and the disappearance of gold coinage is here to stay, just as the passage through security screening for air travellers is. No nation has sufficient military superiority to support monetary trust. On the contrary, an army is a cost, and the payback that a country may expect today will not compensate such a cost in a world where assets are mostly immaterial and there is less value in seizing raw materials. On the contrary also, armies are to protect societies with their philosophies and way of life and all of the goodwill that goes with them. It is a cost of similar nature to the justice department's cost. As a result, money can only be grounded on flows of funds resulting from exchanges. It is a multiform participatory system where no privilege can remain in just one hand. That being said, the problem of the money standard arises again.

Because modern money is simply postings on ledgers, the nature of seignorage has changed. When you are the holder of a book balance with a nominal value on a ledger – even if you have paid more or less of this nominal value for it – accounting-wise it can either stay as it is or be exchangeable into bank bills before its due date (if exchangeable and if it has a due date), or be converted into another instrument, if not into goods or services. If such an event happens at the due date of the financial instrument, the balance (client's or vendor's account on the books) is cleared and the corresponding payment money shows on a bank account or as a substituted instrument reducing another balance. From that process we understand that money creation will result from activity creating receivables and corresponding payables.

If the money floating around in each of the exchangeable categories of money is too significant compared with its conversion possibilities, this trapped money will go directly or through contagion processes to the safest places, to benefit from the expected best contracts in terms of guarantees and return. The production of new financial instruments compared with their final volume will determine a growth or retrenchment from M5 and M6, both as a result of variation in activity volume and prices. When analysing national or transnational (see MGI report in the References) integrated accounts, we see a slow contraction balanced by new governmental issuances, a sign of the slow economic trend in western economies. The new seignorage not only stands as the capability of central banks to issue money, but also at

---

[4] Reminder: payment instrument, measurement instrument and reserve.

the economic agent level to carry on and expand business, or not. The seignorage monopoly has disappeared and is now spread within a circle of companies being able to impose prices. It is rewarded with fees and commissions due to the resulting oligopolies that the remaining bank monopolies and the limited rights to be accepted to a counterpart on markets bring to the management of financial institutions, marketplaces, shadow banking and any financial player strong enough to be accepted as such. Changing the allocation of GDP among societies, they share the seignorage power of governments and their respective central banks. It is never a stable pattern because of technical and market competition. The new pattern is reversible and may include and add to the creation as well as the destruction of money, with changes in prices and valuations of instruments inside the balance sheets. The destruction, and this is key, happens at private household and corporate level, where intercompany credit and receivables from households are two-thirds of the global economy financing.

Centralized monetary policies through the banking system and interest rates are consequently going to have limited impact on monetary volumes. The old seignorage concept of forced value of coins and bills has disappeared with the benefit of the right to impose market conditions when exchanging and being paid. It is included in the exchange prices, meaning the receivables. The sovereign's monopoly to issue money in their nation has disappeared in favour of several new powers that are transnational, raising new concerns as for taxation. Remains or guaranteed issuances by governments and agencies keeping prices up (like for real estate by buying MBSs) are still there for longer-term payments that private sector and financial markets cannot sustain. The capability to levy taxes, regulate instruments and markets to change exchangeability of instruments, as well as to drive a monetary policy that will change the original values of instruments through interest rate policies, are still in the hands of the sovereign and the remaining seignorage rights are shared amongst those in the financial world.

Social Roles of Money: Transferable, Reserve or Bubble? How to Determine Sociological Thresholds from Different Dimensions

Because of electronic markets operating non-stop over days, the matter becomes more of the exchange ratios than the numbering and the standard. Nevertheless, again the trust issue as a social component is there, and human beings need information and explanations. No one wants to have their fate governed by a black box. Money matters, when no longer related to gold, still need to be visible to and understandable by everyone. The only way to gain trust is to be visible, and only figures are visible. The measurement necessity requires a standard to refer to, similar to a calendar, which does not create time or even invent time but is necessary for humans to meet at a particular time. The less money is tangible, the more it needs images to gain the social trust to represent it. It is an efficiency matter conditioning trust and exchanges. It also requires trustable regulation to adapt available quantities to needs and of course a philosophy to determine what such needs are.

The very interesting book *La Monnaie Souveraine* (Sovereign Money), published in 1998 under the direction of Michel Aglietta and André Orlean, includes thorough studies by several sociologists and economists of the sociology and origin of money. After assuming as we do that everything starts with the "debt" concept (and in that sense in line with our view that money is a means to satisfy an obligation), it defines the various understandings of what "money" is and then compares and contrasts them. It distinguishes between the contractual order and money as "a social total"; given the fact that money issuance is a sovereign privilege. The book reminds us that US bills refer to "in God we trust", calling for divine values. It recalls the dual logic of money, both individualist and holistic. It says "money" is a whole set of rules that determine individual adhesion to a market society. By using the word "society", the book refuses to restrict money to a contractual relationship only. It also recalls the dualism of the money from central banks (first-tier banks) and the money from commercial banks (second-tier banks) and the fact that their roles differ significantly as to credit distribution and last recourse. The central bank must satisfy the needs of the nation, and the commercial banks must satisfy the needs of the economy. This dualism is the origin of all the debates between those who would liberate the economy from the government as a right to liberty, and those who believe in some kind of general regulation overriding the monetary system that gold provided at a long-gone point in time. The innovative aspect of the book is that it looks at debts not only as simple contractual monetary commitments but as a more general, understood commitment that at a certain age there is a generation at work and that at another age it retires.

There is a monetary and a corresponding bargaining-power transfer issue at stake that requires legal instruments and legal protections. That approach, called "MGI" (money intergeneration) is to underscore the limits of the purely contractual approach to money that is not sufficient to apprehend the current need for monetary reform. Among other things, it focuses on some consequences of the fact that life expectancy is lengthening and healthcare needs are correspondingly expanding. These facts influence how money should be handled and highlight the need to look at savings and investments, bearing in mind the interplay of demographic factors and production potential.

We don't completely agree with this collective book with regard to its conclusion on the impossibility of an auto-referential currency or with respect to all of the contradictions it points out. We prefer to join Samuelson's approach when he distinguishes between a qualitative dimension to money and a quantitative one.[5] When money is available for use to replace barter with markets, the quantitative aspect of money available is no longer the issue up to a certain threshold. Because of the exchangeability of monetary instruments the threshold is important to determine.

Here, we add a few comments. If, as a separate dimension, money is neutral – if its sampling use is granted the quality factor of stability – it does not mean that the volume dimension is irrelevant to other phenomena like the bubble phenomenon. The issue here is to know how to determine at what volume a reserve ends and a bubble begins, which will differ from one kind of flow to another depending on the purpose of the underlying transaction and the object of the transactions (real estate, credit instruments, shares, etc.), and the participants in the exchange markets. We see the question of differentiating reserves from excess (bubble), as well as the resilience of market actors to variations in prices. Independent of the currency value, the stamping of a figure on an instrument usually corresponds to a limited right to transfer, but not to its market value at the time of an exchange. At this stage, we are again to distinguish the sampling value from prices.

However, the environment in which Samuelson wrote has changed. The speed potential of financial markets has totally revolutionized the matter, reducing the mass of money necessary for them to be operational, and inflation due to the limited offer of industrial products has disappeared with globalization and the resulting overall scale economies. We have explained why the level of prices resulting from transactions will impact balance sheets and behaviour, because of the universal language of accounting and financial analysis. See Figure 8.4.

---

[5] See References: *Classical and Neo-classical Monetary Theory* and also *Economics: An introductory analysis*, where he explains money as an exchange right.

- The stamping privilege and duties: the fixed point

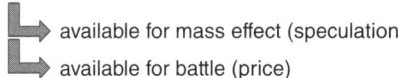 The variable / the value
Non inflationary environment.

A) Stable system = Reserves for:
- adjusting time lags (duration of transport
in the former world)

- adjusting capital needs and time duration of cycles
(intergeneration)

- not foreseeable events

B) Unstable system = Reserves are excessive compared with need and free
of regulation

available for mass effect (speculation)
available for battle (price)

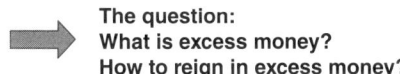 **The question:**
What is excess money?
How to reign in excess money?

FIGURE 8.4   New views on money

Our approach to the definition of money, starting with a contractual approach but considering wider aggregates, changes the entire discussion, as does the increased fluidity of money. This requires, as Christine Lagarde, the IMF General Manager, said, a granular analysis that does not exist. Microeconomic analysis has shown its narrow limits and its incapacity to forecast, with economists just following and trying to make models to explain phenomena after discovering them.

MODELLING THE MONETARY WINDBAG ANALYSIS

We support, as Von Mises did, the social vision of contractual money accepted by a society raising the new issue of diversity. In behaviour, individuals will differ depending where they are located, what their culture is, how remote from each other and how much their stock of money is and what they can freely use or not. This raises questions including the one we have dealt with of reserve and bubble of modelling.

Modelling is used to comprehend all the dimensions we have analysed. The central issue is to understand that value and prices are different, the first being a reality determined by mass and speed, the second being purely contractually human. However, the major result to be researched is the understanding of density and mass independence with, as a result, the disappearance of the relevant monetary system when bubbling and then disintegrating upon reaching a certain price level, triggering a slowdown in rotation. Here again, Douady's work will be needed to determine the instability thresholds (see: The Fair Value Conceptual Mistake Contributes to Instability and Distrust on page 97).

A Tentative Formula: STD (Serval-Tranié-Douady)

We are in the universe of financial statements all expressed in a single monetary unit. From the environment derives all of what was said about contagion. When trying to formalize what has been developed before, we come to the following observation formula:

$$E = (\text{Value} - \text{Price}) \times (S \times \text{M5})$$

where E is the explosion index and S the speed over a period (Revenues/M5) taken as the spread from an optimum target determined later by category of instruments classification of M5. Where Value is the nominal value of the instrument and price the posted amount if different when the instrument has been acquired or exchanged.

The acceleration/deceleration of transactions S' is driven by the following equation:

$$S' = k \times (V - P) \times (S)$$

where (S) is a response function to price/value discrepancy and k is an elasticity coefficient. Typically, (S) is positive between acceptable bounds for each asset class in terms of transaction speed.

The value itself reacts to liquidity, as a function of supply and demand. V is a fast-varying quality following transactions and market sentiment, while P is only reassessed at each transaction on the particular asset. Therefore we can write:

$$V' - P' = h \times (S')$$

These two coupled equations create a joint dynamic of the transaction speed and the value/price discrepancy, the stability of which can be measured by the explosion index E.

The meaning of these equations is that exchanges are done within certain boundaries. The differential value minus price embraces all of them and by itself implicates a minimum volume of financial monetary instruments. We immediately understand, and have experienced, the explosion of bubbles. It is a measurement of the deformation of balance sheets and P&Ls resulting from quantity independence between real economy price determination processes and financial instrument exchange price determination processes. The spread has a limit and to keep exchanges happening we need a certain volume of money. Under that volume the economy dries up, over it is flooded. As monetary instruments can be moved within a certain monetary area and between monetary areas, as well as being exchangeable between themselves, the formula is multidimensional. The derivative equations are continuous; they could also be operated point-by-point within different spaces.

For the understanding of the reader we have to say that the differential between traded prices and face value in our model works as a spark plug. It is a space representation; it does not change the other space representation of the exchanges at nominal value but will change the image of the future. It may further trigger a liquidation mode with crumbling values for some assets. When started, it is difficult to stop and will interconnect with the global model that we have designed to embrace all points and actors with exchanged values. This will operate later in a distinct way that will be observed through accumulations and speed, as already described.

Definition of Aggregates and Functions Used

Value. Value is not fixed data and can be determined using several concepts. It should first refer to physical values expressed with an outside stamping benchmark. A concept close to that of accountants' "fair value" of prices practiced between independent counterparties.[6] As we have

---

[6] Value as it shows in the balance sheets today is totally heterogenous because of being based on banks' individual models and positions taken as to the refinacing (to be kept or not until maturity) (see Chapter 4 for accounting principles and the use of the fair market value standard). We would rather derive it from volumes showing on the P&L compared with prices of inventories and in M5.

seen, because financial market prices are independent of underlying original transactions, we totally disregard accounting standards to link values to flow speed from real exchanges. For the purpose of the equations to determine V we will use two methodologies and compare them thereafter. The first will be the monetary unit, applying last prices checked for significance with rotation indexes to the entire number of existing physical units. The second will be to use the financial instruments' prices, accounted for in the books. Other approaches are possible, differentiating original values for short-term instruments from long-term instruments and apprising all of them at a value depending on rotation. As developed along the book, instruments have also to be differentiated depending on their attached guarantees. With the E index we may, over certain thresholds, have to disregard the equation when S' slowing becomes a macroeconomic threat to values. We then switch to a resolution formula and define what is the current flowing economy that can be saved from disruption from sectors to be dealt with. That would apply to long-term cycles such as real estate, which are necessarily highly weighted in the balance sheets. Value also has to be looked at with pressures, global or sectorial, that will impact the growing of values in monetary units (for instance generating inflation) or collapses.

Prices. Prices are those observed for original transactions expressed in monetary units. (They are not those for transactions on financial instruments). They are the ones generated by real economic transactions.

Exchange ratios. Prices, as already mentioned, determine or are determined by exchange ratios. As a result, the stamped number is no more than a ratio and the monetary unit is irrelevant within a monetary area. The same comment can be made about financial debt or equity instruments.

S. S is rotation over a time period. It is determined space. Or it can be global: Revenue/M5. If the speed goes up or down from the centre, considering each class of financial instruments, this gives a standard speed average A with the consequence S of differential multiples.

M. M is M5. M5 and M6 are defined in Chapter 6. If sufficient quantities M are provided (QE or LTRO), the model does not explode either when the speed is too high or too low. However, in such circumstances, values or prices may become volatile and the differential again to bring the instability that can lead to an explosion as E shows. Minsky's/Douady's approaches apply. We see that if everything goes the same way, the system remains stable, but because of volatility a disconnection may happen between V and P not satisfied by M available volumes. We have already addressed, in Chapter 5, the collection of data process matters, and in Chapter 4 the matter of offsetting balances in balance sheets.

Time. To have the E formula apply, we need to set time and space boundaries. The starting point is given by observation and legal set-up or transfer of property that is the occurring event allowing, according to accounting standards, the posting on financial ledgers. The time exists independent of the set time scale. Like values, its elapsing is not linear. You have a time before the starting set point. For instance, the trading time of one financial market before clearing of instruments has to be observed – the deformation of the time dimension when walking inside the time space where anticipation will influence realities.

M5, M6 and time. M5 and the entire global formula will be walked over a duration scale where production of new instruments and termination (by pure exchange and term combined) will be considered to determine the standard speed to aim for. This will allow a surveillance of discrepancy.

M5 and M6 risk weighting (M5 RWA). In the dynamic use of M5, weighting will be necessary to include the liquidity of underlying guarantees (for instance, distinguishing between governmental direct signature and real-estate leans). The discrepancy between instrumental values and nominal values of guarantees will be looked at either globally or regionally (for those that are regionally linked, such as real estate).

Optimum monetary area. When collecting M5 and derived aggregates, the matter of scope must be considered. The scope is already defined as a whole by the monetary zone systems. This does not mean that it is optimum. It does not mean that it is fully meaningful. For instance, some zones are tightly interconnected and then external exchanges are a matter to be explored. For instance, Mexico is interconnected with the USA, and North Africa or most of Africa with the Eurozone. Some dependence indexes already exist. Several tentative cuts can be made, since these aggregates give the counterparts. The contagious risk approach developed above is also an interconnection over space discovery, which is useful to monitor economic policies.

E. E is calculated for classes of financial instruments (real estate, consumption over LT financing and holders, enterprises and households as counterpart). The time period is a month.

Ex. Exchangeability between instruments is a factor that will be looked at to discriminate, or not, between each category when determining the various volumes of M5 instruments needed for the functioning of a sector of the economy. The speed of exchanges between instruments will have to distinguish two elements – exchanges for the same, a renewal for the same instruments with new similar duration or an exchange for other instruments different in duration, rate and guarantees. Regulation may change the exchangeability (e.g., the switches for stock markets). The actors are the markets when free, market regulation and general authoritative regulation. Usually, laws and regulation will provide for setting the thresholds allocating the power of who is in charge, meaning who holds the seignorage rights. *Ex* will vary at certain thresholds but, when crossing them, will impact the valuation process. When exchangeability is certain, value setting follows, as we have seen, a current pattern. When exchangeability is at stake and reduced, it means the nominal value at term becomes meaningless. The underlying value of guarantees becomes the driver for valuation replacing nominal. This is the reason for us to consider two types of equation to determine the M5 and M6 amounts we are using. Over the exchangeability, which is a function, there is different flexibility showing different categories of bounds for each class of instruments. The interest rates are one of them, like the values.

Seg. Seg is the seignorage right. As a financial instrument becomes money when exchangeable, the seignorage right is exercised through the exchangeability factor. The access to exchanges is also a seignorage right. Where is the seignorage right located? How it is shared may vary. Its mapping will be necessary. As a traffic light, it is where regulation may be exercised.

There is a reason supporting our choices $(V - E)$. Financial instruments have, by contract, a nominal value; the one they are to be claimed at, related to the price of acquired assets or services, but that can also be sold before being satisfied by payment or exchanged at a new, different price. The value amount will represent by difference the non-realized capital gain or loss from the original price. We are no longer within the universe of actually exchanged goods and services, but in the monetary universe of unsatisfied claims that can only be a representation of the first universe. The two universes can, up to a limit, be disconnected within time and distance brackets. Already in Chapter 5 (Figure 5.3), we saw how the difference represents a stress and a risk when velocity slows down.

As there is a need for immediately exchangeable money at certain points in time, liberated from barter exchanges, the monetary universe has to meet the realities of necessary goods (food, housing and tax collection). The instrument itself should become exchangeable for the figure showing on its face – the nominal value. If the differential with the production prices or the usable assets – both nominal and quantities – becomes too high, the implicit exchangeability vanishes and the whole system comes apart both in value and price until a new balance can be found. However, in the meantime, the producers short of cash money cease to produce: the patient is dead.

The spread between value and price is a dangerous one, as it is only a slice of the production of existing goods that are exchanged. To give an example, if, because of cash needs or sheep-like behaviour, everything in a class of assets becomes for sale (as for real-estate assets with the sub-prime crisis), values and prices collapse and production stops. Values and prices will follow similar trends, but not parallel ones, as with differences in timing. If M5 changes in an incoherent manner with speed and production volumes, they are roots for adjustments. Either there is insufficient or excess in *M*, and simultaneously a modification in the exchangeability factor of its components, and there is an effect on prices and values, or the three factors combine and operate in a synchronous manner and nothing has really changed until physical limits are met. The various universes of prices and values cannot be totally disconnected from production of fixed assets (fixed ones, without counterparts) in a unique space.

Debt versus Equity Instruments: The Need for Big Data

Our formula did not consider equity instruments but just what we qualify as monetary instruments. Of course, this does not mean that equity instruments are not exchangeable. Shares in equity were historically the first to be exchanged on stock markets, and the first to exist. But their pricing rules and conduct, long observed, cannot be mixed up as by nature they are not claimable. We now have a second level of observation, with debt operating as guarantees in case debt instruments are linked to these equity instruments either through balance sheet debt ratios or comparative prevailing (in appropriate categories) interest rates. When price thresholds, return flow ratios, leverages or guarantees are breached, it is the interconnection of the system that has to be analysed – not as part of the model but as a possible spark plug operating both ways (from the debt to the equity markets and from the equity to the debt markets; they are not reciprocal). The matrix analysis that we have proposed takes care of that with big data and our analysis.

QUESTIONS AND ANSWERS

The Conceptual Essence of Contractual Money, Constraints and Implications

What is contractual money?
   Contractual money is the result of an exchange where the balance is disclosed with a figure attached to a visible or implied monetary unit ($, £, €, etc.). To have this monetary qualification, the balance figure should be accepted by a sufficient number of market participants not necessarily party to such a transaction.

Why are balance sheets the receivers of these contracts?
   Because of standardization, laws and regulated standards to set these financial statements, balances or total of balances by category (clients, vendors, banks or instruments, etc.) are currently, or potentially, of monetary nature.

How does the contractual approach of money fit into the social, economic and legal environment?
   Contractual money is not antagonistic to laws and regulations; indeed, it results from them. It triggers further regulations to sanction breaches in complying with accounting

and prudential standards. It was seen to be associated with liberty as opposed to central bank monies. It is just the opposite. Social commitments are to be posted (retirement benefits for instance), while central banks don't for the public. Its functioning is as much the development of market economy as regulation. It cannot prosper without regulation, in order to have financial statements of market participants and counterparts or individuals comparable.

What is the ultimate issue of contractual money if it is private money?
The question of the stamping right of the currency unit and the currency definition is at stake. This question is that of the currency chosen by the original participant in the transaction.

What are the remaining requirements with contractual money to have it functioning and adopted over the monetary unit standard and the accounting standards?
The monetary unit used still has to be stable. Otherwise, financial statements cannot be deciphered and the system collapses, no transaction being operated with an obscure balance sheet. Balance sheet acceptance implicates guarantees.

What is the nature of the guarantees that exist?
The nature of the instrument itself and attached leans. If legally protected, the quality of the issuer, for instance, their balance sheet and profits, the depository of the instrument and the market guarantees if tradable, the liquidity of the instrument.

Why is liquidity important, like speed, for mass attraction in physics?
Speed will give an instrument's holder a better capacity to exchange it, making it independent of the issuer.

What are the two ultimate results of this monetary set-up?
The first, due to reciprocity of balances, is that exchangeable money can go from one point in the world to any other one. The variables will be prices for the monetary unit and interest rates working as traditional pricing models, with the interference of taxes (for instance no withholding taxes on public debts and favourable treatment of employees' retirement benefit entities). We call it "The final trap". It explains the need for coherence inside monetary zones, and also the low interest rates on what the financial traders paid to protect assets – called "safe assets".

The second is the seignorage right, now being shared by government as well as tax collectors and debt issuers with underwriters and structured finance specialists. With commissions, the latter with a monopoly to post the balances on the balance sheets, they control seignorage on new money.

What about transferability or exchangeability?
Transferability or exchangeability are now synonyms, since current money is no longer claimable in raw material or precious metals with a monopoly for the central bank to hold such metals.

What has replaced the monetary unit for stamping?
The reciprocity and balancing of post figures for the parties to a transaction.

What are the consequences?
The audit trail is this balancing of figures sentencing the fair value appearance on the books that may not be reciprocal. Trust arises from this reciprocity. A condition of

the transferability is that the original debtor will satisfy, at term, the number and the government will satisfy the stability of the sampling unit. As numbers are arithmetical and unified by essence, modelling is possible.

What about reserves and bubbles?

Money, having changed in consistency and nature, and being relative in its need regarding speed, the question of determining the most appropriate volume for a flowing economy is still there. How to determine the appropriate volume of necessary money and who should be entitled to do such determination is one question. What is a necessary reserve for redistribution and what in case of excess amounts is a bubble showing in prices and the posted money as a result is the second resulting question. These questions lead to the need for sensible measurements and classification of instruments.

What is the ultimate question about speed?

Things being what they are, speed will affect density, values and prices. The entire wind ball air pressure shown in books and records may either flatten or burst, contagion being intrinsic to accounting rules. Determining when instability starts is the key, and supports the idea of full data collection with M5 and M6.

CHAPTER 9

The New Nature of Money in Electronic Times

"Caius Plinius to Julius Valerianus: Hello. It is a small case, but the beginning of a not small business – Pretorian Senator Sollers asked the Senate for authorization to open a marketplace on his land. The Vicentin[1] representatives have spoken against. Tuscillius Niminatus defended the case. The case was postponed..."

— **Pliny the younger, V4,1** (author's own translation)

If money has changed conceptually, it still needs to be organized within a legal set-up to achieve several social goals that require visibility about sampling and sufficient stability for trust. Without the raw material basis that was considered in Bretton Woods times, today's money consists merely of a face value – a number existing along a time dimension – which is different from the concept of a calendar recording our human schedules.

Money's measurement is volatile, and therefore must be based on multiple factors: supply and demand, pressure due to availability over time of both goods and services, and the diameter and length of the pipeline allowing money's flow in determined volumes. This flow, with the speed attached, will determine supply and demand like in a thermodynamic system. The interaction of money with human behaviour must still be comprehended if humans' financial and consumer profiles are to be defined and analysed. Such an analysis is possible today thanks to the evolution of electronic purchasing and resulting marketing strategies. As in the field of marketing, behaviour can be assumed to be stable within determined income brackets, recognizing that such stability factors depend on the general environment, such as the unemployment rate, and that nothing actually remains stable over time.

Today's money is not only a network of individual contracts that parties have accepted in the global context of the social contract that links all of us. It is by its use a description of what we are and what we intend, that profiles and forecasting possibilities are created. They bring hope, but also fear, with respect to individual liberties. Parties do not meet as they used to, and exchanges do not follow the same special stream flows as they used to. As a result, exchanges are mostly a matter of exchange rates. Time, influenced by these new dimensions, has

---

[1] The inhabitants of the village where the market was intended.

different effects. When clarified, the foundational concepts of money open new horizons on how to view exchanges, payment and reserve functions from separate, permanent and simultaneous observations of another time. This can liberate us from the current mixing up of time, value and risk factors in the accounting standards that today guide the observation system. These standards, which are supposed to provide transparent information in financial statements and ratings, can only be inefficient. Worse, by being misleading, they can, without warning, lead to a new catastrophe, as they did in 2007.

The current legal actions against rating agencies, if they provide us with a greater understanding of the processes that led to the mistaken evaluations of sub-prime loans, will show once again the irrationality of the current financial reporting system. They also show that iconic gold and its weight have been replaced by a different concept – the rating and more or less undercover formulae. It is an insult to human intelligence and a breach of fiduciary duty to the public to conceptually mix up numbers, values and formulae to determine a truth that may be believed by the public as transcendental. This is where the frontier between what should be monetary central surveillance and regulation has to be drawn, and is not yet. Money stamping has to be guaranteed as to its stability by democracies' representative bodies. A rating is not a warrantee, and falsely implying such a guarantee in the public's mind creates a systemic risk.

Electronic markets have changed many aspects of the use of money, resulting in behavioural changes from users, and the way to look at regulation set-ups from agencies. No regulation can be effective without considering the legitimate use and purpose of the regulated matter and gaining a deep operational understanding. It also raises the topic of the ultimate social purpose of what is regulated.

NEW HORIZONS CONCERNING EXCHANGES, TIME AND GUARANTEES

Considering money as a contractual link changes everything when clearing is done through electronic platforms. Money is no longer an intermediate requiring the debtor to meet with the creditor to remit coinage or a legal means of payment. The ritualistic process characterizing the ancient world's transfer of ownership – which imposed formalities, intended to demonstrate both the superiority of the regulator or of the gods and to operate as proof when disputes arose – has disappeared. Today's rules are those of the electronic marketplace, in addition to those established by law governing electronic marketplaces, general contract law and the particular rules relating to the property transfers usually specific to each kind of property.

The sale and purchase transaction is faster than any kind of simplified paperwork, and the "trader", by using the electronic marketplace, is just joining a pre-established contractual format they may not really understand in detail. In addition, they are not going to physically touch the product, nor are they going to be able to test it. At most, digitalized images and written descriptions will be available. The trader is also protected with respect to the purpose of the trade. The product may satisfy certain regulatory standards as to its characteristics and attached warranties, and contracts may be standardized by law, regulation or governance rules as to the consequences of the trade. This has several consequences and alters the importance of factors intrinsic to a transaction.

- The fact that parties do not meet each other makes their identification, as well as the identification of the marketplace, a security issue of a new nature, especially regarding the monetary clearing of a transaction. With what and whom will the transaction be cleared?

Forgery of banknotes is no longer the topic. The topic is identification of the actors and their linkage to a transaction.[2] Homogenization of identification is underway for both enterprises and individuals.

- Since the monetary process is electronic, all the issues regarding security of telecommunication and software are present. This also relates to identification, but not only that. It also relates to the matter of ensuring that compliant transactions are not modified after they have been transacted or that marketplace data to record them is not modified independently from any real compliant transaction. The possibility of huge numbers of transactions taking place in infinitesimal time periods raises the issue of how to rank those transactions in the time scale and how to determine what price value to attach to each of them as being the one accepted by the two parties. For instance, on stock markets, should small orders be treated first or should there be a time-of-arrival ranking allowing adjustments between offer and demand?

But this is not all. In reality, it is only an organizational matter, while the essence of the exchange itself has not changed. As for the ancient Greeks, the determination of property ownership is still at stake, and we still have the same kind of ledger that they had to report transfers. We still have a census system as the Romans had to determine taxes to be paid. We still have the same legal system the ancient Romans had to handle monetary exchanges. Plato himself had an idea of several kinds of money depending on whether it was for external uses or internal ordinary domestic exchanges. Only support and technologies have changed. Coins have existed at least since the 6th century BC, letters of credit also, and ledgers appeared at the same time as writing. Modern accounting appeared with the Lombards, and nothing is basically new under the sun except, very recently, for exchange and clearing processes based on telecommunication capacities that did not exist before.

Legal aspects do not support adopting a different perspective. Nor has the purpose of these transactions changed in any way to support taking a different approach. In contrast, with respect to exchanges, the fact that everything is digitalized has changed the monetary means for transactions compared with previous economic organization. The issue has changed for several basic reasons:

- Instead of money being a tool functioning as an intermediate for clearing, the individual or company operating on the markets is now able to make a link between any marketplaces. As a result, most marketplaces are linked, and we have a huge barter system without the hassle of transporting anything or of keeping complicated book ledgers. This linkage includes all organized equity markets through search engines to operate the best execution handled either by the broker dealers or the marketplaces themselves.[3] With respect to a tangible good to be exchanged, markets do not operate physically, and such goods will be delivered directly to the buyer where they want them. The necessary logistics for intangible goods is independent of the trading place. The logistics system is not a trading place like a shop is. Money is no longer the tool for intermediation; the electronic marketplace often uses pictures to make it seem like a shop. The

---

[2] In April 2013 a laundering scandal was revealed in New York City by the Federal Prosecutor, relating to insufficient identification of account holders and consequences of internationalization.

[3] We will note that bond markets are not usually organized and do not fall under this link pattern.

old trade fairs are no longer in existence, no more than are exhibition meetings for people to meet and debate one-to-one, or sell something not on eBay. As physical presence is no longer necessary with modern telecommunications, the individual, as well as the enterprise, can go anywhere in the world to open a trading account after being identified. A trading account is no more than a barter account. Offer competition has not only changed in nature and size but also, because of the necessarily existing par value used for money pricing, a buyer can rank his or her preferences using criteria he or she personally sets (price, quality, availability, volume, delivery date, etc.). Money just becomes an injected bit of data to balance financial statements and comply with rules to determine the exchange ratio. The exchange ratio is again the tangible economic reality. The par value role is reduced, for both buyer and seller, to a sampling measurement tool made for comparison, and not as a payment instrument to satisfy a debt. The time when the acceptance of a banknote was compulsory is still in existence, but it no longer has any substance. The banknote was also claimable. Today's money is exchangeable.

- The banknote system has been replaced by the acceptance by the marketplace of the opening of an account that is linked, among other things, to the subscriber's identity. Because most of an individual's par value income is committed for various periods of time (rent or loan instalments, utilities, insurance premiums, tuition fees for children, etc.), the monetary issue for them becomes the barter both of the money already committed when the commitment ends and the excess money they may use freely. The optimization of economic mechanisms brilliantly described by so many authors must be applied in this new general context. The individual, as well as the enterprise, is exchanging long-term committed goods and services (rent for an apartment, loan reimbursement, tuition for children, insurance premium for the car, compulsory income taxes for public services) against an existing or expected income. The freely usable balance left for the individual is often limited and the space for flexibility and actions is also easy to determine (anniversary dates for tenders, renewal of lease or insurance, etc.). The balance for free action with excess available money (flowers and gifts for known anniversary celebrations, dates and travelling for holidays whose durations are also known) is limited, putting more emphasis on the allocation of individual or collective time than on monetary exchanges and prices. These are not monetary issues but marketing issues, opening up space in which innovations can attract customers. To summarize, the new pattern of exchanges is that the freely usable money under control of the consumer is in the same proportion as it was with the money bills available to them, compared with script money at the bank, and very limited in general. We note also that this vision of exchanges may trigger actions from governments to change the exchange. This is what happened when the regulations governing real-estate loans were changed to increase the volume of lending and to allow S&Ls to operate outside the scope of their original field of competence, which led to rate control actions and protective regulation for the defaulting owner.
- When payments are still separated from an original transaction, several electronic systems, such as swift for banks and others, will ensure the achievement of such payments for both corporations or individuals and therefore there will be an audit trail like when payments are made through a service or payment service provider.
- In addition, because of digitalization, there are some who have knowledge of the actual exchanges between individuals (a general macroeconomic knowledge of consumption not being the same as holding actual data that can be used). The power resulting from this knowledge is huge. It allows economic forecasts, but also interference with individuals.

In this sense, Von Mises and Hayek were visionaries as to the risks of government. They believed that central money would create risk, although they were living in the context of early 20th-century Europe with its rising totalitarian political systems (for Germany, Spain, Italy and Portugal). The money of those times has disappeared. The risk today is greater, but there are, or should be, laws regulating both the uses of information and to whom it should be made available.

- Because of the new aggregated data available for transactions, mathematics to handle forecasts should be used within the above-mentioned limits.

- In addition, with M5 and M6 aggregates and their derivatives, thanks to a better knowledge of exchanges and to what extent exchanges are committed, there is a possibility to build a foundation for the floating ideas of happiness (Joseph Stiglitz and now Ben Bernanke). Dickens was right; in financial terms there is a need for the citizen to have excess cash between income flows and expenses. We should rephrase this simple concept by saying that the liberty to spend money is the source of happiness, in the sense that households need reserves or available cash potential in order to have peace of mind in the face of life's risks. Also, liberty to spend is close to liberty of expression, since in our spending we are able to choose a gift, an unnecessary item or allocate free time for leisure. With knowledge as to the degree of flexibility (or rigidity) of expenses, politicians can pay attention to flexibility and adopt appropriate policies. They have always done so, but without having a global view as to what was possible or impossible because of the insufficient quality and quantity of knowledge and subsequent understanding of money flows. A clear example is the housing expense category, which is a constraint expense category for households. By favouring ownership without limits, founded on an inflationary environment that once existed but has disappeared (at least compared with previously experienced levels), politicians allowed unlimited borrowing (see Table 2.2). In doing so, the issue was not the crisis itself, as written about everywhere, but more the fact that a lack of flexibility was created: the mere commitment to reimburse a loan and, worse, the need to prevent the unhappy event of a family being thrown out of their house. A general policy to ensure that expenses are committed for shorter terms or that commitments can be cancelled in certain circumstances, as well as a policy to ensure the existence of household surpluses and avoid the accumulation of excess money in a few hands, would probably improve happiness for households and individual entrepreneurs. Such strategies are not innovative, but their implementation and the necessary permanent improvement of interactions between interested parties require a conceptual effort from constituents that can only come from knowledge.

- Finally, as we said at the end of Chapter 3, the number now has a key role that may reduce the need for any kind of asset-backed guarantees. The unit used becomes irrelevant, it could be the dollar, euro, renminbi or yen. What counts is the resulting ratio of exchange and the reserve of future exchange that it represents. This is where only a central governmental institution such as a central bank has to intervene subject to democratic control, as when taxes are voted. The exchange ratios may only be changed knowingly and for redistribution purposes, such as for retirement benefits or long-term national investments. It is nothing different from taxes and budget balancing. Attention should be paid to the limits of "virtual money". Being virtual, it may be created by anyone able to raise sufficient attention, credible about the "number's" durability, and therefore to gain acceptance especially when central bank money starts to be criticized. We explained the source of money as being linked to real transactions and being a receivable. Consequently, with a price attached, counterparts and duration for clearing. If not we have M1 money. If not issued by authorities, it should be considered as forged money. Its appearance will show up if quantities are significant in the differential of our risk equation. Legal systems should be adapted to prosecute both issuers and users if not identified and authorized. The breaking of a support, such as a digital cryptographic one, should be prosecutable on a worldwide basis the same as for bank bills nationally.

Time and space are not present in the dispute between those who support the contractual approach to money, who are right, and those who support a regalia approach, who are wrong. But time exists. It exists for both the market players and for observers such as accountants. For money, time has by logical construction the same characteristics as it has in physics. It is the same time and it applies to all humans. If, for practical purposes, time may be taken into account for some calculations, it cannot be mixed up with the measurement standard, such as the nominal value of a debt, which is fixed, but rather must be kept separate for observation and regulation purposes. For instance, the use of a discount rate will not change the date at which a fixed amount is due. Similarly, calendar appointments are meeting points for human beings to satisfy a financial commitment, but the appointment is not the same as time, as we have already explained. Although time has to be measured for calendar purposes, that measurement also has to take into account each particular player, since as everyone knows New York time is not the same as London time or Beijing time.

Today's money, if seen as the means to satisfy, when due, a commitment arising out of a contractual exchange (as distinguished from its reserve function), exists only as an exchange rate at the time of the transaction. The time of exchange, that is the calendar time, is not only rapid but also a one-time event for both parties. All of the market price theories that have been developed over the past years work well if the space they have to operate in is correctly defined by rules. However, market theories are not aggregated into a generally accepted system – a general rule. Once completed, the transaction vanishes as such, and the obligations attached to the delivered goods are not of interest to us here. For our purposes, something new appears when the right for a new exchange in the future is given to a counterparty and not exchanged immediately, creating a face value balance. The open balance is the equivalent of the old money tender. It appears as a "credit" on the statements of one party and as a "debit" for the other party. Clearing houses may offset balances of some of the participants if they are registered with the same platform or if they agree by contract to legally transfer their respective balances between themselves or with third parties. The open balance is an exchange right with time, that is, a future time schedule, attached.

We know that the extension in size and accessibility of marketplaces has changed the frequency of exchanges in the balance of forces between offer and demand. Demand has one computer screen, but offer has control over the system itself. One special pattern already known but more frequent, the adhesion contract, is when a market operates at fixed prices and when the individual participant has no other choice than to accept or refuse the offer by buying at such a price. Because of such accessibility, this pattern has triggered the emergence of service providers who compare quality and prices. This is a new field of action for consumer protection agencies and laws in order to ensure the fairness of competition for the good functioning of the economy.

Time: A Different Dimension

We also know that exchange rates will vary. The important thing to understand, as we explained in our previous book, is that the time component (of an exchange rate) is of no universal value. It is purely attached to the holder of the monetary right, represented by the balance recorded on the statement. It is a social contract. Two or more people may decide that they will look at it and value it the same way, or they may not. For some purposes an authority may decide to set a universal value, what we may call "the time in the day" for instance, and also measure the duration with a physical back-up, but this won't change the fact that time is individual and attached to a purpose. Just as human history and humanity have established "commandments" and defined what natural law is compared with subjective law, we can admit that a society needs some universal language and rules.

We know, for instance, that human beings have to be supported when unable to work because of youth or old age or invalidity at a minimum. This means that time has a value and, in economic terms, that time is attached to an exchange right. Social adhesion to a currency system is simply the boundary, set by contract, between natural law and subjectivity as a sociological matter. But of course laws, regulations and monetary policies can interfere with individual liberty, just like marketplaces can impose a framework on a contract to the extent it is commonly accepted, for practical or economic reasons. Interest is a component of a monetary right that, without time, would not exist. It does not make time universal. Its valuation on markets can only be standardized either by markets or by regulation. The reserve value characteristic of classical money is nothing other than time, which is included as a component of an exchange right. Its value varies continuously as the market for goods and services available for exchanges varies in volume. It becomes a potentially tradable financial instrument. Because it is not a universal value, it can be regulated. The question is, how and when should it be regulated? Should it be stamped, meaning with a regulated value, like a coin? It may or may not. In some fields it is and should be, to an extent, but obviously today's actions to keep debt interest low are difficult to understand as a direct social necessity and probably a mistake due to the incapacity to differentiate different kinds of money as we have seen above. It creates more injustices than it protects borrowers, and will only aggravate the problems of inequity, as laws of physics cannot be avoided. Time cannot be reduced to interest rates. The system is designed to have refinancing made easier to those with financial strength, as they benefit from low rates at wider borrowing scales than the poorest, who cannot borrow as they have no guarantee to provide to the lender. The richest will become richer when, inevitably, the exchange power of money reduces against tangible assets with a new following rise of value in well-located real estate and equity stocks leading, by accumulation, to a further slowdown in money rotation. If so, it is not only the players who should follow an admission process, but also regulatory agencies that should check the players can support any systemic risk during the time lag separating transactions from clearing. The maximum exposure during the time lag should be capped to sustainable amounts for the relevant player.

The time distortion between transactions and their reporting presents specific risks relating to accounting standards. The fair value standard of accounting,[4] implying as it does that market values are more significant than model valuations, is dangerous because, as we said, par values are simply a matter of ratios since they are not cleared in modern reality. The fact

---

[4] Now IFRS 13 is applicable since January 1, 2013 to all IFRS standards where the concept appears.

is that in the absence of tangible operational flow deriving from an asset, in the absence of asset transactions there is no "fair value", and in the case of markets the visible traded value is meaningless when referring to traded volumes. This supports our thesis for a reform of this standard, as for the whole monetary system.

Social Time and Anticipation

Not only is time a separate dimension, but it is also perceived as existing by human beings. In human space, time is looked at as future. As humans are not able to escape from their own space, even if conceptually possible, time only goes in one direction; the future. Deciding otherwise is only a convention between two or more individuals, but not a reality. It is the anticipation process that analysts are applying to interest rates, or accountants when preparing business plans, forecasts and budgets. However, in operating these necessary processes, they are self-prophetic, as we have already seen.

This one-way direction of time is important to understand, and has several consequences when traders, accountants or mathematicians are trying to apply modelling. For instance, observation will show that an uptrend of options' prices will not operate on the same track as back trends, and nothing goes back exactly to the same space spot when moving, except when falling into a black hole of disappearance or zero value. Going to the future is another topic.

Forecasts, in some respects, are images to influence realities. The 2009 de Larosière report (already quoted in Chapter 7) notes, in its introduction, that one of the causes triggering the sub-prime crisis was the 2006 anticipation of an increase in interest rates. This comment is more interesting than the fact, because of the dynamic that is included in money flows. The fact is that such anticipation was logical, but due to the crisis, interest rates had to be cut down as fast as possible. The anticipation was wrong. A simple anticipation of a monetary phenomenon like this one will stop or slow down investments in long-term instruments whose values are very vulnerable to interest increases. Here we again see the psychological impact of excessive debts. When debts are high, interest rates are a rising, driving factor of money flows.

Is it the anticipation or the debt that is the cause? There is no answer to the limits of the curb. In between, the two factors are interlinked. Of course, anticipations have a role in impacting realities to a degree; if realities are not far away they may be aggravated and, independently of any reality, may trigger damages. We believe in what de Larosière says. If no one can escape from our human space, the fact that humans can only go to the future does not mean that they cannot imagine other time spaces or other reverse directions mixing up past and future as similar. If we come back to Chapter 2 we see that however a debt instrument is priced over time, it can either go back to its nominal value at term (the one it had when issued) or, if the issuer failed, to a zero value. When considering the image of the price, the holder or any witness may consider what they will get or another will get for such an instrument by exchanging it or awaiting reimbursement. In doing that, they will consider both the past and the future factor, and project also sheep-like behaviour and the resulting liquidity risk at the end of the considered time space. In an open visible space, doing that, like others, will trigger acceleration of phenomena. Close to the limits, the available time space reduces and vertigo occurs because no one knows if the exchange liquidity will remain, since at a limit it has to disappear (the issuer becomes the only counterparty, or has disappeared).

Speed Efficiency, Risks and Market Switches

Finally, the speed of transactions has changed the purpose of money, as holders can do other things with it than in the past. Because of the difference between the speed of trades and the speed of clearing, there are risks and opportunities for the holders on marketplaces that are not connected to real transactions. We have already discussed the velocity of money as a key factor in the efficiency of money. Are we talking about the same thing here? Between the instant of trade and the time of clearing there will be huge balances presenting default risk. The meaning of legal par value only reappears in case of default, when discovered, or at the time of clearing, when the balance expressed in such value and no longer immediately collectable is determined on the ledgers. In between, during the ongoing period of time elapsing as most transactions expressed at par value are rolled over and legally cleared, the issue is not the par value. The effect of such a velocity independent of anything other than similar transactions is irrelevant to the economy, but traders and the market support the idea that it makes financial markets deeper and therefore more efficient for those who need to hedge their outstanding (but not necessarily recorded) balances. To the best of our knowledge, there is no general proof as to this assessment and to the performance compared with a cost of market intermediation. It is probable that these markets perform an insurance function by being the ones to hedge risk – if they, along with mathematicians, use a model with correctly combined time exposure, interest costs and counterparty risk. They are useful as such to serve the real economy where time cycles (for instance in agriculture) have to be adjusted to the extent that the market is regulated, to ensure that the participant is not taking more risks than the one they are hedging (this is underway on both sides of the Atlantic), both by itself and with civil agencies, in order to limit their purpose to this guarantee of clearing function. What is at stake as questionable over the need for intermediaries to adjust prices and volumes is the need, or not, for speculation to increase liquidity. Certainly, speculators adding capital to the marketplace by taking risks will increase the liquidity of the hedging function. Obviously, liquidity allows participants to exit the market whenever they need to. On the contrary, the margins they have to be rewarded with will need to be disclosed as brokers are probably faster and better informed on market condition changes than the ultimate underlying hedged actor, and sometimes the individual market financial participants. Then, we need to consider and determine the sensible size of the speculation to be allowed. This matter of determination of excessive flows and coherence will need to be addressed.

Time appraisal goes out of control, as it did in the summer of 2008 because, included in the accounting standards wrongly applicable to close the books, there is no other choice for the regulator but to switch off the system. They did so in the USA, the IASB and European Commission followed a few months after. What are the switches? First the applicability of the accounting standard, the applicability of contractual law (for resolution for instance or clearing; a trade can be suspended when price variations are or seem abnormal over certain thresholds), the warrantees (a mutual fund can suspend reimbursements and government guarantees can be suspended). It cannot be a goal, but it may be a system to fight speculation, and also a system to adjust timing differences in trading systems and cycles.

Transparency Effect and Risk of Centralization: The CCP Example

Centralized clearing parties (CCPs) can be classified as an organized switching system. With homogenous instruments, a centralized system of clearing (20 of them currently exist) is certainly an improvement on the over-the-counter system of trading instruments such as

CDSs. Only viable participants agree to gather. Rules about guarantees like deposits and calls for margins are set. Resolution processes are considered. It also brings a mutualization effect to the losses, allowing calls to cover the losses and also back caps to losses. It is a switch on an electrical panel, where you can see what is happening and what kind of default may happen. It will stop, if dimensions are coherent between exposures and guarantees, the contagion effect of a single default of unknown dimension as once experienced with AIG. If the linked depositary system needed knowledge of transactions to allow surveillance, the question to investigate is why and how counterparties have to be guaranteed. As with anything positive for market participants, it may have perverse effects. One of these is the concentration around the table of systemic players. One may say that it does not change the risk, but mutualize it. The mutualization, like any insurance, is a cost but also a process that reduces accountability. It does reduce the volatility of markets as, if there is any variation in deposits' values, concerned participants will be called for adjustments. The ultimate results are still to be appraised, including the matter of resolution of marketplaces. Nevertheless, we believe that knowledge will help. Considering that the real purpose of the swap hedging is purely monetary (naked coverage), it will be obliged to handle exposed volumes to sensible figures.

MONEY ACCUMULATIONS AND INTERACTIONS

Accumulations change value sampling, as does gravity in physics. Money accumulations also play a guarantee role. We have discussed both classical aggregates that consider money as a physical measurement and our proposed aggregates M5 and M6, which are based only on the social relationship that an exchange contract generates with the standardized observation instruments that financial statements are. We have also discussed the determining role of money velocity. However, we have purposely omitted discussing the resulting logic of money accumulation, even though we have touched on the issue of the appropriate amount of reserves, already discussed by J. Tirolle. So many academic works have looked at the consequences of money accumulation and the behaviour of actors that they cannot all be cited here. With respect to the function of sampling, accumulations have no significance in and of themselves, but everyone would admit that they have a role with respect to money rotation and exchanges.

The issue of accumulation is not really new from a raw material and coinage point of view, but in our new monetary perspective it becomes a key topic – especially when considering a monetary rotation slowdown. Deficits corresponding to higher balances as well as the wider economy have, within the last decades, changed the landscape with fiat money accumulations and their interactions with economic health. From a macroeconomic perspective we are talking about 60% of dollar-denominated instruments probably ranking around 1 year of world GDP, that is to say, 85 trillion. Because of regulation, the ultimate power over this money may be said to be held by central banks, as external exchanges are usually under their control. In reality, most is under the control of major financial institutions, transnational companies, that is to say, non-banks.

From Excessive Accumulation Derives Non-level Playing Fields

One billion is not just the product of 1000 and 1000. When trading financial instruments, because of the dual-posting principle explained in Chapter 4, making any transaction reciprocal to the number of holders and the resulting power on exchange ratios will be influenced in a non-linear manner. To illustrate, let's take an example. If a financial instrument is held in one hand in an amount of one million dollars, and the demand for exchange at 1000 dollars is held in 1000 hands, and both benefit from transparency as to such monetary conditions, there is no way that the holder of the monetary instruments will have power to influence the offer, since the 1000 holders will not act as a single holder but will, on the contrary, have differing exchange needs. Some may need more immediate money than others. This person may suffer the imposition of an unfavourable exchange ratio (compared with the reference), but the impact on them may be less significant than on the big holder because the impact is divided among many. The time aspect will appear. We are talking about human beings. To simplify, the single holder needs to eat every day with a cost of a hundred or several hundred if a team. The thousand holders will have a similar need, but multiplied by a thousand, that is to say $1000 \times 1000 = 1,000,000$. The figure will change the balance of forces in the price setting between parties, depending on limits that are different for each of them, and will operate differently in accordance with their cash liquidity, limited availability of product, minimum quantitative needs or production factors as a multiple but different for each of the parties; in an economy with overabundant supply, the bigger the buyer is the better they are positioned. As we know that transactions are the source of gains, the need to act will be more urgent for the thousand. If they know that they have no solution other than dealing with the single holder, they are submitted to a haircut. All conditions will interact, since we are not dealing with physics here but human processes with anticipation capabilities. The quantities of products and services will also interact with speed when we consider not only the actor but also the purpose of the exchange. Time will become a value depending on the need to buy or sell the considered object to the exchange, which is normally a constant. The price for the exchange is the adjustment factor. If you have a crop that cannot be stored, or if storing it entails a cost, you are led to consider time while the party holding the monetary reserves may try to play on the time factor if they can. What differentiates physical masses from monetary accumulations is again this link to human behaviour that is really determined by nature (the need to eat, or to have the cash to do so) and by socially accepted constraints, such as the need for a business to make profits.

Considering money accumulations is, in our opinion, key to understanding markets, price sampling and market oversight. Not only is this the approach that is needed for market surveillance, it is also the way to determine the appropriate levels of firewalls that are needed to guarantee the liquidity of markets at central monetary institutions. Basically, this is the reason why money cannot be left totally to free markets, if anyone thought it could, as if markets were perfect. While parliaments and courts can regulate by law and decisions the exchange of monetary exchangeable instruments, central banks, being independent, are required to stabilize financial markets and to engage in whatever is necessary to maintain the value of their respective currencies for exchanges, including the traditional fight against inflation. These central bank interventions took place during the 2007 crisis that was not predicted by economists, and sometimes add a new goal, such as the fight against unemployment. The interventions were carried out in a disorderly way, without knowing why and for what purpose, besides knowing that books and records are not reliable and that markets need liquidity to substitute for the lack of interbank refinancing – the money contraction effect of interbank refinancing, where tax and regulatory incentives to help public issuance subscriptions have reached their limit. Some of the policies conducted did not produce results, despite encouraging speeches lending them justification. There is an urgent need to understand the role of money accumulation and speed in a context of false recording on financial statements. This is the key for any regulations, since monetary accumulation into a mass will constitute the firewall against speculation. When disclosed, its amount, if appropriate, will operate as a buffer and deter attacks while its absence may generate them. The next question is how to determine the appropriate amounts.

Determining the Appropriate Amounts of Accumulation

The appropriate amount is whatever amount is necessary to hold off an assault on an instrument for a particular period of time. Over this amount, the accumulation cannot be justified. The period of time during which an assault must be held off corresponds to the period of time during which the assailant can maintain their position. An assailant cannot keep their position if they have reached the limits of their borrowing, and to the corresponding costs, and have therefore been obliged to sell their exposure. In this case, the assaulted will probably be able to make the assailant pay, since they will be forced to sell. Another factor will be whether the assaulter, bearing financial instruments, will have the capability to transfer from one financial instrument to another. Convertibility limits, as well as switches to avoid the concentration of means through such transferability, should be established.

These switches, also called "circuit breakers", already exist for some instruments, such as those used by stock exchanges when stock price variations exceed a certain threshold. Trading can be suspended or slowed down by technical measures, for instance by requiring higher cash money deposits from buyers or disconnecting the market.[5] See Figure 9.1.

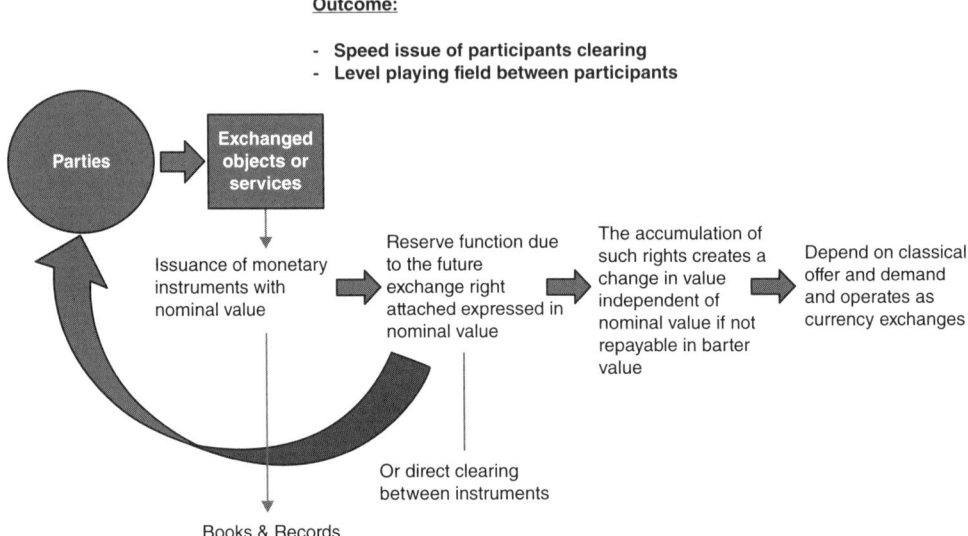

FIGURE 9.1 Outcome

They have been in existence since stock exchanges came into being, but left authorities to be decided. On October 17, 1987, called black Monday, the DJIA on the NYSE fail was 22% in a panic selling process. To avoid the renewal of such an event NYSE, a self-regulatory entity, installed an automatic circuit-breaker limits system. A circuit breaker is a concept whereby trading is halted for a few hours in extreme cases. The day's trade is suspended for a stock if its price increases beyond or decreases below a set value that is determined based on the previous day's closing price. NYSE has chosen variation brackets of 10%, 20% and 30% triggering suspensions of variable duration depending when in the day the limit is breached. But the system is no longer satisfactory considering at the same time the attempt to install bridges between markets, and overall flash trading. The SEC and professionals are currently discussing the topic.

THE PARADOX OF AVAILABILITY OF MONEY MASSES AS A POLICY TOOL FOR THEIR HOLDERS

It is important to repeat here what we said in Chapter 7 about the price determination of financial instruments being independent of the original exchanges that created them. Masses in the hands of their holders are consequently a tool for changing prices just by intervening in financial markets. So when imbalances like deficits create finance instruments such as debt instruments, this generates a paradox. Instead of determining a rise in interest rates to cover increased risk coverage needs, excessive indebtedness may just have the opposite result. Having the capacity to use the existing money issuance capacity, including the mass of their own balance sheet as guarantee, the holder may buy additional debt instruments on the markets to reimburse, partially, their existing debt, whose fluidity is no longer total just because of its excess. Regulatory prudential guidance (such as that of the FED and ECB) may have frozen some of it in representation of financial institution equity, or made their sale process rigid because of duration needs with the tax set-up deemed to favour long-term investments often developed for retirement benefit structures (401ks and insurance contracts). Then, buying these on the market will trigger a rise in their price and reduce the prevailing interest rates. The debt issuers, as most states are, have good reasons for reducing the cost of refinancing to play such an unequal game. The only risk governments take is the limit where free investors quit the playing field for sunnier skies, and leave the other players alone until the market becomes out of control. This paradox is an instability component, as it facilitates increased debt levels and, by artificially modifying the interest scale, disorganizes economic planning calculations for investors with the wrong risk costs. This is an extra reason for better analysis of flows and interactions. Conducting such a policy will lead to further distortion. It will reward the debt holder with increased valuations in their balance sheet and will support its net equity, leading to the convergence of interest between issuer and debtor. Ultimately, it will be detrimental to the economy by deriving money from productive investments to debt financing.

The Implosion Risk of the Money Trap

We have seen the money trap functioning, and the play of humans inside it. We have also seen that if money is trapped, the variable of price reciprocity and time will play with the reimbursement and exchangeability of instruments. However, inside the space of the wind bag, human behaviour will play a role described by the derivative equations or reversal. If a transaction slowdown will have a contraction effect, so will displacement inside the space. Stamping instruments traded separately from any tangible support, just electronic, with numbers, will be self-guaranteeing as numbers are a dimension outside humanity. It may be more trustworthy than central bank money. The emergence of competitive alternative moneys may push the trapped holder of monetary instruments that can only be exchanged using an identified bank account towards them for protection from other species and assets. By such behaviour, it will pull down the price of the usual monetary instruments and raise interest rates. The excess of rate-driven monetary policies combined with the continuous and unlimited issuance of monetary instruments may trigger the successive collapse of both categories of instruments, the limited in quantity ones and the unlimited ones. This model is parallel to the old saying: "bad money drives the good out". Both can operate simultaneously, but as risk. Ultimately debts, if not issued as perpetual, have a term. They could only be bought back by the issuer if they put them in a positive cash flow production position. If not, they must pay the appropriate interest cost to cover their intrinsic risk of default if they cannot reimburse and have to renew. The threshold is the default. Because of market makers' anticipation, the decline in values will come before the explosion. The stability formulas STD (see Chapter 8) if fed with data aggregates globally will operate.

QUESTIONS AND ANSWERS

The New Nature of Money in Electronic Times

What are the effects of electronic communication?
   Market participants do not have to meet to buy, sell, pay or collect.

What are the effects of this change?
   With a worldwide offer economy and lessened trade barriers, competition is wider, prices are not on an uptrend and speed in exchanges has potentially increased tremendously with few limits when exchanges are not physical. Speed is no longer perceivable for human beings, but changes the significance of the monetary unit.

What is the new nature of fraud risk?
   It is to keep track of a not limited number of transactions, to protect them from being spied on and overall to check on the identity of balance holders. The risk of fraud is no longer the forgery of a bank bill – the only crime to be sanctioned by law; it is the use of clearings to launder illegal transactions through non-identified accounts. It is also a question of the safety of the support – now digital, with a cryptographic key that can always be broken. Because it is no longer territorial, there is a lack of jurisdiction to guarantee the support.

What is the new nature of financial risk?
   With more regulation, more transparency and more centralization like with CCPs, the risk becomes systemic. Resolution processes have to be drawn in order to answer to this new environment and, of course, the power of players with accumulations.

How has the monetary unit changed?
   Speed has a key effect on several factors. Among others, the most important one is that volumes of exchanges no longer represent balances when cleared. The unit is only important when the clearing of the balances happens. The size of payment platforms and consumer markets also reduce the meaning of the unit. The unit becomes more of a ratio than a matter of national currency for households who are more interested in their balances than the prices they see on their screen when buying, or using their telephone to pay. If the referential unit changes (national money into the euro) at the same time, nothing has happened besides the psychological effect of numbers and their resulting images.

How have the electronic market platforms and payment platforms changed the monetary world and the way regulation is needed?
   Cleared on interlinked platforms of payments, exchanges have almost no flow and pricing limits. They may become erratic, breaking the stability requirement for sound money. They may trigger a failure, with unexpected flows and balances that prudential regulation may not be able to comprehend or have anticipated. The electronic system or the

modelling may fail, freezing counterparts with contagious effects. Market regulation and switches are necessary. Speed, masses and globalized clearing are putting the emphasis more on numbers than on the attached monetary unit. Ratios are becoming the main indicator. It works as in physics.

What is the ultimate risk?

An implosion of the wind bag by distrust in the central bank stamping tools because of links with public debt issuances and governmental conflicting interest guarantees.

Conclusion

Figure 5.4 shows what the monetary system looks like regarding the use of contracts to exchange compared with the realities of modern exchanges and goals. We have set out all the categories of actors, households and not-for-profit organizations, enterprises and administrations. As a counterpart to these exchange relationships, the enterprises – including both those producing tangible goods and service providers – are shown. These are what the literature calls the market participants, which does not mean very much before it is referred to intermediaries conducting numerous transactions within various marketplaces.

We have explained that their capacity to connect and exchange was established by their mutual reconnaissance, usually materialized by an ID number, and for exchanges a bank account number and a client number with a monetary institution. As soon as any actor is so recognized, they can exchange. Our drawing shows how flows are organized to go to the platform of payment services. This drawing is of key importance to show how the lines have changed over recent years, banks just being reduced to a specific category of enterprises since they have lost their monopoly for payments and now are reduced to receive deposits from actors which are a limited minority share volume of the economic refinancing. Their role is slowly being reduced to that of specialized commissioned intermediaries, and as such is developing in a competitive environment with other actors, even if they still need to open bank accounts for balances.

The monopoly that banks and registered financial institutions had for the financing of the economy no longer exist, since financial marketplaces no longer accommodate them alone, but also many other actors and other monies than bank monies. There is an excess of liquid money floating around the world, with the money production resulting from the long-lasting US and other countries' imbalances. Both trade and budget deficits have fed this production. Held by entities other than banks, and rather by financial corporations, these instruments are on the markets, including dollar ones, and can be used for denominating any kinds of transactions. The accumulation over a long period of time of imbalances becoming for some receivables, and for others debts with a great degree of movement liberty can only be a threat to everyone. They accumulate somewhere and cannot be cleared as money should. Not only is this a threat to the US dollar economy for its refinancing, but to all holders as everyone issues dollar-referenced instruments. The dollar is the reference for between 65% and 75% of balances. This dramatic situation should not be seen as a US governmental responsibility, but one of lack of leadership over the world to rethink the monetary system since the Bretton Woods context has changed. These balances, providing monetary capabilities when flowing, have allowed the development of what are called the emerging economies and BRICS. When discussing US trade deficits, we are looking at existing national geographical and jurisdictional borders that may not have full meaning any longer. Big corporations handling a substantial component of the resulting national trade deficits are global, and if certainly in existence no analysis can be conducted without considering world globalization, specialization and the benefits of scale economies. Acceptance of the parallel-generated imbalances is required. They are merely the result of the achieved strategy and new set-up. Only the limits and political sustainability are at stake, with both employment consequences for education and expertise with long-term effects. There again is an implicit international social contract. Not paying attention to the absence of an internationally agreed-upon set-up would be hazardous. At any time, this set-up could be endangered by a currency war between countries or a liquidity war between separate regulators or speculation using the gap between bank monies and the total of M5 money and such huge accumulations. In this context, the central banks' data – only covering the banking systems and imperfectly the external exchanges – is somehow of little meaning.

Gary G. Gorton raised, in 2009 (for the Congress commission on the causes of the crisis) the question of the regulated perimeter, like we did before him, of shadow banking. However, Gary Gorton's report has no conceptual grounds. As opposed to previous and later literature,[1] it has only the important merit of being a factual description of what happened in 2007 in the USA, without aiming at the impossible target of guaranteeing provided figures. Being the most honest presentation, this report describes the mere result of the banking system's refinancing set-up, due to the remains of the monopolies enhanced by prudential regulation preventing anyone other than financial institutions and banks from distributing loans. The needs of the market economy, available liquidities and low rates triggered a change in the paths of monetary flows towards direct financing on financial markets. Mostly, the report relates to very long-term lending and consequently to huge amounts such as mortgage-backed securities ($11 trillion from guaranteeing agencies in the USA) and monetary money funds, which were the cause for the worse disorder created by governmental and legislative action. By granting privileges to agencies, and by letting central banks change the rules about interest rates, the volatility brought about by the resulting retrenchment of inflated values allowed by wrong accounting standards destabilized the whole system which had just been saved by huge money injections. Prices and values did not match with transactions in a sensible way at that time, and as a result traded volumes on markets shrank. Linked factors to values as a devil's dance just brought collapse. The currently expanding regulations, spilling outside the banking system to shadow banking, will not cure the illness. They grip onto hedge funds, pension funds and insurance companies, as well as monetary treasury funds. They are still trying to follow up on the individual liberty to use money that a free market modern competitive economy needs, but miss direct transactions between companies and most of what is exchanged between households and the corporations or marketplaces. The general mix-up between what is not to be discussed (like numbers) and the realities they apply to has been misleading to the public, professionals and policy makers. By nature, being a breach in fiduciary duty, it will have to be condemned and reformed. This is for proper information on transactions as well as picturing the financial state and perspective of both individuals and enterprises.

Embracing, potentially, almost all receivables, our concept of money and banking activities is different and the concept of shadow money should be modified as it refers to "regular" and "regulation". Virtuality is the essence of the money sampling applied to valuations that happen each time a real exchange occurs. It really exists from the inception of societies where exchanges were conducted. Money as it stands is not a tangible or intangible

---

[1] See footnote 70 in Chapter 3.

good as others are. It is created by the generation of balances of stamped monetary units, money resulting from imbalances. The use of stamping of the debt when sampling the transaction, as we have discussed, is the mere result of central bank setting the monetary unit through their own issuances and actions on the financial markets. It is not value by itself. The stamping by actors is just a derivative measurement and as such can no longer be a set value. On the contrary, the value is the shadow of transaction exchange ratios by itself (see part II of Figure 5.5), representing the ownerships rights on assets and liabilities. The shadow, on ledgers, of such exchange ratios is only given by using central money stamping with reference to a universally transferable instrument, such as a paper bill that a government may guarantee if in a decent fiscal situation or with reserves.

By construction, a book balance (such as a bank statement, for example) is only close to such a bill if current and flowing. The volatility of value is demonstrated by extremes. If there are no flows resulting from an asset exchanged, or not, or no expected flows over time whatever the measurement standard is, this asset has no immediate value. It is attached to the asset. The financial instrument may or not be attached to the value (for instance, ABSs are). If there is unlimited demand with limited availability of such an asset, whatever the standard monetary instrument, transactions jam. In between, all the described factors such as price will interplay. That is why the reference to a compulsory accounting measurement standard of fair value is just a dream designed to satisfy its users, with compensation on bonuses based upwards but cash money not reimbursed when the bubble bursts. It covers two kinds of assets of totally different nature: tangible assets, but usually financial instrument portfolios. The word "fair" refers to market efficiency, something that only exists in stable conditions – a physical state that paradoxically would stop the economy. It is just like mixing up time and calendars. Because of the excessive balances that can fly from one point to another on the globe and accumulate, non-flowing money not carrying the possibility of being reimbursed other than with other issued debts makes the pricing of financial instruments independent of the "real" economy totally volatile and totally unfair. The differential showing values on balance sheets for instruments' real prices at transaction times may not, as it should with passing time, tend to zero but just accelerate. There are stresses and risks. Stress is not uniform, and varies depending on the instruments, the purpose that created them and the guarantees attached, tangible or by signature. This is why we add to the integrated accounts recommended by the G20 a more granular analysis the national accounting systems cannot yet provide. The flows we are looking at are those of financial instruments allowed by M5 and M6. We also see the instruments in their speed. With this information we know about the possibility of changes in value determination between those flowing and those on the hedge of having only a liquidation value based on the attached guarantees, with separate contagious effects if they trigger fire sales of assets (MBS) or counterpart risk.

Money exists since it is issued with denomination in monetary units. It is recorded, posted on books and shown on financials. It is not shadow banking, it is a banking function. Even if segregated, as it should be, to represent that the resulting contracts from exchanges are of different kinds depending on attached guarantees at first row no more than records and statements in the issuer's books and ledgers. Only at the second row is it the issuer's liquidation value that is threatened with no longer being of good standing. Since gold and precious metals have disappeared from the monetary scene as practical instruments and measurement standards, there is no other means to represent money than financial statements that summarize the monetary aspect of contracts by adding nominal value as a derivative of transferability rights resulting from the implicit warrantes given by central banks to intervene on the financial markets in case of a lack of liquidity. This implicit guarantee was reaffirmed by governmental actions during the 2007 crisis, and again with the new Eurozone set-up that was missing it until the agreement on a European stability system ESM. Contracts, if not instantly cleared, are of monetary nature and in opposition to metals, such as gold and silver, are goods like any other. Gold was only a limited but universal social contract by which any trading party recognized the metal both as having an intrinsic value and a weight that was the measurement unit for each of them. Without any possible link with physical measurement – as suddenly happened with the new handling of exchanges that we described – the social contract, imposed by the mere facts that it represents huge progress and hope for human beings to potentially have worldwide remote access to goods and services, and to be able to show and offer them on such a scale, the scope of the social contract has changed both in nature and coverage.[2] The scale effect on markets will contribute to scale economies for producers, and increased competition on price and quality, to the extent regulators are vigilant against excessive consolidation of producers and service providers that would reduce such competition and its beneficial effects for the citizens. The extent of the scale effect has not yet been found in academic papers because the statistics are still mostly national, and cannot yet be comprehended as borderless. Nevertheless, the profitability capacities of big Internet companies, which can be seen on their financials and share prices, or the declining prices of electronic devices and all industrial goods that we can witness, are sufficient to demonstrate such beneficial effect. Attention should be given to the frontier between what is imposed by technology and easiness, and what is accepted wishfully. All of the new resulting seignorage privilege has to be regulated, and that refers to bonuses granted to bankers due to the profits resulting from the effect of bank consolidation and to their monopolistic access to larger financial markets. Scale economies are also beneficial to big companies through sales price setting power, which is also a kind of privilege. To summarize, contracts are not goods, and not one of the concepts of nominal stamping, transfer pricing, value, time, guarantees and masses that should be intermingled when analysing all the social aspects of contracts as of monetary effects. Money appearances are balances on financial statements, those of the banks, the clearing houses and marketplaces, every financial institution. They are the remaining shadows of goods and services exchanged when not cleared.

These balances are money, as they are guaranteed contracts to be used as a reserve and contain a future exchange right. They only differ by the legal support attached to them. They differ on the guarantee attached, which is always of legal nature. They differ by the sponsor of such a guarantee, depending on whether it is a government with a capacity to set taxes and rules or a private person submitted to these. Money always shows a nominal value, even when it is second-hand. Changing this stamped value or exchange ratio right is just a breach in the original contract with the issuer that has been its source. Balances representing the accumulation of flows can only be reduced by reimbursement, failure or a change in the monetary par value like devaluation (money conversion). The effect of any change – explicit or implicit – in value through the balance sheet transmission mode is the centre of any study on money. The way to organize it in a regulated manner will be the centre of any reform. The last studies on carried risk show how any change in value, including currency exchanges, may trigger a shock from one balance sheet to

---

[2] Scale effects have always been studied. The OECD issued Working Paper no. 694, dated April 24, 2009 on the effect of scale: "Structural Reforms and the Benefits of the Enlarged EU Internal Market" by Jens Arnold, Peter Hoelles, Margaret Morgan and Andrea Worgott.

another by interconnection (see Chapter 4).[3] On the contrary, instruments that carry figures and are accepted to satisfy an obligation are not money if not linked to a transaction basing the figure and the terms of clearing. To become money, it should be stamped with a number of units by an appropriate democratically authorized entity, as central bank money is. As explained, sampling is the measurement of the transaction and is attached to the exchange while the stamping goes with the unit itself. This stamping has the same effect as the acceptance of a real transaction by two parties. Subject to such a restriction, virtual money does not contain such acceptance. It does not mirror real transactions that are the guarantees of the instruments' reality if not guaranteed by a third party, and should be considered as fraudulent if not authorized by an elected sovereign authority. The unit matter is only important over time with accumulation when money is not flowing but as a reserve to accommodate intergeneration needs derived from sovereignty or be used as a bumper against variations in speed or production cycle adjustment. We have seen that identification of users will also become of key importance. Central bank money only differs from purely virtual money resulting from the differential between the nominal value of an instrument if any and its posted amount to the extend it carries a guaranteed unit and some kind of exchange guarantee by the mere fact it can be used for the payment of taxes.

To summarize, money instruments seen globally as a system are the mirror of real economic exchanges for the duration of the resulting created instruments. As we have seen, in a global economy composed of national imbalanced economies such as the one we are in, these instruments can live for ever and be priced totally independently of the original transactions creating them. With global deficits combined with the double-entry rule, they are not reimbursable at term but only exchangeable. Over time, the mirror will deform because of changes in interest rates, supply and demand for the instruments, underlying value of the assets and finally anticipations. With a price determination process independent of real economy transactional prices, the image given by the mirror is deforming and the deformation has limits which are instabilities leading to burst outs.

Our graphs (Figures 3.1 and 5.4) do not address this question of the standard to be used for exchanging, the numeration that has to be accepted or made compulsory as legal tender if we want exchanges to happen. Nor do they address the matter of the stability of the withholding for taxes that governments have to levy and the limits to it (Table 3.2). They don't show the fact that many individually identified participants are just conduits hiding behind individuals or corporations. They further do not address the matter of time and the fact that exchanged volumes in the pipes depending on a multitude of actors will not be constant, meaning that if marketplaces are formatted to accommodate and warrantee some players and some volume, they are in definite numbers.

If we look only at traditional aggregates, we see that they represent a small share of the economy compared with what M5 and M6 show. The gap is huge, and we may try to reconcile aggregates with integrated accounts as the G20 recommend (recommendation 15). Specifically looking at M1 (see definitions in Chapter 5) in Europe (Eurozone with 18 countries),[4] we have a figure of 7 trillion euros as of October 2013, M2 stands at 4.1 and M3 stands at 2.2 trillion. These figures, with the growth of M1 from 4.6 trillion last year, show the current preference of actors

---

[3] OECD Working Paper no. 1006, December 7, 2012: "Debt and Macroeconomic Stability: An overview of the literature and some empirics" by Douglas Sutherland and Peter Hoeller; Working Paper no. 970, June 6, 2012: Debt and Macroeconomic Stability, part 7, "International Capital Mobility & Financial Fragility", by Rüdiger Ahrend.

[4] ECB Monthly bulletin of the Euro area.

for liquidity. M1 analysis only brings an idea of the short-term money situation. It shows signs of defiance in the economic outlook, as the preference for liquidity characterizes uncertainty.

We see the importance of the lag between M1 money and what is flowing in the economy by looking at integrated accounts updated month by month giving the detail of all financial assets and liabilities detained by each institutional category of agent (Households, Non-Financial Corporations, Monetary Financial Institutions, Other Financial Intermediaries, Insurance Corporations and Pension Funds, General Government) plus as a whole the rest of the world. Not going into detail, we see the total net financial asset amounts by differential between assets and debts. The rest of the world figure of 17 trillion can only be qualified as significant and not detailed.

EU data in billion euros

	Households	NFCs	MFIs	OFIs	Ins. & PF	Gen. Gov.	Rest of the World
Total financial assets	19,093	16,747	35,442	15,703	7,041	4,198	17,832
Financial net worth	12,234	−9,081	1,077	295	−119	−5,802	

Note: NFCs, non-financial corporations; MFIs, monetary financial institutions; OFIs, other financial institutions; PF, pension funds; Gen. Gov., general government.

If we see that ultimately, and not surprisingly, most of the assets belong to households (knowing that insurance technical reserves are included in their belongings), even if recorded with GDP monthly production, then no direct analysis can be made from details about transactions. If also, not surprisingly, we see EU integration with the rest of the world, this dependency – that is even wider for the US equivalent (see later) – like any dependency, can also be seen as bilateral. Everything is interdependent. Figures are also dependent on tangible assets' valuation grounding as well the GDP's kinetic evolution of the monetary system. These figures as a guarantee for the solvency of the whole system including "the rest of the world" cannot be stated as stable, showing the conceptual weaknesses of the monetary system. There is no determination approach for the necessary link between values and flows and all banking regulations are more assets oriented than flow oriented by the mere absence of conception and related information.

Since 2007, the ECB has kept a fine statistical analysis of the counterparts of M3 showing, as we already knew, a decline or stagnation in credit distribution by MFIs coming from a 10.4% increase rate in 2007 down to 0.9% in 2011 and ranging around 0.5% in 2012, now below the inflation rate. Redemptions in 2012 are higher than issuances and the outstanding amount as of October 2012 stands at 16.789 trillion euros. These clues to difficulties are better known than unknown but they don't reveal the sources and don't allow the transparency that would be sufficient to educate the public to restore confidence in the system and dealing with the social contract. Nevertheless, these statistics and the interagency task force created in 2008 between the US FED and the ECB (at the ECB's initiative allowing, on ECB regulation,[5] "integrated accounts" to be developed) are showing the way to go. As the FSB wrote (see Chapter 3), as well as the IMF General Manager Christine Lagarde said, there is a need for granular observation.

---

[5] ESA 95 and ECB 2002/7, ECB 2005/12.

The US statistical system for the integrated accounts we are interested in is maintained by the BEA and not the central bank. The national accounting system that the BEA has developed (NIPA) corresponds to the structure of the USA (Federal Government and States, Households and Non-Profit Organizations together, Non-Financial Corporate Businesses and Non-Financial and Non-Corporate Businesses), whose sectors cannot, by construction, reconcile easily with the European set-up. If detailed statistics are provided as in the EU system, the US build-up is also different, showing more details on what kinds of instruments are used as financial instruments (mortgage-backed securities, pension plans, mutual funds, bonds, commercial paper, etc.), also corresponding to the US financial organization, wider financial markets and greater disintermediation. Ultimately, if the approach concentrates and should reconcile P&L and balance sheets to explain flows (flow of funds summary statistics), the integrated macroeconomic accounts for the USA – besides giving the same general information on a deleverage of the economy trend – do not give directly sufficient explanation of the flows by type of actors, even with a balance sheet reconciled by income for Households and Non-Profit Organizations, Non-Financial Corporate Businesses and Non-Financial Non-Corporate Businesses.[6] As for Europe, the "rest of the world" column is the most significant with, of course, due to the dollar status, a fine analysis of foreign financial exchanges and detainees of currency. Both systems are missing knowledge of the debits entering each of the categories of receivables and the credits reconciled with the P&L.

The concern over a global understanding of finance instead of old aggregates is not new, even if the M5 and M6 concepts are different and more sophisticated than what was considered after the 2007 crisis. A meeting of the IAG Task Force on Finance Statistics gathered at the IMF in Washington on April 3–4, 2008 where a paper was presented by the ECB.[7] Overall, there is a perimeter issue – statistical agencies only being able to comprehend their national territory.

To our knowledge as in matters of accounting standards, from the statistics published on both sides of the Atlantic we don't see much of a convergence towards a common goal despite similar concerns about giving information on what is happening in the economy to allow the prevention of crises.[8] Comparison between available national figures is not possible while financial markets are international.[9] The rest of the world figures showing on integrated accounts on both sides of the Atlantic are too huge compared with sector classification figures to allow any definitive conclusion on analysis of the former. They only show the interdependency

---

[6] Tables B 100, B 101, 102 and 103.

[7] TFFS 08/09, IATForce.

[8] A recent (April 2013) release from the IPSASB lists the discrepancies between accounting systems used by governments and goals to be set for resolving them. This approach is limited to government accounting and does not cover the entire scope of the economy.

[8] A recent (April 2013) release from the IPSASB lists the discrepancies between accounting systems used by governments and goals to be set for resolving them. This approach is limited to government accounting and does not cover the entire scope of the economy.

[9] The last US statistics available (Q3 of 2012) about net worth wealth show total assets of 78,204 trillion, of which non-financial assets stand at 24,627 and financial assets at 53,577 and liabilities at 13,455, determining a net of 65,749. Regarding non-financial corporations figures: total assets, 31,382; non-financial, 15,513; financial assets, 15,513; liabilities, 13,896 – giving a net financial worth of 1617 trillion. While it is interesting to know that the US citizen is more dependent on financial markets than the Eurozone citizen, it does not provide information about money rotation.

of western economies with the rest of the world. They also show participation "on the fly" for safe assets, providing an explanation of the artificially low level of interest rates on the best western debt governmental securities and money markets.[10] Their insufficiencies are demonstrated by the mere observation of important facts that they don't directly and explicitly point out. One of them is the integration of monies in the single hands of international corporations that are the resulting effect of justified accumulated profits that cannot be invested long term, because of both the lack of appropriate assets for them to invest in with cost savings and/or productivity effects and because of the monetary instability enhanced by tax issues regarding where the money should be stored. *The Wall Street Journal*[11] quotes amounts of $1.7 trillion that American companies say they have invested indefinitely overseas that are deposited in dollars in the US system. This amount not specifically showing has various technical reasons for sitting in dollars. However, its size of over 10% of the US GDP and its liquidity raise a problem of appropriate money endowed and interaction with international competition on taxes. With a theoretical definition of safe harbour instruments and depository custodians, an idea of the threat on stability is given. Any change in corporate taxes or/and monetary regulation may trigger transfers of these monies with currency exchange, bank refinancing and interest rate effects. The need for global knowledge cannot be escaped.

The IAG issued several other papers based on G20 recommendation 15, called the Data Basis Initiative.[12] So far, they have only considered the categories of actors comprehending the flows as all equivalent monetary instruments.

The way we see the monetary economic system is different. Not only is it global as the IAG initiative sees it, but also multidimensional. We have several dimensions:

- Assets with no counterparty.
- Receivables and corresponding debts created by commercial transactions with a rotation.
- A derived world only made through financial transactions simultaneously changing in volume and sampling.

We have also considered modelling, which operates differently depending on the volumes of exchanges having an effect on value determination. All of these dimensions are linked by time elapsing, exchanges of the instruments and by the guarantees attached as derivatives. Another approach is disregard the contractions of interconnected amounts, like the "haircut" phenomenon of REPO processes that triggered the 2007 liquidity crisis at banks.

---

[10] BIS Working Paper no. 399, December 6, 2012: "Global Safe Assets", by Pierre-Olivier Gourinchas and Olivier Jeanne.

[11] *The Wall Street Journal*, Wednesday, January 23rd, vol. CCLXI, no. 18, p. 1 and A12: "Firms keep stockpiles of foreign cash in US".

[12] See papers under IMF/OCDE for the February 28–March 2, 2011 Conference on "Strengthening Sectoral Position and Flow Data in the Macroeconomic Accounts at the IMF" from Mink Shreestha and Reimund Mink. An integrated framework for financial flows and positions on a who to who basis and the last October 11, 2013 paper. Initiative 15 says: "The IAG which includes all agencies represented in the Inter-Secretariat Working Group on National Accounts to develop a strategy to promote the compilation and dissemination of the balance sheet approach flows of funds and sectoral data, more generally starting with the G20 economies data on non-banks should be a particular priority. The experience of the ECB and Eurostat within Europe and the OECD should draw upon in the medium term."

If there is a unique measurement unit, meaning most transactions in the western world are expressed in dollars or euros, values are changing – bringing a risk of disconnection and failure. Flows and exchangeability of instruments being almost free for the financial dimension, available instrument accumulations and change of rotation speed will affect values. This picture allows the necessary risk analysis and appropriate regulation measures about triggering factors.

We think that the implementation of M5 and M6 and derivatives would correspond to the expectation of analysts and allow grounded measurement of monetary flows. As soon as the M5 and M6 concepts of a global observation of all contracts are accepted, as well as the fact that the economy and money are only a social set-up, making products and services to meet consumers' needs and institutions responsible for allocating these and storing the surpluses when possible, there will be no limit to modelling.

The description of money inventories brought about with M5 and M6, combined with the knowledge of connections coming from platforms of payment, allow the build-up of a statistical model. This model will not be satisfactory, as it will not lead to consensus on how the major nations should stay in a sensible channel. That is the reason for this book, to try to cover the monetary issues in our current world. To try to explain, explore and give participants data to be exploited to handle a consensus.

Having a virtual currency, if it allows better creation and use of money and better follow-up, does not make the support issue and its mix up with the unit disappear. It does not avoid the potentiality of fraudulent use. It just increases the impact of the topic of forgery by the extended potential size of a fraud with no existing appropriate judicial counter-power to fight it. To the forging of a coin, a paper or a posting can be added a new means of fraud – the deciphering of a cryptogram protecting digital money created, stored and transported on the Web. Here again, follow-up could be preventative before repression. The need for monetary reform is there, with urgency.

Glossary

ABCP Asset-backed commercial paper. Redeemable financial instrument backed by a guarantee on a portfolio of receivables

ABS Asset-backed securities. Redeemable financial instrument backed by a mortgage or lean on an asset. They are moved off-balance-sheet by banks

ADeS Advanced developed economies. A concept used by the FSB and OCDE. It distinguishes EMDEs and less developed countries

AMF Autorité des Marchés Financiers. French authority in charge of regulating listed securities and financial markets as well as issuers

ANC Autorité des Normes Comptables. French authoritative body for transposing European regulation into French regulation and giving suggestions to international accounting standard setters

APAK German oversight board for the German auditing profession. It is the equivalent to PCAOB in the USA or H3C in France

ARC Accounting Regulatory Committee. Part of the European Union endorsement system for accounting standards

Bancor Proposed by the British economist John Maynard Keynes to create a global bank (the International Clearing Union (ICU)) which would then issue its own currency (Bancor) based on the value of 30 representative commodities including gold, exchangeable against national currencies at fixed rates. All trade accounts were to be measured in Bancor, while each country would maintain a Bancor account with the ICU

BCBS Basel Committee on Banking Supervision. Created inside the Bank for International Settlements (BIS), the BCBS convenes four times a year with four goals: the reinforcement of the safety and reliability of the financial system; the setting up of minimum standards for the control of banks; the release and promotion of the best banking and surveillance practices; and the promotion of international cooperation in the field of prudential control. It is the origin of the "Basel Agreement" that was enforced by a European Directive applicable since January 2008. The following agreement, called "Basel III", will be a progressive enforcement depending on the standard concerned. By definition, the USA, which is not committed by such a Directive, has a follow-up and the FED website, as well as the G20 press release following the Toronto June 26–27, 2009 meeting, indicates that they will go towards the same trend of complying with the new standards set by the Basel Committee over time. US banking agencies, like all BIS participants, are members of this Committee, but issued a press release on November 9, 2012 stating they would not be able to implement Basel III by January 1, 2013 as they had thought

BCFP Bureau of Consumer Financial Protection. A new agency created by Dodd–Frank (the Office of Thrift Supervision being dismantled)

BEA Bureau of Economic Analysis. US governmental statistical organization. Publishes the US National and Production Accounts (NIPA)

BoE Central Bank of England

BoF Banque de France. French central bank member of the European single currency system

BoJ Central Bank of Japan

BIS   Bank for International Settlements. Created on May 17, 1930 to oversee the compensation for war damages, it is based in Basel, Switzerland. It is the bank of central banks. In addition to its clearing role between central banks, it is the home for technical, especially statistical, as well as several international oversight committees. Among these committees, we can cite the Basel Committee on Banking Supervision (BCBS) and the International Association of Insurance Supervisors (AICA). These committees, composed of regulators from member countries, are to elaborate the oversight rules that the G20 countries committed to have their respective banking sectors (Basel II and III) and insurance sectors (Solvency II) comply with (Toronto G20 meeting, June 26–27, 2009 press release)

BOG   Board of Governors of the Federal Reserve System (USA)

Bretton Woods   The Bretton Woods agreements, signed in July 1944 by the 44 allied nations in WWII, set a world currency – the dollar – redeemable in gold, and with which any currency of the signatories was exchangeable. They also set a fixed (at 1%) currency exchange system. These agreements succeeded the pre-war agreements called the "Genoa Agreements" which included the British pound. The unilateral withdrawal of the USA, in August 1971, ended them. Bretton Woods also established the IMF and the World Bank. In 1976, the Jamaica agreements put an end to the fixed currency exchange system as well as gold as a reserve

BRIK   An acronym used by the FSB for Brazil, Russia, India and Korea. It is part of the EMDEs

BRRD   Banking Recovery and Resolution Directive. Refers to the European Directive for the resolution of banks

CAE   Conseil d'Analyse Economique. Independent advisory board to the Prime Minister of France on economic matters

CBO   Congressional Budget Office. Office of Congress in charge of assessing budget projections

CDO   Collateralized debt obligation. Debt instrument guaranteed by a third party

CDS   Credit default swap. Guarantees the reimbursement of a debt by an exchange contract substituting the original signature by a new one in case of default of the issuer

Census Bureau   US governmental statistical organization gathering US data and data by state

CESR   Committee of European Regulators. This committee gathers the European Supervisors of Stock Exchanges

CFTC   Commodity Future Trading Commission. US authority in charge of the surveillance of derivative markets

CRS   Congressional Research Service. Part of US Congress

Deutsche Bundesbank   German central bank. Member of the European single currency system

DFA   Dodd–Frank Wall Street Reform & Consumer Act. Adopted by Congress on May 20, 2010 as a result of the 2007 crisis. With 10 titles and 848 pages, it reinforced the US financial markets' surveillance and the control of banks and insurance, and extended it with orderly resolution processes for banks, the creation of new agencies and increased powers for the FED now covering non-financial institutions

DGS   Directive on deposit guarantee schemes. Directive that organizes the 100,000 euros guarantee per account on cash deposits

EBA   European Banking Authority. Based in London. One of the three European supervisory authorities for the financial sector. With a Board of Supervisors and a Management Board it organizes the QAR, the stress tests, the RWA and transparency exercises. It is now coordinated with the ECB through colleges

ECB   European Central Bank. Based in Frankfurt (Germany), it is the central bank for the 17 member countries of the Eurozone but also the ultimate supervisor of the EU banking system

EFRAG   European Financial Reporting Advisory Group. Independent committee advising the Commission and ARC about accounting standards

EMDE   Emerging markets and developing economies. Acronym now used in FSB papers. It includes the BRIK countries, China and all the Asian countries

EMH   Efficient market hypothesis. Hypothesis set by economists by which markets may be perfect if transparent to determine with exchanges the balanced price

EMIR   European Market Infrastructure Regulation 648/2012. European regulation adopted to fulfil commitments taken by the G20 to regulate private clearing places and have the recording and clearing of derivatives go through them only

EMU   Economic & Monetary Union. Refers to the treaties implementing the Eurozone

ESM   European Stability Mechanism. Created inside the European Union as a bank. It is the Eurozone equivalent of the IMF. It can support a financially troubled country member by way of buying its debt instruments or lending money

ESMA   European Security and Markets Authority. One of the three European supervisory authorities for the financial sector. Based in Paris (France)

ETF   Exchange-traded funds. Trust share instrument exchanged as representing an asset

Eurostat   Statistical institution for the European Union. Based in Frankfurt, Germany

Eurozone   Created in 1991, it is the monetary zone for those European countries which have adopted the single currency, the euro. There are 17 of them today: Austria, Belgium, Cyprus, Estonia, France, Germany, Greece, Finland, Hungary, Ireland, Italy, Luxembourg, Malta, Portugal, Slovenia, Slovakia and The Netherlands. All 27 members of the European Union are potentially members of the Eurozone. The gathering of Finance Ministers of the Eurozone is called the "Euro-group". The Eurozone has 311 million inhabitants

FASB   Financial Accounting Standards Board. Based in Norwalk, CT it is the US accounting standards-setting body

FDIC   Federal Deposit Insurance Corporation. The entity that warrantees the deposits made by the US public at banks. It covers around US$7 trillion

FED   Federal Reserve System. Created in 1913, it is based in Washington, D.C. It gathers the central banks of each of the states constituting the USA. It includes some of the most important commercial banks

Fiat Money   Money with no intrinsic value

FIO   Federal Insurance Office. This is a new body resulting from Dodd–Frank, created inside the US Department of the Treasury to gather statistics on the insurance sector and raise the appearance of systemic risks. It will also represent the USA in international negotiations while the states are still in charge of the regulation for this sector

Firewall   A mechanism designed to stop a financial contagion from failures of price or value. It has to have a triggering mechanism (for instance collapse of a key counterpart, breach of transactional pricing value over a definite period of time (price of shares)). It has to have a mechanism and a tentative rescue and exit process. Switches and market breakers are possible parts of such mechanisms

FSA   Financial Services Authority. UK oversight authority for financial markets and listing of securities. On April 1, 2012 two new authoritative bodies replaced the FSA: the Prudential Regulation Authority (PRA) depending on the BoE to supervise the 1700 main financial institutions and the Financial Conduct Authority (FCA) to protect the consumers and the markets, ensure proper implementation of the regulation and competition

FSB   Financial Stability Board. Created to organize the international coordination of oversight bodies and the follow-up of systemic risks and regulation. Basel based, with the BIS

FSF   Financial Stability Forum. Cooperation body created in 1999 at the international level to promote financial stability. At the beginning, 12 central banks' representatives gathered. The FSB succeeded it

FSOC   Financial Stability Oversight Counsel. Resulting from Dodd–Frank and created inside the US Department of the Treasury, it comprises 10 regulators for coordination purposes. It covers both the banking sector and also the non-bank financial sector. It has the authority to consider when an institution raises a systemic risk and to decide on dismantlement. Works with the Office of Financial Research, also resulting from the Dodd–Frank Wall Street Reform & Consumer Act of 2010

G7 and G20   The G7 was created at the Rambouillet (France) summit in 1975. It gathered the seven most industrial countries as classified by the Bretton Woods agreements: the USA, UK, Canada,

Germany, France, Japan and Italy. This gathering became the G8 with the joining of Russia, present since 1994 but only integrated in 1997, and then the G20 on September 25, 1999 with a Washington meeting attended by new members: China, Brazil, India, Turkey, Australia, Chile, Poland, Pakistan, Saudi Arabia, Mexico, South Africa and Nigeria. Since the 2007 crisis, the G20 has become an institutional body, gathering at least once a year on a work agenda, with the General Manager of the IMF and the European Commission. Decisions taken in this body are publicized with press releases

GAO   Government Accountability Office. This US governmental office is an independent non-partisan agency that works for Congress. Often also called "the congressional watchdog", the GAO investigates how the Federal government spends taxpayers' dollars. In essence, the GAO is the comptroller for the collections and expenditures and an auditor for the budget execution reporting. It also acts as a court for claims regarding bidding processes

GATT   General Agreement on Tariffs and Trade. Created in 1947 to alleviate the barriers to trade, it was the predecessor to the World Trade Organization

GDP   Gross domestic product. This is the adding at market value of the production made and services provided by residents and the property of a country in one year. We distinguish the GDP at current prices or deflated by PPI. Comparisons are difficult because of the different structures of the cost of living between countries. For this reason, most of the provided statistics (see IMF Worldwide Outlook October 2012) are given as the percentage of change from the previous year

G-SIBs   Globally systematically important banks. The FSB organizes the regulation of banks by segregating systemic banks from small ones

G-SIIs   Globally systematically important insurers. Same as for banks, but within solvency for insurance companies

IAG   Interagency group of the G20. It gathers the BIS, ECB, Eurostat, IMF, OCDE, World Bank, UN and finally the FSB secretariat

IAS   International Accounting Standards. Accounting standards issued by the IASB. They are the most used ones throughout the world and outside the USA, which uses the standards issued by the FASB

IASB   International Accounting Standards Board. International accounting standards setter based in London

IFAC   International Federation of Accountants. Gathering in New York most of the national professional bodies of accountants, this institute plays a key role as an interface to the regulators and international institutions. National institutes are usually committed to follow the rules set by the IFAC for the governance, education and ethics of the CPA professions around the world

IFIAR   International Forum of Independent Audit Regulators. Gathers 46 independent regulators

IFRS   International Financial Reporting Standards. Accounting standards issued by the IASB

IMS   International Monetary System. Refers to the rules and institutions for international payments. According to the IMF: "it refers to the currency/monetary regimes of countries, the rules for intervention if an exchange rate is fixed or managed in some way, and the institutions that back those rules if there is a problem (through official credits controls, or party changes)". Based in Washington, D.C.

INSEE   Institut National de la Statistique et des Etude Economiques. French statistical body

IOSCO   International Organization of the Securities Commissions

IPSASB   International Public Sector Accounting Standard Board. Supported by the IFAC, the IPSASB sets International Public Sector Accounting Standards (IPSASs). Being a private organization, even if the IMF, UN, OCDE, World Bank and the Commission of the European Community (EC) participate jointly in the workings of the Board, no nation is individually committed to implement the standards elaborated

ISDA   International Swap and Derivatives Association. Private body created in 1995 and gathering the main private institutions dealing with derivatives. Based in London

Lower Tier 2   Long-term financing considered by the regulator as permanent or additional to permanent. Usually non-claimable

LTRO   Long-term refinancing operation. Linked with ECB monetary policy, it consists of buying public debts on the secondary market. It is the European equivalent of the quantitative easing (QE) policy of the US FED

MFI   Monetary financial institution. Refers to enterprises engaged in the issuance of loans and the trading of any kind of financial instruments and other equities

MGI   McKinsey Global Institute. The business and economics research arm of McKinsey & Company

MIGA   Multilateral Investment Guaranties Agency. A multilateral agency member of the World Bank Group

MOFAs   Majority owned affiliates. Refers to reporting to be filed by US corporations

NBFI   Non-bank financial institution. A definition used to describe the actors of the lending and investment institutions that are not under banking regulation

NIPA   National Income and Product Accounts. US system of national accounting

NSFR   Net stable funding ratio. Acronym used by the Basel Committee and FSB

OCC   Office of the Comptroller of the Currency. One of the three US banking agencies with the Board of the Federal Reserve System (FDRS) and the Federal Insurance Corporation (FDIC)

OECD   Organization for Economic Cooperation and Development. Created by treaty in September 1961 and based in Paris, it is the successor and resulting from the Marshall Plan Administration to reconstruct Europe after WWII. With a staff of 2500 and 34 member countries including the USA and Canada, it now spans a wider space than Europe. Its declared goal is to build a stronger, cleaner, fairer world. Its Statistical Department and Economic Studies Department productions have been of great help for our project

OFI   Other financial institution. Refers to monetary sector analysis

OFR   Office of Financial Research. Created within the Department of the Treasury by Dodd–Frank, it is composed of two sections: a data centre and a research and analysis centre. It is to provide the FSOC with the necessary flow of information to exercise its surveillance duties. The OFR has subpoena powers

OMB   Office of Management & Budget. US civil administration to serve the President of the USA in developing and executing the Federal budget and complementing his vision across the Executive Branch. The OMB is the largest component of the Executive Office of the President. It helps a wide range of executive departments and agencies across the Federal government to implement the priorities of the President. Among five offices, one is in charge of improving performance, another to deal with procurement efficiency and another one to develop e-administration.

ONS   Office for National Statistics. A UK independent statistical agency founded by the taxpayer

PPI   Producer Price Index. Index to deflate current prices from inflation. Often challenged

QAR   Regulation from the EBA obliging banks to be submitted to a quality review of their assets

QE   Quantitative easing. Policy conducted by the FED which consists of buying debts on the financial market in order both to provide liquidities and drive rates

REPO   Sale and repurchase agreement where two parties agree, one to sell some assets to be used as guarantee to the other against a loan and to reverse the transaction at a determined future date

RWA   Risk-weighted assets. Regulation obliges banks to weigh the risks associated with their portfolios

S&Ls   Savings and loans banks. These US banking institutions, specialized in lending for housing, are under the supervision of the Home and Housing Department

Sampling   In this book, refers to the use of a fixed physical referential unit, an etalon, to measure an exchanged good or service. It requires the use of numbers. Weights or lengths are sampling units. Time is not

SCAV   Standing Committee on Assessment of Vulnerability. A committee set within the FSB at the BIS in Basel

SDR   Special drawing rights. An international reserve asset created by the IMF in 1969 to supplement the existing official reserves of member countries

SEC   Securities & Exchange Commission. US supervisory body for securities markets and issuances. Based in Washington, D.C.

SNA   System of National Accounts. Approved in 2008 by the UN Statistical Commission, it was to be enforced in September 2009. It adopts the quadruple-entry principle. This constitutes a comprehensive system of macroeconomic statistics for capturing integrated and consistent information on economic action by all residents as well as non-residents

SRM   Single resolution mechanism. Organization of the resolution and recovery process (the resolvability assessment process) and its surveillance for European systemic banking institutions and transnational banks. It is associated with a single resolution board (SRB) with appropriate authority over national resolution authorities (RA) to regulate a resolution process and a single resolution fund (SRF) to finance the process when needed

SSM   Single supervisory mechanism. Refers to the new EU mechanism intended to coordinate fiscal and tax policies and the banking system within the Eurozone. It is part of the ECB role to operate such a supervisory mechanism through a specialized supervisory board (SB)

Stamping   In the monetary world, this is the action required for the Minting Institute to strike a figure on a monetary instrument to represent the number of units in the currency that such an instrument may be used for. Stamping is usually a privilege granted by constitutions

Tier 1   A category of long-term financing considered by surveillance authorities as permanent. Equity is part of that category, but other instruments non-claimable by holders may be assimilated as perpetual bonds with subordination as to their coupons (LT2, lower tier 2)

Trilogue   A European Parliamentary mechanism by which the European Commission, the Council of Ministers and the Parliament come to an agreement on a draft regulation or Directive

Troika   A Russian word for a carriage pulled by three horses. In the context of this book it is the gathering of the European Commission, the ECB and the IMF organized with experts to follow up on the financial crisis of some troubled European countries to which lending was made under conditions (Greece, Ireland and Cyprus)

USITC   United States International Trade Commission. A US civil agency in charge of performing inquiries in international trade with the USA and competition

Velocity (of money)   The number of times a currency unit is exchanged over a period of time. The follow-up is usually done with M1 and M2 to GDP (see Federal Bank of St. Louis Research Center)

WFE   World Federation of Exchanges. Association gathering 154 stock exchanges throughout the world. Provides statistics and information on listings, capitalizations and trading. Based in London

WRA   Weighted risk asset. Relates to the valuation of financial portfolios, recorded both in balance sheets and "off balance sheets", of banks weighted according to risk. It is used by surveillance to implement adequacy with capital requirements or leverage limits and for stress testing

WTO   World Trade Organization. A statistical organization gathering data on international exchanges and a resolution forum for trade disputes. Geneva based

References

Ahamed, L. *Lord of Finance. The Bankers who Broke the World*. Penguin Press, New York, 2009.

Allais, M. *Traite d'Economie pure*. Editions Clement Juglar, Paris, 1943.

Allais, M. *la crise Mondiale d'aujourd'hui: Pour de profondes reformes des Institutions Bancaires et Financieres*. Editions Clement Juglar, Paris, 1994.

Andreau, J. *Banking and Business in the Roman World* (transl. Lloyd, J.). Cambridge University Press, Cambridge, 1992.

Andreau, J. *Roman Money Brokers (4th Century B.C.–3rd Century A.C.)*. Roman Economy, Rome, 1987.

Andreau, J. *Assets, Exchange and Money Lending*. l'Erma di Bretschneider, Rome, 1997.

Aghion, P., Frydman, R., Stiglitz, J. and Woodford M. (eds). *Knowledge, Information and Expectations in Modern Macroeconomics: In Honor of Edmund S. Phelps*. Princeton University Press, Princeton, NJ, 2006.

Attali, J. *Bruits*. Le Livre de Poche, 2007.

Attali, J. *Une breve histoire de l'avenir*. Fayard, Paris, 2008.

Attali, J. *La crise, et apres*. Fayard, Paris, 2009.

Attali, J. *Survivre aux crises*. Fayard, Paris, 2009.

Aubin, J.-P., Cornet, B. and Lasry, J.-M. *Applied Functional Analysis*. John Wiley & Sons, New York, 1980.

Aubin, J.-P. *Time and Money*. Springer-Verlag, Berlin, 2013.

Baehrel, R. Une croissance, La Basse-Provence Rurale 1789, Paris S.E.V.P.E.N. 1961 Discussion de Emmanuel Le Roy LaDurie 1965 no. 13–14 Etude Rurale.

Banque de France. Focus no. 10, December 5, 2013. Les dangers liés au développement des monnaies virtuelles.

Barrere, A. *Théorie économique et impulsion keynésienne*. Dalloz, Paris, 1952.

Bernanke, B. Non-monetary effects of the financial crisis in propagation of the Great Depression. NBER Working Paper no. 1054. *American Economic Review* 73(3), 1983, 257–276.

Blanque, P. Théorie globale de la monnaie, du cycle et de la mémoire. *Economica,* Janvier 2009.

Bodin, J. Paradoxes de M. de Malestroit touchant le fait des monnaies et l'enrichissement de toutes choses. Les six livres de la Republique. Gallica. Bibliothèque numérique.

Boston Consulting Group. The connected world. The 4.2 trillion opportunity – the Internet economy in the G20. March 2012.

Bottéro, J. *Mésopotamie – l'écriture, la raison et les dieux*. Gallimard, Paris, 1987.

Bottéro, J. *Mesopotamia: Writing, reasoning and the Gods*. Gallimard, Paris, 1995.

Braudel, F. La dynamique du capitalisme (conferences a l'Universite Johns Hopkins 1976: Afterthoughts on material civilization and capitalism). Editions Flamarion, Paris, 1988.

Braudel, F. *Civilisation matérielle, économie et capitalisme, XV–XVIIIeme siecle*. Editions Armand Colin, Paris, 1979.

Braudel, F. *Autour de la Méditerranée*. Editions de Fallois, Paris, 1996.

Braudel, F. *La Méditerranée: L'espace et l'histoire,lLes hommes et l'héritage*. Editions Flamarion, Paris, 2009.

Broadie, S. *Ethics with Aristotle*, Oxford University Press, Oxford, 1991.

Bruun, L.M. *The Roman Imperial Coinage.* London, 1966.

Charles-Picard, G. and Rouge, J. *Texts and documents relating to economic and social life in the Roman Empire 31 BC–223 AD.* Sociéte d'Édition de d'enseignement Supérieur, Paris, 1969.

Choi, Y. and Douady, R. Financial crisis dynamics: Attempt to define a market instability indicator. *Quantitative Finance* 12, 2012, 1351–1365.

Cohen, D. *La prospérité du vice. Une introduction (inquiète) à l'economie.* Albin Michel, Paris, 2009.

Congressional Research Service. US Library of Congress Research Service "Wireless Broadband", 2012.

Conseil d'Analyse Economique (CAE). Note no. 3 "Reinforce Europe", March 2013.

de Larosiere, J. The de Larosiere Group. Report of the High-Level Group on Financial Supervision in the EU, Brussels, February 25, 2009.

Debreu, G. *Theory of the Value; An Axiomatic Analysis of Economic Equilibrium.* Cowles Foundation Monography, 1972.

Depeyrot, G. *La monnaie Romaine.* Edition Errance, Paris, 2006.

Deutsch, E. *La volonté de comprendre, compilation by Haim Korsia.* Les Editions les Rosiers, Paris, 2011.

Diamond, M.A., Flamholtz, M.A. and Flamholtz, D.T. *Financial Accounting,* 2nd edn. PWS Kent Publishing Co., Boston, MA, 1990.

Duncan, R. *The New Depression: The Breakdown of the Paper Money Economy.* John Wiley & Sons, Singapore, 2012.

Du Pont, P.S. *La Physiocratie ou Constitution Naturelle du Gouvernement le plus avantageux au genre humain.* Chez Merlin Libraire, Paris, 1768.

Eday, M. and Hviding, K. An assessment of financial reform in OCDE countries. OCDE/6D(95)60, Economics Department Working Papers no. 164, Paris, 1995.

Emmons, R.W. and Noeth, B.J. Federal Bank of St. Louis issue 4, 2013. Shorts essays related to research on understanding and strengthening the balance sheet of American households.

Escaffe, L., Foulquier, P. and Touron, P. Juste valeur ou non: un débat mal posé. EDHEC Analysis and Accounting Research Centre, 2008.

FASB. Exposure Draft of May 26, 2010 Financial Instruments (Topic 825), Derivatives and Hedging (Topic 815) – file reference no. 1810-100; Exposure Draft of May 26, 2010 Comprehensive Income (Topic 220) – file reference no. 1790-100.

Filippi, C.-H. *L'argent sans maître.* Editions Descartes, Paris, 2009.

Fisher, I. *The Purchasing Power of Money. Its determination and relation to credit, interest and crisis.* Macmillan, New York, 1911.

Fisher, I. *The Money Illusion.* Adelphi, New York, 1928.

Fisher, I. *The Theory of Interest.* Macmillan, New York, 1930.

Fisher, I. *The Debt–Deflation Theory of Great Depressions.* Michael Schemmann, Thailand, 1933.

Foster, B.R. and Polinger-Foster, K. *Civilization of Ancient Iraq.* Princeton University Press, Princeton, NJ, 2011.

Friedman, M. Studies in the *Quantity Theory of Money.* University of Chicago Press, Chicago, 1956.

Friedman, M. and Schwartz, A.J. *A Monetary History of the United States 1867–1960.* Princeton University Press, Princeton, NJ, 1971.

FSB Report 70/2013, September 5, 2013 to G20 leaders on financial regulatory reforms progress. G20 Status (green to amber).

FSB Report April 2009 to G20 leaders on objectives set by G20, Ref. 44/2009.

FSB Global Shadow Banking Monitoring Report 2013. Fourth Progress Report on the Implementation of the G20 Data Gaps Initiative, prepared by the staff of the IMF and the FSB Secretariat, September 2013.

Funari, P.P. and Pollini, A. *Mercato. Le commerce dans les mondes grecs et Romain.* Les Belles Lettres, Paris, 2012.

Gibbon, E. *The History of the Decline and Fall of the Roman Empire.* Penguin Classics, Harmondsworth, UK, 1996.

Godefroy, G. *The Adventure of Numbers.* Library of Congress, 2011.

Godefroy, G. *Les Mathématiques Mode d'Emploi.* Odile Jacob, Paris, 2011.

Hayek, F. *Prices and Production.* Routledge, London, 1931.

Hayek, F. *The Road to Serfdom* (ed. B. Caldwell). University of Chicago Press, Chicago, 2007.

Hayek, F. *The Constitution of Liberty* (ed. B. Caldwell). University of Chicago Press, Chicago, 2011.

Herodotus (around 484–425 BC) (ed. Dewald, C. and transl. Waterfield, R.). *The Histories.* Random House, New York, 2009.

Hicks, J.R. Suggestions for Simplifying the Theory of Money *Economica* 2(5) February, 1935, 1–19.

Hicks, J.R. *Value and Capital: An Inquiry into Fundamental Principles of Economic Theory,* 2nd edn. Nuffield College, Oxford, 1939.

Hicks, J.R. The Long-Term Dollar Problem, *Oxford Economic Papers,* 1953.

Hicks, J.R. The Measurement of Real Income, *Oxford Economic Papers* 10(2) June, 1958, 125–162.

Hicks, J.R. Measurement of capital in relation to other economic aggregates. In Lutz, F.A. and Hague, D. (eds), *The Theory of Capital,* Palgrave Macmillan, 1961.

Hicks, J.R. *A Theory of Economic History.* Oxford University Press, Oxford, 1969.

Hicks, J.R. *Method of Dynamic Economic s.* Oxford University Press, Oxford, 1985.

Hicks, J.R. *Capital and Time. A neo-Austrian theory,* Oxford University Press, Oxford, 1973.

Hicks, J.R. *A Market Theory of Money,* Oxford University Press, Oxford, 1989.

IAG Report of September 2013 from the IMF staff and FSB Secretariat to G20. Released October 11, 2013.

IASB Exposure Drafts.

Juglar, J.C. *A Brief History of Panics and their Periodical Occurrence in the US.* First published in French, 1860. Republished in 2008 by Forgotten Books.

Kagan, D. *Pericles of Athens and the Birth of Democracy.* Free Press, New York, 2011.

Kern, S. Deutsche Bank current issues in global financial markets. Macro-prudential financial supervision in the US. FSOC, April 2012.

Keynes, J.M. *General Theory of Employment, Interest and Money.* Macmillan, London, reprinted 2007.

Kramer, S.N. *History Begins at Sumer.* University of Pennsylvania Press, Philadelphia, PA, 1956.

Krugman, P.R. and Obstfeld, M. *International Economics,* 9th edn. Pearson, London, 2011.

Landes, D.S. Vieille banque et banque nouvelle: La révolution financière du dix-neuvième siècle. *Revue d'Histoire Moderne et Contemporaine* 3(Jul-Sept), 1956, 204–222.

Landes, D.S. *Richesse et pauvreté des nations.* Albin Michel, Paris, 2000.

Lavoisier, A. *Elements of Chemistry in a New Systematic Order, Containing All the Modern Discoveries,* 1789 (transl. Kerr, R.) 1915. William Creed, Edinburgh.

Le Roy Ladurie, E. *Montaillou, Village Occitan de 1294 a 1324.* Gallimard, Paris, 1975.

Le Roy Ladurie, E. *Histoire humaine et comparée du climat,* 3 t. Fayard, Paris, 2004–2009.

Le Roy Ladurie, E. *Histoire et système* (dir.), Editions du Cerf, Paris, 2010.

Lubochinsky, C. *Les marchés financiers dans la tourmente.* PUF Editions Descartes, Paris, 2009.

Locke, J. *Two Treaties of Government,* 1689.

Ludwig, E. *Bismarck.* French edition, 1929. Reprinted by Payot, 2008.

Lund, S., Daruvala, T., Dobbs, R., Härle, P., Kwek, J.-H. and Falcón, R. *Financial Globalization: Retreat or Reset?* McKinsey Global Institute, March 2013.

Malinvaud, E. *Voies de la Recherche Macroéconomiques.* Odile Jacob, Paris, 1991.

Mandeville, B. *A Modest Defense of Publick Stews,* 1723.

Mandelbrot, B. Forme nouvelle du hasard dans les sciences, *appliquées* 26, 1973, 307.

Mandelbrot, B. *Fractal Hazard and Finance.* Editions Flamarion, Paris, 1959.

Mandelbrot, B. and Hudson, R.L. *The (Mis)behavior of Markets: A Fractal View of Risk, Ruin and Reward.* Basic Books, London, 2004.

McCulley, P.A. Teton Reflexion. PIMCO Global Central Bank Focus, May 2009.

Mead, W.R. *God and Gold: Britain, America, and the Making of the Modern World.* Random House, New York, 2007.

Merton, R.K. *Social Theory and Social Structures.* Free Press, New York, 1953.

Milgram, S. *The Individual in a Social World: Essays and Experiments,* 2nd ed (ed. Blass, T.). McGraw-Hill, New York, 1992.

Miller, M. *Merton Miller on Derivatives.* John Wiley & Sons, New York, 1997.

Moller, H. *The Weimar Republic 1919–1933.* Deutscher Taschenbuch Verlag, Berlin, 1985.

Mommsen, T. *Mommsen's History of Rome* (translated Dickson V.P.). Scribner, New York, 1871.

Monnaie de Paris. Catalogue of September–November exhibition. "Trésor de la Monnaie" Récentes acquisitions du musée de la Monnaie (1989–1996). IBSN: 2-11 -089770-8 Septembre 1996- catalogue inventaire.

Montesquieu, C.-L. de Secondat. *Dissertation on Roman Politics,* 1716.

Montesquieu, C.-L. de Secondat. *The Spirit of Laws*, 1748 (transl. Nugent, T.) Digiread.com.

Montesquieu, C.-L. de Secondat. *Considerations on the Causes of the Greatness of the Romans and their Decline,* 1734. Reprinted in English (transl. Lowenthal, D.) Hackett Publishing, 1999.

Mundell, R.A. *International Economics & Monetary Economics.* WW Norton & Co., New York.

Mundell, R.A. *Monetary Theory: Interest, Inflation and Growth in the World Economy.* Goodyear Publishing, Pacific Palisades, CA, 1971.

Neumann, J. Von and Morgenstern, O. *Theory of Games and Economic Behavior.* Princeton University Press, Princeton, NJ, 1947.

Norel, P. *L'Histoire économique globale.* Editions du Seuil, Paris, 2010.

OECD *Central Government Debt.* Statistical Yearbook 2000–2009. See also annual reports.

Patat, J.-P. Monnaie, Systeme financier et politique monetaire. *Economica,* November, 2002.

Paul, R. *End the FED.* General Publishing, Blaine, WA, 2009.

Peters, E. *Chaos and Order in the Capital Markets: A new view of cycles, prices and market volatility.* John Wiley & Sons, New York, 1991.

Petit, P. *Histoire Générale de l'Empire Romain,* 3 vol. Editions du Seuil, Paris, 1978.

Petitfils, J.-C. *Louis XVI.* Perrin, Paris, 2008.

Piketty, T. *Le Capital au XXIième siècle*. Editions du Seuil, Paris, 2013 [English translation by Arthur Goldhammer. *The Capital in XXIst Century*. The President and Fellows of Harvard College].

Pomeranz, K. *The Great Divergence: China, Europe and the making of the modern world economy.* Princeton University Press, Princeton, NJ, 2000.

Popper, K. *The Open Society and its Enemies.* Routledge & Kegan Paul, London, 1945.

Reinhart, C.M. and Rogoff, K.S. *The Second Great Contraction* from *The Time is Different: Eight centuries of Financial Folly.* Princeton University Press, Princeton, NJ, 2009.

Reinhart, C.M. and Rogoff, K.S. *A Decade of Debt.* The Peterson Institute for International Economics, 2011.

Ricardo, D. *The High Price of Bullion: A Proof of the Depreciation of Banknotes,* 1810, classic reprint, Forgotten Books, 2012.

Ricardo, D. *Réponses et observations de M. Bosanquet sur le rapport du Bullion Committee,* 1811.

Ricardo, D. *On the Principles of Political Economy and Taxation,* 1817.

Rickards, J. *Currency Wars. The making of the next global crisis.* Penguin Group, New York, 2011.

Rostovtzeff, M.I. *The Social and Economic History of the Hellenistic World.* Oxford University Press, Oxford, 1941, (monograph reprint 1986).

Rostovtzeff, M.I. *The Social and Economic History of the Roman Empire.* Oxford University Press, Oxford, 2008.

Roux, G. *Ancient Iraq.* Allen & Unwin, London, 1964.

Rovan, J.A. *Histoire de l'Allemagne.* Editions du Seuil, Paris, 1994.

Rozeff, M.S. *Commentaries on Edwin Vieira Jr. Piece of Eight Book.* Von Mises Institute, February 2010.

Saint Marc, M. *Theorie de la monétisation.* Dunod, Paris, 1972.

Saint Marc, M. *Histoire monétaire de la France 1800–1980.* Presses Universitaire de France, Paris, 1983.

Samuelson, P.A. *Economics: An Introductory Analysis.* McGraw-Hill, New York, 1961.

Samuelson, P.A. Classical and neo-classical monetary theory. In R.W. Clower (ed.), *Monetary Theory.* Penguin Education, London, 1973.

Schacht, H. *de l'or pour l'Europe.* Traduction éditée par Editions, Montana Bruxelles [title original: Mehr Geld, Mehr Kapital, Mehr Arbeit].

Schumpeter, J. *Capitalism, Socialism and Democracy.* Harper Perennial, New York, 2008.

Serval, T. The euro: its use and consequences for business. AFEDE Constantin Associates, 1998.

Smith, A. The *Theory of Moral Sentiments,* 1759. Presses Universitaire de France, Paris, 1999.

Smith, A. *The Wealth of Nations. An inquiry into the nature and causes of the income of nations,* 1776. Modern Library Edition, New York, 2000.

Soros, G. The new paradigm for financial market. The credit crisis of 2008 and what it means (2008).

Stiglitz, J.E. *Globalization & its Discontents.* WW Norton & Co., New York, 2002.

Stiglitz, J.E. *The Stiglitz Report Reforming the International Monetary and Financial Systems in the Wake of the Financial Crisis.* The New Press, New York, 2010.

Stiglitz, J.E. *Making Globalization Work.* WW Norton & Co., New York, 2006.

Temin, P. *The Roman Market Economy.* The Princeton History of the Western World. Princeton University Press, Princeton, NJ, 2012.

Theucydides. *History of the Peloponnesian War.* Princeton University Press, Princeton, NJ, 1984.

Tirolle, J. *The Theory of Corporate Finance.* Princeton University Press, Princeton, NJ, 2004.

Triffin, R. *The Gold & Dollar Crisis: The future of convertibility.* Yale University Press, New Haven, CT, 1961.

US Executive Office of the President. Council of Economic Advisors. The economic benefits of the new spectrum.

US International Trade Commission. Digital trade in the US and global economies, Part 1, no. 332–531, July 2013. Part 2 expected in July 2014.

Varenne de, F. L'assurance vie aux Etats-Unis: Histoire d'une crise FFSA. Available at f.devarenne@ffsa.fr.

Veron, N., Autret, M. and Galichon, A. *L'information Financière en Crise: Comptabilite et capitalisme.* Odile Jacob, Paris, 2004. Bruegel Policy Contribution, issue 2013/07, June 2013.

Vieira, E. Jr. *Piece of Eight. The monetary powers and disabilities of the US constitution.* Revised in 2002.

Von Mises, L. *Human Action. A Treatise on Economics.* Scholar's edition, Ludwig von Mises Institute.

Von Mises, L. *On the Manipulation of Money and Credit.* Free Market Books, Dobbs Ferry, NY, 1978.

Wapshott, N. *Keynes Hayek: The Clash that Defined Modern Economics.* WW Norton & Co., New York, 2011.

Williams, A.N. and Russell, B. *Principia Mathematica,* 2010.

Wittgenstein, L. *Tractatus Logica-Philosophicus.* Published in Vienna by Wilhelm Ostwald under the title *Logische-Philosophische Abhandlung – Annalen der Naturphilosopie* (1921).

World Bank. World Development Indicators Database (accessed April 28, 2013).

World Trade Organization Annual Report 2013.

Selected Articles

Borgia, M. and Koncz-Brurer, J. Trends in digitally enabled trade in services. US Department of Commerce. US Bureau of Economic Analysis, 201. Bea.gov/pdf/trends_in digitally_enabled_services.pdf.

Chapter 1

Summary of Eliot, S. (CNRS Lyon – Bibliothèque Nationale), *Catalogue des monnaies de l'Empire Romain* (BNCMER), Vol. XII.1. D'Aurélien à Florien, Paris, 2004, pp. 39–49. **[footnote 28]**

Chapter 2

McKinsey Global Institute (MGI) report of March 2013 on "Financial Globalization: Retreat or Reset". **[footnote 7]**

Bulletin de la Banque de France no. 175, 1st trim. 2009. **[footnote 8]**

Emmons, W.R. and Noeth, B.J., Issue 4-2013, Short essays related to research on understanding and strengthening of the balance sheet of Americans households. **[footnote 9]**

The WTO 2009 report also contains developments on the transformation of international trade because of the rise in integrated groups that would partially explain the more than proportional to GDP growth of exchanges for the period 1948–2009. **[footnote 10]**

OXERA Report 2004, European Commission on the audit market concentration. **[footnote 14]**

EU, Brussels, October 2011, White Paper final – Audit policy: lessons from the crisis. **[footnote 20]**

Chapter 3

IMF website, imsrefor.org/about/glossary – Reforming the International Monetary System, Commonly used terms and concepts. **[footnote 35]**

See further, note 88 in D'Austra and Schlessinger (1993) regarding securitization alongside a parallel banking system, as well as our previous book. **[footnote 52]**

European Market Infrastructure Regulation (EMIR): nude CDS instruments issued on sovereign debt, but released without a hedging basis, are now prohibited on regulated markets in part to avoid speculation. The US equivalent is Title VII of the Dodd–Frank Act adopted on May 20, 2010 with similar approaches. Nevertheless, the allocation of surveillance is different in the USA and EU. **[footnote 58]**

NBER. Paul Allen McCulley, General Manager for PIMCO, notes that he first saw this shadow banking terminology used at the Federal Reserve Bank of Kansas City Symposium of August 2007 held in Jacksons Hole. McCulley missed one document. The most sensitive document and the first known one dates back to 1993. It is published in J.W. d'Arista and T. Schlesinger, "The parallel banking system", Economic Policy Institute Briefing Paper Series 202/775-8810, p. 2. Over the past few decades, the US system has been reshaped by the spread of multifunctional financial conglomerates and the emergence of an unregulated parallel banking system. Along with this powerful trend, like securitization, these events have broken down the carefully compartmentalized credit and capital marketplace established by New Deal legislation 60 years ago. This document nevertheless has been written in the context of the US 1991 banking crisis and the US set-up of monetary mutual funds and specialized financing conglomerates such as GE and GM subsidiaries, at that time non-banks. It does not apprehend, like later papers, the international functioning of shadow banking and the tax implications that we raise, which at that time were refinanced by Japan's balance of payments surplus. A paper of March 2012 by Viral V. Acharya of NY Stern School of Business, "The growth of a shadow banking system in emerging markets: Evidence from India", adds very little to the analysis. M Acharya writes more wisely on a wide range of topics and is more knowledgeable on Korean issues. **[footnote 61]**

Working paper 15787, dated February 2010, nber.org/papers/w15787, see graphic on p. 9. **[footnote 62]**

Working paper 15787 on p. 7 asks: "What is this new banking system, the 'parallel banking system' or 'shadow banking system' or 'securitized banking system'?" **[footnote 63]**

See reports on the FSB website http://www.financialstabilityboard.org/list/fsb_publications/index.htm. The last report entitled "Global Shadow Banking Monitoring" is dated November 14, 2013. **[footnote 67]**

Chapter 4

Multiple papers that did not exist, or were disregarded at the time we published our previous book, now refer to the role of "balance sheets". Among these sources are Ruscher, E. and Wolf, G. (2012), "Corporate balance sheet adjustments stylized facts, clauses and consequences", European Economy, Economic Papers no. 449 and McRosenberg, A., Keller, C., Setser, B. and Rubini, N. (2002), "A balance sheet approach to the financial crisis", IMF Working Papers no. WP/02/210. Already previously quoted by the authors is the OECD yearly 81st 2009–2010 annual report that is also quite meaningful, and which states that: "large mismatches in international balance sheets also create risks" (p. 43). **[footnote 2]**

Shin, H.-S., Sapra, H., and Plantin, G., "Marking to market: Panacea or Pandora's box?", *Journal of Accounting Research*, Princeton University, August 12, 2007, 46: 435–460 (2008). **[footnote 12]**

Severinson, C. and Yermo, J., OECD no. 2/12/12. The effect of solvency regulations and accounting standards on long-term investments; implications for insurers and pension funds. This paper calls for extreme prudence with regard to FMV standards. **[footnote 13]**

Eurostat ECB schedule 3.1, online data: note "general concepts". **[footnote 15]**

Choi, Y. and Douady, R. Financial crisis dynamics: Attempt to define a market instability indicator. *Quantitative Finance* 12, 2012, 1351–1365. **[footnote 17]**

Chapter 5

Tim Congton, British economist, member of the shadow monetary policy committee and author of *Keynes, the Keynesians and Monetarism* as well as author of the article "A decision following Federal reserve decision to discontinue publication of M3 data". **[footnote 9]**

Shin, H.-S. and Tobias, A., Liquidity, monetary policy and financial cycles, *Economics & Finance* Vol. 14, Federal Reserve Bank of New York, Jan/Feb 2008. Extract: "Our findings suggest a need to rehabilitate balance sheet quantities as a relevant measure in the conduct of monetary policy, but with one twist. Rather than reaffirming the conventional monetarist identification of the money stock as an indicator of liquidity our analysis assigns this role to the stock of collateralized borrowings." On a parallel topic, also from Shin: "Procyclality and monetary aggregates", February 2011 and "Monetary aggregates and the central financial stability model", March 2012. **[footnote 10]**

BIS 2010/2012 81st annual report. The 2011/2012 82nd report emphasized the dependency of the entire system on US$ credit lent to the rest of the world, and which "has tended to grow much faster than credit to US residents – a gap that has widened substantially, following the crisis". **[footnote 12]**

EU regulation no. 260/2012 modifying regulation no. 924/2009 on transfers and withdrawals in euros. **[footnote 14]**

Lim, E. and Subramanian, S., Factors underlying the definition of 'broad money'. An examination of current US monetary statistics and practices of other countries, IMF, March 2003. **[footnote 16]**

Gary B. Gorton Report 15787, February 2010: presented to the US Commission on the Causes of the Financial Crisis – National Bureau of Economic Research, *Questions and Answers about the Financial Crisis*, p. 7, www.nber.org/paper/w15787. **[footnote 18]**

European directive addressing markets for financial instruments and derivatives – now under current revision. **[footnote 23]**

Chapter 6

FSB release June 8, 2012. **[footnote 7]**

Edey, M.L. and Hviding, K., OCDE/6D(95) Economics Department Working Paper no. 154, Economic Studies no. 25, "An assessment of financial reforms in OCDE countries", Paris, 1995. **[footnote 9]**

ECB 2005/5 Guideline and ESA 95. **[footnote 14]**

The FSB April 18, 2012 report and OECD annual report complain about the need to improve the data by making it more detailed. **[footnote 15]**

FSB press release of June 8, 2012, "A global legal entity identifier for financial markets". **[footnote 16]**

Shearman and Sterling papers, December 2012 (see Argentina's public bond issues). **[footnote 17]**

Chapter 7

See www.cvce.eu. Interim Committee of the Board of Governors of the IMF. **[footnote 6]**

Los Cabos, June 18–19, 2012 on the IMF and its relationship with the G20. Press release and common press release on Greece with the EU, ECB of October 17, 2012. **[footnote 15]**

European Council release on June 9, 2009 recommending the set-up of a European risk agency that was, thereafter, agreed. **[footnote 16]**

Press release from the European Commission COM/2012 510 (final). **[footnote 27]**

Entretiens du Trésor, November 30, 2012 at the Paris Ministry of Finance. Also present: Mario Draghi, President of the ECB; Mrs Christine Lagarde; Victorrio Grilli, Minister of Finance of Italy; Martin Hillwig, Director of the Max Planck Institute for Research on Collective Goods; Sylvie Goulard, from the European Parliament. Entretien du Trésor held at the Ministry of Finance on December 13, 2013 was more focused on financing the economy, especially SMEs in the context of a wider recourse to financial markets than to bank financing. M. Barnier, the European Commissioner, indicated that he will propose mechanisms for extended securitization of receivables. **[footnote 30]**

CAE Note no. 3, "Compléter l'Euro" (Complete the Euro) has been issued by Conseil d'Analyse Economique, France, which is an independent body set up alongside the French Prime Minister. This note recommends the creation of an independent budget committee. A speech he gave in Paris on April 9, 2013 comments on the note of Jean Tirolle, a member of this council, raising the issue of nationally sanctioning breaches in good governance or risk taking as opposed to having an independent European board. He also raises the topic of financing the guarantees (100,000) given by law to depositors and the difficulty for governments to deal transnationally with already troubled banks. **[footnote 31]**

Cotorelli, G. and Goldberger, C. (2012) Banking globalization and monetary transmission, *Journal of Finance*, vol. 67. **[footnote 41]**

SEC staff release, September 2012. **[footnote 42]**

OECD annual report 2010–2011. **[footnote 52]**

Press release dated August 1, 1975 on previous meeting of the Committee. **[footnote 53]**

Nixon's Secretary of State speech to European leaders in 1971. **[footnote 54]**

Conclusion

OECD Working Paper no. 1006, December 7, 2012: "Debt and Macroeconomic Stability: An overview of the literature and some empirics" by Douglas Sutherland and Peter Hoeller; Working Paper no. 970, June 6, 2012: Debt and Macroeconomic Stability, part 7, "International Capital Mobility & Financial Fragility", by Rüdiger Ahrend. **[footnote 3]**

ECB Monthly bulletin of the Euro area. **[footnote 4]**

ESA 95 and ECB 2002/7, ECB 2005/12. **[footnote 5]**

TFFS 08/09, IATForce. **[footnote 7]**

BIS Working Paper no. 399, December 6, 2012: "Global Safe Assets", by Pierre-Olivier Gourinchas and Olivier Jeanne. **[footnote 10]**

The Wall Street Journal, Wednesday, January 23rd, vol. CCLXI, no. 18, p. 1 and A12: "Firms keep stockpiles of foreign cash in US". **[footnote 11]**

List of Monetary Central Institutions and Others (International and National) with Websites

INTERNATIONAL ORGANIZATIONS OR EQUIVALENT

Bank for International Settlements (BIS)*
www.bis.org

European Central Bank (ECB)*
www.ecb.int

European Commission (EC)*
www.ec.europa.eu

Federal Reserve System
www.fedreserve.gov

International Monetary Fund (IMF)*
www.imf.org

Organisation for Economic Coordination and Development (OECD)*
www.oecd.org

The World Bank*
www.worldbank.org

The World Trade Organization
www.wto.org

INTERNATIONAL STANDARD-SETTING BODIES AND OTHER GROUPINGS

Basel Committee on Banking Supervision (BCBS)*
www.bis.org/bcbs/index.htm

Committee on the Global Financial System (CGFS)*
www.bis.org/cgfs/index.htm

Committee on Payment and Settlement Systems (CPSS)*
www.bis.org./cpss/index.htm

---

* Denotes FSB member.

Financial Action Task Force on Money Laundering (FATF) (EC)
http://www.fatf-gafi.org

International Association of Insurance Supervisors (IAIS)*
www.iaisweb.org

International Accounting Standards Board (IASB)*
www.iasb.org

International Organization of Securities Commissions (IOSCO)*
www.iosco.org

International Association of Deposit Insurers
www.iadi.org

NATIONAL BODIES

Argentina

Banco Central de la República Argentina*
www.bcra.gov.ar

Comisión Nacional de Valores
www.cnv.gov.ar

Ministerio de Economía y Finanzas Públicas
www.mecon.gov.ar

Australia

Reserve Bank of Australia*
www.rba.gov.au

Australian Securities and Investments Commission
www.asic.gov.au

Australian Prudential Regulation Authority
www.apra.gov.au

The Treasury*
www.treasury.gov.au

Brazil

Banco Central do Brasil*
www.bcb.bov.br

Comissão de Valores Mobiliários*
www.cvm.gov.br

Ministério de Fazenda*
www.fazenda.gov.br

Canada

Bank of Canada*
www.bank-banque-canada.ca

Canada Deposit Insurance Corporation
www.cdic.ca

Ontario Securities Commission
www.osc.gov.on.ca

Office of the Superintendent of Financial Institutions*
www.osfi-bsif.gc.ca

Department of Finance*
www.fin.gc.ca

Canadian Securities Administrators
www.securities-administrators.ca

Autorité des marchés financiers, Quebec
www.lautorite.qc.ca

China

People's Bank of China*
www.pbc.gov.cn

China Banking Regulatory Commission*
www.cbrc.gov.cn

Ministry of Finance*
www.mof.gov.cn

France

Banque de France*
www.banque-france.fr

Autorité des Marchés Financiers*
www.amf-france.org

Ministère de l'Economie*
www.minefi.gouv.fr

Germany

Deutsche Bundesbank*
www.bundesbank.de

Bundesanstalt für Finanzdienstleistungsaufsicht*
www.bafin.de

Bundesministerium der Finanzen*
www.bundesfinanzministerium.de

Hong Kong SAR

Hong Kong Monetary Authority*
www.hkma.gov.hk

Office of the Commissioner of Insurance
www.info.gov.hk/oci

Securities & Futures Commission
www.hksfc.org.hk

The Treasury
www.info.gov.hk/tsy

India

Reserve Bank of India*
www.rbi.org.in

Securities and Exchange Board of India*
www.sebi.gov.in

Ministry of Finance*
www.finmin.nic.in

Indonesia

Bank Indonesia*
www.bi.go.id

Capital Markets and Financial Institutions Supervisory Agency (BAPEPAM)
www.bapepam.go.id

Ministry of Finance
www.depkeu.go.id

Italy

Banca d'Italia*
www.bancaditalia.it

Istituto per la Vigilanze sulle Assicurazioni Private e di Interesse Collettivo (ISVAP)
www.isvap.it

Commissione Nazionale per le Società e la Borsa*
www.consob.it

Ministero dell'Economia e delle Finanze*
www.tesoro.it

Japan

Bank of Japan*
www.boj.or.jp

Financial Services Agency*
www.fsa.go.jp

Ministry of Finance*
www.mof.go.jp

Korea, Republic of

Bank of Korea*
www.bok.or.kr

Financial Services Commission*
www.fsc.go.kr

Ministry of Strategy and Finance
www.mofe.go.kr

Mexico

Banco de México*
www.banxico.org.mx

Comisión Nacional Bancaria y de Valores
www.cnbv.gob.mx

Secretaría de Hacienda y Crédito Público de México*
www.shcp.gob.mx

The Netherlands

De Nederlandsche Bank*
www.dnb.nl

Autoriteit Financiële Markten
www.afm.nl

Ministerie van Financiën*
www.minfin.nl

Russia

Central Bank of the Russian Federation*
www.cbr.ru

Federal Financial Markets Service (FFMS) *
www.fcsm.ru

Ministry of Finance*
www.minfin.ru

Saudi Arabia

Saudi Arabian Monetary Agency
www.sama.gov.sa

Ministry of Finance
www.mof.gov.sa

Singapore

Monetary Authority of Singapore
www.mas.gov.sg

Ministry of Finance*
www.mof.gov.sg

South Africa

South African Reserve Bank
www.reservebank.co.za

Financial Services Board
www.fsb.co.za

Ministry of Finance*
http://www.treasury.gov.za/

Spain

Banco de España*
www.bde.es

Comisión Nacional del Mercardo de Valores
www.cnmv.es

Ministerio de Economía y Competitividad*
www.mineco.es

Switzerland

Swiss National Bank*
www.snb.ch

Swiss Financial Market Supervisory Authority
www.finma.ch

Swiss Federal Finance Administration*
www.efv.admin.ch

Turkey

Central Bank of the Republic of Turkey*
www.tcmb.gov.tr

Banking Regulation and Supervision Agency
www.bddk.org.tr/websitesi/English.aspx

Ministry of State in Charge of Economy
http://www.treasury.gov.tr

Turkish Accounting Standards Board
www.tmsk.org.tr/index.php?

The Capital Markets Board of Turkey
www.cmb.gov.tr/

The Undersecretariat of Treasury
www.treasury.gov.tr

Turkish Financial Intelligence Unit (MASAK)
www.masak.gov.tr/

The Saving Deposit Insurance Fund
www.tmsf.org.tr

United Kingdom

Bank of England*
www.bankofengland.co.uk

Financial Services Authority*
www.fsa.gov.uk

HM Treasury*
www.hm-treasury.gov.uk

United States of America

Federal Deposit Insurance Corporation (FDIC)
www.fdic.gov

Office of the Comptroller of the Currency (OCC)
www.occ.treas.gov

Board of Governors of the Federal Reserve System*
www.federalreserve.gov

Federal Reserve Bank of New York
www.newyorkfed.org/

Financial Accounting Standards Board
www.fasb.org

US Commodity Futures Trading Commission
www.cftc.gov

National Association of Insurance Commissioners (NAIC)
www.naic.org

US Securities & Exchange Commission (SEC)*
www.sec.gov

US Department of Treasury*
www.treasury.gov

savings and loans banks (S&Ls) 60, 96–7,
 218, 245
scale economies 7–8, 178, 191–2, 199–203,
 232, 234
Schacht, Hjalmar H. 32, 42, 98
Schumpeter, J. 46
scriptural money 10–11, 28–9, 30–1, 36–7,
 39–43, 44–7, 49, 53, 62–5, 70–5,
 104–27, 133–47, 218–19
secondary markets 54–60, 123–5, 245
secured lending 20–1
Securities & Exchange Commission (SEC)
 23, 61–2, 83, 142–3, 150, 163–7, 179,
 189–90, 226, 246, 263
securitization 25, 53–60, 63–9, 74–5,
 96–100, 118–27, 130–47, 186–8,
 195–213
 see also asset-backed...;
  disintermediation; mortgage-backed...;
  'shadow banking'
 concepts 54–60, 63–4, 65–6, 74–5, 96–7,
  118–21, 132–3, 144–7, 186–8
 critique 54–60, 74–5, 186–8
 guarantees on receivables 59–60,
  195–213
 implementation methods 56–8
 origins 54–6, 74
 taxes 57–8
seignorage privilege 9, 43–7, 62–4, 70–5,
 97–8, 120–5, 126–7, 184–5, 190–2,
 204–13
 see also issuance...; stamping concepts;
  trust factors
 history of money 9, 43–7, 63–4, 73–4
 modern times 44–7, 62–4, 73–5, 97–8,
  120–25, 126–7, 184–5, 190–2, 204–13
selected articles 253–5
self-interests 153
self-prophetic issues, anticipation processes
 222–4
self-reform problems 162–7, 184–6
self-regulation problems 23–4, 28–9, 162–7,
 226
service industry overvaluations,
 manufacturing industry undervaluations
 10–11, 16–17
service sector 10–11, 14–25
 see also financial...
Sesterce 29, 41

'shadow banking' 58–60, 63, 65–9, 75,
 112–27, 132–3, 135–47, 165–7, 232–9
 see also non-bank financial institutions;
  parallel banking systems; securitization
 concepts 65–9, 75, 115–18, 132–3, 135–6,
  144–7, 165–7, 232
 definition 69, 75, 115–16, 145–7
 interconnectedness concerns 68–9, 145–7,
  235
 regulations 68–9, 165–7
 statistics 66–8, 132–3
silver, history of money 2–5, 29–37, 39, 40,
 70–2, 73–5, 152
Singapore 64, 163, 261
Single Euro Payment Area (SEPA) (EU no.
 2007/64) 36, 133–4
Single European Act 1987 182
Single Resolution Board (SRB) 171, 172–3,
 246
single resolution mechanism (SRM) 171,
 180–1, 246
single supervisory mechanism (SSM)
 169–73, 246
Six-Pack regulations 174–5
slavery 6
slowdowns 132–3, 136–47
Smith, Adam (1723–1790) 6, 198
'Smithsonian Agreement' 33–4
social considerations 9–11, 12, 27, 145–7,
 175–7, 181–8, 193–213, 221–2, 232–3,
 239
social contracts 9–11, 12, 27, 145–7, 175–7,
 193–213, 221–2, 232–3, 239
social obstacles of monetary unification
 181–8
social time 222–4
social unrest, history of money 10–11
'society' 205–7
sociologists 205–6
Solon (640–558BC) 5–6, 10, 181
Solvency II 137, 158, 161, 166–7, 179,
 184–5
Soros, George 133
South American colonization from 1492,
 history of money 9–10
South and Central America
 see also individual countries
 exports 18–19
sovereign debt, CDSs 61–2